A HISTORY OF THE ENGLISH PEOPLE
IN THE NINETEENTH CENTURY

A HISTORY OF THE ENGLISH PEOPLE
IN THE NINETEENTH CENTURY

WILLIAM LAMB, 2nd. VISCOUNT MELBOURNE

J. Partridge

(National Portrait Gallery)

A HISTORY OF THE ENGLISH PEOPLE
IN THE NINETEENTH CENTURY — III

THE TRIUMPH
OF REFORM
1830—1841

by

ELIE HALÉVY

Translated from the French by
E. I. WATKIN

ERNEST BENN LIMITED
LONDON

First published in French   1923
First published in English   1927
Second (revised) Edition   1950

Published by Ernest Benn Limited
Bouverie House, Fleet Street, London.
Made and printed in Great Britain by

STAPLES PRESS LIMITED
at their Rochester, Kent, establishment

Translator's Note

HALÉVY wrote no special introduction to this third volume of his history. What introductory remarks he desired to make he prefaced to the second volume of which the present is simply the continuation. The translation of the present, as of the two previous volumes, has been read by Madame Halévy, to whose kindness I owe a very large number of valuable suggestions and criticisms.

E. I. WATKIN.

Contents

Illustrations

PART I

THE FIRST REFORMED PARLIAMENT
(1830-1834)

The July Revolution in England

I THE WHIGS IN OFFICE

I

IN 1829 King Charles X had placed in office a Government of ultra-conservative ministers with the Prince de Polignac as prime minister. When the Deputies refused his cabinet their confidence he dissolved the Chamber. The new elections were held in July 1830 and in spite of ministerial pressure the Opposition increased its strength by fifty votes. Thereupon Charles issued four decrees dissolving the new Chamber before it met, restricting the franchise and abolishing the freedom of the press. In Paris the party of the tricolour replied by a rebellion whose issue was still uncertain when in England the borough elections began on July 30. But when the first county elections were held on August 5 Charles X had fled and Louis Philippe was lieutenant-general of the kingdom. Two days later he was king of the French.

The news of these events provoked in England a bewildering storm of popular feeling, which swept the country and was most unfavourable to the Government. A legend sprang up and was widely believed to the effect that Wellington was Polignac's accomplice in his *coup d'état*. His brother, Lord Cowley, was ambassador at Vienna, his brother-in-law Sir Charles Bagot minister at the Hague. Was it so incredible that he maintained through these channels close communications with that alliance of monarchs which for the past decade had placed the absolutists in power in Spain, in Portugal, and finally in France? Moreover, Polignac had been the French ambassador in London when Charles X had made him prime minister. Wellington's frequent guest and intimate friend, he had no doubt returned to France encouraged by his good wishes and primed with his advice. What if the *coup d'état* he had tried to carry through in Paris should prove the prelude to a similar *coup d'état* which Wellington, a former soldier, would attempt at some future date in London? Indeed, was not the hasty dissolution of Parliament itself an attempt to override the will of the people? Fortunately

Polignac's failure and Charles' fall had frustrated the plot and the new Parliament would certainly not prove so amenable as the Parliament of 1826.

To be sure the existing franchise and the disintegration of both the traditional parties did not permit of a regular battle between two groups of candidates each furnished with a programme identical throughout the entire kingdom. The Opposition was composed of very disparate groups, containing as it did Radicals, orthodox Liberals, aristocratic Whigs, Canningites, and ultra-Tories, and during the past months the Whigs had by no means shewn uncompromising hostility to Wellington. Such indeed was the confusion, which prevailed during the contest, that the ministerialists could even claim to have increased their strength. But reliable calculations showed that, if they had gained twenty seats, they had lost fifty, a loss of about thirty seats. Moreover, the composition of their majority, if indeed they still possessed one, requires examination. The Government secured a powerful majority in Ireland, where the disappearance of the forty-shilling freeholders[1] had rendered the influence of the great landlords preponderant, every seat in Scotland, where the elections were a farce, and a considerable number of English pocket boroughs. But it was significant that of the 236 members returned by con-stituencies where the franchise was more or less open only 79 were supporters of the Government, 16 were neutral, 141 belonged to the Opposition.[2] Further what were the subjects which filled the candidates' addresses? Until the closing days of July the abolition of slavery and the necessity of retrenchment. But as soon as the revolution broke out in Paris the constitutional question took precedence over every other. To be sure the attack was not as in France directed against the person of the sovereign. George IV was dead and the new king popular; he was considered with or without justification as a friend of reform. It was the privileges

[1] *The Result of the General Election: or What has the Duke of Wellington gained by the Dissolution?* pp. 10 sqq.: Brougham to the Duc de Broglie, August 15, 1830 (*Wellington, Despatches Cont.*, vol. vii, p. 174). The Government claimed a net gain of twenty-one seats. (*The Result of the General Election*, p. 10.) Cf. Reply to a Pamphlet entitled *What has the Duke of Wellington gained by the Dissolution?* by a Graduate of the University of Oxford; or even twenty-three (Lord Grey to Princess Lieven, September 3, 1830: *Correspondence of Princess Lieven and Earl Grey*, vol. ii, p. 76). See also on this election: *The Result of the Pamphlets*, or *What the Duke of Wellington has to look to:—The Country Without a Government*; or *Plain Questions upon the Unhappy State of the Present Administration* (by Brougham); *The Duke of Wellington and the Whigs*; *The Country Well Governed*; or *Plain Questions on the Perplexed State of Parties in Opposition.* [2] *The Result of the General Election*, pp. 18–19.

of the aristocracy which were the object of attack, the excessive influence it was in a position to exercise over an unduly restricted electorate. In every constituency where the elections were more than a form the candidates found themselves obliged to promise more or less explicitly a reform of the franchise.

The Radicals were triumphant. In their view the July Revolution was the renewal of 1789; they saw France and the whole of Europe in her train following the example of the United States of America and advancing towards a system of unqualified democracy. In London and Birmingham they displayed once more, as in 1819, the tricolour flag, organized mass meetings of sympathy with the Parisian rebels[1] and opened subscriptions for the victims of July.[2] Their representative in Paris was Doctor Bowring, translator of the Marseillaise, who boasted that he was the first Englishman to be granted an audience by the new king Louis Philippe;[3] and three still very young and raw Radicals, John Mill, John Roebuck, and John Austin undertook a joint pilgrimage to Paris, were applauded in the theatre and officially received by La Fayette.[4]

It was with more mixed feelings that the Whig aristocracy, the middle class, and in general the moderate elements of the nation, learnt the news from Paris. Who could tell during the summer and autumn months whether the French were not preparing to repeat 1792 after 1789 and give the signal for a class war in France to be followed by a crusade throughout Europe?[5] Indeed, in August the news of the revolution at Paris produced a panic on the Stock Exchange.[6] But on the whole public opinion was unfavourable to the Bourbons. For *The Times*, a non-party organ, Charles X from the moment of his flight was plain Charles Capet, who had no claim to anything beyond the hospitality of Great

---

[1] H. Jephson, *The Platform, Its Rise and Progress*, vol. ii, p. 63—*Political Register*, August 21, 1830: To the Readers of the Register. On the Dinner at the London Tavern on the 16th instant. (Vol. lxx, pp. 225 sqq.)   [2] Ibid., August 21, 1830 (vol. lxx, p. 249).

[3] William Carpenter, *Anecdotes of the French Revolution of 1830*, pp. 269 sqq.—With portraits of Louis Philippe and La Fayette and Bowring's translation of the Marseillaise. The sale, according to Carpenter, reached 6,000 copies.

[4] R. E. Leader, *Life and Letters of John Arthur Roebuck*, pp. 29–30. J. S. Mill, *Autobiography*, p. 172.

[5] Lord Grey to Princess Lieven, August 19, 1830: 'What you say as to the existence of strong and unanimous feeling in England in favour of the change in France was quite true in the beginning but is no longer so now. The Court and the Ultra-tories are both inimical and any manifestation of interest is now confined to the lower classes.' (*Correspondence of Princess Lieven and Earl Grey*, vol. ii, p. 58.)

[6] Lord Brougham's *Recollections of a Long Life*, vol. iv, pp. 44, 52.

Britain.[1] The Liberals continued to cherish the hope that Louis Philippe's experiment would prove successful, and the July Revolution be a revolution at once liberal and conservative, would in fact revive not 1789 or 1792 but 1688 and thus be a French tribute to the political wisdom of the English.

A few diehards here and there ventured to defend Charles X and his ministers—but only two papers represented this point of view—one daily, the *Morning Post*, and one weekly, *John Bull*. It was quite otherwise with the overwhelming majority of the Tories. The greater their alarm at the march of events the more severe their condemnation of the blunder committed by Charles X. On many occasions during the fifteen years which had elapsed since Waterloo the English Tories had fraternized with the French legitimists and had supported their criticisms of the democratic spirit which animated the Code Civil. But they were now obliged to admit that they had been mistaken when they believed that the same profession expressed the same faith. The methods of continental absolutism were unintelligible to the English gentry. Wellington, who unknown to the public had for months past been at variance with Polignac, whose foreign policy—an understanding with Russia, annexation on the Rhine, and expansion in the Mediterranean—excited his strong disapproval, officially recognized Louis Philippe's Government.[2] In common with all his followers he awaited with alarm the effects upon the European situation of Charles X's foolhardy stroke.

2

Only a month indeed had passed since the outbreak at Paris when the revolution spread beyond the French frontiers. The same results followed as had followed the revolution at Madrid in 1820. But since Paris was now the seat of the infection its ravages were far more extensive. The revolutionary fever took possession of the Swiss Cantons, the free city of Hamburg, Hesse, Saxony, and Brunswick. Then in the second week of September it broke out in Belgium, where the Belgian Catholics and Liberals combined to raise Brussels and the other large towns against the King of the Netherlands. Britain thus found herself faced with a

---

[1] *The Times*, August 5, 14, 1830.

[2] See his letter to Lord Aberdeen, August 13, 1830 (*Despatches, Cont.*, vol. vii, p. 159), also his important Memorandum upon the existing state of our relations with France, founded upon the treaties of 1815–18, August 14, 1830 (ibid., pp. 162 sqq.).

grave problem. Charles X had excited British apprehensions by his ambitious aims. Was there not reason to fear that revolutionary France would, as in 1792, display the same ambitions under a more dangerous form? Any day the French might intervene in Belgium. Ought not England to declare war on France? But the country was radically opposed to war on any pretext, and for the past two months the most active political groups had shown a tendency to regard an alliance with the new France as an inviolable tenet of their political creed. Wellington negotiated an armistice between the Dutch army and the Belgian insurgents. No doubt he cherished the intention to effect later an agreement between Belgium and Holland by which the former while retaining its autonomy should accept a Dutch protectorate. But that did not alter the present fact that the Tory Government had made a further concession to the revolution and had recognized, provisionally at least, the independence of Belgium.

The movement now reached England itself. In Kent at harvest time some farmers attempted to replace English labour by Irish, the latter being extremely cheap. The English farm-hands expelled the Irish by force. When the time came to thresh the corn the farmers attempted to reduce their wages bill by the use of machinery. The labourers broke the machines. The disturbances spread to Sussex, Hampshire, and Wiltshire. The agitation then turned northward into Berkshire and Oxfordshire, and from there reached the eastern counties, Buckinghamshire, Huntingdon, and Northamptonshire. Sixteen counties in all were affected.[1] The farm labourers intimidated the Irish immigrants, broke the agricultural machinery, and burned the mills. An imaginary 'Captain Swing' played the part which 'Captain Ludd'[2] had played in the north twenty years earlier and terrorized the countryside. Bands of labourers traversed the country districts spreading alarm by their violent language and behaviour. They attacked the overseers of the Poor Law, whom they charged with

[1] The best account of the agricultural disturbances will be found in William Carpenter's *Political Letters*, October 15, 21, November 6, 11, 18, 25, December 7 and the end of December, 1830. See also *Political Register*, November 13, 20, December 4, 11, 25, 1830 (vol. lxx, pp. 722 sqq., 784 sqq., 872, 899 sqq., 929 sqq., 971 sqq., 1077 sqq.), January 5, 31, 1831 (vol. lxxi, pp. 80 sqq., 182 sqq.). H. of L., November 2, 1830: Speeches by Lord Winchilsea, Lord Camden and the Duke of Richmond (*Parliamentary Debates*, 3rd Series, vol. i, pp. 18 sqq.), further Extracts from Informations . . . as to . . . Poor Laws, 1833 (pp. 14, 27, 30 sqq., 76, 136, 144, 178–9).
[2] In agricultural parlance the word Swing denoted the swinging stick of the flail.

excessive harshness in enforcing the regulations.[1] They denounced the farmers and obtained by threats an increase in their wages[2] of 2s. or more a day. In some instances they declared themselves the farmers' allies and espoused their cause against the Anglican clergymen. When the latter came to receive their tithe they offered violence and compelled them to abandon a third or even a half of their due.[3] This was the first open display of anti-clericalism witnessed in rural England.

Economic causes alone cannot account for this sudden outbreak; no new economic factor came into play just at this moment to render the position of the agricultural labourer in the southern counties more insupportable than it had been for months, indeed for years, previously. The factor which turned the scale was the example of France. Two years earlier the peasants of Picardy and the district around Boulogne had burned the mills. After the July revolution it seemed natural to the Kentish labourers to imitate their French comrades.[4] It was after a tour undertaken by Cobbett, the Radical orator, that the disturbances broke out in Kent, Sussex, and Hampshire. The manifestoes circulated through the country-side copied the stereotyped formulas of French Jacobinism, and the common people were exhorted to remember Brussels and Paris.[5] When the Government decided to take severe measures it was often found that the suspects were not agricultural labourers but smiths, joiners, artisans of every trade whom political passion not poverty had turned into agitators.[6] The Tories maintained that this rustic rebellion had been the work of French agents. These assertions of Lord Eldon and Lord Falmouth[7] were unsupported by a shred of evidence. But if

[1] *Political Register*, November 13, 1830 (vol. lxx, pp. 724–6).

[2] J. L. and B. Hammond, *The Village Labourer*, pp. 232–6 (Sussex), 241–2 (Hampshire).

[3] See the manifesto circulated in Hampshire in December 1830: 'The flags of freedom and liberty are flying over the *churches* and *steeples* on the continent; rise, Englishmen and assert your rights and *pull down priestcraft* and oppression. The Reform Bill is only a stepping-stone to our future advantages. Down with the *tithes*! down with the taxes! down with the places! and down with the pensions!' (*Pol. Reg.*, August 3, 1833, vol. lxxxi, p. 300).

[4] Harriet Martineau, *Hist. of the Thirty Years' Peace*, Book IV, Chap. i., ed. Bohn, vol. ii, p. 397. J. A. Roebuck, *Hist. of the Whig Ministry of 1830, to the passing of the Reform* vol. i, p. 334.

[5] Carpenter's *Political Letters*: A letter to Earl Grey, November 25, 1830.

[6] Report from the Select Committee appointed to inquire into the state . . . of Houses in which Beer is sold, Min. of Ev.: evidence given by the Rev. Robert Wright (*Pol. Reg.*, August 3, 1833, vol. lxxxi, p. 287).

[7] H. of L., November 29, 1830 (*Parliamentary Debates*, 3rd Series, pp. 680, 682).

France did not affect England by direct propaganda, she did so by the contagion of her example.

The riots were of a very mild description. The agricultural labourers confined themselves to looting, and if occasionally they employed personal violence against some particularly unpopular landlord, they were content with knocking him about. If a country house here and there were attacked, a few young men armed with fowling-pieces were sufficient to subdue the mob. And the disorders were after all confined to particular areas. The manufacturing districts of the north and north-west, which had now recovered from the crisis of 1825 and were once more enjoying a period of prosperity, were entirely unaffected.[1] But it happened that the districts over which the disorders occurred were those in the immediate neighbourhood of the capital. The citizen of London, seeing himself surrounded by a circle of riots, could hardly avoid the impression that rural England as a whole was in a state of anarchy. He demanded a remedy which the Tory Government decided that it was not in a position to provide. The economists ascribed the demoralization of the working class in the southern counties to the lax administration of the Poor Law in those areas. Should the Poor Law then be rendered more stringent? The Cabinet felt itself already too unpopular to incur the further unpopularity of such a measure, and in any case the medicine would require time to produce its effects. Were they to call out the troops, imprison and hang the rioters? The least step in this direction and Wellington would be accused of attempting the role of a British Polignac and might well find that instead of repressing riot he had provoked revolution. He prepared to resign.

3

The opening of the next session was at hand. The question of parliamentary reform would inevitably be raised. It was discussed by the group over which Lord Althorp presided at the Albany, and Brougham, who had just been returned amid every circum-

[1] *England in* 1830; being a letter to Earl Grey, laying before him the conditions of the people as described by themselves in their petitions to Parliament, 1831. These are the 185 petitions utilized by the Rev. W. N. Molesworth (*The History of the Reform Bill of 1832*, 1865, pp. 73–95). But his extracts from the petitions tell us nothing at all of Lancashire or Cheshire, nothing of any importance of Yorkshire. All the complaints come from the agricultural districts.—A Prentice, *Hist. Sketches of . . . Manchester*, p. 173. In the great manufacturing districts there was no rising; the people there better knew the cause of the rioting.

stance which could attract public attention by the enormous constituency of Yorkshire, where the franchise was popular, was commissioned to introduce a motion to that effect. To be sure the Whigs displayed no anxiety to take office. They would willingly have left to the Tory Government the responsibility of settling this difficult question. They had seen Wellington in the course of the summer negotiate with the Huskisson group. This surely was a sign that he had made up his mind to compromise with liberalism. The dramatic death of Huskisson, crushed by an engine the very day when he was to be publicly reconciled with Wellington at the opening of the railway from Liverpool to Manchester, had not interrupted the negotiations. It was Huskisson's followers who had finally retreated.[1] The Opposition continued to cherish the belief that the Government would take the initiative and bring forward a measure of moderate reform.

Parliament met on November 2 and it was immediately evident that Wellington had decided otherwise. The Speech from the Throne promised financial economies and the repression of the agrarian disturbances but was silent on the question of Parliamentary reform. On the subject of Belgium an expression was employed which alarmed the Liberals. In the course of the debate which followed, Wellington made an explicit statement of his intentions. 'The legislature,' he declared, 'and the system of representation possessed the full and entire confidence of the country—deservedly possessed that confidence. If at the present moment he had imposed upon him the duty of forming a legislature for any country . . . he did not mean to assert that he could form such a legislature as they possessed now, for the nature of man was incapable of reaching such excellence at once; but his great endeavour would be, to form some description of legislature which would produce the same results. . . . Under these circumstances he was not . . . only not prepared to bring forward any measure of this nature (of parliamentary reform), but he would at once declare that so far as he was concerned, as long as he held any station in the government of the country, he should always feel it his duty to resist such measures when proposed by others.'[2] Imprudent words whose effect he had

---

[1] Sir G. Cornewall Lewis, *Administrations of Great Britain from 1783 to 1830*, p. 471. Sir H. L. Bulwer, *Life of Viscount Palmerston*, Book VI.
[2] H. of L., November 2, 1830 (*Parliamentary Debates*, 3rd Series, vol. i, p. 53).

certainly never calculated. Had he been content to express in terms carefully weighed his distrust of reformist principles and his conviction that it was not for the party which he led to embark upon experiments in his opinion fraught with danger he would have spoken the language of a statesman. For the events which had taken place in France had undoubtedly weakened his position, already weaker in July than it had been six months or a year earlier, and, even if he were willing to undertake parliamentary reform, the Whigs would not display the gratitude they had shown in 1829, when he emancipated the Catholics. At the present juncture their sole motive in urging this course upon him was the desire to humiliate and overthrow him.[1] But what purpose was served by this haughty and unmeasured language in which he seemed to take delight in irritating public opinion?[2] Since the days when Canning, the liberal Tory, had spoken with impunity in the same strain too many grave events had occurred, in England Catholic Emancipation two years before, in France quite recently the July revolution. Wellington's words added fuel to the revolutionary conflagration. At the Rotunda, near Blackfriars Bridge, Jacobin speeches were delivered every evening and tricolour cockades distributed. A demonstration of hostility to Wellington was arranged for the ninth of November, when the King and his ministers were to attend a banquet at the Guildhall. A rumour spread among the populace that Peel was arming

[1] Lord Grey to the Princess Lieven, October 7, 1830: 'You are greatly mistaken if you think this will assist the Ministers, as the Catholic question did. I certainly shall support a proposal for Parliamentary Reform, but the Ministers will not find in me, in this as in the former occasion, a personal defender. If moves of the kind are in contemplation, be assured that those who make them feel that they are nearly reduced to checkmate, which is inevitable without a false move on the part of their adversaries.' (*Correspondence of Princess Lieven and Earl Grey*, p. 104.) Brougham to Chalmers about the same date: 'Really slavery cannot now expect much longer protection from a Government so weak, that it is even about to give Parliamentary Reform as a sop, and to save itself for a few months.' (Rev. W. Hanna, *Memoirs of the Life and Writings of Thomas Chalmers*, vol. iii, p. 289 *n*.)

[2] Wellington's conversation with his intimate friends and his correspondence leave no doubt of his sincere determination not to yield an inch. See the letter from Princess Lieven to Lord Grey, November 9, 1830: 'The Duke of Wellington has told me that all would go off well: that he was sure of his position: that he would carry out all his intentions: that reform could no more be carried through without him than the Catholic question; that he would have nothing to do with it; and consequently that nothing would be done. In a word, he feels perfectly sure of his position.' (*Correspondence of Princess Lieven and Earl Grey*, vol. ii, p. 115.) A few months later he is less optimistic, but equally obdurate. He writes to the Duke of Buckingham on April 2, 1831: 'I am opposed to all reform; and can, without personal or, indeed, public inconvenience, avow my opinion. Indeed, I believe, that some advantage is gained by the knowledge which the public have of my opinion on this subject.' (*Wellington, Despatches, Cont.,* vol. vii, p. 423.)

his police with cutlasses to suppress the demonstration. And the ministers on the other hand were informed that the Radicals were preparing not a peaceful demonstration but a rebellion. Were they less numerous or worse organized than the republicans of Paris, who had succeeded in overthrowing the Government and establishing another in its place? If Wellington attempted resistance had he as many troops at his disposal as Polignac? The Cabinet after prolonged discussion decided on the eve of the fateful day that the royal visit to the City should not take place. A Government at once arrogant and feeble was obviously condemned to a speedy doom. Brougham's motion was set down for November 16. On the fifteenth the Government on a motion by Sir Henry Parnell respecting the civil list was defeated by 29 votes. The following day Wellington resigned, only too thankful that he had been defeated on another question than parliamentary reform[1] and by a scratch majority whose nucleus consisted of ultra-Tories. But he strangely miscalculated if he imagined that the solution of the problem could be postponed any longer when once the forces released by the July revolution had carried the Whigs into office almost in spite of themselves.

Public opinion pointed unanimously to Lord Grey as Wellington's successor. When in 1827 Lord Lansdowne and the group represented by the *Edinburgh Review* had rallied to Canning's policy, he had stood out for the independence of the traditional party. He had, it is true, since contemplated later the possibility of an alliance with Wellington,[2] but since Wellington had never for a single moment entertained the idea of negotiating with him his reputation as a politician of rigid consistency remained unimpaired. He was the typical Whig. Nor could it be denied that during the forty years which had elapsed since that distant period when he began his political career by denouncing the abuses of the franchise his zeal for parliamentary reform had often relaxed. Since 1822 he had taken no action whatever on its behalf and in 1827 had gone out of his way to insist that if he was obliged to break with Canning that question played no part in their disagreement.[3] But the July revolution had reconverted him, and during the debate on the address he had bound himself to the

---

[1] Wellington to the Duke of Northumberland, November 17, 1830 (op. cit., vol. vii, p. 361).   [2] H. of L., May 10, 1827 (*Parliamentary Debates* ,N.S., vol. xvii, p. 731).
[3] H. of L., May 10, 1827 (ibid., N.S., vol. xvii, p. 731).

reformers by an unequivocal declaration. When he was summoned by the King, he made his acceptance of office subject to one condition and one alone, that he should be allowed to form an administration unanimous on the question of Reform. The King consented and by his consent accredited the report that he was himself a convert to the Liberal cause. In two or three days the new Cabinet was complete.

The formation of Lord Grey's ministry amounted to a revolution in polite society. For the first time for fifty years the great Tory families fell from power, and Devonshire House, Lansdowne House and Holland House became the ministerial salons. Lord Grey was an aristocrat of the old school, genuinely persuaded that by placing himself and his clique at the head of the reformers he was destined to revive in all their ancient lustre the eighteenth-century traditions of the Whig aristocracy. He began by making liberal provisions for all his followers. Lord Durham, who for years past as John George Lambton had fought the battle of parliamentary reform, was given the privy seal and a seat in the Cabinet. Lord Howick, Ellice, Lord Duncannon, George Barrington, George Ponsonby, and Wood received positions which if less important were extremely lucrative. Lord Althorp took the Treasury and became leader in the Commons. Lord Lansdowne was made president of the Privy Council, Lord Holland Chancellor of the Duchy of Lancaster. The Duke of Devonshire became Lord Chamberlain, Lord John Russell Paymaster of the Forces. Full satisfaction was given to the group of noble families known as the Stafford Interest. Sir James Graham received the Admiralty and Stanley was made Secretary for Ireland. Both Graham and Stanley had been among the most prominent debaters during the session of 1830.

Wellington had owed his defeat to a coalition. The Cabinet therefore even contained a Tory, the Duke of Richmond. The Canningites, left without a leader by Huskisson's death, rallied to the Whigs and were richly rewarded. William Lamb, who had become Lord Melbourne on his father's death two years earlier, became Home Secretary, Lord Goderich Colonial Secretary. Grant went to the Board of Control, and Lord Palmerston became Foreign Secretary. Lord Grey had indeed wished to give the Foreign Office to Lord Lansdowne or Lord Holland and it was only on their refusal that he offered it to Palmerston.[1] The latter had occupied a very subordinate position, as Secretary for War, in the successive administrations in power between 1809 and 1828; but on quitting office with Canning's other followers had suddenly attracted public attention by the vigorous speeches he had delivered in the Commons during 1829 and 1830 denouncing the foreign policy of Wellington and Lord Aberdeen as a violation of the principles for which Canning had stood.[2] Thus by the choice of his foreign secretary Lord Grey, whether he liked it or not, paid tribute to the memory of the statesman whom he had once attacked so bitterly in concert with Wellington. This apparent miracle was the work of the July revolution. A disciple of Canning would it was hoped be in a better position than a member of any other group to adopt a firm line towards the northern Powers and maintain friendly relations with the new Government in France.

Was the new Cabinet then entirely devoid of new blood? A few concessions were made to the Whig intelligentsia. One of these might seem at first sight important. Brougham became Lord Chancellor. But the appointment was motived by the desire to get rid of his embarrassing presence in the Commons, and his departure could not be purchased at any cheaper rate. Without being in the strict sense members of the Cabinet Jeffrey and Cockburn became respectively Lord Advocate, and Solicitor-General for Scotland, and the *Edinburgh Review* joined the new coalition. On the other hand Poulett Thomson, the Manchester free-trader, became Vice-President of the Board of Trade. He was exposed to mortifying sneers when, a plain merchant, he took his seat on the Government bench.[3] But this was all. Mackintosh was obliged to content himself with a subordinate position on the Board of Control. Never had a more aristocratic administration governed the country. Of the fourteen members of the Cabinet only four sat in the Lower House. And of these four Palmerston held an

[1] Lord Tavistock to Lord John Russell at the end of 1830: '. . . Lord Grey . . . informs me that the Foreign Office is now quite out of the question for you. Lords Lansdowne and Holland having declined it, they have given it to Palmerston—not a very popular appointment, I fear.' (Spencer Walpole, *Life of Lord John Russell*, vol. i, p. 160.)

[2] *Greville Memoirs*, June 11, 1829. 'Palmerston's speech . . . they say was exceedingly able and eloquent. . . . He has been twenty years in office and never distinguished himself before . . . but . . . the great men having been removed from the House of Commons by death or promotion, he has launched forth, and with astonishing success.'

[3] Croker to Lord Hertford, November 22, 1830 (*Croker Papers*, vol. ii, p. 78).

Irish title and was an important landowner, Sir James Graham was a baronet and another great landlord, and Lord Althorp, appointed leader in the Commons, was heir to a great family, the Spencers.[1]

II FIRST REFORM BILL

I

The programme of the new Government could be reduced to three heads—peace abroad, retrenchment at home, parliamentary reform. But to apply that programme, indeed to draw it out in detail, needed time. For the moment the task facing the Government was, in the most elementary sense, to govern.

To put down the agrarian disturbances the ministers did not ask Parliament for new legislation. They simply undertook to apply without hesitation the existing laws, and strengthened by the assistance rendered, not without an ironic amusement, by the Tory gentry they kept their word. The new Home Secretary, Lord Melbourne, who passed for an indolent man of fashion, astonished his colleagues by the energy he displayed. Circulars were dispatched to the Lord-Lieutenants of the counties and the Justices of the Peace, urging them to proceed with the utmost severity.[2] Large numbers were arrested, 900, it was calculated, in December alone.[3] The same magistrates who in October had acquitted eight men who had broken machines changed their line of action towards the close of November, and committed the accused for trial at the assizes. And to obviate the necessity of waiting until the assizes were held, a 'special commission' was bestowed upon a number of justices empowering them to try the accused summarily.[4] Before the end of December the death sentences began. Usually the death penalty was commuted. Three persons however were executed. Four hundred and fifty-seven were transported.[5] The riots ceased immediately, arson a little later. The suppression—assisted we must add by a considerable

[1] Sir James Walsh, *Observations on the Ministerial Plan of Reform*, 1831, pp. 24–5. 'As a body,' adds Sir John Walsh, 'with the exception of the followers of Mr. Canning, who do not appear to be the leaders now, they are totally inexperienced and untried in their management of state affairs.'
[2] *Political Register*, Dec. 4, 1830 (vol. lxx, pp. 919 sqq.). *Annual Register*, 1830, Chron., p. 200.
[3] Carpenter's *Political Letter;* to the right hon. Wilmot Horton, end of Dec. 1830.
[4] *Ann. Reg.*, 1830, Chron., December.
[5] J. L. and B. Hammond, *The Village Labourer*, p. 284.

increase of the labourers' wages[1]—had thus proved successful.
But it was strange inauguration into office for a party which posed
as the popular party! At the same time the manufacturing
districts which until November had remained quiet began to
cause anxiety to the Government. They were agitated by a
number of conflicting movements with which the ministers felt
themselves powerless to cope. They were in the first place
economic. The mines of Cornwall and Wales were the scene of
disturbances.[2] In the Manchester district an extensive strike began
among the cotton spinners; the son of one of the leading manufacturers was murdered, and the danger to law and order to be
apprehended from the Trade Unions once more engaged public
attention.[3] But these popular movements also possessed their
political aspect. All over the country Political Unions sprung up
modelled upon the Political Union of Birmingham. Their
programme was far more democratic than any which Lord Grey
could possibly bring forward and after the events in France the
English agitation for reform assumed a revolutionary character
which no one could mistake. In Staffordshire the rumour spread
that tricolour flags were being prepared and seditious pamphlets
circulated by mysterious agents.[4] At Preston, in Lancashire,
Stanley, who was obliged to seek re-election on his appointment
as Secretary for Ireland, found himself opposed by an unexpected
candidate in the person of the agitator Henry Hunt. And Hunt
was returned.[5] On the other hand these Political Unions might
in certain circumstances prove indispensable allies of the Cabinet
against the party of Wellington and Peel. For since the July
revolution they had lost the Tory character which in January
1830 Thomas Attwood had imparted to the Birmingham Union,

[1] In October 1833 Cobbett estimated at £18,000,000 the total amount of additional
wages received since 1830 by the agricultural labourers. (*Political Register*, Oct. 12, 1833,
vol. lxxxii, p. 122.) Cf. Lord Melbourne to Wellington, Nov. 10, 1832. The concessions which were made to violence in the year 1830 have, I fear, had a permanently bad
effect upon the character of the agricultural population (*Lord Melbourne's Papers*, p. 152).
But when the magistrates contemplated the legal regulation of wages Lord Melbourne
dissuaded them from the attempt. (J. A. Roebuck, *History of the Whig Ministry of 1830
to the passing of the Reform Bill*, vol. i, p. 337.)

[2] *Annual Register*, 1831, Chron., Feb. 22. *Pol. Reg.*, Jan. 15, 1831 (vol. lxxi, p. 187).

[3] For this movement, which was led by Doherty, see vol. ii, p. 287. Cf. *Greville
Memoirs*, January 25, 1831. *Ann. Reg.*, 1831, Chron., January 3; *Pol. Reg.*, January 15,
1831, vol. lxxi, p. 183. Carpenter's *Political Letters*, December 18, 1830, January 7, 1831.

[4] *Pol. Reg.*, October 30, 1830 (vol. lxxi, p. 597).

[5] For Hunt's election see ibid., December 18, 25, 1830; January 1, 8, 1831 (vol. lxx,
pp. 991, 1069; vol. lxxi, p. 118).

and by providing popular feeling with a political outlet they might perhaps divert most opportunely the attention of the people from a propaganda which in Lancashire and Yorkshire was gaining ground every day. A committee which, it was remarked, included Tories had undertaken a campaign for the legal restriction of the hours of labour in factories. In the public meetings it organized language more violent than any which had been previously heard was addressed to the factory owners, and the country gentlemen seemed rather pleased than alarmed. Fortunately trade was prosperous, and there was practically no unemployment: for the revolutions on the Continent, by bringing industry to a standstill in France and Belgium, had provided employment for the workers of Yorkshire and Lancashire.[1]

Even in London the revolutionary agitation gathered strength. Cobbett emerged from the obscurity in which he had lain for several years. To his *Political Register* he now added another and a cheaper publication, *Twopenny Trash*, in which every week he dealt out his invectives impartially to Whigs and Tories alike. Another journalist, William Carpenter, revived in October an old idea of Cobbett's and evaded the stamp duty by publishing several times a month but at irregular intervals open letters addressed to an individual politician of either party. These letters, which were periodicals without being periodicals, scored immediately an enormous success and from the end of October had a regular circulation of 20,000 copies. During the following months a host of Radical and republican papers came into existence—for example, *The Ballot*, *The Voice of the People*, and Carlile's *Prompter*. All these papers if they did not directly incite the agricultural labourer to burn mills and break machines excused acts of disorder which would compel the governing classes to give heed to the sufferings of the people. Demonstrations on a large scale proved how fertile was the soil into which the seed

---

[1] *Westminster Review*, January 1831, 'The Wellington Administration' (vol. xiv, p. 244). 'Let us for a moment consider the state of the two great divisions of the labouring order. The manufacturers, at present in comparative comfort, are experienced in organization and assured of their strength. The agricultural labourers sunk to the last depth of misery, and breaking into desultory violence. Whenever these two extremes meet—for extremes they are—the one class resorting to force from the extreme of misery and degradation, and the other in an extreme condition of power, from the best management of their means of strength—what will be the state of society, tossed upon these vast and furious elements?' For wages at this date (real wages were declining, according to the author) see the interesting details furnished by Carpenter's *Political Letter* of January 21, 1832, entitled 'A Political Herald'.

fell which the Radical press was scattering broadcast. On December 13 over 10,000 skilled workmen headed by the tricolour beset St. James' Palace.[1] On January 10 Hunt, just returned for Preston, made a triumphal entry into London.[2]

Panic took hold of the party in office.[3] While the friends of the Government who were not bound by the ties of party betook themselves to the more moderate Radicals—the Benthamites— and implored them to prove to the people by speech and writing the absurdity of smashing machinery, the Cabinet decided to prosecute Cobbett and Carlile. On January 10 Carlile was tried for two articles alleged to be seditious and the jury after long hours of anxious deliberation made it possible for the judges to sentence him to two years' imprisonment and a fine of £200.[4] But the prosecutions were fruitless; and the unstamped press went on its triumphant way. New papers came into existence: the *Radical*, the *Republican*, and, most important of all, Hetherington's famous publication, the *Poor Man's Guardian*, 'a weekly newspaper for the people established contrary to law to try the power of might against right'. In July no less than thirty-two unstamped journals were being published in London. For the French word journals was used to describe them instead of the English word newspapers, and it was the fashion in Tory circles to decry what was called the spirit of journalism.[5] And the republican journals of

[1] Croker to Lord Hertford, December 14, 1830 (*Croker Papers*, vol. ii, p. 81).

[2] *Political Register*, January 15, 1831 (vol. lxxi, p. 79).

[3] See the alarmist letter written by a very advanced Liberal, Sir William Napier, to his wife in January 1831: '. . . before spring all Europe will be in war and turmoil. Here in London men speak sedition openly in the clubs and secretly in the streets; every person is prepared or preparing for a great change. . . . Public opinion is at last ripe for a revolution, and the first great man that steps forward will be sovereign of this country, or he will found a republic' (*Life of Sir William Napier*, vol. i, p. 336). On February 23 he warned his wife and daughter to get ready for exile. It was unfortunate that France was so unsafe, America so distant (ibid., p. 344). [4] *Annual Register*, 1831, Chron., January 10.

[5] *Ann. Reg.*, 1831, p. 111: 'the spirit of journalism, to use a foreign phrase'. *Morning Chronicle*, April 23, 1833: 'His (Sir R. Peel's) maledictions against Journalism and Democracy remind us of the maniac raving against his keepers.' April 25: 'Sir Robert Peel . . . an enemy to the liberty of the Press, which he chooses to term *Journalism* . . . He talked on Friday of the "despotism of journalism".' For a depreciatory use of the word 'journal' see *Ann. Reg.*, 1831, pp. 241, 283, 295; 1832, pp. 2, 100, 131, 147. Cf., on the other hand, *Westminster Review*, Jan. 1833, 'Journalism' (vol. xviii, p. 195): '*Journalism* is a good word for the thing meant. A word was sadly wanted: *Newspapers* and *newspaper writing*, not to mention that they have a bad odour, only imperfectly described the thing intended. The intercommunication of opinion and intelligence, as maintained in England and other countries by means of journals, is too important to pass without a name and that a good one. . . . It is not very usual to find any one who will allow his connexion with a newspaper, and if it were avowed, it would certainly operate to the disadvantage of the party so avowing. . . . In France, on the contrary, to be a journalist, is to be a person of note . . . the title of a journalist, implies education, character and perhaps disinterested enthusi-

Paris were in fact the models which the London revolutionaries imitated and in consequence of the prevalent unrest imitated successfully.

Upon Ireland also the French and Belgian revolutions—the latter especially, for the Belgian revolution had been largely Catholic—had their repercussion. The peasants refused to pay the tithe and demanded reductions of rent. In January a series of agrarian outrages was inaugurated by the first murder and there were signs that a famine was imminent. Meanwhile, O'Connell had placed himself at the head of another agitation, of a political not a social nature, whose object was the repeal of the Act of Union. Scarcely had one association which he founded been dissolved than he founded another which pursued the same object under a new name. It was dissolved in its turn and the farce continued. Then the Government proscribed *en bloc* all associations founded by O'Connell. He at once devised other methods of agitation. One day he would advise the Irish to withdraw all the gold they had deposited in the banks, another day to abstain from the commodities on which they must pay a tax to the English treasury. On January 18 the Chief Secretary Stanley and the Lord-Lieutenant Lord Anglesey imprisoned him together with seven of his colleagues. No sooner released on bail he recommenced his legal antics. A section of the Cabinet seemed bent upon securing his condemnation, another hesitated and negotiated with him through his son.

2

Such was the condition of the United Kingdom when Parliament reassembled on February 3. Deplorable in itself, it reflected the utmost discredit upon the Administration. Without a majority in Parliament, unable to count upon the support of the clergy, the courts, or the magistrates the Cabinet was incurring the hatred of the lower classes by a high-handed method of government which Wellington had not dared to employ. 'The real battle,' wrote Jeffrey to a friend, 'is not between Whigs and Tories, Liberals and Illiberals and such gentlemen-like denominations, but between property and no property—Swing and the law.'[1]

asm.' The writer of the article protests against the unfavourable sense which usually attached to the term, while pointing out pretty clearly its French origin. The *Westminster Review* was Radical and favourable to the French.

[1] Jeffrey to Empson, January 31, 1831 (Lord Cockburn, *Life of Lord Jeffrey*, vol. ii, p. 233).

If these were the thoughts of a leading representative of the party in office how could the ministers be expected to show any zeal to carry out their positive programme of peace, retrenchment, and parliamentary reform?

Peace indeed was maintained in spite of gloomy forebodings amply warranted by the disturbed condition of Europe. The months passed by and the general conflagration was not kindled. In November Poland rose in rebellion against Russia, in January a Russian army invaded Poland. When Modena and Parma revolted and the inhabitants of the Romagna threw off the authority of the Pope, an Austrian army hastened to restore everywhere legitimate Government. Palmerston, faithful to Canning's tradition, protested against the Russian and Austrian invasions. But he had the prudence to be satisfied with a verbal protest and liberal France did no more.

The situation in Belgium presented difficulties which seriously threatened the understanding between Whig England and Orleanist France. For we must not be deceived by the lively debates which the question raised in Parliament. The Belgian policy of Lord Grey and Palmerston was in reality scarcely distinguishable from the policy which Wellington and Lord Aberdeen had followed in September. Their Liberal profession no doubt made it easier for the new ministers to declare themselves in favour of Belgian independence. But their Tory predecessors had already recognized the autonomy of Belgium, and Grey and Palmerston fully shared their desire that the new state should as far as possible belong to the sphere of Dutch rather than of French influence. For Belgian sovereign they proposed the Prince of Orange, the son and heir of the King of the Netherlands.[1] The Belgian National Congress disregarded the wishes of Great Britain and offered the throne to the son of Louis Philippe. The prudence

[1] Contemporary documents enable us to follow during this January Lord Grey's change of opinion in regard to the candidature of the Prince of Orange. On the fifteenth he seems still to have been in favour of the Prince's claim (*Diary of Sir John Hobhouse*, January 15, 1831; Lord Broughton's *Recollections of a Long Life*, vol. iv, p. 79). Fifteen days later he was discouraged by the inactivity shown by the supporters of the Prince. He wrote to Princess Lieven, January 30, 1831: 'We still hear of the Orange party, but it does nothing and does not advance a step. This, therefore, may be put out of your calculation and the best thing now to be done—the neutrality being new established, which creates the best barrier that existing circumstances afford against her [France], if she passes it— is to take any King the Belgians will choose, who can be accepted without dishonour' (*Correspondence of Princess Lieven and Earl Grey*, vol. ii, p. 150). The next day he expresses his fear lest the Orange party should embarrass British diplomacy by some inopportune step (Lord Grey to Princess Lieven, January 31, 1831, ibid., p. 151).

which the latter displayed in yielding to the British protest, and the accession to office of Casimir Perier paved the way for a peaceful solution of the Belgian question by the choice of Prince Leopold of Saxe-Coburg, a candidate agreeable to England and not distasteful to France. Was this settlement a victory for England, a defeat, or an honourable compromise? The question was left to the diplomatists to discuss. Public opinion, wholly absorbed by domestic problems, attached no importance to this dynastic arrangement. The nation wanted peace and imposed its will upon Lord Grey as upon Wellington before him. 'I have no fear,' Lord Grenville wrote in December to the Duke of Buckingham, 'of anybody involving us in war. The truth is (I should be sorry that France or America overheard me), our entering on any such course is as much a physical impossibility as it would be for me to set about drilling my servants and labourers.'[1]

If the country demanded peace, it equally demanded retrenchment and a reduction of taxes. The financial question had exerted a considerable influence upon the late election and it was by the demand that the items of the civil list should be examined by a parliamentary committee that Sir Henry Parnell on November 15 had obtained the vote which placed Wellington's Cabinet in a minority. But as the result of two months' study of the financial position, Lord Althorp, the new Chancellor of the Exchequer, had reached the conclusion that it would be difficult to satisfy the hopes his party had raised, impossible to improve in this direction on the policy of the late Government. The July revolution, by reviving the Belgian question, had compelled the Government to arm, and, even if peace were preserved, the taxpayer must shoulder the cost of the additional forces. Only one resource remained at the Chancellor's disposition—to lighten the burden by shifting its incidence, in other words to reform instead of reducing taxation. Lord Althorp introduced an ambitious budget inspired by the ideas of Sir Henry Parnell. It proved an utter failure and collapsed under the criticism of the House of Commons. Already at the close of February Lord Althorp, Chancellor of the Exchequer and Leader of the Commons, weary of his important offices was considering the best way to secure the Government an honourable demise.

[1] Lord Grenville to the Duke of Buckingham, December 7, 1830 (Duke of Buckingham, *Memoirs of the Courts and Cabinets of William IV and Victoria*, vol. i, pp. 161–2).

3

But when Lord Althorp was despairing, Parliament had not even discussed the third plank of the ministerial programme and it was this which engrossed the attention of the country. By innumerable public meetings and petitions the public demanded a House of Commons truly representative of the entire people, a reduction of the interval between elections and voting by ballot. This political agitation, weak in the country districts where the labourers were in revolt against their employers, was very powerful in the manufacturing districts, where to a large extent it provided a safety-valve for the workers' discontent, liable otherwise to take a violent form. No doubt recourse to violence was in contemplation should the Cabinet betray the mandate of the nation. But for the moment an impenetrable obscurity shrouded its intentions.

If Denman, the Attorney General, declared himself opposed to the ballot,[1] Lord Althorp eight days later spoke in its favour.[2] A rumour circulated at the beginning of January that the Cabinet had asked the two democrats who represented Westminster, Burdett and Hobhouse, whether they would accept a £10 qualification for the franchise.[3] Did the Government then propose only to enlarge the boundaries of the existing boroughs and in these enlarged boroughs establish on that basis a democratic franchise? Or did they intend to undertake on a large scale a redistribution of the constituencies? On January 31 Lord Grey was in Brighton laying the Government's bill before the King, and as soon as he returned to the House it was known that the King had accepted it. Did that mean that it was extremely moderate?

Throughout the entire month of February—the discussion of the bill was not to begin until March 1—the uncertainty continued. Not a single indiscretion shed any light on the mystery. However, the debate upon the budget had issued in a victory for the Tories, and as less was now heard of parliamentary reform, they indulged the hope that the nation was losing interest in the question. Peel, a more able speaker than any of the ministers, shielded them with his scornful patronage. What difficulties

[1] H. of C., November 22, 1830: Denman added: 'Though he must confess himself quite open to conviction upon the subject' (*Parliamentary Debates*, 3rd Series, vol. i, p. 627).
[2] *Political Register*, December 11, 1830 (vol. lxx, p. 945).
[3] Croker to Lord Hertford, January 3, 1831 (*Croker Papers*, vol. ii, p. 96).

would face them the moment the Reform Bill was introduced! The proposed reform might be radical. In that case what hope had they of getting the Commons to accept it? Or it might be moderate. In that case the democrats throughout the country would be in arms against the Cabinet. From a liberal administration they would not accept the minor reforms they would have welcomed from a Tory Government. Then Peel's hour would strike. 'If there is not a revolution,' wrote Greville, 'Peel will assuredly be Prime Minister.'[1]

On March 1 Lord John Russell addressed a crowded and expectant House. He proved that parliamentary reform was founded on the principles of justice, was reasonable and an urgent necessity. The confidence of the nation in its representatives must be restored by a reform which 'without endangering the settled institutions of the country' would satisfy 'every reasonable man'. Lord John proceeded to explain the measure under three heads.[2]

In the first place the Government proposed to disfranchise wholly or in part all those boroughs too tiny to be safe from illegitimate influences, whether the domination of a powerful family or the corruption of the electors. Every borough whose population as ascertained by the census of 1821 was less than 2,000 would be completely disfranchised. This would affect twenty boroughs returning at present 120 members. Every borough whose population according to the same census was above two and below 4,000 would in future return one representative instead of two. This would involve a further decrease of forty-six members. And Weymouth would henceforward return two instead of four members. In all 168 seats would be abolished that is to say, more than a quarter of the House of Commons.

In their place it was proposed to create a number of new seats. Nine large towns headed by Manchester, Birmingham, and four metropolitan districts would return two members, eighteen other towns one member. Twenty-six counties would return

---

[1] *Greville Memoirs*, December 19, 1830. Cf. Croker to Lord Hertford, January 11, 1831: 'I hear less and less every day of the Duke, and in the House of Commons men begin to look *exclusively* to Peel' (*Croker Papers*, vol. ii, p. 97); to the same correspondent, March 1, 1831: For the last week every one, Court, City, Ministers, Tories, all agree that the Government holds its seat at the mercy of *Sir Robert Peel* (ibid., p. 108).

[2] We have followed the provisions of the bill (reproduced in its entirety in Cobbett's *Political Register*, March 19, 1831, vol. lxxi, pp. 714 sqq.). These provisions do not agree in detail with the explanations of Lord John Russell's speech as reproduced in *Parliamentary Debates*, 3rd Series, vol. ii, pp. 1061 sqq., nor these with the data of the *Annual Register*, 1831, pp. 8 sqq.

four instead of two representatives, Yorkshire six instead of four. In all ninety-eight new seats.

In the third place it was proposed to introduce a uniform franchise for every county and a uniform franchise for every borough. Henceforward, in the boroughs the franchise would be given to every householder who had occupied for at least six months previous to the annual revision of the register a house whose rental value was not less than £10. Since the former franchise was so diversified the establishment of this uniform franchise might have the effect in a certain number of boroughs of reducing the number of electors. Steps would be taken to prevent the decrease being too sudden or too extensive. Every British subject who at present possessed the borough franchise would retain it for life provided that, if he possessed it in virtue of membership of a corporation, he continued to reside in the locality. In the counties the freehold franchise would be extended to include those who in the language of English law held their land in copyhold or leasehold.

A number of subordinate provisions laid down the procedure, of an extremely simple character, to be followed in revising the register every year. To prevent rioting at elections the duration of the poll both in the boroughs and the counties was limited to two days. In the counties provision would be made that no voter need travel more than fifteen miles to record his vote.

The new English franchise would be extended to Wales, Scotland, and Ireland. Only one new seat would be given to Wales, five to Scotland, and three to Ireland.

To the House Lord John's speech came as a thunderbolt. He was heard with stupefaction. The members of the Tory Opposition, silent at first, decided, as the explanation proceeded, to receive each new provision with an outburst of scornful laughter. They could scarcely believe their own ears. Could it be possible that the project was meant seriously?

How ever could the Cabinet have reached an agreement to introduce so extensive a measure? The answer was not known until several years later; so well was the secret kept.[1] The draught-

---

[1] We can follow the stages by which this Cabinet's secret was gradually revealed. (1) Lord Durham's speech at Gateshead, October 23, 1833 (Stuart and Reid, *Life and Letters of Lord Durham*, vol. i, pp. 344 sqq.). (2) Brougham's article, *Edinburgh Review*, October 1834 (vol. lx, pp. 249–50). See also the letter which, as a result of this article, Lord John Russell wrote to Lord Durham, October 19, 1834, to fix his memory of what passed in

ing of the bill had been entrusted in December to a committee of four—Lord John Russell, Lord Durham, Sir James Graham, and Lord Duncannon. On this committee Lord John and Lord Durham represented the left wing, Sir James Graham and Lord Duncannon the moderates. But Sir James was under the influence of Lord Althorp, who was the convinced supporter of a comprehensive reform. The unqualified abolition of the nomination boroughs was accepted without discussion and a uniform qualification of £10 soon gained the support of the entire committee,[1] though Lord John, faithful to the views he had expressed in 1822, advocated at first a 'diversified' qualification. It was a qualification which would satisfy the Benthamites.[2] But at this point Lord Durham intervened and asked the committee to consider the other articles of Bentham's programme, the reduction of the legal life of Parliament, and the introduction of the ballot.

For the past fifteen years Bentham and his friends had valued the ballot more highly than even the extension of the franchise and for the past year or two it had assumed an additional importance in their eyes. We have already seen the distrust with which towards the close of 1829 the editors of the *Morning Chronicle* regarded the agitation conducted by the Tory demagogue the Marquis of Blandford. And what on the other hand was the lesson to be drawn from the events which had taken place before their eyes in France? They had witnessed a Chamber of Deputies elected on a narrowly restricted franchise defy for months Polignac's reactionary cabinet. It had been dissolved and the same electorate had acted in complete independence of the

the Committee of Four (*Early Correspondence of Lord John Russell*, vol. ii, pp. 41 sqq.). (3) Lord John Russell's speech at Stroud, July 28, 1837 (*The Times*, July 31, 1837); also the altercation which, as a result of this speech, took place on the subject of this speech between Sheil and Sir J. Graham, H. of C., June 18, 1839 (*Parliamentary Debates*, 3rd Series, vol. lviii, pp. 488 sqq.). (4) The information supplied by Sir J. Graham to Roebuck, Jan. 2, 1851 (C. S. Parker, *Life and Letters of Sir James Graham*, vol. i, pp. 114 sqq.), and utilized by Roebuck (*Hist. of the Whig Ministry of 1830*, pp. 225 sqq.). (5) The complete text of Lord John Russell's first draft in the final chapter of the new edition published in 1865 of his *Essay on the History of the English Government and Constitution*, pp. 225 sqq. (6) The text of the report presented by the four members of the committee in the *Correspondence of Earl Grey with William IV*, vol. i, pp. 461 sqq.

[1] This figure seems to have been reached after some discussion. Lord John originally proposed that the register of electors should be identical with the jury list. It was recommended by the example of Norwich, where all the £10 householders were entitled to vote for the guardians of the poor. That is to say, 4,000 out of 11,000 householders possessed the franchise, and the qualification had worked well. (H. of C., February 3, 1832. Lord John Russell's speech: *Parl. Deb.*, 3rd Series, vol. i, p. 1235.)

[2] *Westminster Review*, January 1831: 'Parliamentary Representation in Scotland' (vol. xiv, p. 145).

Government and returned a Liberal majority to the Palais Bourbon, because it was secured against official pressure by the ballot. 'France, happy France,' exclaimed Bentham, 'to what but the Ballot is it indebted for its salvation?'[1] The committee decided to reduce the duration of Parliament to five years and to propose the introduction of the ballot. To offset these concessions the qualification was raised from £10 to £20. A uniform franchise narrowly restricted and the ballot: the plan of reform as it left the committee was directly modelled on the French system.

But when the scheme was submitted to the Cabinet Lord Grey flatly refused even to consider reducing the duration of Parliament or introducing the ballot. He wished to abolish the pocket boroughs to diminish the influence which Court and Cabinet exercised over the elections, but to maintain public voting to preserve unimpaired the influence of the great landowners over the elections in the counties and even in the smaller boroughs. His views carried the day. By way of compensation the Cabinet returned to the Committee's original proposal and restored the £10 franchise. All the members of the Cabinet, even the recruits of the Canning group, finally accepted more or less willingly Lord Grey's contention that it was advisable to introduce an imposing measure of reform if public opinion were to receive the satisfaction it had demanded since July, and effect a final[2] settlement of the question, such that the Radicals could not demand its revision in the near future. How are we to explain the fact that when the Cabinet had adopted this plan of reform, without any further delay the King gave his unconditional assent? Recent memories of the senile obstinacy displayed on several occasions by George IV, and gratitude that the bill made no attempt to

---

[1] *Westminster Review*, October 1830: 'Mr. Brougham and Local Judicatories' (vol. xiii, p. 457). Cf. ibid., January 1831; article quoted in the preceding note: 'The ballot is a question of *principle* and not of *detail*. It is *the* question—the all important question. . . . We are convinced that no scheme of reform without the ballot will satisfy public opinion' (vol. xiv, pp. 144–5).

[2] This term, which had a history before it (see below, p. 290), was employed for the first time by Lord Grey in a letter in which he communicated to Lord Durham the King's opinion of the ministerial plan (*Earl Grey to Lord Durham*, January 31, 1831): '. . . . He [the King] was particularly pleased with your report, and entirely concurred in the statement so clearly and powerfully made in it of the necessity of doing something, and that something should be effectual and final' (*Corr. of Earl Grey with William IV*, vol. i, p. 91). Cf. H. of C., March 1, 1831, Lord Althorp's speech: he thought it would be a final settlement (*Parliamentary Debates*, 3rd Series, vol. ii, p. 1143); also June 5, 1832, Stanley's speech: 'He must say that, so far as rested with the Government, the present was a final measure' (ibid., 3rd Series, vol. xiii, p. 439).

introduce manhood suffrage or the ballot, were no doubt motives which played their part in a decision so rapid that the ministers themselves were astonished. Thus William IV, in reality a convinced Tory, encouraged the popular belief, a belief very useful to the Cabinet, that for the first time for a century the sovereign belonged to the popular party.

4

Nevertheless, since the Government's bill did not bestow upon the country manhood suffrage and the ballot it was not in the strict sense a Radical measure. Outside the House would it receive the approval of the democratic press and the popular speakers? Immediately after the sitting Hobhouse rushed off to Francis Place, anxious to learn the opinion of the great electioneering agent of his constituency. He found him delighted with the bill.[1] A few days before, Cobbett had announced that he would not support any measure which did not introduce the ballot.[2] In spite of this he gave his unqualified approval to Lord John's bill[3] and abused Hunt for his attempt in the House to criticize the measure in its present form as a piece of middle-class legislation.[4] Although the bill maintained in Ireland the disfranchisement of the forty-shilling freeholders O'Connell became its enthusiastic supporter. The Cabinet concluded a tacit alliance with him and the prosecution was dropped. According to Lord John's explanation, the bill would double the number of voters, raising it from 500,000 to 1,000,000.[5] Thus the English 'Reform', occasioned by

[1] Lord Broughton's *Recollections of a Long Life*, vol. iv, p. 88.
[2] *Political Register*, February 26, 1831 (vol. lxxi, pp. 532–4).
[3] See the article entitled 'My Triumph': to the readers of the *Register* on the Destruction of the Boroughmongers, ibid., March 5, 1831 (vol. lxxi, pp. 624 sqq.).
[4] To the People of Preston On the Parliamentary Reform now under discussion, and on the Conduct of the Preston Cock with regard to the Measure (ibid., March 12, 1831, vol. lxxi, pp. 661 sqq.). See especially p. 662: 'This measure is one the adoption of which will form a really NEW ERA in the affairs of England, aye, and of the *world* too: it will produce *greater effects* than any that has been adopted since the "PROTESTANT REFORMATION": it will be called . . . "THE REFORM", as the change made in the time of Henry VIII is called "THE REFORMATION", and as that made in 1688 is called "THE REVOLUTION".'
[5] H. of C., March 1, 1831 (*Parliamentary Debates*, 3rd Series, vol. ii, p. 1083). In exact figures Lord John forecast an increase of 455,000 voters: 110,000 in the boroughs which were already represented, 50,000 in the new boroughs, 95,000 in London, 60,000 in Scotland, 40,000 in Ireland, and 100,000 in the counties. Since the number of voters before 1832 was approximately 435,000 in England, 3,600 in Scotland, and 25,000 in the Irish counties (the figure for the Irish boroughs cannot be ascertained), the total number of voters was decidedly below 500,000. In fact, the actual increase in the number of voters proved to be less than Lord John Russell had expected (in London, for example, the

the example of the Parisian 'Revolution', promised to prove in certain respects a bolder venture than that Revolution itself. With the corporation boroughs the bill swept away the abuse of the non-resident freemen, and at one blow got rid of all the nomination boroughs. This was by itself sufficient to justify the general delight. In every town and shire mass meetings were held to support the Reform and they were not confined to the Liberals. Tories also participated in the meetings. The King, only too pleased to see revolutionary Radicalism swamped by this great movement of public opinion, was well satisfied with the decision he had taken.[1] The ministers had the entire nation at their back.

The Tories in the House put up the best fight they could. The debate on the bill continued for eight days. The Opposition speakers maintained that to abolish the nomination boroughs without compensation was to weaken the social structure by violating the right of property.[2] They denied that a bill of this kind could effect a final settlement. Whenever the distribution of the population changed, the distribution of seats must change with it. Indeed, the bill had already become obsolete before it was passed, since it was based upon the returns of a census ten years old.[3] A 'diversified' franchise, they insisted, was an essential feature of the British system of representation.[4] In one place the right to send a representative to Parliament belonged to the noble patron of a close borough, in another to all the ratepayers, sometimes even, at Preston for example, to all the inhabitants. The new bill was a levelling measure. In every constituency throughout the Kingdom it created two legally defined classes, the one above, the other below, a definite standard of property, the former possessing political rights, the latter excluded from their

increase amounted only to 44,000 instead of 95,000; H. of C., April 18, 1836, Duncombe's speech; *Parliamentary Debates*, 3rd Series, vol. xxxii, p. 1170), and the total number of electors was only 813,000. This, however, was a considerable increase. It will help us to understand these figures if we remember that as a result of the July revolution the qualification for the franchise in France was merely lowered from 300 to 200 francs. In consequence of the change, out of a population of 31,000,000, 160,000 possessed the vote. One vote for every 200 citizens. In England, with a population of 24,000,000, there were 800,000 voters. One voter for every 30 citizens.

[1] The King to Lord Grey, March 3, 1831 (*Correspondence of Earl Grey with William IV*, vol. i, p. 136).

[2] H. of C., March 2, 1831. Speech by H. Twiss and Lord Darlington; March 1831, Sir James Scarlett's speech (*Parl. Deb.*, 3rd Series, vol. ii, pp. 1130, 1177; vol. iii, pp. 771 sqq.).

[3] H. of C., March 2, 1831, C. B. Wall's speech; March 7, 1831, Colonel Sibthorp's speech (ibid., 3rd Series, vol. ii, p. 1171; vol. iii, p. 123).

[4] H. of C., March 3, 1831, Baring's speech (ibid., 3rd Series, vol. ii, pp. 1305 sqq.).

enjoyment.[1] The Government was preparing to replace the old constitution with its confused outlines by a brand new constitution whose worst defect would be its rigid, clear-cut demarcations. At the top would be an aristocratic House of Lords, a little lower a middle-class House of Commons, at the bottom the disfranchised masses. It was an arrangement likely to endanger social order. At the very moment when the French were attempting—with what success the future would show—to carry out a revolution on the English pattern to defend their constitutional rights against the encroachments of absolutism, the English were proposing to effect a doctrinaire reform in the French style. At the first economic crisis the poor would rise against the rich and that day would see the end of the monarchy, the nobility, and the middle classes themselves. Nevertheless, very few of the critics believed that an obstinate resistance had any prospect of success. Very few dared to take up Wellington's attitude and deny that even a moderate reform was inevitable. Peel in particular was remarkable for his frank admissions.[2] When, on March 9, Lord John obtained leave to introduce his bill, the Opposition would not risk a division. On March 14 the Commons passed the first reading of the bill by show of hands. When at last on March 22 the Opposition voted against the bill on the second reading the Government obtained a majority of one—302 against 301 votes.

This result was a disappointment to the diehards. They blamed

[1] H. of C., Mar. 3, 1831, Sir Robert Peel's speech (*Parliamentary Debates*, 3rd Series, vol. ii, pp. 1336, 1346). Cf. April 18, 1831. M. T. Sadler's speech (vol. iii, p. 1559). Hence the curious effect of the Reform already mentioned, namely, that in certain constituencies it actually reduced the number of voters. Here, however, we must be on our guard against exaggeration. It is true that the franchise was restricted in forty-three English and Welsh boroughs out of the 156 which kept their representation. But of these forty-three boroughs, twenty-seven in England and three in Wales had been before the Reform Act corporation boroughs. In the majority of cases the reduction in the number of voters was the effect of depriving the non-resident freemen of the vote—at Canterbury, for example, where the number of voters fell from 2,325 to 1,511; at Dover, where it fell from 2,385 to 1,651; at Gloucester, where it fell from 1,900 to 1,527; at Lancaster, where it fell from 4,000 to 1,109; at Maldon, where it fell from 4,000 to 716; at Sudbury, where it fell from 1,000 to 509; and at York, where it fell from 3,750 to 2,873. Among the remaining thirteen boroughs, if we leave out of consideration those in which the number of voters (a small body before the Reform) remained about the same, only varying by a few dozen, there were only two where an important decrease in the electorate was clearly due to the restriction introduced by the new franchise. At Preston, theoretically a borough which possessed universal suffrage, the number of voters fell from 7,500 to 6,352; at Westminster, a scot-and-lot borough, from 16,000 to 11,576 (*Return of the number of electors . . . in the years 1815, 1830, 1832–3 and 1839–60.* 1860).
[2] H. of C., December 16, 1830 (*Parl. Deb.*, 3rd Series, vol. i, p. 1227); March 3, 1831 (ibid., 3rd Series, vol. iii, p. 1337); March 24, 1831; debate on the Irish bill (ibid., 3rd Series, vol. iii, p. 912).

Peel, once more unpopular with his own party,[1] for not having attempted a vote of censure on the Government at the beginning of the month. Against such a charge Peel could have made a convincing defence. Had the Government been placed in a minority at the beginning of March, he might have replied, a dissolution would have been inevitable, to be followed possibly by an attempt at revolution, certainly by an overwhelming defeat at the polls. Now, on the contrary, the Cabinet, still indeed in possession of a majority but a majority of only one, was condemned to continue interminably the debates on the Reform Bill and, moreover, under the most unfavourable conditions. What would be left of Lord John's bill after it had been debated clause by clause for one or two months?

When Parliament reassembled after the Easter recess Lord John on April 18 reintroduced his bill with a few trifling amendments.[2] Five boroughs which had been totally disfranchised were to retain one member. Seven boroughs which had been deprived of one representative were to retain both. Seven additional boroughs were enfranchised, but by way of compensation Halifax was to return only one instead of two members. Eight counties unaffected by the original bill were given three instead of two representatives. The qualification for the franchise was also slightly modified. The children of resident freemen alive at the passing of the bill would be entitled to the vote on attaining their majority, and all apprenticed at that date would be entitled to vote on becoming freemen. The county franchise was extended to two further classes of leaseholders: every extension of the county franchise was acceptable to the Tory opposition. In the boroughs the £10 franchise was no longer confined to householders, but was extended to the occupier of a warehouse or counting-house. The effect of this provision, which appeared at first sight a further concession to Liberal principles, would be to establish a plural vote in favour of the capitalist who possessed besides his residence a warehouse or an office. But it was immediately evident that these amendments were insufficient to strengthen

[1] Croker to Lord Hertford, March 22, 1831: 'Peel comes to me very often and kindly. He is sore perplexed. I suppose his conscience tells him that he is the primary cause of all the mischief' (*Croker Papers*, vol. ii, p. 112). *Greville Memoirs*, March 24, 1831: 'I continue to hear great complaints of Peel—of his coldness, incommunicativeness and deficiency in all the qualities requisite for a leader, particularly at such a time. There is nobody else, or he would be deserted.' Cf. ibid., March 18, 1831.

[2] H. of C., April 18, 1831 (*Parliamentary Debates*, 3rd Series, vol. iii, pp. 15 sqq.).

the position of the Government in the House; and Peel had already secured an undertaking that the ministry would submit to the vote the provision by which the number of representatives for Scotland and Ireland was increased while the representation of England and Wales was diminished by thirty seats.[1] It was clever tactics to raise this point—and for two reasons. In the first place the Tories seemed to know instinctively where the weakness of the Whigs lay and would continue to lie. In a nation formed by the 'union' of three distinct Kingdoms, it was a skilful move to exploit English patriotism in the narrow sense against the Scotch and Irish tendencies of the popular party. And in the second place the ministers had expressly declared that they had no objection to increasing the number of representatives provided by the bill if the increase were in favour of the industrial centres or important counties. It would be difficult, therefore, for the Government to allege that the amendment now proposed endangered the existence of the bill. Thus, from the very first day the Tories took the lead in debate. When a Tory member of the Commons, General Gascoyne, called upon the House to vote against any decrease in the representation of England and Wales the Cabinet declared by the mouth of Stanley that if his motion passed they would consider the bill rejected.[2] By a majority of eight the House accepted the motion. The Cabinet was now faced with the alternative of resigning or, if they could retain the King's confidence, obtaining his consent to dissolve. For the past three months William had declared himself flatly opposed to dissolution.[3] But when the moment came to decide he gave way. Unaccustomed as yet to govern, and obliged to learn the art in the midst of a political crisis, his fear of provoking a revolution by dismissing his Cabinet finally prevailed over his fear that dissolution would be followed by a revolutionary election.[4] While he was making up his mind confused and disorderly debates continued at Westminster in both Houses. On the 21st the House of Commons in defiance of Lord Althorp refused to continue the discussion of the budget. In

[1] H. of C., April 13, 1831: Sir Robert Peel's question and Lord Althorp's reply (*Parliamentary Debates*, 3rd Series, vol. iii, pp. 1273–5). Cf. Sir Robert Peel to Croker, April 15 (? 14), 1831 (C. S. Parker, *Sir Robert Peel*, vol. ii, p. 181).
[2] H. of C., April 12, 1831; Lord John Russell's speech, April 13, 1830; Stanley's speech (*Parl. Deb.*, 3rd Series, vol. iii, pp. 1242, 1264).
[3] The King to Lord Grey, March 21, 1831 (*Corresp. of Earl Grey with William IV*, vol. i, p. 177).
[4] The King to Lord Grey, March 21, April 21, 1831 (ibid., vol. i, pp. 177, 227).

the House of Lords Lord Wharncliffe introduced a motion calling upon the King to refuse dissolution, and it was set down for debate on the 22nd. That very day, as the two Houses took their seats, the sound of a cannon was heard. It was the signal that the King had left St. James' Palace and was on his way to Westminster to dissolve Parliament in person. Every shot was greeted by the ministerialists with cheers, by the Tories with shouts of anger. 'The next time you hear these guns,' was the taunt addressed by a Tory member to his exultant opponents, 'they will be shotted and take off some of your heads.'[1] The tumult was still raging when the King entered the House of Lords and did not cease until he had taken his seat upon the throne to declare Parliament prorogued 'in view of its immediate dissolution'.

III SECOND REFORM BILL

I

The dissolution was received with outbursts of popular rejoicing. In London and in the large provincial towns the news was celebrated by a general illumination. Then the nation plunged into feverish preparations for the election, which was to take place at extraordinarily short notice—only a week after the dissolution. Both parties, whom the present situation had divided far more sharply than at any previous election—on one side the supporters of the bill, on the other its opponents—made hasty attempts to organize their forces. The democratic organs denounced a certain 'Conservative Senate' in daily session, so it was said, in London,[2] while the Tories denounced a 'Parliamentary Candidate Society' founded by the Radicals for which Bentham drew up a manifesto.[3] The election presented an altogether exceptional character. For the Parliament now to be elected would not be a legislature empowered to govern the country for a term of years. It would be a species of Constituent Assembly entrusted with the task of passing the Reform after which it must

[1] Lord Broughton's *Recollections of a Long Life*, vol. iv, p. 106. Cf. *Greville's Memoirs*, April 24, 1831: 'Those who were present tell me it resembled nothing but what we read of the "Serment du Jeu de Paume", and the whole scene was as much like the preparatory days of a revolution as can well be imagined.'

[2] *Political Register*, April 30, 1831 (vol. lxxii, p. 273).

[3] Proceedings of the Parliamentary Candidate Society instituted to support Reform by promoting the Return of Fit and Proper Members to Parliament, 1831. Cf. *Bentham Works*, vol. xi, p. 66, and Graham Wallas, *Life of Francis Place*, pp. 260 sqq.

make way for a Parliament chosen by the new electorate. Consequently, the electioneering device of the ministerialists was 'the bill, the whole bill, and nothing but the bill'. The election resulted in an overwhelming victory for the Government, and by its condemnation of the existing franchise went near to justify the plea of its Tory defenders.

In the English counties the Tories were almost annihilated. Of eighty-two seats they kept only six, all in unimportant counties. In the boroughs the Whigs were equally triumphant. Not only did all the important towns return supporters of the bill (Gascoyne was defeated at Liverpool), but the Government won seats for rotten boroughs and close boroughs. There was money in the Treasury to purchase the former and at least one Tory landlord sold his seats to the ministry.[1] In Ireland O'Connell's assistance combined with departmental pressure secured a gain of ten seats. Even in Scotland, thanks to the small number of the electorate, the influence of the Government could prevail over Tory gold. There was a gain of eight seats and a majority in favour of the Reform Bill. And the voters may have been intimidated by the disfranchised masses. That this was in fact the case is suggested by the scenes which occurred in many constituencies where the Tory candidate was returned. At Edinburgh the life of the newly elected member was in danger for several hours.[2] On the morrow of the election it was calculated that the Government had secured a majority of 140 votes. And when the Reform Bill was actually put to the vote of the new Parliament it was passed on the second reading by 367 to 231 votes, a majority of 136.[3]

The debate which opened on June 24 continued throughout an entire summer of exceptional heat and was not concluded until September 21. At first Lord John Russell was in charge of the bill. When he succumbed beneath the heavy burden Lord Althorp took his place. His parliamentary reputation had been considerably damaged by the debate on the budget. He contrived to regain the position he had lost and by speaking the blunt language of

[1] *Greville Memoirs*, April 29, 1831.
[2] *Annual Register*, 1831, pp. 152–3; *Law Cases*, pp. 311 sqq.
[3] For the text of the bill as submitted to the Commons in June, see *Parliamentary Debates*, 3rd Series, vol. iv, where it is printed separately at the beginning of the volume. For an abridged text of the bill as it left the House in September, see *Ann. Reg.*, 1831, 'Public Documents', p. 336.

the country squire endeared himself to a parliament of gentlemen farmers. As the debates were protracted the reformist press and the Political Unions showed signs of impatience.[1] But were three months really too long a time to discuss a bill of such exceptional importance? A host of detailed objections arose on each of the three fundamental points of the proposed reform.

There were, in the first place, difficulties respecting the new distribution of seats. On this matter only one alteration had been made in the March bill. Two additional boroughs were disfranchised. The Opposition speakers pointed out how arbitrary were the lines of demarcation drawn between the boroughs which preserved their present representation intact, those which kept one out of two members, and those which lost both and showed that those responsible for draughting the bill had based their work on unchecked statistics, often highly debatable and inspired by party considerations. But the only way to obviate such objections entirely would have been to adopt Bentham's system and divide the country into equal constituencies each returning one member or the same number of members. The moment the borough representation was maintained inside the county areas and the traditional boroughs as far as possible preserved, many anomalies became inevitable. Yield an inch, and the retreat would become a rout. The ministers and their supporters were inflexible. With the exception of a single borough, transferred from Schedule A to Schedule B—that is to say, retaining one member instead of being totally disfranchised—both Schedules were passed in the exact form in which Lord John had presented them to the House.

Besides the difficulties relative to the boroughs wholly or partly disfranchised there were others concerning the new boroughs. Why were so many boroughs disfranchised in the south of England, so many created in the north? The effect surely must be to upset the balance of representation to the prejudice of the agricultural interest and in favour of the manufacturers.[2] Why should the London area receive so many new representatives? To give London a number of representatives proportionate to the population would disturb the balance of

---

[1] *Annual Register*, 1831, p. 193. H. of C., July 26, 29; August 2, 15, 27, 1831 (*Parliamentary Debates*, 3rd Series, vol. v, pp. 328, 520, 588; vol. vi, pp. 7, 701). *Political Register*, July 23, 30, August 6, 1831 (vol. lxxxiii, pp. 209, 285, 341).

[2] H. of C., July 27, 1831: Sir Robert Peel's speech (*Parl. Deb.*, 3rd Series, vol. v, pp. 410 sqq.).

representation to the detriment of the provinces and by giving the opinion of the capital an excessive weight in the deliberations of Parliament increase the danger of insurrection, a danger whose gravity was attested by the recent events in Paris.[1] And why on the other hand were members granted to towns of 30,000 or even 16,000 inhabitants whereas only one member was allotted to a group of Staffordshire towns with a total population of 50,000 and in Lancashire towns with a population of 40,000 were left without a representative? To these criticisms the ministers replied that the increased number of county seats for which the bill made provision gave agriculture all the influence it ought to possess, that the danger of insurrection would be increased not diminished if the metropolis were refused the representation to which it was justly entitled, and further that if there were any anomalies in the distribution of the new seats it was because population was not the sole basis on which it had been made. And if the bill were not a levelling measure which sacrificed everything to equality, the Tories were the very last people entitled to complain. Schedule C (the new boroughs returning two members), Schedule D (the new boroughs returning one member), and Schedule E (the counties whose representation was increased) passed the Commons without the least alteration.

The voter's qualification occasioned further debate.

The principle of a uniform borough franchise of £10 was maintained. It was in vain that the Opposition called attention to the real inequalities disguised by the uniform qualification, and pointed out that payment of a rent of £10 did not imply the same amount of wealth in London and in the provinces, in a large town and in a small borough. In vain they proposed that a graduated qualification should be established rising from £10 or even £5 to £15 or £20 according to the size of the borough.[2] Had their objections been successful, the qualification would have been raised wherever a £10 qualification conferred the vote upon members of the working class.[3] But they went unheeded.

---

[1] H. of C., August 3, 1831: Sir Robert Peel's speech (*Parliamentary Debates*, 3rd Series, vol. v, pp. 667 sqq.). Cf. Croker to Lord Haddington, April 7, 1832 (*Wellington, Despatches, Cont.*, vol. viii, pp. 273–4).

[2] H. of C., August 24, 25, 1831 (*Parl. Deb.*, 3rd Series, vol. vi, pp. 576 sqq., 599–600).

[3] *Political Register*, Nov. 12, 1831 (vol. lxxiv, pp. 393–4): 'Even according to the rejected bill, there are many *whole counties* in which not a single working man would have had a vote. . . . There were none but these populous spots [London, Norwich, Bristol and Staffordshire, Derby, Nottingham, and the large towns in Lancashire, Yorkshire, and

The new bill however defined the £10 qualification more stringently than the former had done, and important consequences followed from the stricter definition. In the large towns a custom sanctioned by statute[1] made the landlord, not the tenant, responsible for the rates on house property let at a low rental. By the amended form of the bill these tenants were disfranchised: for no one was now qualified to vote who did not pay his own rates. Moreover, the new bill prescribed that to confer the franchise the rent must be paid half yearly. But a very large number of tenants paid their rent every quarter and in the North it was common to make weekly payments. Thus while the £10 franchise was scrupulously respected the number of voters had been reduced by indirect methods.

The Radicals were up in arms. The Birmingham 'Political Union' addressed a formal protest to Lord Grey against the clause prescribing half-yearly payment of rent and he thought it necessary to write a personal letter to the President of the Union to explain that the clause had been inserted by an oversight and promise that the bill should be amended.[2] In the form in which it was finally adopted the measure was in two respects more liberal than the original draught. Not only was the provision that the rent must be paid half yearly dropped, no actual payment of rent was any longer required. It was sufficient if the rates and taxes

further to the North, including the large towns in Scotland, and four or five large towns in Ireland] in which there would have been one single working man entitled to vote.' H. of C., December 17, 1831, Lord John Russell's speech: 'The town of Leeds has been regularly canvassed for the purposes of the election . . . The result of (the) canvass has been, that in the quarters inhabited by the working classes, not more than one in every fifty householders will have a vote under the £10 clause . . . The working classes in Leeds almost all live in houses of from £5 to £8 rent; out of 140 householders, heads of families (including several overlookers employed in the mill of Messrs. Marshall & Co.), not more than two will have votes . . . In Manchester the case is somewhat different. From personal examination it appeared that, in a manufactory, where 702 persons were employed, 108 were householders, thirty-one of whom pay a rent of £10 and upwards. In another, where 530 persons were employed, seventeen stated that they pay a rent of £10 and upwards' (*Parliamentary Debates*, 3rd Series, vol. ix, pp. 498-500).

[1] 59 Geo. III, Cap. 12, s. 18 (*The Sturges Bourne Act of* 1819; see vol. ii, p. 42).

[2] *Annual Register*, 1831, pp. 162-3. H. of C., July 4, 1831 (*Parl. Deb.*, 3rd Series, vol. iv, pp. 654 sqq.); Le Marchant, *Memoirs of Viscount Althorp*, p. 325. *Political Register*, July 9, 1831 (vol. lxxiii, pp. 68 sqq.). The protest made by the 'Political Union of Birmingham' criticized several other provisions of the bill. It is regrettable that historians of the Reform Act have concentrated their attention almost exclusively upon the abolition of the rotten boroughs and the pocket boroughs. Owing to this limitation of interest they have all omitted to relate the 'technical' history of the £10 franchise, though it also possesses considerable importance. Even Mr. J. R. M. Butler is guilty of this neglect, and has therefore failed to write the definitive history of the Reform which he might otherwise have written.

were paid by the tenant. But on the other hand to keep the body of voters free of elements 'far from respectable', two new clauses, of the utmost importance, were inserted. No longer as in the first bill was six months' residence sufficient, twelve months' residence was now required. And since the twelve months were to be reckoned from the annual revision of the register, residence for a period of almost two years would in some instances be necessary in order to qualify. Nor was any one entitled to vote unless during those twelve months he had occupied the same domicile without interruption.[1] And in the course of the debate an amendment was introduced, adopted by the Government and passed by the House, disqualifying any one who during his twelve months' term of residence had been in receipt of poor relief.[2]

As regards the county franchise the attitude of the two parties was by no means the same. The Tories desired to enlarge the electorate and the Liberals must either satisfy their wishes or place themselves in a false position. The former bill had conferred the franchise on leaseholders whose rent, if the lease were held for life, was not less than £10 per annum. And it had also provided that a shorter lease should confer the franchise if the rent were not less than £50 per annum. The Cabinet had reserved the right to determine later the period of these shorter leases. It was now proposed to fix a term of seven years.[3] It was a very brief term, so short indeed that it astonished Peel. Why, he asked, should they not go further in the same direction and grant the franchise to every tenant without exception, even to those who held their lease on an annual tenure? Were they afraid that such tenants would be unduly exposed to the influence of their landlords? Those who held a seven-year lease would be scarcely more independent.[4] The Marquis of Chandos moved an amendment to this effect,[5] which the Cabinet opposed in vain. They were abandoned by the Radicals, who favoured every extension of the

[1] For these provisions see H. of C., August 13, 1831, Lord Althorp's speech; August 23, 1831, debate on the amendment. John Campbell's amendment requiring quarterly payment of rent as a condition of the franchise; August 20, 1831 (*Parliamentary Debates*, 3rd Series, vol. v, pp. 1373 sqq.; vol. vi, pp. 600 sqq., 670 sqq.).
[2] H. of C., August 26, 1831: Praed's amendment (ibid., 3rd Series, vol. vi, pp. 686–7).
[3] H. of C., June 24, 1831: Lord John Russell's speech (ibid., 3rd Series, vol. v, p. 339).
[4] H. of C., August 17, 1831: Sir Robert Peel's speech (ibid., 3rd Series, vol. vi, p. 202).
[5] H. of C., August 18, 1831: Colonel Sibthorp's amendment reintroduced by the Marquis of Chandos (ibid., 3rd Series, vol. vi, pp. 202, 278).

franchise. The amendment was passed by a majority of eighty-four, and adopted by the Government. On this occasion, under Peel's leadership, the Tories employed the tactics advocated by the Marquis of Blandford, and the gentry pursued a democratic policy as a weapon against a Liberal policy conceived in the interest of the middle class.

2

When the House of Commons had finally passed the Reform Bill, and the debates had concluded with two eloquent speeches, by Macaulay in favour of the Reform, by Croker against it,[1] Lord John took the Bill on September 21 to the Lords. The Lords passed the first reading on the 22nd and the second reading was fixed for October 3. A harassing fortnight followed.

It was an anxious time for the supporters of the Reform Bill. The bill had successfully passed the first stage, the second was still to come, and here the dangers were far greater. What would the Lords do? Debate the bill clause by clause and amend it out of recognition? Or would they reject the entire bill without more ado on the second reading? From the record of previous divisions it would appear that the House of Lords was about equally divided between the two parties, and the new peerages created in June, and more recently still at the coronation, which the Government had finally decided to postpone no longer, were not believed to be sufficient to turn the scale in favour of the Reform.[2] Should the Government secure the passage of the bill by a further creation? Optimists calculated that five or ten new peers would suffice. A pamphlet published at this juncture, which without mincing matters bade the Lords do their duty and pass the bill, was universally attributed to the Lord Chancellor.[3] The meetings organized by the Political Unions and the newspapers which

[1] H. of C., September 20, 1831 (*Parliamentary Debates*, 3rd Series, vol. vii, pp. 297 sqq., 311 sqq.).

[2] Five were created on June 16. 'Nobody, I think,' wrote Lord Grey to Princess Lieven, 'can object to these names, and it may be taken as a hint that more will be made if necessary' (*Correspondence of Princess Lieven and Earl Grey*, vol. ii, p. 242). Sixteen on the Coronation day ('a set of horrid rubbish most of them', Greville wrote on September 17, 1831). 'For the creation of so many as sixteen new peers the ministers invoked the precedent of George IV's coronation, conveniently forgetting that of the eighteen peers created in 1821 only nine were not already members of the Scotch or Irish peerage, and were therefore added to the existing nobility' (*Wellington to Lord Strangford*, January 12, 1832: *Despatches, Cont.*, vol. viii, p. 156).

[3] 'What will be done with the Lords?' Question to the Lords generally, more especially to Lords Eldon, Londonderry, and the Duke of Newcastle, what will be done with their Lordships? 1831.

supported the bill—they were the vast majority—spoke a threatening language. In his great speech in the Commons Macaulay had advised the peers of the United Kingdom to behave prudently unless they wished to suffer the fate which had befallen the French nobility forty years earlier.[1] But it was, in truth, unnecessary to go so far back in French history to see the dangers which in Western Europe awaited an aristocracy too haughty to obey the popular will. The French election in July had turned on the abolition of the hereditary peerage. The Chamber of Deputies had just opened on September 20 a debate on the question and Casimir Perier was prepared to overcome the resistance of the Upper Chamber by the creation of new peers.

The Tories were equally anxious. But their anxiety was due to a very different reason. The ministerialists were growing alarmed, the Tories recovering hope. Since the general election they had won all or almost all the bye-elections.[2] These victories were plausibly interpreted as a sign that the public was losing interest in the fate of the Reform Bill. Moreover, during the protracted debates in the Commons the tolerant attitude adopted by Lord John Russell and Lord Althorp towards the Opposition had displeased many Reformers. The Radical press had criticized the Government, and even the bill itself. In reality this divergence of opinion among the Reformers signified that the bill was the minimum which Radical opinion would accept. But the Tories understood it as an indication that the party in favour of Reform was weakening and began to hope that they might avert defeat by winning over their more moderate opponents. The King, as they well knew, was definitely hostile to a further creation of peers. Indeed, he had already shown his dislike of the peers whose patents he had signed in June and September. And when the time actually came, Lord Grey and the other heads of the great Whig houses might be expected to share the sentiments of their sovereign. All these considerations encouraged the belief that if the Lords had the courage to resist they would not be left without support.

[1] H. of C., Sept. 20, 1831 (*Parliamentary Debates*, 3rd Series, vol. vii, pp. 313–414).
[2] Weymouth, August 1; Great Grimsby, August 10; Dublin, August 18; Carmarthenshire, August 25; Dorsetshire (Lord Ashley returned), September 30; Forfarshire, October 3. Against these victories of the Anti-Reformers, the Reformers could only place a solitary gain at Wallingford on September 21 (*Standard*, October 24; *The Times*, October 26, 1831), and the Anti-Reformers scored a further success at Liverpool on October 21 But on November 1 their hopes were dashed by a defeat in Cambridgeshire (*The Times*, November 1, 1831).

The debate in the Lords opened on October 3, and continued for five days. If his language was very moderate, Lord Grey none the less made it quite plain that he was not prepared to yield any essential point. If their Lordships hoped to satisfy the public by substituting some more moderate measure for the Government's bill he would not accept the responsibility.[1] On the other hand, though Brougham used more violent language than the Prime Minister his position was far more conciliatory and excited Radical protests.[2] Wellington, without explicitly stating his hostility to every project of reform, manifested once more in opposing the measure his determination to concede nothing.[3] Finally, in an all-night sitting, October 7–8, the division was taken, and on the morning of the 8th the reformist press in black-edged editions informed capital and provinces that the bill had been rejected by a majority of forty-one.

The excitement aroused throughout the country by the news was the more violent because it came as a surprise to the vast majority of Englishmen. Indeed, even the best-informed journalists and members of Parliament were astonished at the size of the majority against the bill. When the state of feeling which prevailed in the suburbs of London and to an even greater degree in the provinces became known moderate men of both parties were terrified by the immediate prospect of revolution and cursed the Lords' imprudent action. One thing was evident from the beginning: the King would not ask the Cabinet to resign nor would the ministers tender their resignation. The Government knew that it could count on the unflinching support of a majority in the Commons. On the 10th Lord Ebrington moved on the order of the day a vote of confidence in the ministry and his motion was passed by a majority of 131. On the 11th Lord Grey saw the King at Windsor and obtained the immediate dismissal of Lord Howe, the Queen's Chamberlain, for his vote against the bill. On the following day the King and Queen returned to London. Cobbett in his *Register* compared their return with the

---

[1] H. of L., Oct. 3, 1831 (*Parliamentary Debates*, 3rd Series, vol. vii, pp. 928 sqq.)

[2] H. of L., October 7, 1831 (ibid., 3rd Series, vol. viii, pp. 220 sqq.). *Political Register*, Oct. 15, 1831 (vol. lxxiv, pp. 142 sqq.).

[3] H. of L., October 4, 1831 (*Parl. Deb.*, 3rd Series, vol. vii, pp. 1186 sqq.). *Greville Memoirs*, October 10, 1831: 'The Duke of Wellington's speech was exceedingly bad: he is in fact, and has proved it in repeated instances, unequal to argue a great constitutional question. But his language a few days later was less decided.' H. of L., October 7, 1831 (*Parl. Deb.*, 3rd Series, vol. viii, pp. 338 sqq.).

return of Louis XVI to Paris in October 1789.[1] Delegates from every parish in London marched in procession to present addresses to the King and his reply was considered satisfactory. But the same day a persistent rumour was current that the ministers intended to prorogue Parliament until after Christmas and then introduce in the Commons a new bill better calculated to secure the adhesion of the Upper House. At eleven o'clock that night the London streets once more presented a scene of tumult. Lord Grey was awakened by a group of politicians from Westminster, headed by Francis Place, who demanded a plain statement of his intentions and his evasive replies increased the public fury.[2] On the 17th he found it necessary to state definitely in the House of Lords that 'he would never be a party to, or recommend any measure of Reform which was not founded on similar principles, and as effective as regarded its declared object, as that which was lately before Parliament'.[3] Two days later Parliament was prorogued not until January but until November 22.

3

The prorogation was inevitable if order were to be maintained. Alarming intelligence was being received from the provinces. At Derby the crowd released from prison some rioters who had been arrested and with them the entire contents of the gaol, the military were summoned, and several among the mob were killed.[4] At Nottingham, the castle, the property of the Duke of Newcastle, who was notorious for the number of pocket boroughs in his possession, was burned to the ground.[5] Incendiarism broke out afresh in the southern counties.[6] Moreover, the present insurrection, graver than any which England had witnessed since 1815, presented a new feature in which it resembled the revolutions on the Continent. The popular fury turned against the clergy of the

---

[1] *Political Register,* October 15, 1831 (vol. lxxiv, p. 177).
[2] Graham Wallas, *Life of Francis Place,* pp. 278–9.
[2] H. of L., October 17, 1831 (*Parliamentary Debates,* 3rd Series, vol. viii, pp. 850–1).
[4] *Annual Register,* 1831, Chron., October 8, 9, p. 161.
[5] *Pol. Reg.,* October 15, 1831 (vol. lxxiv, pp. 179–80).
[6] County Fire Office to the Home Office, December 15: 'The burnings of the present season far outnumber those of last winter' (J. R. M. Butler, *The Passing of the Great Reform Bill,* p. 327 n.); also Cobbett, *Pol. Reg.,* January 7, 1832 (vol. lxxv, p. 102): 'The Fires are blazing more furiously than they were last year at this time.' According to Cobbett the London Press maintained a conspiracy of silence about these acts of incendiarism in the country districts.

established Church. As measures of pacification Catholic Emancipation and the abolition of the Test Act had proved a failure. On the contrary, they had stimulated to further activity the two groups who had benefited by them—the Irish Catholics and the English Dissenters. The decision just taken by the House of Lords had the effect of uniting Catholics, Dissenters, and demagogues in a common opposition to the Establishment. As we have just seen the majority which on October 8 threw out the Reform Bill on the second reading was a majority of forty-one. But of the thirty prelates, archbishops, and bishops who sat in the House of Lords only two had voted for the bill. Seven had abstained from voting. Twenty-one—seventeen English and four Irish bishops —had voted against the bill. If these twenty-one bishops had voted the other way, it would have been passed by a majority of one. Therefore the bishops were responsible for the rejection of the bill.

In the course of debate Lord Grey had warned the bishops of the danger in which they stood.[1] His warning was justified by the event. When they returned to their dioceses after the prorogation their appearance in public was greeted with booing and more than once they believed their lives in danger.[2] In London a newly erected church remained closed because the Bishop dared not come to consecrate it.[3] When a preacher attempted to defend the bishops' vote, the entire congregation rose and left the church.[4] On the anniversary of the Gunpowder Plot it was not Guy Fawkes but a mitred bishop that was burned in effigy by the urchins. Bristol was the scene of far more serious disturbances. Prominent among those who had most stoutly opposed the Reform Bill in the House of Commons was Sir Charles Wetherell, who held a judicial position at Bristol. On October 29 Sir Charles arrived at Bristol to perform his official duties, was received in state by the corporation, but hooted by the mob. The same evening during the official banquet the excitement assumed a threatening aspect. Next day the mob broke open and burned the gaols and set fire to the town hall. The riot then took an anti-clerical turn and the bishop's palace was burned to the ground. It was not until the following day that the troops succeeded in restoring

[1] H. of L., October 3, 1831 (*Parliamentary Debates*, 3rd Series, vol. vii, pp. 967–8).
[2] Jeffrey to H. Cockburn, October 9, 1831: 'Then several bishops will die (or be killed)' (Lord Cockburn, *Life of Lord Jeffrey*, vol. ii, p. 239).
[3] *Annual Register*, 1831, Chron., October 21.
[4] J. R. M. Butler, *The Passing of the Great Reform Bill*, p. 206.

order. According to the official figures twelve persons were killed and ninety-four wounded. The burning of the bishop's palace at Bristol reproduced in England the sack of Saint Germain l'Auxerrois and the Archiepiscopal Palace in Paris. But although the disturbances presented a political and anti-clerical aspect, they had not lost in the England of 1831 the social character, as a rising of the working class, they had possessed in 1816 and in 1819. The Government could no longer maintain as during the previous winter that trade and industry were prosperous. The same report came in from every mining and manufacturing district: fall of prices; lowering of wages; workmen dismissed; factories closed. For the workers to attempt to secure higher wages by striking was now out of the question—the difficulty was to find employment.

Was the political crisis then the result of the economic? Yes, but only in part. For the economic crisis was itself the repercussion of the political which had continued for over a year. In France, one month after the Bristol mob burned the bishop's palace, the insurrection which put the silkweavers in possession of the city of Lyons reproduced in a more serious form those risings of the working class which during the past twenty years had come to be regarded as characteristic of northern England. The 'Ligue de la Résistance Bretonne' and the 'Société aide-toi le ciel t'aidera' (the Help-yourself-and-heaven-will-help-you Society), unions of the middle class, which had been founded before July to refuse to pay taxes if the Charter were violated, were replaced by new unions, the 'Amis du Peuple' and 'Droits de l'Homme', which drew a portion of their membership from the working class, were frankly republican and displayed, what were beginning to be called, socialistic tendencies. The sense of insecurity which oppressed the whole of western Europe diminished the consumption of goods and at the end of a few months production suffered accordingly. Thus the history of the two great nations of the West seemed to be following the same path. On both sides of the Channel a political had given birth to a social crisis, and the social crisis in turn aggravated the political.

Both the middle class and the proletariat were represented in the ranks of the reformers. The former constituted the membership of the Political Unions and by a number of channels, especially through Bentham and his subordinates, maintained unbroken contact with the governing class and the ministers. The revolutionaries on the contrary, advocates of the working class from which usually they had themselves sprung, were regarded with terror by the ministers and their sole point of contact with the Government was the prosecutions to which they were subject. The Whig Ministry were not content with disappointing popular hopes by refusing to repeal the Stamp Act of 1817; it put the Act into execution with the utmost rigour; and if middle-class juries were disposed to acquit revolutionaries of their own class—Prentice, for instance, at Manchester[1] and even Cobbett[2]—they had no mercy for those sprung from the working class—Carlile, Taylor, Carpenter, and Hetherington.[3] It is not surprising that these leaders of the proletariat, sensible, as they were, that they were every bit as cultivated as their middle-class allies were disposed to renounce the alliance, form their own organizations, and utilize for their own benefit the methods of agitation and intimidation which the middle-class democrats were employing against the aristocracy and the boroughmongers. And in fact in the summer of 1831 the workmen, who had learnt from Robert Owen his doctrine of 'co-operation'—today we should call it, as indeed Owen would shortly call it himself, 'socialism'— repudiated one of the fundamental articles of his creed and combined with their social propaganda those political claims which he persisted in treating as unimportant, if not positively mischievous. An Association bearing the title 'The British Association for the Spread of Co-operative Knowledge' gave birth to an Association, whose objects were undisguisedly political, which called itself at first 'The Metropolitan Trades Union' then the 'National Union of the Working Classes'. After considerable debate it was decided to exclude manual workers from membership. But the ban remained a dead letter and in fact the Union consisted entirely of working men.[4]

[1] *Political Register*, July 23, 1831 (vol. lxxiii, pp. 239–40). A. Prentice, *Hist. Sketches* . . . *of Manchester* (pp. 386 sqq.). This was not a prosecution instituted by the Government, but a charge of defamation brought by a member of the opposite party.
[2] *Annual Register*, 1831, Chron., July 7. *Pol. Reg.*, July 16, 1831 (vol. lxxiii, pp. 128 sqq.).
[3] *Life and Struggles of William Lovett*, pp. 59 sqq. *Ann. Reg.*, 1831, Chron., July 4.
[4] *Life and Struggles of William Lovett*, pp. 68 sqq. This Association was organized somewhat on the plan of the Methodist Connection. *Class leaders* were appointed at public meetings of the members in the proportion of one for about every thirty or forty members; the class leaders mostly meeting with their classes weekly at their own houses. Graham Wallas, *Life of Francis Place*, pp. 269 sqq.

By October it possessed a dozen branches in London and held weekly meetings at the Rotunda, near Blackfriars Bridge. When on the prorogation of Parliament the Radicals of the middle class decided to unite all the political unions of the Kingdom in one single 'National Political Union', they found themselves faced by the opposition of the 'National Union of the Working Classes'.

The middle-class members of the National Political Union embodied in its constitution a declaration that its sole aim was 'to support the King and his ministers against a small faction in accomplishing their great measure of Parliamentary Reform'.[1]

The workers who belonged to the rival Union replied by a manifesto which affirmed a sacred right to all property 'honestly acquired', the equal, natural, and inalienable rights of all men alike, declared 'all hereditary distinctions of birth' inequitable, and far from accepting the Reform Bill as a satisfactory measure demanded manhood suffrage, the ballot, and annual Parliaments.[2] When at the end of October the Political Union called a meeting of its supporters to pass the statutes, the members of the Union of the Working Classes threw the meeting into confusion. Blows were exchanged and it was finally agreed that half the seats on the Council of the Union should be held by manual workers. To be sure the organizers cleverly contrived to fill these seats with working men who did not subscribe to the revolutionary tenets of the Rotunda. Nevertheless many of the middle-class members took alarm and after some weeks of friction Sir Francis Burdett, who had consented to become president of the Union, resigned.[3] 'If the ministers flinch,' wrote the young John Stuart Mill to a friend, 'or the Peers remain obstinate, I am firmly convinced that in six months a national convention, chosen by universal suffrage, will be sitting in London.'[4]

The Government was therefore obliged to fight simultaneously on two fronts, to combat the revolutionaries organized in their

[1] See the full text of the statutes, *Annual Register*, 1831, Chron., October 31.
[2] *Life and Struggles of William Lovett*, pp. 72 sqq.
[3] Diary of Henry Hobhouse, November 4, 11, 1831 (Lord Broughton's *Recollections of a Long Life*, vol. iv, pp. 146–7, 151). G. Wallas, *Life of Francis Place*, pp. 278 sqq.
[4] John Stuart Mill to John Sterling, October 20–22, 1831 (*Letters of John Stuart Mill*, vol. i, p. 7). Cf. Lady Cadogan to John Hookham Frere, November 1831: '. . . For the first time I believe we are in a bad way, for I always felt that we were secure amidst the crash of other Governments, but now . . . This is awful . . . and awfully like 1792 in France' (G. Festing, *John Hookham Frere and His Friends*, pp. 239–40).

Unions and the reactionaries whose stronghold was the House of Lords. Lord Melbourne, at once the most conservative and the most sceptical member of the Cabinet, took action against the revolutionaries with the same energy he had displayed the previous year. A meeting of the Union of the Working Classes had been arranged for November 7, and as the date drew close ugly rumours were current in the metropolis. It was reported that cudgels, sword-sticks, and pikes adorned with the tricolour were being sold at Bethnal Green. Would London witness a repetition of the scenes which had so lately disgraced Derby, Nottingham, and Bristol? On November 2 a royal proclamation appeared calling upon the magistrates throughout the country to suppress every attempt at disorder, and upon every loyal citizen to assist them in the task.[1] In the capital itself the ministers took Wellington into their counsels and in full view of the public put the troops in readiness to disperse the meeting which the local authorities had declared illegal. The organizers thought it wise to postpone the meeting. On November 21 a second proclamation was issued declaring 'unconstitutional and illegal' all political associations which 'were subject to the general control and direction of a superior committee or council without having received the express sanction of the Government'.[2] The Political Union, which, equally with the Union of Working Men, was condemned by the proclamation, attempted to evade the blow by declaring that its terms were inapplicable to itself and to the vast majority of the existing Unions.[3] Nevertheless, the parent Union at Birmingham deemed it advisable to drop a plan of organization it had just prepared.[4] And in December special commissions were nominated to try outside the regular period of the assizes the rioters of Bristol, Nottingham, and Derby.

On the other hand the majority of the ministers were aware that it would not be possible to obtain from the King a promise to create new peers on the large scale—about fifty—which the vote on October 8 had shown to be necessary. They did not even desire it themselves, for they were too loyal to their order and too proud of their position as noblemen to wish to see the peerage

[1] See the text of the proclamation, *Annual Register*, 1831, Chron., November 2.
[2] Ibid., 1831, Chron., November 21.
[3] J. R. M. Butler, *The Passing of the Great Reform Bill*, p. 317.
[4] Without referring to the proclamation and probably in concert with Cabinet. H. of C., Dec. 16, 1831: Croker's speech (*Parliamentary Debates*, 3rd Series, vol. ix, p. 300).

cheapened.[1] Towards the middle of November Palmerston, Stanley, and Lord Grey himself entered into negotiations with two Tory peers, Lord Harrowby and Lord Wharncliffe, in the hope of reaching a compromise.[2] The conversations continued for more than a month, in fact until the meeting of Parliament. The negotiation failed. Peel and Wellington had been consistently opposed to it. But it was not therefore fruitless. The advances made by Lord Wharncliffe convinced the Cabinet that the Lords' opposition to the Reform Bill was not insuperable, and that the battle might be won without resorting to such a revolutionary expedient as the creation of new peers.

IV THIRD REFORM BILL

I

The opening of the new session had been fixed for November 20. The ministers who wished to reach an agreement on the alterations which might be made in the Reform Bill without defeating its purpose attempted indeed to secure a longer period for deliberation and once more the rumour spread that they contemplated postponing the session until after Christmas. But the public displeasure was too marked, and on December 6 the two Houses assembled to hear the King's Speech. On December 12 Lord John Russell presented his Reform Bill to the Commons for the third time.[3] The bill had been considerably amended and embodied the concessions which the Cabinet had offered privately a fortnight before but which had failed to satisfy Lord Wharncliffe and those whom he represented. In the first place it was admitted that the figures on which Schedule A had been based the

[1] Lord Grey to Sir H. Taylor, October 8, 1831: 'I do not know that anything more is required to be said, than that the amount of the majority puts all notions of our attempt to counteract it by a further creation of Peers quite out of the question' (*Corr. of Earl Grey with William IV*, vol. i, p. 366). The account of the matter given by Lord Grey's son (*Edinburgh Review*, 1871, vol. cxxxiv, p. 291), according to which Lord Grey was determined to create the peers if necessary, but considered it a tactical blunder to create them immediately, as he would thus deprive himself of a means to exert further pressure —is difficult to accept.

[2] See the documents communicated by Lord Harrowby to Wellington, November 22, 1831 (*Wellington, Despatches, Cont.*, vol. viii, pp. 81 sqq.); also in the *Corr. of Earl Grey with William IV*; *Minutes of Conversation between Lord Grey and Lord Wharncliffe*, November 16, 1831—further, Lord Wharncliffe's *Plan for the Alteration of the Reform Bill*, November 23, 1831 (pp. 464 sqq., 471 sqq.).

[3] For the text of the Reform Bill as presented to the Commons on December 12, see *Parliamentary Debates*, 3rd Series, vol. ix, where the bill is printed separately at the beginning of the volume; *Political Register*, December 21, 1831 (vol. cxxiv pp. 705 sqq.).

year before were not altogether satisfactory. The returns of the census of 1831 were now available and were utilized for the purposes of the bill. Nor was population any longer the sole criterion by which to decide whether a borough should keep or lose the franchise. The wealth of the inhabitants as calculated by the total amount of taxes paid by each borough was also taken into consideration and a definite rule laid down to estimate the claim to the franchise on that basis. But the bill was not radically altered as a result of these modifications. Of the fifty-six boroughs originally enrolled under Schedule A fifty-one kept their place. Moreover, to prove that the Government had no intention of weakening the measure five new boroughs were added to the list, and thus the number of boroughs totally disfranchised was still fifty-six.

In the second place, the Government accepted the principle laid down in the Gascoyne amendment, which eight months before they had treated as fatal to the integrity of the bill. England and Wales were now to retain the full number of seats they possessed before the reform. This necessitated the provision of twenty-three additional seats. Eleven boroughs were withdrawn from Schedule B and kept two representatives. This was a concession to the Tories. But to balance it the twelve remaining seats were obtained by raising from one to two the members to be returned by certain boroughs in Schedule D, that is to say the additional seats were utilized to strengthen the representation of the large towns.[1]

In the third place the electoral qualification was modified in certain respects. The original bill had continued the franchise of resident freemen only during the life of those who actually held it when the bill became law. In April the franchise had been extended to their children and apprentices living when the act was passed. As reintroduced in December the bill maintained the franchise of resident freemen in perpetuity. This, however, was the sole concession made to the Tories. The latter had desired a restriction direct or indirect of the £10 franchise. So far was the new bill from meeting their wishes that the indirect restrictions of the franchise contained in the bill of September were considerably attenuated. The rental value of houses was often assessed for poor

---

[1] In spite of Lord Palmerston's and Lord Melbourne's protests (Lord Grey to Sir Herbert Taylor, December 3, 1831; *Corr. of Earl Grey with William IV*, vol. ii p. 8).

rate below the true figure. A clause of the new bill protected certain classes of small tenants against deprivation of the vote on this account. The exercise of the right conferred by the September bill upon the small tenants to pay their own rates in spite of the custom which made their landlords responsible for payment was facilitated. Moreover, the continuous occupation of the same tenement for a year was no longer necessary to qualify for the franchise.[1] Lord Grey, personally it would seem in favour of restricting the £10 franchise,[2] attempted to reassure the Tories[3] and quiet his own scruples by the argument that it was sufficiently restricted already by the provisions of the Bill as passed by the Commons in September. His contention was apparently justified by the event. In March 1831 Lord John had foreseen the addition of about 1,000,000 voters to the electorate as a result of the Reform. In spite of the adoption of Lord Chandos' amendment and the liberal provisions of the third Reform Bill the actual increase does not appear to have much exceeded 800,000.[4]

The debate on the second reading was brief. It terminated on the morning of the 18th by a new victory for the Government. In June 598 members had taken part in the division, on this occasion only 486 voted. Evidently the House was growing weary of the

[1] According to Brougham this last amendment involved an addition of 100,000 to the electorate (H. of L., May 25, 1832; *Parliamentary Debates*, 3rd Series, vol. xiii, p. 112).

[2] Lord Wharncliffe relating to Lord Harrowby (November 23, 1831) a conversation which he had held with Lord Grey, stated that '. . . the regulations under which the £10 franchise should be given were points upon which he [Lord Grey] was quite willing that discussion should take place. . . . I am satisfied that he would be willing to give way a good deal, provided that in some way the £10 stood as the apparent amount of the qualification' (*Wellington, Despatches, Cont.*, vol. viii, p. 82).

[3] Lord Grey to Sir Herbert Taylor, November 30, 1831: 'The danger, or rather, the inconvenience, of too large a constituency will probably be obviated, I think certainly, by requiring the paying of the rates as well as the taxes by the occupiers of a £10 house and by the required residence of one year previous to registration, which will in effect be a residence of nearly two' (*Corr. of Earl Grey with William IV*, vol. i, pp. 452–3). The new facilities which the third bill granted to the small ratepayer failed to satisfy the Radicals. Some of these would even appear to have been afraid that under a system of public voting the greater the number of poor voters the more they would be exposed to forms of corruption only too familiar to the Westminster politicians. See Francis Place's address to the Council of the National Political Union, December 14, 1831 . . . he alluded particularly to instances of former elections in Westminster, which had come under his own cognisance, where a Government was entitled to the vote of many a poor victim, because he at the moment of election paid any poor rates due, but where similar votes were tendered and refused to the popular candidate' (*Morning Chronicle*, December 15, 1831).

[4] The difference was attributed to the reasons which we have already stated by Colonel Evans, H. of C., June 18, 1833, June 19, 1834 (*Parl. Deb.*, 3rd Series, vol. xviii, pp 961-2; vol. xxiv, p. 562) and T. S. Duncombe, H. of C., April 18, 1836 (ibid., 3rd Series, Vol. xxxii, pp. 1168 sqq.). It is not an easy task to control these statements by exact statistics —but at least they do not appear to have been contested either by the ministers or by the Conservative speakers.

interminable question. On the former occasion the Government had obtained a majority of 136. Now the bill was passed by 324 to 162 votes, a majority of 162 votes, a majority of two to one. The Tories, that is to say, had suffered the most numerous defections.

But the contest became more animated when the clauses were discussed separately, and the debate continued for more than two months, from January 17 to March 23. No doubt many among the more moderate supporters of either party desired a compromise. But the position of the thorough-going reformers was strengthened by the inflexible attitude adopted by Peel as leader of the Opposition. There is, indeed, evidence that in October 1830 he was prepared in his capacity as leader of the Tories in the Commons to take the initiative in accepting a moderate measure of reform. Unfortunately Wellington had overruled his wishes and he could not resign himself to a change of front within the space of a few months. His recantation in the matters of Catholic emancipation was too fresh in the public memory, and in December had been the subject of Macaulay's rhetoric.[1] He did not wish to give any ground for the suspicion that he was on the verge of a second conversion on the subject of Parliamentary Reform and was therefore compelled to adopt an attitude of unbending Toryism. If the House wished, let them pass the bill as it stood and let the Government bear the entire responsibility; he and his followers would have nothing whatever to do with it.[2] Only once during the entire period covered by the debate was the Cabinet placed in a minority, and obliged to whip up its recalcitrant supporters to obtain a majority of thirty-seven in the Lords.[3] But this was on an issue of foreign policy—the attitude adopted by the Government in the matter of Belgium. And although for a few hours the incident made a stir in Parliamentary circles, it passed unheeded by the country and was completely forgotten the next day. What did Belgium matter? What did anything matter except the Reform Bill? The situation in March repeated the situation of the previous September. The same question awaited solution. What would the House of Lords do?

[1] H. of C., Dec. 16, 1831 (*Parliamentary Debates*, 3rd Series, vol. ix, pp. 380–1).
[2] Sir Robert Peel to Arbuthnot, October 13, 1831; to Lord Wharncliffe, November 23, 1831; to Lord Harrowby, February 5, 1832 (C. S. Parker, *Life of Sir Robert Peel*, vol. ii, pp. 189, 194, 199). See the angry comments of Greville on this letter of February 5 which was communicated to him (*Greville Memoirs*, February 7, 1832).
[3] H. of L., January 26, 1831: Lord Aberdeen's motion (*Parl. Deb.*, 3rd Series, vol. ix, pp. 834 sqq.).

2

The debate in the Commons had been a formality, for the result was a foregone conclusion. In protracting the discussion the Tories had only one end in view—to strengthen the resistance of the Lords. After a moment of despair Tory politicians had begun once more to entertain the belief that public opinion would support the Lords in rejecting the Bill. The disturbances of October and November were at an end and it had proved a very easy matter to restore order. At Bristol an officer and a single company of troops had sufficed to quell the riots. At Lyons the same task had required an army of 40,000 men under the personal command of the heir to the throne and the minister for war. During the month of January four executions had taken place at Bristol and three at Nottingham, and although the Political Unions had petitioned for the pardon of the condemned, the petitions were couched in the most moderate language and had not occasioned a single disturbance. By the beginning of March the Tories in Cambridgeshire and Hampshire had gathered sufficient courage to hold meetings and sign petitions against the Political Unions.

If the Tory diehards believed that the country had lost interest in reform they grossly miscalculated. Had they forgotten that twice already, in 1831, they had made the same mistake and on each occasion had been speedily undeceived? Nevertheless the speed with which calm succeeded the storm in January 1832, as previously in March and July 1831, was extremely significant. For it afforded a striking proof how little the British people resembled their French neighbours. Since the crisis began in 1830, religious enthusiasm had apparently gained ground and kept pace with the revolutionary propaganda. Never had the book of Daniel and the Revelations been studied more diligently. Irving, in Scotland at first, then in London, drew the attention of the crowd by his mysterious prophecies. He announced the approach of the millennium and his disciples believed that they had received the gift of tongues like the Apostles on the day of Pentecost.[1] 'Distress seems to increase hereabout and crime with it,' wrote

[1] John Stuart Mill to John Sterling, October 20–22, 1831: . . . . no one can tell [the future of European politics] except Messrs. Drummond, MacNeal, Irving and others who profess [to know?] the hidden key to the Prophecies' (*Letters of John Stuart Mill*, vol. i, p. 9). *Greville Memoirs*, March 26, 1832: 'As to madness, Dudley has gone mad in his own house, Perceval in the House of Commons and John Montague in the Park, the

Greville in his Diary. 'Methodism and saintship increase too.'[1] The strength of the religious revival was revealed when in February the Asiatic cholera, a novel epidemic which had for months past been extending its ravages on the Continent, reached England. The previous winter 'Saint' Perceval, a son of the Prime Minister assassinated in 1812, and a follower of Irving, had asked Parliament to appoint a day of public fasting and humiliation. The proposal had been received with shouts of laughter. This winter he took the opportunity of the cholera epidemic to repeat his request in a lengthy and extravagant religious rant; and the ministers made haste to secure themselves against any charge of irreligion by declaring that the proposal was superfluous, since it had been granted before it was made; it was the intention of the Government to appoint a national fast.[2] It was in vain that the London revolutionaries Benbow Lovett and Watson organized by way of protest a parody of the fast day, which they called the farce day.[3] For the fast day was not an official formality imposed by the Government upon a hostile public. On the contrary the Government had yielded to the pressure of Evangelical opinion. The great Liberal organ, the *Morning Chronicle*, which was consistently hostile to the Evangelicals, had gauged the situation correctly when in 1830 on the very morrow of the July Revolution in an article which sought to determine the significance of the event from its own standpoint it had delivered itself as follows: 'We may consider the great events of Paris as having given a decisive blow to superstition. The evil was not as in this country, in the people themselves. The French are not like the English, under the influence of a gloomy fanaticism. . . . All that is required in their

two latter preaching, both Irvingites and believers in "the tongues".' Edward Bickersteth (Balleine, *Hist. of the Evangelical Party in the Church of England*, p. 137) wrote in 1831: 'The good folks here [in the Midlands] are all afloat in prophesying and the immediate work of the Lord is disregarded for the uncertain future.' Balleine here adds a list of the literature produced by this extravagant religious movement: Hartley Frere, *A Combined view of the Prophecies of Daniel, Esdras, and St. John*, 1815; Basilicus (Lewis Way), *Thoughts on the Scriptural Expectations of the Christian Church*, 1823; and, beginning in 1826, the periodical published by the banker Drummond, *The Morning Watch*. For Thomas Erskine Campbell and the beginning of Irving's preaching, see Rev. W. Hanna, *Memoirs . . . of Thomas Chalmers*, vol. iii, pp. 245 sqq.

[1] *Greville Memoirs*, January 1, 1832. In current parlance the term 'saint' designated a pietist of the evangelical school of religion.

[2] For Perceval's extravagant speeches see H. of C., December 23, 1830, February 7, 1831, and especially February 14, 1831, and January 26, 1832 (*Parliamentary Debates*, 3rd Series, vol. ii, pp. 81, 205, 541; vol. ix, p. 895).

[3] *Poor Man's Guardian*, March 24, 31, 1832. A number of arrests were made, but the accused were acquitted on May 16 (*Political Register*, July 7, 1832, vol. lxxvii, p. 44).

case is, that the Government should not cram Priestcraft down their throats. With us it is another affair.'[1]

Inside the Cabinet the extremists who desired to break the resistance of the Lords by a creation of peers were becoming ever more impatient and clamorous. But they were faced by the opposition of Lord Grey supported by the majority of his colleagues. The latter party argued—and the argument was certainly plausible—that it was far from certain that a creation of peers would after all prove effective. Many peers who had voted in October for the Reform Bill threatened to change their line of action as a protest against the attack upon the honour of their order. What a magnificent piece of work would have been achieved, if for every new peer created a peer who had hitherto voted for the bill voted against it! At this juncture the intervention of the moderate Tories proved most opportune. They offered if the project of creating peers were dropped to vote for the second reading of the bill. Even so it was uncertain what would happen when the House of Lords came to discuss the clauses individually. Lord Grey was convinced that the essential provisions of the bill could be saved provided the Government were prepared to jettison the whole of Schedule B as they had already thrown it over in part. And when many of his colleagues were sceptical his optimism induced him to make them a promise which he never expected to be called upon to honour. If after passing the second reading of the Reform Bill the Upper House attempted to mutilate it by amendments, he undertook to ask the King to create sufficient peers to ensure the passage of the bill in its integrity.

On March 26 the bill was brought up to the Lords. Lord Harrowby and Lord Wharncliffe announced their intention to vote for the second reading.[2] The Bishop of London made a liberal speech.[3] Wellington though speaking against the bill did not declare himself opposed in principle to any measure of Reform.[4] The second reading, originally set down for April 5, was postponed until the 9th in virtue of an agreement between Lord Grey and Lord Wharncliffe; for negotiations were still proceeding with the 'Waverers' in the Tory ranks. The Government made ostensible preparations to create new peers in case the

[1] *Morning Chronicle*, August 3, 1830.
[2] H. of L., March 16, 1832 (*Parliamentary Debates*, 3rd Series, vol. xi, pp. 862–3).
[3] H. of L., March 26, 1832 (ibid., 3rd Series, vol. xi, p. 864).
[4] H. of L., March 26, 1832 (ibid., 3rd Series, vol. xi, p. 869).

bill were defeated and drew up a list of the peers they intended to create. The bluff was not without the desired effect on the Tories. On April 13 after five days' debate the second reading was passed by 184 to 175 votes, the Government thus obtaining a majority of nine. Progress had been made since October. The discussion of the clauses in detail was postponed until after the Easter recess and fixed for May 7.

3

The debate opened on the appointed day but immediately came to an abrupt conclusion. The first clause of the bill provided for the total disfranchisement of a number of boroughs. Speaking as the mouthpiece of the Tories Lord Lyndhurst proposed that a different procedure should be adopted from that which had been followed in 1831, that the discussion of the clause should be left to the last, and the House should not decide what boroughs should be inserted in Schedule A until they had passed all the other clauses of the bill. From this move it appeared that the Tories intended to reserve the liberty after accepting with the necessary modifications the electoral qualifications proposed by the Whigs to reject, if they thought fit, the clause abolishing the nomination boroughs. Lord Grey declared that he could not accept the amendment and was defeated by 116 to 101 votes. He immediately rose to demand an adjournment. After a year's interval the episode of the Gascoyne amendment had repeated itself. But in the former case the Government was able to employ against a refractory House of Commons the weapon of dissolution. Against a refractory House of Lords they had only one resource—the creation of new peers. On May 8 Lord Grey asked the King to create the necessary peers. He refused. King William was too prudent to break the promise which Lord Grey had already wrung from him by meeting his demand with an unqualified refusal. But he objected, as he had consistently objected during the past two months, to the excessive number of new peers which the Cabinet asked him to make.[1] Thereupon Lord Grey offered his own and his colleagues' resignation. It was immediately accepted. The Prime Minister had thus taken the decisive action which

[1] The King to Lord Grey, May 9, 1832 (*Corr. of Earl Grey with William IV*, vol. ii, pp. 395–6). Lord Grey asked for fifty new peers. The King would create only twenty, all of whom were to be taken from the Irish and Scottish peerages. (See especially the King's long letter to Lord Grey of April 5, 1832: *Corr. of Earl Grey with William IV*, pp. 311 sqq.)

had been expected from him in October. But we must not imagine that his motive in resigning was to make the King feel his power and prepare a triumphant return to office. He was weary of so heavy a burden of responsibility. Lord Althorp shared his feelings.[1] These two noblemen, whom circumstances had placed at the head of a movement which threatened at times to prove the prelude to a revolution, regretted those happy days when they were leaders of the Opposition and all the cares of government were borne by the Tories. Among their colleagues some had never liked the bill for which they accepted the responsibility, and would have been delighted to see the Tories carry out a more moderate reform. And even among the Radicals there were some who were alarmed by the prospect of revolution. James Mill visited Brougham and obtained his promise not to adopt a policy of obstruction if the King formed a government of moderate reformers. It was only by degrees that the commanders of the Liberal army regained confidence or rather were once again driven forward to victory by the determination of their troops. The Tories on the other hand were at first exultant. The King, his wife, his brothers, and his illegitimate children, made no attempt to conceal their delight. Unintentionally the waverers had played into their hands. By passing the second reading of the bill they had released the King from his promise and set him free from the yoke of the Whigs. The Tories could now mutilate the bill at their pleasure. They were speedily disillusioned.

Public anger, already aroused by the news of Lord Grey's resignation, assumed alarming proportions when it became known that on the successive refusal of Lord Lyndhurst, Peel, and Manners Sutton, Wellington had accepted the task of forming an administration. Nightly in churches up and down the Kingdom the bells were rung. Everywhere work ceased, everywhere there were rumours that the people were arming. On the 11th monster petitions reached London from Birmingham and Manchester. Revolutionary manifestoes were displayed in London itself—and placards shown in the windows bearing the inscription 'No taxes paid here'. The Common Council of the City called upon the House of Commons not to pass the budget until the Reform Bill had been passed. The King, the princes of the blood, and above all the Queen, 'the German frow', were caricatured and insulted

[1] Le Marchant, *Life of Lord Althorp*, p. 420.

not only by the revolutionary press but even in the organs of the middle class. On Wednesday Lord Lyndhurst had advised the King to retire to Windsor. On Friday he advised him to return to London,[1] and on Saturday the royal coach was followed by the hoots of the mob all the way from Hounslow to St. James' Palace. The King and Queen already saw themselves going into exile, perhaps even to the scaffold, and the court made preparations for flight.

Nevertheless there was no repetition of those violent and aimless explosions of popular fury which had occurred in October at Derby, Nottingham, and Bristol. Throughout the length and breadth of the country there was not a single case of incendiarism, not a single assassination. The National Union took charge of the movement, kept it under strict discipline, and gave it a definite and immediate objective. Their aim was not to prevent a military *coup d'état* by an armed rising. A *coup d'état*, which even in France had proved impossible in July 1830, was out of the question in England. Who could dream of keeping down by force 15,000,000 Englishmen with an army of 11,000 of which only 7,000 were stationed in London? The object of the Union was to bring home to the Tories the absurdity of their designs, and the radical weakness of their position by organizing throughout the country a species of political strike. Until the Reform Bill passed, all over England the taxes must be refused and in every town the political Unions must take the local government into their hands. Against a universal movement of this kind a mere handful of aristocrats supported by 11,000 mercenaries, whose fidelity was by no means above suspicion, were powerless. The leaders of the movement boasted that a large number of retired officers had placed their services at the disposal of the Union, and were prepared to take command of bodies of civic guards. Moreover, they had accomplices among the Whig ministers. Lord Durham gave them every encouragement in his power. Sir John Hobhouse, who had been at the War Office since January, kept them informed of everything that passed in the deliberations of the party.[2] On Sunday, May 13, members of Parliament, in spite of the growing agitation, were still sufficiently blind to the facts of the situation as to entertain the belief that a Tory Cabinet would be able to pass a modified Reform Bill and that the ultra-Tories, who in 1829 had

[1] Croker's *Diary*, May 9, 11, 1832 (*Croker Papers*, vol. ii, pp. 154, 157).
[2] Graham Wallas, *Life of Francis Place*, p. 304.

raised the question of Reform to embarrass Wellington, and in 1831 had become reconciled with him on account of his uncompromising opposition to the reform bill, would now help him to carry a measure of moderate reform. Wellington, who still shared or tried to share these illusions, was engaged in a series of difficult negotiations with Lord Lyndhurst, Alexander Baring, whom he wanted to place at the Exchequer, and Manners Sutton.[1] The Whigs held a stormy meeting at Brooks Club, and Stanley, who terminated a very violent speech with an extremely moderate conclusion, carried a motion assuring a possible Tory cabinet of the tolerance of the reformers.[2] But on the morrow, the great day of public debate, the combination broke down. The adherents of the National Union had met on the Saturday at Francis Place's shop and arranged a new method of agitation to destroy the position of the Bank of England by withdrawing deposits on so vast a scale that the Bank would be threatened with failure. And the whole of London was in fact covered with posters calling upon Englishmen to withdraw their deposits. 'To stop the Duke, go for gold.' The manoeuvre was successful.[3] By noon on Monday its effect was felt in the Commons.

The Radical Duncombe delivered an attack upon the Tories which was received with cheers. A Tory member, Sir Henry Inglish, declared that if Wellington introduced a Reform Bill however moderate he could not support him without dishonour.[4] Alexander Baring in whom Wellington hoped to find his Chancellor of the Exchequer entreated the Whigs to save the country from revolution by returning to Office.[5] Faced by this wholesale desertion by the Tories, Wellington could only abandon an impossible task. On the 15th he informed the King that he was unable to form an administration. The King recalled Lord Grey.

During the next four days the crisis continued. But the result was no longer doubtful. In spite of himself[6] Lord Grey remained

---

[1] Wellington to the King, May 13, 1852 (*Wellington, Despatches, Cont.*, vol. viii, p. 314).
[2] Le Marchant, *Memoir of Viscount Althorp*, p. 429.
[3] Graham Wallas, *Life of Francis Place*, pp. 308–9.
[4] H. of C., May 14, 1832 (*Parliamentary Debates*, 3rd Series, vol. xii, pp. 944 sqq.).
[5] H. of C., May 14, 1832 (ibid., 3rd Series, vol. xii, pp. 953 sqq.).
[6] See the letters to Lord Holland quoted by G. M. Trevelyan (*Lord Grey of the Reform Bill*, p. 398), May 13, 1832: 'I begin to be afraid the attempt [Wellington's attempt to form an administration] may fail.' May 14, 1832: 'I wish to God they [the Tories] were fairly in office.' May 15: 'I believe all you say is quite right: the truth is that never was a captive more desirous of escaping from prison than I am from my present situation. But I will do my duty.'

in possession of the field. When Wellington retired he promised the King that he would abandon active resistance to the Reform Bill and when it was again submitted to the Upper House would abstain from voting. If a sufficient number of peers would consent to follow his example, the victory of the bill was assured, and William IV dispatched a species of circular to the most influential peers asking them to adopt Wellington's attitude. But a mere hope was not sufficient for Lord Grey. He desired Wellington to give a public undertaking. When however, Wellington spoke in the House of Lords on the Thursday he failed to make the declaration which was expected of him. Lord Grey considered the omission a betrayal and betook himself to the King who was obliged to give a written promise to create the necessary number of peers 'if any obstacle arose during the debate upon the bill'. On receipt of the news Wellington at length consented on the 19th to give the undertaking required.

In less than a week a half empty Chamber had finished the discussion of the bill. On June 4 it passed the third reading by a majority of 106 to 27 votes.[1] A few insignificant amendments[2] introduced by the Lords were accepted without debate by the Commons and on June 7 the bill received the royal assent.[3]

This was the issue of a crisis which had lasted almost two years. But was it the conclusion of a crisis which had been no more than the passing repercussion of a continental revolution, or was it only the prelude to fresh upheavals? In spite of the reassuring symptoms we have already noticed there remained many grounds for anxiety. When the bill passed, London was still uncertain what would be the result of the serious rising which had broken out at Paris on June 5 on the occasion of the burial of General Lamarque. Even if, as appeared likely, the throne were sufficiently

---

[1] Five bishops who had voted against the bill in 1831 now voted for it, one who had voted against it abstained from voting, and four who had abstained from voting voted for the bill.

[2] Among them was the following. In defining the house property, occupation of which conferred the franchise, the original bill had said simply 'a house'. In April 1831 the ministers added 'warehouse or counting-house'. The third Reform Bill, as laid before the Commons in December, added the words 'or shop'. Finally, the Lords added the further words 'and other buildings'. 'As this amendment,' Lord John Russell declared, 'was an extension, not a limitation of the franchise, he was sure it would be gladly accepted by the House' (H. of C., June 5, 1832; *Parliamentary Debates*, 3rd Series, vol. xiii, p. 408). The effect, however, of the amendment was not to extend the suffrage, but the plural vote for the benefit of voters who occupied more than one tenement.

[3] 2 and 3 Will. IV cap. 45. Act to amend the representation in Scotland. 2 and 3 Will. IV, cap. 65—in Ireland 2 and 3 Will. IV, cap. 88.

strong to suppress the insurgents the situation in France offered no security for the future. And if two years after the successful revolution of July France was still a prey to such grave disorders, what fare could be augured for England, where apparently a rebellion had been averted only at the last moment by a reform—which many Englishmen regarded as revolutionary—of the entire system of representation?

CHAPTER II

The Policy of Reform

I THE STATE OF PARTIES IN 1833

I

PARLIAMENT was prorogued on October 16 and dissolved on December 3. Widespread anxiety was felt. The first elections conducted under the new system and on the morrow of so grave a crisis might well give rise to disorder if not to riots.[1] There was reason surely to fear that the Political Unions which had played such an important part in securing the reform but had not obtained for all their adherents the civil rights to which they aspired might organize disturbances at the hustings when the votes were being recorded, intimidate the voters and wherever the prospects of their candidate were unfavourable attempt to bring the proceedings to a violent close. When the time came these alarmist predictions were fulfilled at most in some ten constituencies in the north and midlands. In London the election passed without the least disorder.[2]

In the counties the duration of the election had been reduced to two days; and doubts were felt whether in that short space it would be possible to get to the polls the large number of voters whose names had been hurriedly placed on the new registers. But everything passed off without a hitch. For except in Scotland where hitherto the boroughs had never been represented in any real sense, there was no British subject who had not already, either as an actor or a spectator, taken part in an election. To be sure the new franchise had profoundly altered the conditions

[1] For these prognostications and the conditions under which the elections were actually held, see two articles in the *Edinburgh Review*, October 1832: 'Working and Prospects of the Reform' (vol. lvi, pp. 245 sqq.) and January 1832: 'The Reformed Parliament—The Ballot' (vol. lvi, pp. 543 sqq.).

[2] *Ann. Reg.*, 1832, pp. 303 sqq. Lord Grey to Princess Lieven, December 12, 1832: 'Never was there anything so completely successful as the London elections. Not one Radical returned, not one soi-disant Conservative; not a symptom of violence or tumult. Nobody who passed through London would have known that an election was going on . . . I really believe that there has not been a disturbance anywhere, except where it was provoked by the Tories, whom God seems to have blinded for their destruction' (*Corr. of Princess Lieven and Earl Grey*, vol. ii, pp. 428–9).

under which an election was held. But the voter did not find himself in a new world.

By December 24 all the returns had been received except from a few remote constituencies in Scotland and Ireland. The country therefore knew the complexion of its future government. The sole comfort left to the 'Conservatives' (the Tories had thought it politic to adopt this new name) was the knowledge that their rout had not been complete. When the county franchise was extended to the occupiers of a tenement of which the rental value was at least £50 the avowed motive of the change had been to secure the influence of the landowners, and it had in fact saved several county seats for the Opposition. In this way they kept one seat in Cumberland, one in Essex, one in Dorset, one in Buckinghamshire, one in Lancashire and two in Westmorland and Lord Althorp shared with a Conservative the representation of Northamptonshire. The new qualification had continued in existence a large number of small urban constituencies in which not more than a few hundred ratepayers possessed the vote, and under a system of public voting the Conservatives were plentifully provided with the means of exerting pressure on the voters. In two or three instances they even succeeded in returning their candidates for a large town, namely at Bristol, Liverpool, and Norwich, where both the Tory candidates were elected. It goes without saying that the Universities remained true to the Tory flag.[1] But when all their successes were counted the Tories hardly mustered more than 150 members of the new House. Of its 658 members, the same number as in the unreformed Parliament, over 500 belonged to the party which had carried the Reform. Of the 101 Irish members twenty-five Conservatives were returned, in Scotland at most ten out of fifty, in Lancashire and Yorkshire six or seven out of seventy-two, and London did not return a single Conservative.[2]

[1] For these Conservative successes see *Annual Register*, 1832, pp. 301–2.
[2] Since at this date the party organization was still somewhat fluid, it is impossible to obtain absolutely accurate figures. Lord Mahon, in a letter to Robert Peel, January 8, 1833, gives the following estimate: Conservatives 150; Ministerialists, 320; Radicals, Repealers, etc., 190 (C. S. Parker, *Sir Robert Peel*, vol. ii, p. 209). Goulburn, as we learn from a letter written to him by Peel on January 3 (ibid., p. 214), estimated the number of Conservatives at 140. The *Edinburgh Review* (January 1833, 'The Reformed Parliament: The Ballot'; vol. lvi, p. 562) speaks of '. . . 130 or 140 Tories who . . . are avowedly members of that party', and in addition '15 or 20 wavering and uncertain men who deny their being Tories'. J. Grant, writing a few years later (*Random Recollections of the House of Commons*, 1836, pp. 87–9), estimates at 192 the number of Tories in the first Reformed Parliament.

What then were the elements of which this enormous, almost unwieldy, majority was composed? The reform of 1832 had been at once the victory of a political group—a group of great Whig families—and the victory of a class—the vast middle class electorate, the farmers, bond holders, manufacturers and shopkeepers, who henceforward enjoyed the franchise on the same terms throughout the entire country. We might well have expected that victory once secure this class would revolt against the group whose conduct they had followed while the issue was still doubtful, that the House of Commons would be suddenly filled with financiers, merchants and manufacturers. Nothing of the kind took place. The number of business men in the House remained after 1832 practically the same as before.[1] The election revealed an even more characteristic feature of the new system. In every borough, the Nonconformists formed the back-bone of the majority. In every constituency they were probably the majority of the Liberal party and in some places perhaps the majority of the electorate.[2] They should in consequence have been largely represented in the reformed Parliament. Had this been the case, the invasion of the House by Dissent would have amounted to nothing less than a social revolution. But no such

[1] In the Parliament of 1818 (see vol. i, p. 145) we found twenty-three bankers and thirty-five representatives of trade and industry, among the latter six manufacturers, twelve merchants, four brewers and two directors of the East India Company, etc. The Black Book of 1835 (p. 686) gives the following figures for the Parliament elected in 1830: East India Interest sixty-two; West India Interest thirty-five; Bankers thirty-three. The statistics given by Carpenter for the same election in his *Political Letter* of November 6, 1830, are as follows: Merchants and Traders eighty-two, Bankers thirty-six. For the Parliament of 1833 Wade (*British History*, p. 929) gives the following figures: thirty-three Merchants and Tradesmen, thirty-six Bankers. *The Rotten House of Commons*, 1837, p. 20, enumerates for the Parliament elected in 1835: thirty-five Bankers; thirty-five East India proprietors; 14 West India proprietors. In the House of Commons returned in 1837 we have found the names of ninety-seven business men, of whom twenty-nine were bankers, twenty-six merchants, and fourteen manufacturers. The increase is as yet hardly perceptible. (*The Assembled Commons: or Parliamentary Biographer*, with an abstract of the law of election and the usages of Parliament by a member of the Middle Temple, London, 1838.)

[2] See in the *Morning Chronicle*, January, February, March 1834, the figures by which the Dissenters attempted to prove that their numbers exceeded the membership of the established Church. Obviously, statistics of this kind can be utilized only with due precaution. See, however, the figures given for Leicester (March 10), which appear to be reliable. 'The number of the electors who polled at the last contest for that town was 2,260; of these 1,107 are Dissenters, 936 are Churchmen and 167 of unknown religious opinions. Of the 1,107 Dissenting voters, 1,024 gave their suffrage in December 1833 in favour of the Ministerial Candidates; on the other hand, 811 Churchmen voted for the Anti-Ministerial Candidate; and of the 167 nondescript electors, 100 voted with the Dissenters as above and 67 for the political adversary of the Cabinet.' In these statistics the Catholics are counted among the Dissenters.

invasion took place. If we except the group—itself tiny—of those who called themselves Unitarians but were in fact free-thinkers and deists who found it convenient to bear the name of a Christian denomination,[1] only two members of the Evangelical sects took their seats in the new Parliament—the Quaker, John Pease, and the Methodist, John Wilks, to be joined a few months later by the Congregationalist, Edward Baines.

The new House contained sixty-four army officers, nineteen naval officers, forty-five officers of the militia and the yeomanry; over 400 members who followed no profession, and nearly 200 relatives or clients of peers. That is to say, the first Reformed Parliament, returned by a middle-class electorate, was like its predecessors a Parliament the overwhelming majority of whose members were country gentlemen and members of the aristocracy. On the morrow of the election the Conservative press called attention to the fact not without sarcasm. According to these journals the sole intention of the Whigs when they worked out a complicated system to determine what boroughs were unworthy of the franchise, had been to suppress the boroughs whose members were nominated by Tories and preserve those subject to the influence of some important Whig family of the neighbourhood. They even published lists of constituencies with a population below, often far below, 300 which had nevertheless kept their two representatives—to swell the Government majority.[2] There was perhaps some justification for these criticisms. But the Conservatives were the very last people to complain, for it was they who benefited by the aristocratic composition of the new Parliament. When the House proceeded to the choice of a Speaker the ministers proposed the Speaker of the

[1] G. W. Wood, Brotherton, D. W. Harvey, Faithfull, Gillon. Cf. *Eclectic Review*, October 1833, 3rd Series, vol. x, pp. 303 sqq. 'How can Dissenters expect to exercise any influence upon the national councils and institutions but through their representatives? Do they dream of obtaining the recognition of their rights, or promoting the advance of their principles, by petitions, or resolutions, or conferences with the Premier? . . . Should we wrong the Reform Government by expressing the suspicion that for orthodox Dissenters, as a body, they incline to entertain a not uncourteous, but very aristocratical feeling of contempt? And truly, if Dissenters can show no better front in Parliament, they must submit to the sort of feeling which is naturally excited by the display of either political weakness or a supineness bordering on imbecility. Their exclusion under the old system was no indication of their relative strength, and involved no dishonour. But their self-exclusion from a *bona fide* national representation will inevitably produce, in the minds of both our legislators and the Government, the impression that they are entitled to small consideration.'

[2] *Quarterly Review*, April 1833: 'The Present and Last Parliaments' (vol. xlix, pp. 255 sqq.).

last Parliament, Manners Sutton, a Tory, and only a handful of Radicals protested against this act of courtesy to the defeated party. And it would be absurd to ascribe the social complexion of the new Parliament to a fraudulent manipulation of the Reform Bill. For it was not only in the small boroughs which even after the reform continued to be fiefs of the nobility, it was also in the popular constituencies that the English middle class remained so often loyal to the old families.

2

Such are the reflections suggested to-day by an analysis of the list of the members who composed the first reformed Parliament. But contemporary observers were very far from viewing the situation in the same light. Englishmen of moderate views, if temporarily reassured by the peaceable conduct of the December election, found a new subject of alarm in the sudden increase in the number of Radical representatives.

Who in fact were these Radicals? They were in the first place the men whose names had been on the lips of the crowd during the meetings which preceded the passage of the Reform Bill. If Hunt had not been returned for Preston, which under the new franchise no longer possessed universal suffrage, Sir Francis Burdett, Thomas Attwood, and William Cobbett had taken their seats in the new Parliament. And if Sir Francis, disillusioned, aged, and on the eve of deserting the Radical cause, played a very subordinate part, Attwood and Cobbett showed themselves intent on causing trouble. The latter opened his parliamentary career by taking his seat on the front bench of the Opposition by the side of the Conservative leader Peel. We need only mention in passing members to-day practically forgotten but not without influence in their time: Warburton, Clay, Whittle, and Harvey. But in the new house sat John Fielden, the great Lancashire factory owner, a consistent defender of the operatives. And there were the philosophic radicals, Bentham's disciples. Before the reform their sole representative in Parliament had been the aged Joseph Hume. Now, six months after Bentham's death, six young disciples made their appearance at Westminster; Roebuck, Sir William Molesworth, the banker Grote, Leader, Charles Buller, and John Romilly. And Edward Lytton Bulwer the novelist and his brother Henry were in very close connection with the Benthamites. All these men were men of ideas, 'philosophers' as they entitled themselves, and, though repudiating the use of violent methods, had inscribed upon their programme the complete abolition of aristocratic institutions. And finally, there were the Irish followers of O'Connell. It was all very well for their leader to pose as an English Radical, a political disciple of Bentham. He was in reality the national hero of a foreign people. His relatives—four O'Connells were returned in December 1832—and his followers drawn indifferently from every rank of society, and having no other programme than obedience to the orders of the great demagogue, made up a group—'O'Connell's tail'—who were a clan rather than a political party and constituted a species of foreign body lodged in the entrails of the British Parliament.

All together the Radicals were few in number, not above fifty or sixty at the most, but they were noisy and always on the war-path, and it was their intervention which caused the disorder which marked the debates of the Reformed Parliament. We can picture the aspect presented by the old 'St. Stephen's Chapel' when Parliament was in session. The House consisted of 658 members but there was sitting room for no more than 400. The remainder stood and blocked the gangways. Where such confusion prevailed, it required only a score of riotous Radicals or twenty ill-bred Irish members bent upon a row and the tone of the assembly became deplorable. Tiresome speakers could not obtain a hearing and were obliged to address the House amidst a hubbub of private conversation broken from time to time by the Speaker's monotonous and unavailing calls to order. Unpopular speakers were interrupted by gross insults, yells, and imitations of the cries of animals.[1] It was years before the 'reformed' House of Commons recovered its balance.

---

[1] For these scenes of rowdyism, see *Sketches by Boz* (Charles Dickens), 1836, Chapter XVIII; J. Grant, *Random Recollections of the House of Commons*, 1836, pp. 61–2, 72 sqq. S. Warren, *Ten Thousand a Year*, 1841, vol. ii, pp. 79 sqq. Cf. Croker to Lord Hertford, January 25, 1833: '. . . For two nights and a half the vehemence and disorder were so great that people began to think the National Convention was begun. Peel told me that it was "frightful—appalling" ' (*Croker Papers*, vol. ii, p. 202). *Greville Memoirs*, April 4, 1835: '. . . in better, or at least more gentleman-like, times, no noises were permissible, but the cheer and the cough . . . Now all the musical skill of this instrument is lost and drowned in shouts, hootings, groans, noises, the most discordant that the human throat can emit, sticks and feet beating against the floor. Sir Heworth Williamson, a violent Whig, told me that there were a set of fellows on his side of the House whose regular practice it was to make this uproar.' *Diary of Charles Edward Poulett Thomson*, September 21, 1839: 'I will give up the Cabinet and Parliament . . . The interruption and noise which prevails so much in the House *cows* me' (G. Poulett, *Scraps Memoir of . . . Lord Sydenham*, 1843, p. 103).

And if at present the Radicals were few, were they not likely
to increase? The majority just returned to Westminster had been
elected to carry out a programme of reform. One of two things
must therefore happen. The new members might keep their
promises in which case, whatever the name by which they might
elect to be known, they would be in fact Radicals. They might
on the other hand make no attempt to carry out the programme
forced upon them by their constituents. What would be the
effect on public opinion? During the weeks immediately preceding the election of 1832 Radical voters had done their utmost
to secure the assent of candidates to the theory of the mandate,
of pledges.[1] Would not members who failed to honour their
election pledges be regarded as defaulting agents? In the large
towns and especially in London the contest in December had no
longer been a contest between Whigs and Tories, Conservatives
and Liberals, but between Liberals or moderate Reformers and
Radicals. It might reasonably be expected that before many
years had passed the elections would present the same character
in every constituency throughout the Kingdom.[2] This was the
forecast of the leader of the Opposition, and whatever his alarm
at the prospect he sought to adapt his policy to the new conditions.
He formed the design of placing himself at the head of a large
party, which would not be Tory or reactionary, but 'Conservative',[3] a party which would become the party of order and

[1] *Annual Register*, 1832, pp. 299–300. *Quarterly Review*, October 1837: 'Prospects of
the Country' (vol. lix, pp. 555–6).

[2] *Greville Memoirs*, April 1, 1834: 'Lord Wharncliffe ... like Harrowby, is very dismal
about the prospects of the country and thinks we are gravitating towards a revolution.
He says that the constituency of the great towns is composed of Ultra-Radicals, and that
no gentlemen with really independent and conservative principles can sit for them, that
the great majority of the manufacturers and of the respectable persons of the middle class
are moderate, and hostile to subversion and violent measures, but that their influence is
overwhelmed by the numerical strength of the low orders, who want to go all lengths.'

[3] The idea of using the term Conservative to denote a rejuvenated Tory party is usually
and correctly attributed to Croker. See *Quarterly Review*, January 1830, 'Internal Policy'
(vol. xlii, p. 276): '. . . We now are, as we always have been, decidedly and conscien-
tiously attached to what is called the Tory, and which might with more propriety be
called the Conservative Party; also January 1831, 'Parliamentary Reform' (vol. xliv,
p. 595): 'It would ill become those who desire to cherish the *Conservative Principle* to
withhold, in circumstances like the present, on any mere party considerations, their
cordial support from any Government which should evince a fixed determination to
uphold that principle. The alternative use of the words "conservative" and "conservator"
reveals the Continental and French derivation of the new term.' Cf. Baron Vincent to
Wellington, January 4, 1819: '. . . *La bonne cause, les principes conservateurs, ont en vous un
fort et noble appui*' ('The good cause and conservative principles possess in yourself a
powerful and distinguished supporter') (*Wellington, Despatches, Cont.*, vol. i, p. 3). H. of
C., April 16, 1823, Lord John Russell's speech: 'In 1820 the Emperor of Russia had

rally to its support every enemy of revolution. Whether the supporters of the new party chose to term themselves Whigs or Tories was a matter of no importance. They would be united by a common hatred of revolutionary or 'destructive' radicalism.[1] And even at present though the Radicals were so scantily represented at Westminster, was there no danger that the Radical members would exercise an influence in the House disproportionate to their number by claiming to represent the disfranchised masses in an Assembly elected on a restricted franchise? In May 1832 the nation by the use of unconstitutional methods and the threat of revolution had successfully intimidated the House of Lords and compelled it to surrender. It might well be feared that this 'pressure from without', to employ Lord Grey's already classical formula,[2] exerted, not as in the past spasmodically but 'constantly and actively', would permanently influence the

issued his first manifesto respecting the Spanish affairs, in which he laid down the principle —that "institutions emanating from thrones were conservative, while those which sprung up from popular effort were calculated to engender a new chaos" ' (*Parl. Deb.*, N.S., vol. viii, p. 1038). (Wellington to Lord Londonderry, April 20, 1827: 'Rely upon it, dear Charles, the object of the great aristocracy and of the *parti conservateur* of this country is to secure the crown from the mischief with which it is threatened, by moderation, by consistency, by firmness and good temper' (*Wellington, Despatches, Cont.*, vol. iii, p. 655). Lord Londonderry to the Duke of Buckingham, January 5, 1831: '. . . it appears to me that if there were means of bringing about a complete reconciliation between the ultras and Peel's party—a reconciliation founded on the necessity of a loyal and constitutional party adhering together—to which (by the bye) Grey might come, if forced by the Liberals—it would be the best *puissance conservative* for the next session' (Duke of Buckingham, *Memoirs of the Courts and Cabinets of William IV and Victoria*, vol. i, p. 190). The word 'conservator' is still used by Wellington on April 23, 1831: 'We are . . . the conservators of the Constitution' (*Wellington, Despatches, Cont.*, vol. vi, p. 432), and by one of his friends, the Rev. R. L. Freer, in a letter to the Duke, of May 14, 1832: 'Birmingham is far from being *radical*, the majority of respectable persons being decidedly *conservators*.' (ibid., vol. viii, p. 319). The word is employed by the *Standard*, December 24, 1831, as if already in current use (the Conservative Party). After the election of 1832 its position was established, for the same paper employs it exclusively in place of the word Tory (see especially December 26, 28, 29, 1832). Nevertheless, the term is still felt to be a neologism. See Lord Grey to Princess Lieven, December 12, 1832: 'Never was there anything so completely successful as the London election. Not one Radical returned, not one soi-disant Conservative' (*Corr. of Princess Lieven and Earl Grey*, vol. ii, pp. 428–9); Peel to Goulburn, January 3, 1833: 'that party which is called Conservative' (C. S. Parker, *Sir Robert Peel*, vol. ii, p. 212); also *Edin. Rev.*, January 1833, 'The Reformed Parliament': 'what has of late been called *Conservatives*' (vol. lvi, p. 563).

[1] See the important speech in which he announced his intention to vote in favour of the address whose text the ministers had submitted to the approval of the Commons, and laid down the principles which would govern his policy (H. of C., February 7, 1833; *Parl. Deb.*, 3rd Series, vol. xv, pp. 366 sqq.).

[2] In using the expression Lord Grey seems to have alluded to a saying of Lord Chatham's quoted by Cobbett a few months earlier in his *Political Register* (March 19, 1831, vol. lxxi, p. 711): 'Lord Chatham said more than fifty years ago that "if the House did not reform itself from within, it would be reformed from *without*, with a vengeance". It *will* be to a certainty reformed from *without*.'

proceedings of both Houses. Parliament had scarcely assembled when it was deluged with petitions of every description, and it was decided, if not to restrict the right of petitioning, at least to make such alterations in the standing orders of the House as would diminish the time wasted in reading and discussing these innumerable documents.[1] Many of them had been sent up by the Political Unions, which Lord Grey had expected to be dissolved when the Reform Bill passed[2] but which continued in existence to pursue the accomplishment of their complete programme. The first Reformed Parliament had not been in session two months before a campaign of public meetings opened in the large towns, for example at Birmingham and Newcastle, to demand the resignation of a Government deemed too moderate. The plan was again brought forward, which had already in 1819 found favour in revolutionary circles, of electing delegates who in opposition to the members of Parliament returned on a restricted franchise would be the genuine representatives of the people. These delegates would set up in London a National Convention to combat the middle-class Parliament at Westminster. On May 13 a mass meeting was held in London in defiance of a prohibition by the Government at which all those republican emblems were displayed which had been seen so often during the past three years. A skirmish with the police ensued, one policeman was killed, several wounded, and for months to come the Courts were employed in trying the rioters who had taken part in 'the battle of Calthorpe Street'.[3]

The new members—those at any rate who composed the Government's majority—found themselves on the whole in a false position. Drawn from the same class as their predecessors they had been sent to Westminster under novel circumstances and with a democratic programme. For the reform had not only been, as we have already pointed out, the victory of a party and a class, it had also been the victory of a political doctrine. We have seen the part played during the crisis by Bentham and his disciples. Now when the new franchise had been established the

[1] J. Redlich, *Procedure of the House of Commons*, vol. i, p. 76.
[2] Lord Grey to Sir H. Taylor, June 5, 1832 (*Corr. of Earl Grey with William IV*, vol. ii, p. 461).
[3] For the Calthorpe Street riot, see *Annual Register*, 1833, Chron., May 7; also *Political Register*, June 29, 1833 (vol. lxxx, p. 778), July 6, 1833 (vol. lxxi, p. 11); and for the case, arising out of it, of the agent-provocateur, Popay, see ibid., July 20, August 10, 17, 31, September 7, 1833 (vol. lxxxi, pp. 130, 324, 562, 585, 628–9).

of the July revolution compelled Palmerston to adapt the principles of Canning's foreign policy to an entirely new state of European affairs. As a Liberal power, France was now in the nature of things the ally of a Liberal England. Nor could England treat France as she treated her client states Portugal and the South-American Republics. On the contrary, France might even be in a position to contest with her the protectorate of the small nations. What then could be done to secure that in the Franco-British alliance, which circumstances rendered inevitable France should remain as far as possible, in the eyes of the world, the subordinate partner? The problem was not easy to solve. 'Paris,' Palmerston wrote to his brother, 'is the pivot of my foreign policy.'[1]

2

Casimir Perier had laid the foundations of the 'good understanding', the 'entente cordiale', with England.[2] If the French alliance was useful to the Whig ministry, the new Government in France during those early years when its existence was still precarious could not dispense with the support of the London Cabinet. The first strain upon the Anglo-French understanding arose out of the Belgian question; for the French acceptance of Prince Leopold's candidature had not removed all difficulties. When a Dutch army invaded Belgium, a French army drove it back and proceeded to lay siege to Antwerp. Then the plenipotentiaries, weary of the fruitless endeavour to secure the conclusion of a treaty between Holland and Belgium, brushed aside Dutch opposition and drew the frontier between the two peoples in the 'Treaty of twenty-four Articles' of October 15, 1831. When Austria, Russia, and Prussia hesitated to sign it, France and England signed it by themselves. Faced with this quasi-alliance of the two nations, the three continental Powers gave way and ratified the treaty. It was completed by the conclusion of a military convention between France and England, and British opinion allowed a French army to enter Antwerp. Finally Holland concluded an armistice with Belgium to be succeeded

[1] To William Temple, June 29, 1834 (Sir H. L. Bulwer, *Life of Viscount Palmerston*, ed. 1870, vol. ii, p. 196).
[2] The term was not in official use until 1842, but we already come across it in 1832. 'Cordial union' (Lord Palmerston's speech, H. of C., February 9, 1832; *Parliamentary Debates*, 3rd Series, vol. x, p. 159). 'Good understanding' (Lord Grey's speech, H. of C., February 27, 1832; ibid., 3rd Series, vol. x, pp. 727, 730). 'Friendly understanding' (Lord Grey to the King, April 17, 1832; *Corr. of Earl Grey with William IV*, vol. ii, p. 360).

five years later by a formal treaty. The Belgian question was settled. It had been settled by the establishment between France and Holland of a buffer state whose neutrality was guaranteed. This arrangement had averted the danger of a European conflagration. By the pacts which she concluded with Great Britain, France gave an implicit undertaking to abandon all projects of aggrandizement towards the Rhine. Louis Philippe, however, found himself obliged to make some satisfaction to French patriotism and the public opinion of the capital. Casimir Perier and those who inherited his policy turned their attention to the Mediterranean. They aimed at making it, according to the Napoleonic formula, a French lake, and the Whigs deemed it advisable to leave this outlet open to French ambition.

It was already certain that the French occupation of Algiers would be permanent; and once installed in Algiers the French cherished the dream of building up a colonial empire along the northern coast of Africa. Level-headed observers were consoled by the thought that the peace of Europe would benefit. The more French troops in Algiers, the fewer on the Rhine. In Italy the Emperor of Austria aimed at preserving peace and order by the establishment under his patronage of a species of Italian confederation. The British Government was opposed to a union of this kind, and Seymour at Florence and Rome, and Palmerston's brother, Sir William Temple, at Naples,[1] openly worked against Austria. But it was left to Casimir Perier to adopt the bold measure of opposing Austrian intervention by French counter-intervention. By occupying Ancona, France became the most powerful factor in Italian politics: Palmerston's agents received orders to raise no opposition.

In the Levant Greece was established as an independent state to be governed by a German prince with the title of King. It was a victory at once of British diplomacy and western Liberalism. But the recognition of Greek autonomy did not restore peace in the Levant. The two Ottoman powers lately united against Greece were now at war. Ibrahim Pasha, the son or adopted son[2]

[1] Lord Palmerston to William Temple, October 8, 1833: 'I am glad to hear the King of Naples perseveres in his conciliatory system: pray encourage it as far as you can without appearing to meddle too much in matters which do not concern us.' Cf. his letters to Sir W. Temple of December 3, 1833, April 21, 1834, June 27, 1834 (Sir H. L. Bulwer, *Life of Viscount Palmerston*, ed. 1870, pp. 166, 174, 180, 194).

[2] [Which is uncertain.—*Trans. note.*]

of the pasha of Egypt, Mehemet Ali, at the head of an Egyptian army of 50,000 men, annihilated the Sultan's army and encamped before Brusa. The Sultan sought help from Russia, a Russian fleet was despatched to the Bosphorus and 15,000 Russians landed at Scutari. Finally, through the mediation of a French diplomatic agent, Sultan Mahmoud concluded a treaty with Mehemet Ali by which he abandoned to the latter all the territory he claimed. And on the other hand he concluded with the Czar the treaty of Unkiar Skelessi, which established in fact if not in name a Russian protectorate over Turkey and closed the Dardanelles to the fleets of Britain and France. Under these circumstances what action could England possibly take? When the Egyptians reached Brusa and the Russians Scutari, there was not even a British ambassador at Constantinople. As a result of British inaction Russia's influence was supreme at Constantinople and French influence at Cairo. In the Levant to all appearance England had ceased to count.

In Spain and Portugal British influence had not been so completely eclipsed. But since the Peninsular War the entire diplomatic situation had undergone a strange transformation.

The Portuguese Government was no longer the client of England, shielded by British protection from French ambition. It was divided between two warring parties, and the same party received at the same time the support of the British and French Governments, the Absolutists before, the Liberals after, July 1830. When Don Miguel assumed with the royal title the leadership of the Absolutist party he came into conflict both with London and Paris. He was compelled to yield to the successive issue of a British and a French ultimatum supported in either case by a naval demonstration.[1] Civil war ensued and Dom Pedro came from Brazil to uphold against Miguel the rights of his daughter Donna Maria. He failed to secure any direct assistance from the British or French Government. The principle of non-intervention was maintained. But he was permitted to enlist freely the necessary troops. British naval officers commanded his fleet in turn; and veterans of the Napoleonic war who had served under Massena or Wellington formed a corps of 15,000 men which was the backbone of Donna Maria's army.

---

[1] Lord Palmerston attempted to prevent the naval demonstration by France. See his letter to Lord Granville, June 10, 1831 (Sir H. C. Bulwer, *Life of Viscount Palmerston*, ed. 1870, vol. ii, p. 86). But when it took place he refused to disavow it.

In Spain Ferdinand VII yielded to his wife's wishes and annulled the Salic law. By this step he disinherited his nephew, Don Carlos, the head of the Absolutists, and assured the succession of his daughter Isabella, the hope of the Liberals. He was no sooner dead than Don Carlos towards the close of 1833 raised his standard in the northern provinces. Spain now presented the same problem as Portugal and, if the good understanding between England and France were to continue, their respective Governments must agree upon a common policy. This was not easy in a country where French and British influence were traditionally opposed. Metternich made it easier. At Münchengrätz the Emperor of Austria and the King of Prussia concluded a treaty undisguisedly directed against the two western powers. The latter realized the necessity of a counter stroke.

Joint action was not easily taken. At the very moment when the Franco-British entente was to issue in a formal undertaking its weakness was painfully evident. The Duc de Broglie and Talleyrand proposed to Palmerston a general treaty of alliance between France and England. He refused. He did not wish to commit the country so far. He had decided upon a different policy and had draughted a treaty of alliance between England and the two Governments of Donna Maria and Isabella. England would cease to collaborate with France in the peninsula and once more take Spanish and Portuguese Liberalism under her sole protection. Only when the treaty had been signed would France be invited to give her adhesion. In his turn Talleyrand protested. Finally a treaty of alliance whose scope was confined to Spain and Portugal was concluded on an equal footing by the four contracting powers France, England, the Government of Isabella, and the Government of Donna Maria.[1] The Quadruple Alliance therefore represented a compromise between the rival policies of two statesmen who were drifting into a position of hostility and was a partial defeat for both parties. But on its first publication in April and May the treaty aroused the enthusiasm of those who were unacquainted with the intrigues which had

[1] See the correspondence which passed between December 1833 and April 23, 1834, between Talleyrand and the Duc de Broglie, Talleyrand and the Comte de Rigny, Talleyrand and Palmerston (*Mémoires du Prince de Talleyrand*, vol. v, pp. 269–385). Thureau-Dangin utilized these documents before their publication (*Histoire de la Monarchie de Juillet*, vol. ii, pp. 376 sqq.). But the secret history of the Quadruple Alliance had been already related in outline in 1841 by Duvergier de Hauranne in an admirable article entitled 'De l'Alliance anglo-française' (*Revue des Deux-Mondes*, vol. lxvii, pp. 469 sqq.).

produced it.[1] For public opinion it was a reply to Metternich which arrayed the Liberal nations in a solid phalanx against the league of absolute monarchs. Palmerston took the entire credit.[2] It was the first of the long series of dramatic surprises which would distinguish his foreign policy.

3

It was the obvious tactics of the Conservative opposition to charge Palmerston with sacrificing the interests of the country to maintain the understanding with France. To be sure the Conservatives did not ask for a declaration of war against Liberal France, but they considered that friendship with France was purchased too dearly by a breach with all the great powers[3] and witnessed with alarm the Russian, Austrian, and Prussian ambassadors withdrawn in turn from London, a procedure which placed Palmerston in a state of diplomatic isolation. They wounded his vanity by representing him as once more the dupe of the great statesman who represented France in London. The expulsion of Dom Miguel and Don Carlos would, they declared, be 'the *coup de main* of Talleyrand's political life'.[4] The British ministers were 'moved at pleasure like the puppets of this skilful diplomatist's will'. The Conservatives were equally dissatisfied with the solution of the Belgian question. They depicted England forsaking her weak and faithful allies Portugal and Holland to win the friendship of a nation far more powerful and therefore far less reliable. They accused the Whigs of returning to the foolish policy of the Stuarts and allowing the French to reduce Holland

---

[1] *Morning Chronicle*, April 24, 1834: 'The policy which has dictated the Treaty appears, as far as we know of its provisions, to be some reparation for the timid, busy and neverending system of negotiation and interference which has latterly distinguished the management of our "Red Tapists" at home.' *The Times* adopted a far more reserved attitude and restricted its remarks to two short notices of fourteen and eleven lines respectively at the beginning of the leader on April 23 and April 24, 1834. On April 23 it consoles its readers by the assurance that in any event 'armed interference will not be resorted to'.

[2] To William Temple, April 21, 1834: 'I carried it through the Cabinet by a *coup de main*, taking them by surprise, and not leaving them time to make objections ... I reckon this to be a great stroke. In the first place, it will settle Portugal and go some way to settle Spain also. But what is of more permanent and extensive importance, it establishes a quadruple alliance among the constitutional States of the West, which will serve as a powerful counterpoise to the Holy Alliance of the East' (Sir H. L. Bulwer, *Life of Viscount Palmerston*, ed. 1870, vol. ii, p. 180). To the same, May 12, 1834: 'This treaty was a capital hit and all my own doing' (ibid., p. 186); also June 27, 1834 (ibid., p. 194).

[3] H. of C., March 17, 1834, Sir Robert Peel's speech (*Parliamentary Debates*, 3rd Series, vol. xxii, p. 339).

[4] H. of L., May 6, 1834, Lord Londonderry's speech (ibid., 3rd Series, vol. xxiii, p. 590).

under cover of the British fleet.[1] In their eyes Belgium was merely a French province masquerading as an independent nation.[2] It was impossible to look on without dismay while Leopold married Louis Philippe's daughter, demolished the forts recently erected on the southern frontier of his kingdom to protect Germany against another French invasion, and obtained officers from Paris to train his army on the French system. If this was the severity with which the Conservatives criticized the policy Britain adopted in Belgium, Spain, and Portugal the reader can imagine the anxiety with which they witnessed the annexation of Algiers, the occupation of Ancona, the complete eclipse of British influence on the Dardanelles, the growth of French influence at Cairo.

Nor were the politicians alone in their fears. The merchants and manufacturers were equally alarmed. English exports to Spain fell by a half. Portugal imposed a uniform tariff on all imports thus depriving British goods of the preference guaranteed by treaties concluded in the eighteenth century. The English embargo against Holland brought to a standstill for months the entire trade of the east-coast ports. Belgium concluded a commercial treaty with France. It had been hoped that a France converted to political liberalism would have been converted at the same time to free trade. The hope had not been realized. John Bowring, Bentham's disciple and friend, who was sent on an economic mission to Paris, brought back nothing more substantial than promises in return for a reduction of the British duty on wines.[3]

These criticisms can hardly have left Palmerston unmoved. For they were the very charges he had himself brought in 1829 and 1830 against his present opponents, Wellington and Lord Aberdeen. And their effect may be seen in an incipient breach

---

[1] H. of L., January 26, 1832, Lord Aberdeen's speech (*Parliamentary Debates*, 3rd Series, vol. ix, p. 835).

[2] 'King Leopold the First was just as dependent on the French Cabinet as any Nabob on the Ganges was on our East India Company' (H. of C., March 26, 1832, Baring's speech; ibid., 3rd Series, vol. xi, p. 908).

[3] For the economic relations between France and England, see *First Report on the Commercial Relations between France and Great Britain*, by George Villiers and John Bowring. With a supplementary report by John Bowring, 1834. The first report is dated November 26, 1832. Also *Second Report on the Commercial Relations between France and Great Britain; Silks and Wine*, by John Bowring, 1835 [January 24, 1834]. For more information about the trade negotiations between England and France from 1830 to 1840, see Raymond Guyot's well-informed book *La Première Entente Cordiale*, 1926, pp. 105 sqq., 139 sqq.

with Louis Philippe and Talleyrand, a breach partly due to the causes which in the spring of 1830 had set Wellington at variance with Polignac. One thing at any rate is certain. For the moment public opinion was not seriously disturbed. The memories of 1830 were too recent, and France and England were bound together by a very close tie. Even more ineffective were the protests of the advanced Liberals for whom the attitude adopted by England and France towards Metternich and Nicholas was too timid and who reproached Palmerston for betraying in Poland the cause of freedom.[1] The country was bent on peace. Every war whose memory lived in the minds of Englishmen had been a war with France. Therefore the good understanding with France was a sure guarantee that peace would be maintained, and public opinion asked for nothing further. In fact, the Opposition leaders did not venture to brave public opinion. Questions of foreign policy were seriously discussed only in the House of Lords, where Lord Aberdeen or Lord Londonderry took the initiative in debate. It was the House of Lords which in June 1833 took the bold step of appealing to the King to ensure the genuine neutrality of the British Government towards the factions at war in Portugal.[2] In the House of Commons if a few isolated remarks were made at wide intervals on questions of foreign policy, a debate on the subject was extremely rare, and it was very seldom that Peel or some other speaker of repute would intervene in the discussion. For Peel was well aware that it would be imprudent tactics to deploy his troops on this ground. Provided peace were maintained, the nation was indifferent to questions of foreign policy. Men's thoughts were fully employed elsewhere.[3] A host of domestic problems engaged their exclusive attention.

[1] To the Congress of London the nternational law of Europe is indebted for a new principle, that of non-intervention; a principle which keeps oppressed subjects apart because the Holy Alliance is no longer strong enough to keep the oppressors together (*Westm. Rev.*, October 1831, 'France and her Revolution'; vol. xv, p. 430). Cf. ibid., January 1831, 'European Revolution' (vol. xiv, p. 249): 'What would be the consequence in common life, if the principle of non-interference was acknowledged and acted on; if there might be a Holy Alliance of thieves, but only a Non-Interference Society of honest men?'

[2] H. of L., June 3, 1833 (*Parliamentary Debates*, 3rd Series, vol. xviii, pp. 238 sqq.).

[3] Lord Palmerston to Lord Granville, March 1, 1831: 'Cowley's statement that Austria does not mean to meddle with the Pope's territory is satisfactory and relieving. We are all too busy with reform to make it possible to give you instructions about Italy.' Also on March 9, 1831, the significant statement: 'I have been too busy to write to you for some days' (Sir H. L. Bulwer, *Life of Viscount Palmerston*, Book VIII).

4

One of the first problems which faced the Reformed Parliament—a problem however, of colonial policy rather than a
domestic question in the strict sense—was the abolition of slavery.
The problem had been almost ripe for solution before the July
revolution broke out and it was only that event which relegated
the question to a subordinate place in the candidates' programmes
at the general election. But the abolitionist propaganda far from
slackening assumed, under the influence of the political situation,
a revolutionary character. At first the Whig administration was
content to carry further the policy of moderate reform inaugurated by Canning and Lord Bathurst. In the old West
Indian Colonies economic advantages (for example, a reduction
in the duty on sugar) were promised to the planters if they would
consent to adopt the legislation which royal decrees had promul-
gated in the Crown Colonies by which slave labour was subjected
to legal regulation.[1] At the same time the Government proclaimed
the emancipation of all slaves owned by the Crown.[2] But the
immediate result of these measures was to provoke an insurrection
among the slaves. The West Indian negroes knew that the
Government had taken action on their behalf but did not understand its nature. A rumour gained currency among them that the
King of England had proclaimed the emancipation at Christmas
of every slave. In December a formidable insurrection broke out
in Jamaica, and for ten days the island was abandoned to pillage.[3]

Martial Law was proclaimed and the Colonial Militia restored
order. In London the group known as the West India Interest
attempted to make use of the outbreak to postpone emancipation.
But the Abolitionists, who were led in the Commons by Buxton,
were on the watch and they knew that the present conjuncture
was favourable to their designs. For the influence which the West
India Interest exerted in Parliament was due to its ability to purchase for ready money the representation of a number of rotten
boroughs. When the final battle which preceded the passage of
the Reform Bill was in progress during April and May 1832 it

[1] *Annual Register*, 1832, Public Documents, pp. 282 sqq. Cf. H. of C., April 15, 1831:
Lord Althorp's speech; March 23, 1832: speeches by Lord Althorp and Lord Howick
(*Parliamentary Debates*, 3rd Series, vol. iii, pp. 1423; vol. xi, pp. 807, 815).
[2] H. of C., August 17, 1831: statements made by Lord Howick in reply to a question
by Burge (ibid., 3rd Series, vol. vi, p. 160).
[3] *Ann. Reg.*, 1832, Public Documents, pp. 286 sqq.

LIBERALISM OF THE GOVERNMENT

became clear that to combat slavery was to deprive the Tories of an instrument of corruption. Lord Harewood was a prominent defender of the planters in the House of Lords. He was also the head of the Tories in Yorkshire, a county devoted alike to the cause of reform and the cause of emancipation. In the Commons the Marquis of Chandos took the lead among the supporters of slavery. He was also the most energetic and the ablest opponent of the Reform Bill. 'Pull down an abuse when you can,' wrote Perronet Thompson in the *Westminster Review*, 'especially when it is one, like that of slavery in the West Indies, whose supporters support all the rest.'[1] Cobbett, who had long been an opponent of emancipation, as in the bottom of his heart he would always remain, rallied for a time to its support. By his change of front he gratified his political hatreds.[2]

Moreover, the contest between the abolitionists and the defenders of slavery assumed the aspect of a religious struggle. The Nonconformists sects, among whom the missionary spirit had been active for the past half century, were hard at work converting the West Indian negroes to Christianity. In England they constituted a rallying point for the shopkeepers and artisans, in the West Indies for the slaves. The Methodist and Baptist preachers did not incite the slaves to rebel. But they made them more convinced every day that in the sight of God they were equal to the whites and held out promises of speedy emancipation, informing them of the untiring campaign which the Evangelicals at home were conducting on their behalf. It is therefore hardly surprising that when the servile war broke out they found themselves exposed to the slave-owners' fury. In January 1832 fourteen chapels were destroyed by the colonists, who formed themselves into a Church Union to wage unrelenting war upon the Dissenters.[3] Thus battle was joined between the Nonconformist sects and the Anglican Church at the very moment when the position of the latter was threatened by the unpopularity it had incurred.

[1] Article by Colonel Thompson in the *Westminster Review* quoted by A. Prentice, *Hist. Sketches of . . . Manchester*, p. 352.
[2] *Political Register*, Aug. 4, 1832: 'It now appears that, in fact, these slaves are in general *the property of the English boroughmongers*, that they are so in great part at least and that the fruit of the labour of these slaves abroad, has long been converted into the means of making us slaves at home . . . their continuing to hold slaves cannot be good to the people of England' (vol. lxxvii, p. 261).
[3] H. of C., May 24, 1832: Fowell Buxton's speech (*Parliamentary Debates*, 3rd Series, vol. xii, p. 41).

The Wesleyans, the most Conservative of the sects, who abstained on principle from intervention in party strife, regarded slavery as a religious and moral rather than a political question and advised their members to exact from every candidate as a condition of receiving their vote an undertaking to support its unqualified abolition in the colonies.[1] The resistance of the Church was weakened by the fact that on this, as on so many other questions, the Evangelical party was in agreement with the Methodists. A prominent Evangelical, who had made his mark at the bar, Stephen by name, sacrificed a promising and lucrative career to enter the colonial ministry and work for the speedy emancipation of the negroes. So long as Lord Goderich remained at the Colonial Office the department wasted much time in a fruitless attempt to secure the planters' assent to legislation which would pave the way for emancipation of the slaves without inflicting too heavy loss upon their owners. But in March 1833 he was replaced by Stanley, whose relations with O'Connell had become so strained that it was no longer possible to leave the administration of Ireland in his hands. Stanley wished to redeem his failure in Ireland by some brilliant achievement in his new capacity. In less than two months he had produced unassisted a bill of emancipation.[2]

It provided in the first place that every child who should hereafter be born or who was less than six years of age when the bill became law should be declared unconditionally free. This enactment was identical with Buxton's proposal ten years earlier. The Government had repudiated Canning's temporizing policy and accepted the Radical measure advocated by the abolitionists.

However, its operation postponed complete emancipation for a considerable period. For in default of further provision, every slave above six years of age when the act was passed was condemned to permanent slavery. To afford them some relief Stanley established a system of legally controlled apprenticeship. The working day must not exceed ten hours. For three-quarters of that period the slaves would be at the disposition of their owners, who however were obliged to make them a fixed payment either in kind or in money. The remaining quarter belonged to the slave himself to employ as he pleased and he might set

[1] Wesleyan Methodists, Minutes of Conference, vol. vi, p 613 (Conference of 1830); vol vii, pp. 66–7 (Conference of 1831) and 175–7 (Conference of 1832).

[2] H. of C., May 14, 1833: Stanley's speech (*Parliamentary Debates*, 3rd Series, vol. xvii, p. 1193 sqq.).

aside the money thus earned to purchase his freedom. The wages payable for these two hours and a half of work were to be such that, if the entire amount were taken by the owner, the slave would be free at the end of twelve years. This system of legal apprenticeship embodied the principle which had inspired Canning's entire policy in the matter of slavery. But whereas Canning had instituted a system of modified and legally regulated slavery in the hope of finally inducing the owners to emancipate their slaves voluntarily, Stanley set up the new system as a transitional system which, at the will of the slave, would automatically be replaced in twelve years' time by complete freedom.

Finally, to indemnify the owners against the risk of uncertain and remote payment the state intervened between master and slave. The slave owners would receive immediately from the Government the sum of £15,000,000, which was estimated to represent the total cost of redeeming every slave. And officials whose impartiality would be above suspicion would be despatched to the West Indies by the Government to receive the payments with which for twelve years the slaves would purchase their freedom.

The colonists protested that £15,000,000 was too small a sum and asked for £20,000,000. Nor would they accept a 'loan' even though, under the Government scheme, it was nominal. They demanded an unconditional gift. Cabinet and Parliament conceded their demands and made them a gift of £20,000,000.[1] The abolitionists on the other hand accepted only under protest Stanley's system of apprenticeship, though it gave effect to the suggestions they had made themselves ten years before. They found fault with a mongrel system, which, they maintained, would fail in practice to satisfy either the masters or the slaves. The slaves would have no motive to work, and would not work. The masters would weary the home Government with complaints which it would be impossible to satisfy since the responsibility for the slaves' idleness would lie not with themselves but with the system to which they were subject. Moreover, since the sum paid to the planters was no longer a loan but a gift and since it had been arbitrarily raised from £15,000,000 to £20,000,000, there was no longer any reason to fix at twelve rather than at any other number the years which must elapse before the 'apprentice'

[1] H. of C., June 10, 1833: Stanley's speech (*Parliamentary Debates*, 3rd Series, vol. xviii, pp. 547 sqq.).

became a free man. The Government took account of these criticisms, and the duration of the new system of apprenticeship was reduced from twelve to seven years for slaves employed on the land, and five years for the rest.[1] Thus amended the bill had an easy passage through both Houses and was passed by enormous majorities. The Jamaica insurrection, the aftermath of the July revolution, must therefore be considered as an instance, exceptional among so many contemporary revolts which failed, of a revolt which succeeded. But to understand the delight with which the emancipation of the negroes was greeted, the rejoicings which took place on a large scale throughout the entire country when a year later the act came into force, we must remember that the abolitionist campaign had been first and foremost a Christian movement. What the liberal bourgeoisie of contemporary France failed to do for the slaves in the West Indies, the Evangelical middle class dared to accomplish in England; and when Wilberforce died within a few weeks of the passage of the bill his deathbed was consoled by the knowledge that the victory won for the blacks had been won by his efforts. No doubt the organ of the Benthamite group, the *Westminster Review*, was wholehearted in support of emancipation. But even here religious influences were at work. The editor, John Bowring, was a Liberal Christian, who did his utmost to modify the hostile attitude towards Christianity which the group had inherited from their master. On the other hand Joseph Hume in the House of Commons had never ceased to preach the necessity of caution: 'they ought not to rush headlong into an abyss'.[2] Among the professional politicians Brougham had distinguished himself side by side with Wilberforce and Buxton by his zeal, it is true, for emancipation. But the *Edinburgh Review*, in an article which passed in review all the reforms accomplished during the first session of the new Parliament, while expressing its satisfaction at the abolition of slavery, did not conceal its apprehensions, recognized 'the extraordinary difficulty of the question'; 'so difficult a subject never was attempted by human legislation', and deplored 'the extravagance of the anti-slavery party.'[3] Too much importance must not be attached to

[1] H. of C., July 24, 1833: Fowell Buxton's amendment; July 25, 1833: Stanley's speech (*Parliamentary Debates*, 3rd Series, vol. xix, pp. 1184 sqq., 1238–9).
[2] H. of C., June 7, 1833 (ibid., 3rd Series, vol. xviii, p. 459).
[3] *Edinburgh Review*, October 1833, 'First Session of the Reformed Parliament' (vol. lviii, pp. 206, 207).

these reservations. Liberals and Evangelicals worked together to secure the passage of the law. It is nevertheless a significant fact that the first great measure of emancipation passed by the reformed Parliament was due to the co-operation of political Liberalism and Evangelical piety.

5

To study an aspect of the new Liberalism devoid of the slightest tinge of Christian feeling we must go to the economists. Not only the Benthamites, the writers of the *Westminster Review*, but ordinary Liberals, for example the contributors to the *Edinburgh Review*, were disciples of Adam Smith and Ricardo. The optimists believed that the interests of individuals are naturally harmonious, and that it was only the interference of the State which prevented the harmony being realized. Others—the economists who were most faithful to the doctrines of Ricardo—took a more pessimistic view, frankly recognized the existence of a natural conflict of interests between the capitalist and the worker, the landlord and the capitalist, and were even inclined to believe that the progress of mankind, far from abolishing the conflict, would exasperate it. But they agreed with the optimists in holding that State interference must inevitably be unscientific, and therefore could only make the situation worse. Both parties therefore were united in putting forward a programme of economic freedom. It was to satisfy the economists that the Government abolished privileges of landed property which had survived from the feudal system, by enacting that henceforward sporting rights should not be confined to those who owned the land over which they were exercised, legalizing trade in game,[1] and granting creditors the same claims upon the real estate of their debtors as they already possessed upon their personal.[2] It was also under their inspiration that it carried further the process of abolishing monopolies, which trammelled the freedom of the individual, his freedom to consume or produce, his freedom to buy or sell. And it happened that two most important monopolies expired in 1833 and 1834, the monopoly of the East India Company and the monopoly of the Bank of England.

The East India Company continued to govern India under the control of the India Office according to the system established in

[1] 1 and 2 Will. IV, cap. 32.　　　　[2] 3 and 4 Will. IV, cap. 104.

85

the reign of George III. But it lost its monopoly of trade and navigation with China.[1] It was estimated that whereas the population of Great Britain during the past thirty years of the century had increased by a half, the consumption of tea had increased by no more than a twelfth. That the increase was so small was no doubt due to the imposition of higher duties on tea,[2] but the monopoly of the East India Company was a contributory factor. Everyone agreed that the monopoly must be abolished, and even before the Whigs came into office Wellington had the matter under consideration. Although the introduction of the new system would strike an immediate blow to the entire body of trade which gravitated around the Company's offices in the Port of London, the representatives of the East End were among those who voted for the reform.[3] The measure was in fact passed almost without discussion by an empty House,[4] and has barely left a trace in the published debates.

But the monopoly of the Bank was quite another matter. If the Government were faithful to the teaching of Ricardo, the statute of 1819 restoring specie payment must be completed by a further enactment abolishing the privilege of the Bank. A State Bank whose sole function was the issue of paper money would suffice to perform the only useful function at present performed by the Bank of England. What reason could there be to delegate that function to a deposit bank, whose interest might conflict with the interest of the State?[5] But the Bank was a powerful corporation, with which, for many a long year, the Exchequer and the world of industry and commerce had been accustomed to deal. Its directors' honesty and ability were universally admitted even by those who objected to the privilege accorded to the Bank. The crisis of 1825 was already forgotten, and since the danger had been temporarily removed the need of a remedy seemed less urgent. Moreover, time pressed and it seemed hardly possible to settle so weighty and intricate a question within the few months yet to elapse before the privilege expired. A secret committee of inquiry was appointed in 1832 over which the Chancellor of the Exchequer presided. But the following year the Chancellor decided

---

[1] 3 and 4 Will. IV, cap. 85.
[2] Sir Henry Parnell, On Financial Reform, 3rd ed., 1831, pp. 40-1.
[3] Quarterly Review, January 1834, 'Free Trade to China' (vol. l, p. 431).
[4] Greville Memoirs, September 3, 1833.
[5] H. of C., May 31, 1833: Hume's speech (Parl. Deb., 3rd Series, vol. xviii, p. 202).

to bring its work to an end, and after some hasty negotiations concluded on his personal responsibility an agreement with the Bank which on May 31, 1833, was laid before the Commons.[1]

The Bank accepted a reduction of £120,000 per annum in the amount it received for its service of the National Debt. It undertook to publish a quarterly statement of its reserve, its note issue, and its accounts. Further, it consented to the abolition of a monopoly it had assumed on the strength of an erroneous interpretation of the law. A provision of the Act expressly permitted other joint-stock banks to compete in future with the Bank of England even within the radius of sixty miles from the City, where the Bank would henceforward possess only a monopoly of issuing notes. Though the monopoly of the Bank was not directly extended, two clauses of the new act facilitated its operations. Under the existing law the sole means by which the Bank could restrict the currency was to refuse discount. In future it would be entitled to raise the charge for discount and was no longer confined to the legal rate of interest. As we should have expected, this provision, the first step towards the abrogation of the usury laws, aroused no opposition. It was otherwise with the second clause. To prevent a repetition of the disaster of 1825, when the panic of the provincial banks exhausted the reserves of the Bank, it was provided that in future Bank of England notes should everywhere, except at the Bank itself, be legal tender for any sum not less than £5. At first sight this provision was tantamount to repealing the Act of 1819: Cobbett and Attwood were triumphant[2]: Peel raised vehement protests.[3] But the repeal was after all merely apparent, for the bank note was still exchangeable for gold at the Bank of England. The sole effect of the clause was that the Bank at the very moment when it lost its monopoly in London as a deposit bank acquired a sort of universal monopoly as a bank of issue. In short, with the reservations above mentioned, the privilege of the Bank was renewed for a period of twenty years, Parliament reserving the right to alter its conditions at the end of ten. The Liberal Government, taken by surprise, had until 1844 shelved the problem of organizing the banking system raised by the crisis of 1825.

[1] 3 and 4 Will. IV, cap. 98.
[2] H. of C., Aug. 19, 1833: Cobbett's speech (*Parliamentary Debates*, 3rd Series, vol. xx, p. 764); Aug. 9, 1833: Th. Attwood's speech (ibid., 3rd Series, vol. xx, pp. 465 sqq.).
[3] H. of C., June 28, July 1, 1833 (ibid., 3rd Series, vol. xviii, pp. 1337-68).

6

If there was a yoke which ever since 1815 had been felt as intolerable by every Englishman it was taxation. The heavy taxes were obviously a legacy of the long war waged against France, and since the Tories were proud to claim responsibility for the war, they must be held equally responsible for the heavy burden the country was obliged in consequence to bear. It was evidently the duty of the Liberal party when it took office to free the nation from this financial bondage. We have already noticed the complaints which at the opening of 1830 Sir Henry Parnell and Poulett Thomson had urged against the existing system of taxation. Now the latter was president of the Board of Trade, and therefore preeminently qualified by his position to assist in drawing up the budget. Sir Henry Parnell, it is true, was not invited to join the administration. But when Lord Althorp found himself dumped upon the Exchequer with no special qualification for the office, and introduced his budget in February 1831, he expressly stated that he had taken his 'general view of finance'[1] from Sir Henry. The budget embodied an extremely bold and ambitious financial policy. For the new administration, which had taken office to carry out a double programme of retrenchment and political reform, probably attached equal importance to Lord Althorp's budget and Lord John Russell's Reform Bill.[2] Little did they foresee that Lord John's bill would prove the sole means of saving a Government whose position had been endangered by the failure of Lord Althorp's budget. For the budget had hardly been introduced when it was pulled to pieces by the criticism of the House. The Liberal campaign had opened with a serious blunder. According to Sir Henry Parnell it was possible both to lighten the taxpayer's burdens and increase in the long run the resources of the State. But only in the long run; and it was evident that fiscal reform was no easy matter unless at the outset the State disposed of a considerable surplus. Otherwise the taxes which were abolished must be replaced by others, that is to say the Government must adopt what was termed in current parlance a 'commutation of taxes'. Unfortunately there was no surplus in 1831. The receipts for 1830 had indeed risen to £50,600,000. But the

---

[1] H. of C., February 11, 1831 (*Parliamentary Debates*, 3rd Series, vol. ii, p. 407).
[2] H. of C., February 11, 1831: Lord Althorp's speech (ibid., 3rd Series, vol. ii, pp. 403 sqq.).

Tory cabinet, to satisfy the demands of the Opposition, had consented to such a reduction of taxes that the receipts for 1831 were not expected to exceed £47,150,000, that is to say, the estimated surplus would barely amount to £300,000. If, in spite of this unfavourable situation, the Government decided to reform the system of taxation, would it have the courage to tackle the powerful combinations whose interests stood in the way of a satisfactory reform—the timber merchants of Canada, the sugar planters of the West Indies, the owners of agricultural land at home? Lord Althorp attempted to modify the tariff to which timber was subject. We shall soon see what blunders he committed in the attempt. But this was not the moment to antagonize the West Indian planters, already threatened by the campaign against slavery. And no politician in his senses could possibly contemplate any interference with the corn laws, an attempt which would destroy any prospect of passing the Reform Bill by driving into the Tory camp the agriculturalists, who formed the majority of the House.

Under these circumstances Lord Althorp's budget was a series of random blows. He reduced several taxes—the tax on tobacco, and the tax on advertisements—in the avowed hope that the reduction of the tax, by ultimately increasing the consumption, would one day produce an increase of revenue. He abolished a tax obviously unfair since it was levied exclusively on a limited number of taxpayers, the tax on coal brought by sea to London. And he abolished several taxes considered to be detrimental to trade and to cost the nation more than they brought in to the Government; the taxes on candles, printed calicoes, and glass. The total amount of revenue thus sacrificed amounted, according to Lord Althorp's calculation, to £3,170,000, a sum equal to ten times the paltry surplus at his disposal.[1]

Should the deficit be supplied by reimposing the income tax? This was the course advocated by Sir Henry Parnell, and the Radicals of the Bentham group and the ultra-radicals went further in the same direction. Not content with proposing an income tax, they desired a graduated income tax. In the spring of 1831

[1] See the petition from Wilton presented by Hobhouse, Feb. 14, 1831 (*Parliamentary Debates*, 3rd Series, vol. ii, p. 487). Cf. Benham *Traités de Législation civile et pénale, Principes du Code Civil le Partie*, Chap. VI (vol. i, p. 186; *Works*, vol. i, p. 305). But the *Edinburgh Review*, April 1833 (vol. lvii, p. 162), opposes the tax on the ground that it is calculated to 'depress one class and elevate another'.

Lord Althorp had had the imprudence to avow that on this matter also he was a follower of Sir Henry. But Poulett Thomson had always been careful not to commit himself in favour of the tax and Lord Althorp could not fail to perceive that if he attempted to introduce an income tax into his budget he would have to face the unanimous opposition of the Cabinet and the Whigs. He was therefore compelled to have recourse to other expedients.

Great Britain had adopted for certain classes of goods a system of preferential tariffs calculated to encourage the trade of particular colonies or client states to the disadvantage of the rest of the world. In two respects Lord Althorp proposed to modify this system of preference and thus give some satisfaction to the theorists of free trade. But we must notice the exact nature of his proposals. If he reduced the duties on French wines, he would compensate for the loss of revenue by raising the duties on other foreign wines and on the wines of the Cape. All would in future pay the same duty. The change benefited the French producer, not the English consumer. He attempted to diminish the difference between the duty levied on Canadian timber and the duty levied on timber from the Baltic. But he raised both. He estimated that these two revisions of the tariff would produce an increase in the revenue of £840,000.

In the second place he proposed the introduction of several new imposts: a duty on raw cotton; a duty on the export of coal; a tax on journeys by steamboat varying in proportion to the distance traversed; a duty of half per cent on all transfers of property whether real or personal. All these imposts, from which he expected an increase of revenue amounting to £1,900,000, were obviously violations of the economic principles taught by Sir Henry Parnell and Poulett Thomson.

In short, he proposed a reduction of taxation to the amount of £3,170,000, and the imposition of fresh taxation to the amount of £2,740,000, a net reduction of £430,000. There would therefore have been a deficit of £130,000. But it happened that apart from any changes in the taxation a sum of £580,000 derived from arrears on the Excise was at the disposal of the Exchequer as an exceptional source of revenue, and he estimated that his budget would therefore produce an actual surplus of £450,000. But the budget had been barely introduced when vehement protests were raised on all sides against his new imposts[1] and he saw himself compelled to pull his budget to pieces. He abandoned the proposed tax on transfers of property, and to compensate for the revenue lost, the proposed reduction of the tobacco duty and the abolition of the duty on glass, changes which involved a reduction and an increase of revenue amounting altogether to £1,000,000.[2] He abandoned the tax on steamboat travel and consented to a reduction of the duty to be levied on raw cotton.[3] He succeeded without much trouble in carrying his revision of the duties on wine, though he was obliged to lower slightly the duties on wines imported from the Cape.[4] But his attempt to revise the duties on timber failed entirely. It was in vain that he tried to save his proposal by a double amendment. The duties on Canadian timber would not be raised and the duties on timber from the Baltic would be gradually reduced. He was defeated.[5]

Thus the budget as passed by Parliament bore little resemblance to the budget draughted by Lord Althorp, which had been an attempt, as hasty and unintelligent as it was showy, to make the financial system of the country conform in some measure to the new doctrine of free trade. At the same time the ministry underwent a further humiliation, also on a matter of finance. In November Wellington had been defeated on a motion by Sir Henry Parnell for the revision and reduction of the civil list. The committee of inquiry which was consequently appointed was content to make a few insignificant suggestions which William IV refused to accept and his ministers dared not force upon him. They were content to reform the system of accounts and to detach from the civil list the salaries paid to officials in the diplomatic service and a few other disbursements of the same nature whose inclusion in the list was a relic of the old days of absolute monarchy.[6] But this reform, however excellent in itself, did not afford taxpayers the relief they had expected.

---

[1] H. of C., February 11, 1833: Speeches by Goulburn, Sir Robert Peel, etc. (*Parliamentary Debates*, 3rd Series, vol. ii, pp. 418 sqq.).

[2] H. of C., February 14, 1833: Lord Althorp's speech (ibid., 3rd Series, vol. ii, pp. 491 sqq.).

[3] 1 and 2 Will. IV, cap. 16.

[4] 1 and 2 Will. IV, cap. 30.

[5] H. of C., March 11, 15, 18, 1831 (*Parl. Deb.*, 3rd Series, vol. iii, pp. 367, 455, 540).

[6] H. of C., February 4; March 25, 28, 1831 (ibid., 3rd Series, vol. ii, pp. 152 sqq.; vol. iii, pp. 959 sqq., 1102 sqq.).

7

The budget of 1832 introduced and passed in the very midst of a political and economic crisis was merely a provisional measure. But during the spring of 1833, in a Parliament returned by a new electorate, finance reassumed all its importance. The economic crisis had been surmounted and the financial position had enormously improved. The surplus for the last financial year which had been estimated at £800,000 had amounted to £1,487,000. Under these circumstances it was easy for Lord Althorp without repeating the dangerous experiment of a 'commutation of taxes', to pursue the policy whose principles had been laid down by the Opposition in 1830 and which the Tory Cabinet had put into practice the same year, the policy of utilizing the surplus to reduce taxation rather than the National Debt. He reduced or entirely abolished a number of excise duties and assessed taxes, for example exempting tradesmen from paying the window tax.[1] He removed the duty on raw cotton imposed in 1831.[2] He abolished the duty on tiles[3] and reduced by half the duty on soap.[4] He proposed to sacrifice a total revenue of £1,056,000 and since the estimated surplus was £1,572,000 a margin of £500,000 remained at his disposal.

But an outcry arose immediately. It was no longer, as in 1831, against the imposition of new taxes that the taxpayers protested. The new electorate displayed its power by indiscriminate and intemperate demands for a far more radical reduction of taxes.

Agriculture was passing just then through a difficult period. Every year between 1832 and 1835 the harvests were good and bread was cheap, the manufacturers profited, the farmers suffered. The prediction had been freely made—whether in hope or fear—that it would not be long before the passage of the Reform Bill was followed by the repeal of the Corn Laws. These hopes and fears were not destined to be fulfilled, and the circumstances of the moment permitted the Cabinet to treat the question as purely academic, an 'open question' on which ministerialists and even ministers were free to vote in accordance with their private convictions. It was the agriculturalists who wearied the Government with their complaints. They demanded that the malt tax

[1] 3 and 4 Will. IV, cap. 39.
[3] 3 and 4 Will. IV, cap. 11
[2] 3 and 4 Will. IV, cap. 10.
[4] 3 and 4 Will. IV, cap. 16.

should be totally remitted or at least reduced by half. It was
difficult for the Chancellor of the Exchequer to meet their wishes.
The malt tax produced an annual revenue of almost £5,000,000.
Was it possible to sacrifice the whole or even the half of so large
a sum? Could they count upon an increase of consumption to
cover sooner or later so enormous a loss? Could they meanwhile
devise some form of 'commutation', or even go to school with
the Radicals and introduce an income tax? Lord Althorp refused
to abolish or even reduce the tax on malt; he would promise only
a reform of the tithe and the Poor Law, and the appointment
of a Committee to inquire into the agricultural depression.[1] Yet
he was well aware what dangerous enemies the agriculturalists
might prove. They were strongly represented in the new House
of Commons and not only on the Opposition benches. Their
influence was supreme in the rural constituencies, and if the
Government failed to do justice to their complaints the entire
county representation might perhaps be Conservative after the
next election.

In the towns dissatisfaction with the present system of taxation
assumed another form. The taxpayers clamoured for the abolition
of the assessed taxes, in particular of the tax on house property.
The tax was rendered still more unpopular by its unfair incidence.
The assessment method was such that country estates and even
the mansions of the nobility practically escaped payment. The
towns on the other hand were assessed very heavily. It was
calculated that the county of Middlesex paid over half the tax.[2]

[1] H. of C., February 14, 1834: Lord Althorp's speech (*Parliamentary Debates*, 3rd Series,
vol. xx, p. 367); also the debate in the House of Commons, April 26, 1833 (ibid., 3rd
Series, vol. xvii, pp. 678 sqq., esp. p. 681).

[2] Facts (founded upon Parliamentary Returns) illustrative of the great inequality of the
Taxes on Houses and Windows, showing how unjustly and oppressively they bear upon
the middle and industrious classes, 1833. See the extracts from this pamphlet in the
Political Register, March 30, 1833, April 6, 1833 (vol. lxxix, pp. 804 sqq.; vol. lxxx,
pp. 37 sqq.). Cf. in ibid., January 26, 1833 (vol. lxxix, pp. 208 sqq.), the report of a meeting of delegates from the London parishes, and on May 18, 1833 (vol. lxxx, pp. 426 sqq.),
the report of the Southwark meeting, especially Paul's speech: 'In the county of Radnor
there was not a house rated beyond £20 per annum; yet in that county there were
numberless gentlemen's seats, parks, and all that could tend to the luxuries of life. But
in London there was hardly a person who had a house over his head who was not obliged
to pay £20 per annum in these taxes' (p. 431). See also the text of the first resolution
passed by the meeting . . . That the Marquis of Westminster, having expended about
£1,000,000 on Eaton Hall, in the county of Chester, is rated at only £300 per annum
and chargeable thereupon with the annual payment of £42 10s., while any person
expending the like sum on 500 houses in London at £2,000 each, would be, allowing
for ground rent, assessed at the yearly sum of £64,000 and would, therefore, be chargeable
with the annual sum of £9,066 13s. 4d. (pp. 430-1).

Even before the introduction of the budget one of the four City members announced his intention to demand the remission of the assessed taxes; and a deputation which included thirteen representatives of metropolitan constituencies went to Downing Street to urge Lord Althorp to abolish the hated imposts.[1] The demand was as embarrassing to the Government as the agriculturalists' demand for the abolition of the malt duty. How could it be conceded without destroying the balance of the budget? But on the other hand was it prudent to resist an agitation whose headquarters was the capital? The memory of the Paris revolution was still fresh and the events of 1830 and 1832 had thrown the ruling classes into a state of panic which we can hardly conceive to-day, terrified as they were lest at any moment England might take the revolutionary infection from the Continent.

Lord Althorp's tactics consisted in playing off the two groups of malcontents against each other. On April 26 when the House of Commons had adopted by a majority of 162 to 152 votes a motion of Sir W. Ingilby, a ministerialist county member for Lincolnshire demanding the reduction of the malt tax by half, he gave way for the moment while deploring a vote which had placed him in a very difficult position.[2] But three days later he announced that when Sir John Key's motion to abolish the assessed taxes came up for discussion he would move an amendment rejecting both proposals alike—the reduction of the tax on malt and the abolition of the assessed taxes. For, as he pointed out in moving his amendment, so much revenue could not be sacrificed without substituting an income tax, and it was inopportune to undertake the reorganization of the national finances which such a step would involve.[3] On April 30, the amendment was accepted by a majority of 355 votes to 157.[4] The Conservatives headed by Peel had retreated, and abandoned the attempt to reduce the tax on malt. For they were afraid that if they pressed their claim to relief they might encourage the Radical agitation of the towns.

[1] See the account of the proceedings at the interview, *Political Register*, March 23, 1833 (vol. xxix, pp. 710–14).
[2] H. of C., April 26, 1833 (*Parliamentary Debates*, 3rd Series, vol. xvii, p. 716).
[3] H. of C., April 29, 1833 (ibid., 3rd Series, vol. xvii, pp. 728 sqq.).
[4] H. of C., April 29, 30 (ibid., 3rd Series, vol. xvii, pp. 728 sqq., 769 sqq., and 832–4).

8

For the moment Lord Althorp had won the parliamentary battle. But the agitation continued. At the meeting between the London delegates and Lord Althorp, Sir John Hobhouse had distinguished himself by the energy with which he pleaded their cause. He had since been appointed to succeed Stanley as Irish secretary. But when Lord Althorp in concert with his colleagues met the demand for the abolition of the assessed taxes with an unqualified refusal, he left the Cabinet and even gave up his seat in Parliament. The step was a solemn profession of faith in the doctrine of the mandate; rather than be false to the pledges he had given his constituents Hobhouse submitted himself anew to their choice. But after a series of disorderly meetings at which he was not even allowed to speak he was defeated by Colonel Evans, a more uncompromising Radical than himself.[1] Six months after the general election the electorate gave their representatives a serious warning.

In the large towns of the Midlands, at Birmingham,[2] for example, and at Hull,[3] but above all in London, the opposition to the taxes assumed a definite shape. In the London parish of Marylebone an association was founded whose members agreed to refuse to pay their taxes. It soon had a membership of 2,000. By this attitude the taxpayers obliged the authorities to summon them for default of payment and distrain upon their goods, and when the distraint was attempted they expelled the officers by force.[4] Then Lord Althorp gave way. On January 5, 1834, the financial position was even more favourable than in 1833. There was a surplus of £1,513,000. At the beginning of February, Lord Althorp announced his intention to remit taxation to the amount of £1,200,000. What taxes would he remit? 'If,' declared Lord Althorp, 'I were to look at the question simply as a financial question, I think there are other taxes the repeal of which is more desirable. . . . But I feel it very strongly that it is one of the ingredients in the impropriety of a tax, that it is most exceedingly unpopular. Taking all the circumstances into consideration . . . I do think that the best suggestion I can make is that the House Tax

[1] *Annual Register*, 1833, pp. 158-9.   [2] Ibid., 1833, p. 159.
[3] *Political Register*, August 24, 1833 (vol. lxxxi, p. 489).
[4] *Ann. Reg.*, 1833, Chron., October 26, November 2. *The Times*, October 3, 10, 11, 12, 15, 17, 25, 1833.

should be repealed.'[1] The agriculturalists demanded the abolition or at least the reduction of the malt tax, the shopkeepers the reduction or even the total remission of the assessed taxes. The Whig statesmen decided to gratify the urban in preference to the rural electorate. They were prepared in the event of a general election to lose the counties rather than allow the Radicals to swamp the Whigs in the boroughs.

Looking back at the end of 1834 on the four financial years during which the Liberals had held office what should be our judgment upon their performance as a whole? The ministerial organs did not want arguments to prove that they had carried out faithfully their programme of retrenchment. They had effected drastic economies in the Government departments. When Lord Althorp introduced his budget in 1833 he informed the House that 1,387 places had been suppressed since 1830, a reform which had effected a saving of almost £200,000.[2] Expenditure on the army and navy after a slight increase in 1831—when the disturbed posture of affairs had justified additional precautions—had rapidly decreased. The army estimates which in 1830 amounted to £7,000,000 had fallen in 1834 to £6,500,000, the naval during the same period from £5,300,000 to £4,500,000, and the amount spent on the artillery from £1,600,000 to £1,100,000. The total expenditure of the nation had progressively fallen from £52,019,000 in 1830 to £51,711,000 in 1831, £51,523,000 in 1832 and £49,166,000 in 1833.[3]

Moreover, the condition of trade and manufacture was so prosperous and the receipts produced by the taxes so high that in the space of three years the Government was able without endangering the balance of the budget[4] to reduce taxes to the amount of £3,335,000, and by the further reductions in the budget of 1834 the Treasury sacrificed revenue to the amount of

[1] H. of C., Feb. 14, 1834 (*Parliamentary Debates*, 3rd Series, vol. xxi, p. 365). When after a considerable delay (it was not until July) the Government actually introduced their budget, Lord Althorp could reckon upon a surplus of £1,620,000. And it was calculated that a revision of the duties on spirits would produce an additional £195,000. The total surplus would therefore amount to £1,815,000, which made it possible to reduce the taxation by the amount of £1,581,000, of which £1,200,000 represented the proceeds of the house tax.

[2] H. of C., April 19, 1833 (ibid., 3rd Series, vol. xvii, p. 326).

[3] Public Expenditure of the United Kingdom of Great Britain and Ireland in the year ended January 5, 1831, 1832, 1833, 1834. N.B.—After 1832 the financial years ended in April instead of in January. But the annual reports issued by the Exchequer continued to state the expenditure from January to January.

[4] H. of C., February 14, 1834 (ibid., 3rd Series, vol. xxi, p. 361).

£1,581,000. We have already seen what were the most important of these reductions. Moreover, Poulett Thomson, by two statutes passed respectively in 1832[1] and in 1833[2], lowered a considerable number of duties levied upon articles of restricted consumption which therefore produced a very slight return but which nevertheless interfered to a marked degree with the national production. The duties on 217 articles were reduced in 1832, on 63 in 1833.[3] And in 1834 the duties on sixteen articles were reduced. Thus Poulett Thomson continued at the Board of Trade the work of tariff reform begun by Huskisson.

All this is true. Nevertheless, the policy of the Liberal Cabinet was by no means a matter for unmixed congratulation. No doubt the Whigs had economized the national resources. But their Tory predecessors had also practised economy and never more strictly than during Wellington's administration. The Whigs, it is true, had effected larger reductions of taxation. But was this policy prudent? They had taken advantage of a temporary boom in trade. If later trade experienced another depression and the budget produced a deficit would there not be reason to regret the loss of so much revenue that might have been employed in an annual reduction of the national debt? And even if the principle on which Liberal finance was based was sound, had it been successfully applied? Once, in 1831, Lord Althorp had attempted a comprehensive measure of financial reform. He had failed; and since the passage of the Reform Bill neither he nor Poulett Thomson had shown the least desire to repeat the experiment. The great monopolies—sugar, timber, and corn—had not been touched. The Government was satisfied to effect a number of minor reforms. Here and there particular burdens were removed as the immediate interest of the Ministry in Parliament or in the constituencies seemed to demand. It was a financial policy at once imprudent and unattractive.

---

[1] 2 and 3 Will. IV, cap. 84.   [2] 3 and 4 Will. IV, cap. 56.

[3] The revision effected in 1832 concerned a larger number of articles than the revision of 1833. But whereas the act of 1832 was a mere amendment of the existing statutes, the statute of 1833 was a substantial measure which revised and consolidated the entire code of legislation by which the customs were regulated. It thus resembled the statute of 1825 (3 and 4 Will. IV, cap. 51–60). See J. D. Hume, *The Laws of the Customs*, 1833, Introduction.

III THE BEGINNINGS OF ADMINISTRATIVE CENTRALIZATION

I

These were not the only charges to which the Government's financial policy was exposed. The Opposition detected and denounced an incipient tendency, which if allowed to develop would in time more than compensate for the systematic retrenchment for which the Government claimed so much credit, the tendency to set up new administrative machinery and impose a bureaucracy on the nation. The House of Commons had scarcely begun to discuss the Reform Bill before this tendency began to make itself felt and arouse protest. The Bill provided for the creation of a large number of new constituencies. Who would be entrusted with their demarcation? The Cabinet proposed at first to commit the task to a body of 'commissioners' nominated by the Government,[1] and it was only Conservative protests which induced the ministers to abandon their intention and agree that the boundaries of the new boroughs should be drawn by a statute passed by both Houses according to the traditional usage.[2] Further the Bill provided that public registers of those qualified to vote should be compiled and annually revised. Who was to compile them? The officials already in existence, the parochial overseers? That was in fact the procedure laid down in the first draught of the Reform Bill. But were these small farmers and shopkeepers capable of performing the task it was proposed to allot to them? In consequence of this objection new officials were set up by the bill, entrusted with the duty of settling on appeal all questions which concerned the compilation of the registers, a body of 300 barristers who would be paid a salary of five guineas a day, and would be nominated by the Judges of Assize, the nominations to be confirmed by the Lord Chancellor. Though the provision was carried it was sharply criticized in the course of debate.[3] Objections were raised to the enormous increase of influence, 'patronage' to use the accepted phrase, which would accrue to the Cabinet from its power to appoint the 300 officials.

[1] H. of C., September 1, 1831 (*Parliamentary Debates*, 3rd Series, vol. vi, pp. 981 sqq.).
[2] H. of C., December 12, 1831: Lord John Russell's speech (ibid., 3rd Series, vol. ix, p. 169). 2 and 3 Will. IV, cap. 64.
[3] H. of C., September 3, 5, 1831 (ibid., 3rd Series, vol. vi, pp. 1069 sqq., 1147 sqq.); February 8, 10, 1832 (ibid., 3rd Series, vol. x, pp. 82 sqq., 217 sqq.).

Henceforward complaints of this nature were a favourite theme with the Opposition. To prepare its various reforms the Government appointed a series of important commissions of inquiry, staffed by the ministers' personal friends, which though theoretically unpaid, in reality cost the nation very dear. Statistics compiled in 1834 estimated at above £53,000 the cost during the last three years of ten large commissions. And if the commissions were a temporary evil, the Government was also creating permanent offices, and in rapidly increasing numbers. Only two in 1831 and 1832 as against 1,100 places suppressed, but in 1833, 128 for 201 suppressed, and in 1834, 110 for 155.[1] The day might well be approaching when the number of places created would exceed the number suppressed.

It was very easy for the Conservatives to exploit this administrative policy against the Ministerialists. They were now the upholders of the genuine Liberal tradition, the old system of aristocratic self-government with its unpaid officials against a new system of bureaucratic despotism administered by salaried officials. The system had not been invented by the self-styled Liberals in the Cabinet. They had borrowed it from the continental nations. The *Quarterly Review*, the organ of the Conservative party, was delighted to be able to quote from a book written by a German traveller the passage in which, explaining English political life to his fellow countrymen, he described the Whig party as the German or Prussian party.[2] More frequent and even better adapted to prejudice public opinion against the Whigs were the charges of 'gallomania' brought against the Cabinet. Young Disraeli made a speciality of this sort of criticism. It was certainly true that the Liberals were disposed to put forward Prussian or French institutions as models for British imitation. Moreover, this new aspect which the policy of reform was assuming represented a genuine, perhaps even the most characteristic, aspect of the

[1] An account of every Increase and Diminution which has taken place within the year [1831, 1832, 1833, 1834] in the number of Persons employed or in the Salaries, Emoluments, Allowances and Expenses, in all Public Offices and Departments. The *Quarterly Review* estimates at 270 the number of new places created during the one year, 1833, but the estimate has apparently been exaggerated for polemical purposes (October 1837: 'Lord John Russell's Speech at Stroud', vol. lix, pp. 533–4).
[2] *Quarterly Review*, July 1836, Raumer's 'England in 1835' (vol. lvi, pp. 569–70). The passage quoted, which was translated by Mrs. Austin, runs as follows: 'The contest (between parties in England) *really is*, whether England shall *germanize* herself. *Germany stands exactly at the point towards which Whigs are steering*, and at which Tories can discern no land.'

doctrine of the orthodox Radicals, of Bentham and his followers.

The 'utilitarian' philosophy was not solely, nor even perhaps fundamentally, a liberal system; it was at the same time a doctrine of authority which looked to the deliberate and in a sense the scientific interference of Government to produce a harmony of interests. As his ideas developed, Bentham, who as a young man had been an advocate of 'enlightened despotism', was converted to democracy. But he had reached the latter position by what we may call a long jump, which carried him at a bound over a number of political doctrines at which he might have been expected to halt—aristocracy, a mixed constitution, the balance of powers, and the doctrine that the statesman's aim should be to free the individual by weakening the authority of the Government and as far as possible dividing its powers. In Bentham's view, when the authority of the state had been reconciled by a universal or at least a very wide suffrage with the interests of the majority there was no further reason to hold it suspect, it became an unmixed blessing.[1]

This was the spirit in which Bentham, already a septuagenarian, composed the 'constitutional code' which occupied the closing years of his life. New collaborators helped him in his task. One of these was a Unitarian, Thomas Southwood Smith, a doctor, philanthropist, and philosopher, who was dominated by the conviction that it was imperative to extend the functions of the state in the domain of public health.[2] Another was Edwin Chadwick, a young publicist and a contributor to the *Westminster Review*, who was a determined opponent of the aristocratic self-government which prevailed in England, and a zealot for uniformity and administrative centralization.[3] In his Code Bentham sketched a

---

[1] We have called attention to this double aspect of Bentham's philosophy in our *Formation du Radicalisme Philosophique*, 3 vols., 1901-4. Cf. A. V. Dicey, *Lectures on the Relation between Law and Public Opinion in England*, 1905, lecture IX: 'The Debt of Collectivism to Bentham' (pp. 302 sqq.). See also B. L. Hutchins, *The Public Health Agitation*, 1833-48, 1909. Edwin Chadwick, *The Health of Nations*. A review of the Works by Edwin Chadwick, with a biographical dissertation by B. W. Richardson, 2 vols., 1887. 'This book is practically a biography of Mr. Chadwick and was largely dictated by him' (T. Mackay, *History of the English Poor Law*, vol. iii, p. 138 n.). Cf. Sir William J. Collins, 'The Chadwick School of Thought', 1913 (*Journal of the Royal Sanitary Institute*, vol. xxxiv, n. 7, pp. 315 sqq.).

[2] He had been on the staff of the *Westminster Review* from its foundation. See his articles, *Westm. Rev.*, January 1824, 'Literary Education'; July 24, 'Use of the Dead to the Living' (vol. i, pp. 43 sqq.; vol. iii, pp. 59 sqq.).

[3] See his article, ibid., April 1828, 'Life Assurance' (vol. ix, pp. 384 sqq.). He had also, according to his biographer, contributed to a journal called the *London Review*, edited in 1829 by Whately, Blanco White, and Nassau Senior, two articles entitled 'Preventive Police' and 'Public Charities in France'.

complete plan of local government. Local assemblies were to be set up, to be elected by universal suffrage, which he termed sub-legislatures. They would pass local bye-laws and employ a body of salaried officials to carry them out.[1] These officials would be themselves subject to the Government departments and Bentham proposed to establish an entire series of new departments: a ministry of 'Preventive Service', of 'Interior Communication', of 'Indigence Relief', of 'Education and Health'.[2] 'Wherever,' to quote the words of an intelligent exponent of the Master's thought, 'you see a good and a salutary constitution *there* you see the great masses of the population wedded to and mingled with the State; there must be energy to insure prompt and efficient legislation: energy exists not where unity is wanting.'[3] Thus on the morrow of the Reform Bill the contradiction between the doctrine of complete free-trade and the system of organized democracy was revealed, the contradiction inherent in the development of western civilization in modern times, and permeating its entire course.

The victory of 1832 was therefore scarcely won when the Radicals made a systematic effort not only to make the state democratic but to make it strong. The attempt aroused among Conservatives and ordinary Liberals alike the opposition only to be expected where for a century and a half the national tradition had demanded a State so weak that its existence was barely felt.

2

Brougham was Lord Chancellor. Though he had already alarmed his colleagues by his extravagant ambitions and intemperate language he contrived notwithstanding to present for a year or two the semblance of a great man. Gifted with a marvellous capacity for work and an equally marvellous flow of eloquence he was prepared to speak in the House of Lords, where he presided, on any topic, and he contrived if not, as he boasted, to

[1] *Const. Code*, chaps. xxix, xxx (*Works*, ed. Bowring, vol. ix, pp. 640 sqq.).

[2] *Const. Code*, chap. xi (*Works*, ed. Bowring, vol. ix, pp. 428 sqq.).

[3] Edward Lytton Bulwer, *England and the English*, Book V, chap. viii (ed. 1, vol. ii, p. 308). The entire book should be read if we would understand the attitude of the philosophic Radicals in England after 1832. Though Bulwer Lytton was not in the strict sense a member of the group, he was nevertheless in a wide sense a disciple of Bentham and Mill. In his *Autobiography* (pp. 192-4), John Stuart Mill, after he has analysed their point of view, relates how it was only by reading the works of the French historian de Tocqueville that he realized the dangers attaching to centralization.

clear up entirely, at least very considerably to reduce the arrears of business which blocked the Court of Chancery. He believed himself destined to be a second Bacon, at once a great lawyer, a great statesman, and a great philosopher, and dreamed of devoting his scanty hours of leisure to the composition of a Novum Organum adapted to the needs of the nineteenth century. Moreover, as a former journalist he took care to nurse his fame by keeping on good terms with the Press, and at that date every Liberal organ, and in particular the *Times*, was celebrating his praises. More than any of his colleagues he was designated both by his past history and by the office he filled to undertake the practical application of Bentham's principles.

As far as the penal code was concerned Peel had left his successor very little to do. Brougham abolished the death penalty for a number of crimes Peel had overlooked.[1] By the appointment of a Commission on which the Benthamite Austin had a seat he took the first step towards the codification of English law. And the reader may remember that in an important speech he had himself sketched a plan on which to reform the entire judicial system and had secured the appointment of two important commissions to inquire respectively into the procedure of the common law courts and the law of real property. To carry out the suggestions these commissions had made, he established a uniform procedure in all the Courts of Westminster,[2] and deprived the landowners of certain privileges which had the effect of immobilizing their estates.[3] He reformed the Court of Chancery by abolishing a number of sinecures,[4] substituted fixed salaries for fees in the Westminster Courts and elsewhere,[5] reformed the Privy Council,[6] and established a Bankruptcy Court[7] and a Central Criminal Court in London to try offences committed in the metropolis.[8] He was only twice defeated: but his failures were significant. For the opposition by which he was vanquished was not simply that of individuals with a personal

---

[1] 2 and 3 Will. IV, cap. 34, 62, 123; 3 and 4 Will. IV, cap. 44. These enactments abolished the death penalty for housebreaking, horse stealing and sheep stealing, coining, and almost all cases of forgery.

[2] 2 and 3 Will. IV, cap 39; 3 and 4 Will. IV, cap. 67.

[3] 3 and 4 Will. IV, cap 27, 74, 104, 106, 108.

[4] 2 and 3 Will. IV, cap 110; 3 and 4 Will. IV, cap. 84.

[5] 1 and 2 Will. IV, cap. 35; 2 and 3 Will. IV, cap. 51, 116, 122.

[6] 3 and 4 Will. IV, cap. 41. Cf. *Greville Memoirs*, March 13, 1833.

[7] 1 and 2 Will. IV, cap. 56.

[8] 4 and 5 Will. IV, cap. 36.

interest in maintaining abuses but the deeply engrained prejudice which clung to the old decentralizing liberalism.

He wished to carry out a proposal made by Bentham and compile a survey of all the real estate in the country. He hoped in this way to clear up the inextricable confusion which in England attended every attempt to investigate the title to the ownership of land. At his desire his brother, William Brougham, introduced in the Commons a bill to this effect. Lord Althorp dared not adopt it and it was rejected by the House. Yet another department, was the cry, in which a host of officials furnished with inquisitorial prerogatives will keep under their perpetual scrutiny the management of every estate in the country ! 'What a fine instrument in the hands of the Government !'[1] Brougham also wished to ease the congestion of the Westminster Courts by setting up 'local courts' in which judges appointed and paid by the Government would try without a jury certain specified cases. A bill to this effect passed the House of Commons but got no further. For the revolutionaries it was a preparatory step towards the institution of that rural police the ministers had promised to establish at the first opportunity. For the country gentlemen it was a threat to the unpaid and aristocratic jurisdiction of the Justices of the Peace. The Opposition speakers maintained that Brougham's sole motive in putting forward the scheme was the desire to multiply the places at his disposal. And the hackneyed cries did duty once more. The project was copied from a French model, and thus came from a country whose judicial system was characterized by the immunity of the rich and powerful, gross partiality and a corruption practised or at least taken for granted.[2] One of the provisions of the bill had been borrowed from Denmark. 'I wish these fellows,' exclaimed Cobbett, 'would cease to refer us to the "Continent" for examples for us to imitate. There is something suspicious in the very circumstance, that the scheme seems to come from the hellish governments of Germany.'[3] The Lords knew that they could throw out the bill without risking the displeasure of the public.

[1] *Political Register*, June 22, 1833, vol. lxxx, p. 725. Cf. *The Times*, May 9, 1834: 'The *Times* while deploring the defeat of the bill, recognizes the reality and strength of the prejudices to which it was due.'

[2] H. of L., July 9, 1833: Speeches of Lord Lyndhurst and Lord Brougham (*Parl. Deb.*, 3rd Series, vol. xix, pp. 312 sqq., 343 sqq.). *Quarterly Review*, October 1833, 'The Reform Ministry and the Reformed Parliament' (vol. l, pp. 24–5). *Greville Memoirs*, July 12, 1833.

[3] *Pol. Reg.*, July 13, 1833 (vol. lxxxi, p. 101). It must be admitted that the *Standard* expressed dissatisfaction with the action of the House of Lords (June 13, July 4 and 10, 1833).

3

On the whole then the reform of the judicature had succeeded. In the rare instances where it had failed it had been defeated by the national prejudice against centralization. But there was a domain in which the situation was reversed, and the policy of administrative reform pursued by the Whig administration failed almost completely because immediately and all along the line it came into conflict with the same prejudice.

The leaders of English Radicalism wished to see the people 'enlightened', enlightened as to their true interests and the means to secure them. But their desire could be fulfilled only by State intervention, for the first condition of its accomplishment was a system of compulsory public education. The Government of 1830 effected very little towards this end.

In their disappointment the Radicals and advanced Liberals were loud in their complaints, whose bitterness indeed is almost disconcerting. For as we listen we can scarcely avoid the impression that the intellectual life of Great Britain was in a state of almost irresistible decline. Yet it was at this very time that Lyell published his *Principles of Geology*, and Faraday revolutionized our knowledge of electricity by a series of remarkable discoveries. But the complete indifference of the Government to literature and science scandalized Liberal and Radical thinkers. They saw contemporary France after 1830 governed by philosophers, fostering literature and art, and eagerly engaged in the task of organizing a system of national education. And more often still their thoughts turned towards Prussia, that puzzling state, aristocratic but seeking to promote the welfare of the poor, despotic but at the same time progressive. Though the great age of German poetry had passed, her historians and jurists placed Germany in the first rank of European nations. Boeckh, Niebuhr, Grimm, Ottfried Müller, Heeren, Savigny, and Gans found translators and readers in London and the two Universities. And it was on the model of a German institution that Sir David Brewster, weary of waiting in vain for assistance from the State, founded with the voluntary collaboration of all the men of learning in Britain the celebrated 'British Scientific Association'.[1] Austin, Bentham's young disciple, prepared a course of lectures on the

[1] *Edinburgh Review*, January 1835, 'The British Scientific Association' (vol. lx, pp. 363 sqq.).

philosophy of law which he was to deliver in London as professor of jurisprudence by a visit to the University of Bonn. It proved a revelation. 'The men,' he declared on his return, 'who could do these great things did not exist in the country.'[1] 'In Denmark and Prussia,' wrote Lytton Bulwer, 'is the form of absolute monarchy. But what of that? Nowhere are the people happier or more contented . . . the State protects, educates, and cherishes them all.'[2] The *Edinburgh Review* echoed these aspirations. Would England, it asked, ever experience so glorious a consummation, 'the blessed triumph of a paternal government'.[3] By this imprudent language the Liberals and Radicals deliberately incurred the charge of 'gallomania' and 'prussomania'.

Was then the Whig Cabinet prepared to attack the root of the evil by endowing England with the national education, the system of primary education, organized and financed by the State, which was at present non-existent? Brougham, banished to the House of Lords, and moreover absorbed in his reform of the penal code and legal organization, no longer as in the period before the Reform Bill took the initiative in this department.[4] But in 1833 a disciple of Bentham, a young Canadian, Roebuck, who hoped one day to become the leader of an organized Radical party, laid before the Reformed Parliament the educational programme of his group. His language which was brutally frank, was calculated to excite instead of calming Liberal prejudices. He denounced the idol of liberty. 'We every day coerce the people by laws and rob them of freedom. . . . Freedom in itself is not a good thing.'[5] He invited his fellow countrymen to copy the

[1] J. S. Mill, *Autobiography*, pp. 176-7. Cf. J. S. Mill to T. Carlyle, April 11 and 12, May 18, 1833 (*Letters*, vol. i, pp. 45, 51). Cf. *London and Westminster Review*, January 1836, 'Local Government of the Metropolis' (vol. xxv, pp. 101-3): 'Those who may one day see a Prussian revolution, will never witness the scenes of violence and bloodshed, in that country, which prevailed in France. The next generation in Prussia will, to a man, have had the benefits of an enlightened system of education. They will have been accustomed to govern themselves in their own local affairs, and when the people discover that the national affairs may as well be governed upon the same principles, the object will be noiselessly effected with a single effort.'

[2] E. Lytton Bulwer, *England and the English*, Book V, chap. viii (1st ed., vol. ii, p. 307).

[3] *Edinburgh Review*, January 1835, 'The British Scientific Association' (vol. lx, p. 364): 'Great as have been the improvements of our social institutions, Europe has not yet achieved in any of her states the blessed triumph of a paternal government. The events which now agitate England indicate her distance from so glorious a consummation.'

[4] See, however, his speech, H. of L., June 20, 1834 (*Parliamentary Debates*, 3rd Series, vol. xxiv, pp. 616 sqq.) and Greville's eulogy of his speech, June 24, 1834.

[5] H. of C., July 30, 1833 (ibid., 3rd Series, vol. xx, p. 154). Cf. *London and Westminster Review*, January 1837, 'Fallacies on Poor Laws' (vol. xxvi, p. 377): '. . . We advocate, both for England and Ireland, the necessity of a national provision for the moral and

Prussian model and thus imitate the example set by France sufficiently magnanimous to rise superior to national prejudice and send Victor Cousin to Berlin to study Prussian educational methods[1] and which had just carried out the suggestions contained in his report by enacting an important measure of primary education. Roebuck asked that education should be made compulsory between the ages of seven and fourteen, and that the Government should provide infant schools, schools of industry, evening schools, Sunday schools, holiday schools for adolescents, and '*écoles normales*' (he used the French term) for the training of masters and mistresses. The whole of England should be divided for educational purposes into districts, each provided with at least one school controlled by a local body elected on a democratic basis. At the apex of the entire system would be placed a minister, possessing a seat in the Cabinet, who would supervise all the schools in the Kingdom, authorize the construction of new schools, allocate the funds granted by the State, manage the normal schools, and draw up the syllabus to be followed in the National Schools.

Roebuck was faced by the opposition of the entire House. He was opposed not only by Peel but by Lord Althorp who expressed his fear that a system of State-controlled primary education by discouraging private initiative might do more harm than good. And if the proposal was attacked by Sir Robert Inglis, a Tory and an orthodox Protestant, O'Connell, who denounced Prussian drill and French impiety, was no whit more friendly.[2] At the instance of Lord Althorp, Roebuck withdrew his motion. The Government was satisfied with appointing a committee the following year which did not even issue a report but merely published the evidence given by the witnesses and asked for a further inquiry.[3] The great reform was postponed.

What in view of this failure was the Government's educational

industrial training of the young. In the old we cannot hope for much improvement. But the new generation springing up might be modelled to our will.'

[1] Victor Cousin's report marked an epoch not only in French, but in British education. Issued in 1833, it was translated in 1834 by Sarah Austin, the wife of the jurist. Cf. *Edinburgh Review*, July 1833, 'Cousin on German Schools' (vol. lvii, pp. 505 sqq.), and October 1833, 'National Education in England and France' (vol. lviii, pp. 1 sqq.).

[2] H. of C., July 30, 1833 (*Parl. Deb.*, 3rd Series, vol. xx, pp. 167, 169, 170, 172).

[3] Report from the select Committee of Inquiry into the Present State of the Education of the People in England and Wales, and into the Application and Effects of the Grant made by Parliament for the Erection of Schools, 1834. This so-called Report has no right to the name.

achievement? In 1832 a Board of National Education had been formed in Dublin. In schools which received a grant from the Board extracts from the Bible selected so as to give no offence to Catholics were read without comment twice a week in school hours. On the other days even the Bible might be read only outside school hours. It was a feeble attempt to effect a compromise between Catholic and Protestant intolerance.[1] In England the Government accomplished even less. The reformers could obtain nothing more than an annual grant of £20,000 from the budget, first made in 1834, to be divided between the voluntary societies engaged in the work of public education, the English National Society and the Nonconformist British and Foreign Society. Was this all? No, not quite all. For the Radicals made an attempt to achieve their object indirectly under cover of two important measures passed to improve and regulate the condition of the people. These were the Factory Act of 1833 and the Poor Law of 1834. Knowledge of the conditions under which these two statutes were passed and the economic principles they embodied is indispensable if we would understand the spirit which inspired the party to which the election of 1832 had committed the government of the nation.

4

Imagine yourself in Yorkshire on the morrow of the general election of 1830. For months, nay for years past, that large county had been the scene of a campaign against slavery conducted by the Evangelicals, both Anglican and Nonconformist. It occurred to two of these pietists, a Bradford manufacturer named John Wood and a land agent named Robert Oastler, that in England and even in Yorkshire there were human beings whose lot was as hard as that of the West Indian negro, the children compelled to work day and night for fourteen, fifteen, even sixteen hours at a stretch—the little white slaves of the factories. Oastler was a Tory. John Wood's political opinions are unknown. But there is no evidence that when they opened their campaign political considerations played any part. It was in the columns of the great Liberal organ of Leeds, the *Leeds Mercury*, that Oastler launched his agitation. A group of Bradford manufacturers took the movement under their aegis and signed a petition, which Lord Morpeth,

[1] For Protestant opposition to the compromise of 1831, see Rev. W. Hanna, *Memoirs of Thomas Chalmers*, vol. iii, pp. 249 sqq.

a Liberal member for Yorkshire, undertook to present to the House of Commons in their name. They asked that the statutes already in operation in the cotton industry should be extended to the Yorkshire woollen industry. Hobhouse, a Radical member for Westminster, who had already in 1825 and in 1829 procured two acts for the protection of children employed in the cotton mills[1] drew up the new bill.[2] It forbade the employment at night of persons under twenty-one, and no worker under eighteen might work more than twelve hours. These provisions were to extend to the entire textile industry, to the manufacture of wool, hemp, linen and silk as well as cotton.

This hopeful beginning was followed by speedy disappointment. The Scottish manufacturers rose as one man against the bill.[3] Their equipment was inferior to that of their Yorkshire rivals and they no doubt believed that only by ruthless exploitation of their hands could they hope to compete with them. And even in Yorkshire the progressive manufacturers who had initiated the movement were opposed by the majority of their fellows.[4] In the end after protracted debate[5] Hobhouse gave way. The bill[6] as finally passed by both Houses was no more than a statute consolidating previous measures and confined exclusively to the cotton industry. Moreover, the present statute in common with all its predecessors omitted to set up any machinery to secure obedience to its provisions; and therefore even in the case of the workers in the cotton mills could amount to nothing more than a barren declaration of principles.[7]

The effect of this defeat[8] was to stimulate the agitation in

---

[1] 6 Geo. IV, cap. 63; 10 Geo. IV, cap. 51. For the sake of accuracy we must add 10 Geo. IV, cap. 63, which, however, was a mere formality validating the preceding statute which had been passed without the observance of the requisite forms. See Diary of J. S. Hobhouse, June 19 and 23, 1829 (Lord Broughton's *Recollections of a Long Life*, vol. iii, p. 323).

[2] H. of C., July 10, 27, 1831 (*Parliamentary Debates*, 3rd Series, vol. iv, p. 1447; vol. v, p. 388).

[3] Alfred, *Hist. of the Factory Movement*, vol. i, pp. 95, 199. [4] Ibid., vol. i, p. 108.

[5] See the extremely imperfect reports, H. of C., June 30, July 18, July 30, 1831 (*Parl. Deb.*, 3rd Series, vol. iv, pp. 501, 1446; vol. v, p. 558). [6] 1 and 2 Will. IV, cap. 39.

[7] Kirkman Finlay, *Letter to Lord Ashley*, 1833, p. 16: 'So little were the laws on this subject ever regarded in these districts, that I assert without fear of contradiction, the provisions of the Acts of Sir Robert Peel and Sir John Hobhouse were till lately unknown to many and disregarded by a great proportion of the Spinners and Manufacturers in them.'

[8] Strickland's speech introducing a petition from the town of Leeds (H. of C., March 20, 1833, *Parl. Deb.*, 3rd Series, vol. xvi, p. 879): He regretted that the bill introduced some years back by Sir John Hobhouse had met with the opposition it experienced; for he was confident that it was the limitation of that bill to the cotton manufacturers which had excited a great part of the present discontent.

Yorkshire which as it became more powerful changed its form. The country was in the midst of a political crisis. The gentry who had long been at mortal enmity with the parvenus of the factory were alarmed to see them making use of the Reform Bill to raise their political and social status, and as though to take their revenge for the agitation which had carried reform threw themselves heart and soul into the agitation against the factory system. And at the same time the revolutionaries of the working class were refusing to collaborate any longer with the Liberals in the defence of a Reform Bill which benefited only the middle class and therefore failed to satisfy their wishes. For the past two years factory legislation had been the programme put forward by a powerful union of Lancashire cotton spinners.[1] It was therefore easy to unite Yorkshire and Lancashire in the pursuit of this common object. The operatives, it is true, were seeking a restriction of working hours for themselves, not for the children who were very often the victims of their brutality rather than of the employers' tyranny.[2] But the number of children employed in the factories was so great in proportion to the adults that it was out of the question to restrict the working hours of the latter without restricting at the same time the hours of the former.[3] It was for the children that Oastler sought to awaken the pity of the English middle class, but his aim was the legal protection of the adult worker.[4]

The movement quickly assumed the aspect of a Radical and Tory coalition. Oastler put himself into touch with the working class, organized among the operatives Short Time Committees to undertake the necessary propaganda, spoke at open-air meetings, and adopted the methods of a revolutionary agitator. But when he needed a member of Parliament to carry on the campaign in the House in place of the unworthy Hobhouse, his choice fell on Michael Thomas Sadler, a Leeds banker, and like himself a Tory, who had attracted wide attention by the celebrated works in which he criticized Malthusianism and the new

[1] S. and B. Webb, *Hist. of Trade Unionism*, 2nd ed., 1920, pp. 116 sqq.
[2] A. Ure, *Philosophy of Manufactures*, pp. 298 sqq.
[3] Fielden, *Curse of the Factory System*, 1836, p. 34: 'Any Factory Bill to be effective, must restrict the labour, not only of children, but of those older hands with whom they worked; for that the work of both was so connected, that it could not be carried on by the adult hands without the assistance of the younger. But this fact our adversaries always attempt to turn against us.'
[4] Factories Inquiry Commission. First Report of Central Board of Commissioners, p. 47.

political economy,[1] owed his seat in the Commons to the influence of the Duke of Newcastle and had resisted Catholic emancipation to the bitter end. Like Oastler, Sadler was an Evangelical. His first book which he had written as a young man had been an apologia for Wesley. He was a friend of Wilberforce and had acted as his political agent in Yorkshire. And he was the superintendent of a large Sunday School in Leeds.[2] A contemporary has painted his picture for us. It is the picture, almost the caricature, of an Evangelical preacher. 'In his countenance there was such a seriousness and solemnity that a stranger might have mistaken him for a clergyman. . . . His voice was full and distinct, but it had a species of twang about it very much resembling that which is so often heard in the pulpit.'[3] The historian of the movement which produced the factory acts must not forget the many tributaries which swelled the stream. But the source of the river was the piety and Christian sentiment of the Evangelicals.

Sadler lost no time in bringing the subject before the House of Commons,[4] obtained the appointment of a parliamentary committee of inquiry, presided over its labours, and finally draughted the bill which embodied its recommendations. The bill, which included in its scope every branch of manufacture in the Kingdom, prohibited the employment at night of persons under eighteen, and any employment of children under nine, made regulations to safeguard the health and safety of the operatives and provided penalties for breach of the statute which might extend in the case of a second conviction to two months' imprisonment, to be inflicted on the sentence of two Justices of the Peace.[5]

The December election supervened. Sadler came forward as candidate for Leeds and was defeated by the ministerial candidate, the youthful Macaulay. The supporters of the ten-hour day were therefore compelled to find another spokesman in the reformed Parliament. They might have chosen Fielden, the Radical manufacturer, a zealous advocate of legal protection for the workers,

[1] See especially his book entitled *Law of Population*: a Treatise in Six Books in Disproof of the Super-Fecundity of Human Beings and developing the Real Principle of their Increase, 1830, which was honoured by a refutation from the pen of Macaulay. *Edinburgh Review*, July 1830 (vol. li, pp. 297 sqq.). For his first statement of his social philosophy in Parliament, see H. of C., October 11, 1831 (*Parliamentary Debates*, 3rd Series, vol. viii pp. 498 sqq.).
[2] *Memoirs of the Life and Writings of M. T. Sadler*, pp. 11, 19.
[3] [J. Grant], *Random Recollections of the House of Commons*, p. 102.
[4] H. of C., March 16, 1832 (*Parl. Deb.*, 3rd Series, vol. xi, pp. 340 sqq.).
[5] A summary of the bill may be found in the *Poor Man's Guardian* for March 30, 1833.

who had practised what he preached by introducing the ten-hour day into his own factory. They preferred Lord Ashley, who like Sadler was a Conservative and an Evangelical. Two Evangelicals conducted the negotiations between Sadler and Lord Ashley. One of these, Sir Andrew Agnew, was a Whig and a member of the ministerial majority in the Commons. The other, the Rev. G. S. Bull, was an Anglican clergyman, who in Yorkshire had taken an active part in the campaign conducted by the Short Time Committees.[1]

The decisive moment had come. What attitude would the new Parliament, the first Parliament elected since the Reform Bill, adopt towards the claims of the working class? The opponents of the Ten Hours Bill attempted at first to get rid of Lord Ashley's bill which with a few trifling modifications was a copy of Sadler's by bringing forward in its place a bill introduced by Lord Morpeth which merely extended to the entire textile industry the provisions enacted for the cotton manufacture by Hobhouse's bill of 1831.[2] The manoeuvre failed and Lord Ashley's bill was given precedence over Lord Morpeth's. Then the manufacturers put forward a motion to submit the question to the examination of a Royal Commission and on April 3 in a House three-quarters empty it was carried by the insignificant majority of 74 to 73 votes.[3]

5

The check aroused violent protest. What need could there be of a new inquiry after that which Sadler had conducted in 1832? And if it were necessary why should it be entrusted not to a simple Parliamentary committee but to a Royal Commission, a mere delegation of the executive, whose procedure was represented as inquisitorial, since the witnesses were heard behind closed doors and the evidence was not taken down in shorthand? In brief the complaints were raised which were always heard when a Liberal government appointed a commission. But this time they came from the working class. When the commissioners divided

[1] E. Hodder, *Life and Work of the Earl of Shaftesbury*, pp. 80–1. In the House of Lords the leading advocate of factory legislation was Lord Kenyon, also an Evangelical.
[2] H. of C., February 8, 1833 (*Parliamentary Debates*, 3rd Series, vol. xv, p. 390). For Lord Morpeth's bill see *Leeds Mercury*, January 12, February 9, 1833; *Leeds Intelligencer*, February 14, February 23, 1833.
[3] H. of C., March 20, 1833 (*Parl. Deb.*, 3rd Series, vol. xvi, p. 1001); April 3, 1833, Wilson Patten's motion (ibid., 3rd Series, vol. xvii, p. 79).

between them the industrial districts of Great Britain and visited each in groups of three they were everywhere met with the organized obstruction of the workmen. Their arrival was greeted by hostile demonstrations, almost by riots. They were burned in effigy.[1] Everyone regarded the commission as a mere device to shelve the question, and thus postpone indefinitely a reform the workmen regarded as urgent. In fact the commission accomplished its task with extraordinary speed. When on June 17 Lord Ashley's bill came up for the second reading, Lord Althorp was able to announce that its report would be very shortly before the House, and to publish, even before it was completed, the substance of the conclusions reached by the commissioners. For the latter were not opportunists who were trying to reach a compromise between the workers' demands and the employers'. Of the three members who composed the central board of the commission—those who remained in London while their colleagues conducted their tour of inquiry in the provinces—two, Southwood Smith and Edwin Chadwick, were disciples of Bentham, committed to a definite political and economic creed. We have made their acquaintance already. The secretary of the central board, John Wilson, also belonged to the group of Bentham's friends, and, like Austin, had just returned from a visit to Germany.[2] They proposed to replace Lord Ashley's bill by another based on a different principle.

They objected to Lord Ashley's bill that it was a dishonest measure which, while professing to protect children, was in reality intended to secure the legal restriction of the adults' working day. The Benthamites, agreeing on this point with the Liberals, regarded every restriction of this kind as impracticable or mischievous. The commissioners therefore proposed that the law should regulate the labour of children up to the age of thirteen, but not of older boys and girls until the age of eighteen or twenty-one. When Lord Ashley's bill was again debated in the House of Commons on July 18, Lord Althorp carried by a very

[1] Alfred, *Hist. of the Factory Movement*, vol. ii, pp. 33 sqq. For the incidents which occurred at Huddersfield, see the account by an eyewitness in Hanna, *Memoirs of Thomas Chalmers* (vol. iii, p. 366), also the *Poor Man's Guardian*, June 29, 1833.

[2] J. S. Mill to Sterling, October 20–22, 1831 (*Letters of John Stuart Mill*, vol. i, p. 18). Cf. his letter to Carlyle of April 11–12, 1833: 'It is a real satisfaction for me to know, and in some cases to have even been somewhat to help on several men who are now gaining, by dint of real honesty and capacity, a considerable and increasing influence, though not an externally visible one, over the underworkings of our government' (ibid., vol. i, p. 45).

large majority, 238 to 93 votes, an amendment which embodied the commissioners' proposal. At this point Lord Ashley abandoned the contest and left Lord Althorp to carry on the debate.[1]

On the other hand for the very reason that the real object of the bill was to protect the adults, it failed to protect the children sufficiently. It laid down the principle of the ten hours' day for workers under eighteen years of age; but ten hours' work a day was too much for a child of ten or eleven. According to the teaching of Bentham the State possessed the right of interference to protect those who obviously could not be considered free agents capable of making a contract. The commissioners proposed —and on this point also with success—that the maximum working day for children under thirteen should be reduced to eight hours. Lord Ashley's bill suffered from another serious defect. It did not concern itself with the use the child worker should make of his hours of leisure when his day's work was over.[2] The commissioners proposed that every child employed in a factory should be compelled to attend a school, and the bill, as finally passed, provided that the children whose work was restricted to forty-eight hours a week must attend school for two hours every working day.

The measure was obviously defective. The State provided no funds for the children's education. The provision of the schools was left to the manufacturers, who were to recover the cost out of the wages paid to the children in their employment.[3] Nevertheless, the 'Prussian' principle of compulsory education had won its first victory.[4] At the very moment when one disciple of Bentham,

[1] H. of C., July 18, 1833 (*Parliamentary Debates*, 3rd Series, vol. xix, p. 913). Cf. Factories Inquiry Commission: *First Report of Central Board of Commissioners*, pp. 33–4. One concession was made to Lord Ashley, Fielden, and their friends. The principle of a maximum day of twelve hours up to the age of eighteen was introduced into the bill. That is to say, the provisions of the Act of 1831 were extended to the entire textile industry. (S.3.) Cf. Factories Inquiry Commission: *Supplementary Report*, pp. 14–15.
[2] See the evidence given by Rowland Detrosier, Factories Inquiry Commission. *First Report of the Central Board*, evidence taken by Central Board, p. 19: 'The evils of the factory system are twofold: they are physical and moral . . . I am not sure that the difference of two hours would produce all the sanative effects that are anticipated by the humane individuals who are endeavouring to obtain the passing of that bill. . . . To render that measure really efficient it must be accompanied by educational provisions, and those, too, of a compulsory nature, independent of sect or party.'
[3] The House of Commons had inserted a clause which authorized the necessary grant. It was deleted by the Lords on the motion of Lord Salisbury (*London and Westminster Review*, October 1836, 'The Factories'; vol. xx, pp. 205–6).
[4] H. of C., August 13, 1833 (*Parl. Deb.*, 3rd Series, vol. xx, pp. 585–6). MacCulloch to Lord Ashley, March 29, 1833 (E. Hodder, *Life and Work of the Earl of Shaftesbury*, pp. 85–6).

THE POLICY OF REFORM

Roebuck, had failed to secure its adoption by the House of Commons, two others, Southwood Smith and Edwin Chadwick, introduced it into the law of the land under cover of the Factory Bill. And these provisions of the new statute received the enthusiastic support of many Radicals or advanced Liberals in the House, men such as Hume and Poulett Thomson, who were opposed on principle to factory legislation in any shape or form.[1] Tufnell, a member of the commission, who shared their point of view explained that the reason why he could accept the bill and share the responsibility for it was that rightly considered it 'had no more claim to be called a factory bill than an education bill'.

On yet another point the influence of the Benthamites made itself felt. On several occasions since the century opened factory acts had been passed. But they had remained a dead letter. To secure the present measure from the same fate the commission proposed the institution of a body of officials to inspect factories and see that the law was obeyed. It was absurd to leave the task of punishing offenders to the magistrates who lacked the necessary qualifications and were often manufacturers before whom the injured parties would not dare to bring their complaints.[2] There could be no better opportunity than the present to carry out the favourite plan of Edwin Chadwick and replace the Magistrates by salaried officials appointed to perform this particular task. They need not be local officials permanently resident in the industrial districts. Parliament would have shrunk from the cost. But there should at least be a small body of officials resident in London and making periodical tours of inspection in the provinces. Four inspectors were appointed by the act, who divided the country into four circuits. It was the victory of one of the fundamental principles of Bentham's political philosophy, the principle of administrative centralization.

These facts show that the statute of 1833 had a double origin. As first draughted the Factory Bill was the work of the Evangelicals who were so strongly represented in every section of the

[1] Factories Inquiry Commission. Supplementary Report of Central Board: Report by Mr. Tufnell, p. 227: 'This measure has no more claim to be called a factory bill than an education bill.' This was the standpoint adopted by the *Eclectic Review* in an excellent article in praise of the new law (January 1839, 'National Education on Just and Comprehensive Principles, 3rd Series, vol. ix, pp. 1 sqq.). See also for the view of the bill taken by the group of orthodox Benthamites. *London and Westminster Review*, October 1836, 'The Factories' (vol xxvi, pp. 174 sqq.).

[2] Factories Inquiry Commission, *Report of Central Board of Commissioners*, p. 69.

middle class. It was in response to the demands of a humanitarian piety that the first Reformed Parliament passed in the space of a few weeks the statute abolishing slavery and the statute protecting the children employed in the factories.[1] Nevertheless, there was a difference between the two. The former was a measure of emancipation equally dear to the Liberals and the pietists. The second was a measure of State interference, and on that score might have been expected to offend the Liberal economists. But although in many respects the disciples of Bentham were also disciples of Adam Smith and Ricardo, they were very far, as we have already had occasion to discover, from professing that systematic dislike of any and every form of State interference which thirty years later would be characteristic of Richard Cobden and Herbert Spencer. And it was they who under the circumstances just related gave the bill its final shape. Nor was the Benthamite bill merely a mutilated version of the Evangelical. It was a completely different measure. In some respects it was an improvement on Lord Ashley's bill even from his own stand-point; for its provisions were more stringent. And they would have been even more stringent than they were if Parliament had given effect to all the suggestions made by Southwood Smith

[1] Edward Lytton Bulwer, *England and the English*, Book III, chap. iv (1st ed., pp. 335–6): 'Even where, in the case of the loyal and subordinate Wesleyan, the politics generally may incline to the powers that be, some individual point, some isolated but stirring question—to-day the Slavery question, to-morrow the Factory Bill—occurs on which the Wesleyan no less than the bold and generous "Independent" is united with the most popular opinions.' The Wesleyans, however, it need hardly be pointed out, did not fight as a body for the liberation of the little factory slaves as they had fought as a body for the liberation of the West Indian negroes. There were too many Wesleyan manufacturers. A Nonconformist organ, the *Patriot* (January 19, 1833), mentions a case at Bradford in which the Wesleyans had refused the use of their chapel to the organizers of a Ten Hours Bill meeting. The Primitive Methodists, however, came forward to offer what the Wesleyan Methodists had refused. The *British Magazine*, an organ of the High Church party, was definitely hostile to factory legislation (March 1, 1833, vol. iii, pp. 318 sqq.; November 1, 1833, vol. iv, pp. 365–6; January 1, 1834, vol. v, pp. 59–60). On the contrary, the *Eclectic Review*, the organ of the Liberal Dissenters, was favourable to the reform (October 1832, 3rd Series, vol. viii, pp. 328–49). Cf. *Patriot*, January 9, 1833. The part taken by the Wesleyans in the agitation which led to the passage of the Anti-Truck Bill of 1831 (1 and 2 Will. IV, cap. 37) is also worth study. The leading supporter of the bill was a Nonconformist, W. Smith, who brought it forward in the first place on behalf of the Wesleyan ministers of Dudley. See H. of C., March 16, 1830, W. Smith's speech: 'The petitioners . . . expressly state in their petitions that they are much disinclined to meddle in political matters, but being continually made sensible of the distress arising from the system, they thought themselves bound to lay their petition before the House' (*Parl. Deb.*, N.S., vol. xxiii, p. 387). To the Factory Act must be added the two statutes passed to regulate, and later to abolish altogether, the employment of children as chimney sweeps (4 and 5 Will. IV, cap. 1; 3 and 4 Vict., cap. 85). For the details of the second of these acts, see H. of C., April 14, 1840, Lord Ashley's contribution to the debate; also H. of L., July 6, 1840 (*Parl. Deb.*, 3rd Series, vol. liii, p. 1092; vol. lv, p. 433).

and Chadwick. The inspectors would have received more extensive powers to control the hygiene of the factories, and the employer's liability for accidents which befell his employees in the course of their work would as early as 1833 have been legally enacted.[1]

6

Such as it was the bill gave satisfaction. A handful of Radicals in the House criticized it as a measure too timid to be adequate.[2] But a few feeble protests were powerless against the considered purpose which animated the Benthamites. The great Tory organ the *Standard* continued to demand Lord Ashley's original bill, but the Conservatives in the House of Commons supported the ministerial measure. Nor would it appear that Lord Ashley himself found much difficulty in accepting the defeat of his bill. He was no doubt alarmed by the violent language of Sadler and Oastler. Strange to relate, the new act was well received by the London revolutionaries. They had little love for Sadler and Oastler, and when a Yorkshire journalist accused them of appropriating a portion of the funds they had collected for purposes of propaganda Hetherington, the editor of the *Poor Man's Guardian*, lost no opportunity of publishing these defamatory reports. He seemed delighted to do anything which might encourage the working classes to throw off the yoke of these two 'Methodists'.[3] Moreover, the act was drawn up in such terms that, skilfully exploited, it afforded the workers a most serviceable weapon with which to fight for claims which no one expected. It had scarcely become law when it gave birth to a new agitation.

Both commissioners and ministers had attempted to reassure

[1] Factories Inquiry Commission: *First Report of Central Board of Commissioners*, p. 73: 'We conceive that it may be stated as a principle of jurisprudence applicable to the cases of evil arising from causes which ordinary prudence cannot avert that responsibility should be concentrated, or as closely as possible apportioned on those who have the best means of prevention of the mischief. . . . It is only the proprietor of the machinery who has the most effectual means of guarding against the dangers attendant upon its use.'

[2] See, for instance, H. of C., August 12, 1833: Torrens' speech (*Parliamentary Debates*, 3rd Series, vol. xx, p. 53).

[3] *Poor Man's Guardian*, July 6, September 7, 28, November 2, 1833. See especially the article of November 2: 'We have long been accustomed to hear the changes rung on Oastler and Sadler and Sadler and Oastler, *ad nauseam*. They have had the patronage of the Factory Exchequer; and all the swaddlers—the humbugs—and the money-loving London Press, who, without any real feelings on the subject, but for the base purpose of courting popularity, have been loud in their applause of these *Wilberforces the second*. . . .' For the attacks made upon Sadler and Oastler in Yorkshire (the Foster affair), see the *Morning Chronicle*, December 17 and 25, 1833. The two agitators seem to have been innocent of anything worse than extreme carelessness in keeping their accounts.

the manufacturers by pointing out that the reduction of the working day for children did not involve a corresponding reduction of the working hours of the factory. They were at liberty, if they pleased, to employ on the same day two consecutive shifts of children, and the machines could thus continue in use for sixteen hours.[1] The machines no doubt; but what of the adult workers? Were they also to work sixteen hours?[2] Had the children's working day been reduced to eight hours only that the adults' might be increased to sixteen? The Factory Act enabled the workers to avoid that danger. For the first time it laid down the principle of the eight hours' day. To be sure the principle was applied only in the case of children under thirteen, but it could be made generally applicable, and extended to adolescents and even to adults. The act came into force on March 1, 1834. On that day let the workers of every age refuse to work more than eight hours and quit the factory at the same time as the children who were the subject of its provisions. Thus the agitation for an eight hours' day began. The suggestion was approved by Fielden, who promised to carry out the reform in his own factory on the appointed day. He put himself in touch with Cobbett, who had never shown any zeal for factory legislation—no doubt the movement contained too many Methodists for his taste—but who suddenly decided to support the new agitation. They were joined by Robert Owen.[3] Owen had been as it were submerged by the powerful wave of democracy which had swept over England between 1830 and 1832. Now the workers were returning to him, disabused of their belief in political action and once more attracted by the prospect of social or, as we should now call it, direct action. He incorporated the eight hours day in the programme of the 'Society for National Regeneration', which he had just founded. But the society pursued a far more ambitious aim, to unite the entire working class in a single trade union which on a given date, promised by Owen for the near future, would assert its power by declaring a general strike and transform itself into an enormous co-operative society which would take control of all the means

[1] Factories Inquiry Commission: *Report of Central Board of Commissioners*, pp. 53, 58–9, 64. See further the debate, H. of C., August 12, 1833 (*Parl. Deb.*, 3rd Series, vol. xx, p. 530).
[2] *Political Register*, December 14, 1833: Mr. Fielden's 'Letter to Mr. Cobbett' (vol. lxxxii, p. 652). Cf. *Leeds Intelligencer*, June 22, 1833.
[3] For a full account of the design, see *Poor Man's Guardian*, December 28, 1833; *Pol. Reg.*, December 7, 14, 21, 1833 (vol. lxxxii, pp. 624 sqq., 641 sqq., 752); *Morning Chronicle*, December 7, 8, 1833, January 23, 1834 (a protest by Ebenezer Elliot and a few others).

of production. During the early months of 1834 the workers flocked into Owen's Grand National Trades Union.[1] Nor was the movement confined to the workers in the factories. It embraced the agricultural labourers as well. Unions sprang up all over the southern counties where the landlords and farmers had attempted to withdraw some of the concessions they had made to their labourers in 1832. And the agrarian disorders of 1830 and 1831 broke out afresh.[2]

To combat a movement which was beginning to alarm the middle class, Lord Melbourne asked for no new legislation. Neither did he take any direct steps to suppress it. But he encouraged the local authorities to enforce the existing laws with the utmost rigour. In March, 1834, six Dorsetshire labourers, inoffensive Methodists (two of whom were local preachers), were sentenced on a charge of administering illegal oaths to seven years' transportation. On March 18, the sentence was passed and by April 15 they were on their way to Australia.[3] The sentence aroused the intense indignation of the Radicals.[4] But we cannot deny that Lord Melbourne's methods were successful. The workers were thrown back upon the defensive. Nothing more was heard of the eight-hours' day, and the only demonstration of the working class which took place in the spring of 1834 was an enormous procession of the guilds through the streets of London to protest against the condemnation of the six Dorchester Labourers. The huge numbers who took part in the procession, 100,000 according to the more irresponsible estimates, certainly not less than 30,000, alarmed the middle classes.[5] The classes who governed England could not forget the example set by the revolutions in Paris; Lyons had just revolted and it is quite possible that individual revolutionaries in London entertained the project of a violent insurrection.[6] But the peaceable nature of the demonstration allayed their fears.

[1] S. and B. Webb, *Hist. of Trade Unionism*, 2nd ed., 1920, pp. 133 sqq.
[2] *Morning Chronicle*, November 5, 26, 1833; *Political Register*, November 23, 30; December 14, 1833; February 1, 8, 1834 (vol. lxxxii, pp. 468 sqq., 524 sqq., 670 sqq.; vol. lxxxii, pp. 259 sqq., 332 sqq.).
[3] S. and B. Webb, *Hist. of Trade Unionism*, 2nd ed., 1920, pp. 143 sqq. For the legality of the condemnation of the Dorchester labourers, see the curious correspondence which passed between Lord John Russell and Lord Melbourne, October 2, 6, 9, 1835 (*Early Correspondence of Lord John Russell*, vol. ii, pp. 132, 138, 143)).
[4] See *Westminster Review*, July 1834, 'The Dorchester Labourers' (vol. xxi, pp. 52 sqq.).
[5] *Morning Chronicle*, April 22, 1834.
[6] See *The Autobiography of a Working Man* (by A. Somerville), pp. 389 sqq.

Was it, however, sufficient to put down disorders when they actually broke out, only to see them recur a year or two later? Was it impossible to discover and remedy their cause and thus bring the evil to a final end? The disorder which caused such anxiety at this period to the ruling classes was not the chronic unrest which kept the manufacturing districts of the north in a state of almost perpetual ferment. The great disaster which haunted the imagination of every statesman was the French Revolution, whose recurrence in the near future seemed to be foretold by the events of July, 1830. But the French Revolution had opened with an agrarian rising and a rising of the Parisian mob. The two perils, therefore, which at the present juncture wore so menacing an aspect were the revolutionary temper of the London Radicals and the lawlessness which prevailed in the country districts around the capital and appeared to invest it with a ring of anarchy. Nor was there any doubt as to the causes of the disorder. If the southern counties were infected, while the northern counties were free, it was because in the former the practice had been introduced, which did not exist in the latter, of distributing relief to the labourers whenever their wages fell below a particular amount which was accepted as the standard wage. The result had been the demoralization, the exorbitant demands and the revolutionary attitude of the agricultural labourer. The remedy was to reform the law under which public relief was granted, the notorious Poor Law.

7

As early as February, 1832, three months before the Reform Bill was finally passed, the Liberal government had appointed to investigate the question an important Royal Commission, which contained bishops, barristers, economists, politicians, and Sturges Bourne, the author of the Act of 1819. The inquiry was comprehensive and thoroughgoing. In February, 1834, the commission issued its report,[1] and the Cabinet decided to lose no time in giving effect to its recommendations. On April 17, Lord Althorp brought in a bill. On August 13, the Poor Law Amendment Bill passed its third reading in the House of Lords. Thus, in spite of a

[1] *Report from H.M.'s Commissioners for inquiring into the administration and practical operation of the Poor Laws*, 1834. See also the official publication: *Extracts from the information received by H.M.'s Commissioners as to the administration and operation of the Poor Laws*, 1833.

political crisis which suspended the debate for a fortnight at the beginning of July, it took less than four months for Parliament to enact what was termed the New Poor Law. 'The great achievement of the Whigs since their accession to the government,' wrote a contemporary, whose sympathies were not wont to be given to the Liberal party, 'is the passing of the English Poor Law. This is their true Reform Bill; and if the measure more distinctively so called possesses any real value, it is chiefly as having paved the way for the passing of the other.'[1]

The luminary of the commission was Nassau Senior, an Oxford professor, and at that time the accepted authority on economics. When the agrarian troubles broke out towards the close of 1830, he had published a portion of his lectures on political economy to advocate a theory which MacCulloch had originated and which was destined to become famous, the theory of the 'wages' fund'. Since the fund was fixed before the work began, the share which each labourer would receive was necessarily equal to the entire fund divided by the number of labourers, and it was absurd to hope that by any means whatsoever, whether the action of a trade union or assistance by the State, wages could be raised, so long as the number of labourers remained the same, and the wages fund also remained the same.[2] At the same time he had been officially consulted by the Government as to the best means of putting an end to the right to strike without restricting the liberty of combination so recently granted.[3] As regards the Poor Law he had publicly expressed the opinion that it should not be reformed but abolished altogether.[4] In advocating this Radical solution he followed the principles of Malthus. Nor did he stand alone; Harriet Martineau[5] and Brougham[6] were of the same opinion. But was it practical politics at one blow to sweep out of existence a vast fabric of legislation to which the country had been accustomed for more than two centuries? And if principles known *a priori* proved in advance that no right to relief ought to be conceded, of what use was this lengthy inquiry?

[1] *Annual Register*, 1837, p. 128.
[2] *Three Lectures on the Rate of Wages, delivered before the University of Oxford in Easter Term*, 1830. *With a preface on the causes and remedies of the present disturbances.*
[3] S. and B. Webb, *Hist. of Trade Unionism*, 2nd ed., 1920, pp. 139–40.
[4] *Three Lectures* . . ., p. xi.
[5] *Poor Laws and Paupers illustrated*, 1833–4: four 'tales' told to 'illustrate' the true economic doctrine on the subject of Poor Relief.
[6] H. of L., July 21, 1834 (*Parliamentary Debates*, 3rd Series, vol. xxv, pp. 219 sqq.).

The conclusions therefore reached by the commission were necessarily more moderate. The commissioners insisted that the lax application of the law which since the days of Pitt had wrought such mischief in the country districts must be abandoned. The local authorities must no longer be permitted to recognize the right to a standard wage, and it must be clearly understood that the Poor Law was not and was not intended to be a cure for poverty but merely a means of relieving temporary distress. In conformity with this principle the commission asked that the spirit of Elizabeth's original statute should be strictly observed and the able-bodied pauper compelled to earn his relief in a work-house. The recommendation was enforced by the new Poor Law.[1] Moreover, the report insisted that the pauper in receipt of poor relief should be subject in the workhouse to such treatment that his condition would be evidently less desirable than that of the poorest labourer not in receipt of relief.[2] Indeed, the commissioners even went so far as to suggest that relief should be given only as a loan and the pauper who obtained work should be obliged to repay the amount it had cost the ratepayers to relieve him.[3] But Lord Althorp did not dare to incorporate this suggestion in the bill.

On a second point, less fundamental but important nevertheless, the commissioners admitted that as a result of the inquiry the Malthusians had been obliged to modify their doctrine in certain respects. According to Malthus the worst fault of the Poor Law was that it stimulated artificially an excessive growth of population. But it was obvious that the population of England in 1832 was not excessive, as was proved by the constant demand for Irish labour. According to the commission the worst fault of the Poor Law was that it produced an uneconomic distribution of the population. As the disorders proved, there were too many workers in the rural counties of the south, too few in the manufacturing districts of the north. The cause of this undesirable distribution must be sought in the state of the law regarding 'settlement'. Labourers acquired the 'settlement' in a parish which carried with it the right to receive relief, if they, born in that parish or apprenticed there, had rented a domicile for at least a year or owned the most infinitesimal strip of ground. These provisions

[1] 4 and 5 Will. IV, cap. 76.
[2] Poor Law: Report from H.M.'s Commissioners, pp. 128 sqq.
[3] Poor Laws: Report from H.M.'s Commissioners, Ninth Recommendation, pp. 190–1.

though apparently liberal restricted the circulation of labour; for
the parish authorities refused to admit new workers for fear that
as soon as they were thrown out of employment the rates would
be burdened with their support. The effect of this attitude was to
confine the poor to their own parishes, and check the free movement of labour. To render the law more liberal it must be made
apparently more stringent. The commission proposed that the
law of settlement should be radically simplified, and that in
future a settlement should be acquired only by birth. The Cabinet
and Parliament adopted the suggestion but with certain modifications; apprenticeship for instance continued to confer the right
to relief.

On a third point the commissioners, faithful in this to the
teaching of Malthus, proposed an alteration of the existing law.
For the operation of the measure the reform did not possess the
same importance as the law we have just enumerated; but it was
the most warmly debated. The bastardy laws sanctioned the
search for the father of an illegitimate child under conditions
glaringly unjust to any unfortunate man whom the mother might
accuse. According to the commission the existing legislation had
the effect of putting a premium upon illegitimate births and thus
indirectly encouraging an excessive increase of population. For
the inquiry had revealed the extent to which sexual immorality
was rife among the lower classes of Great Britain. The commissioners proposed that illegitimate children should be chargeable to the mother and that she could obtain relief for her child
only by entering the workhouse herself. The numerous amendments introduced both by the Commons and the Lords did not
alter the fact that the proposal was in principle adopted. On this
minor point the reform of 1832 followed the example set by the
French Revolution forty years earlier and abolished search for
the father.

8

It was all very well to lay down these rules. It was another
matter to ensure that the local authorities obeyed them. It was
not to be expected that the plain country gentlemen from whom
the magistrates were taken should possess the necessary competence, or that the petty traders who sat on the parochial vestries
should be sufficiently disinterested, to distribute relief with un-

swerving adherence to a strict rule. And since their functions were unpaid they could hardly be asked to give the necessary time. All previous reforms of the Poor Law had shattered on this rock. There was only one way by which the difficulty could be overcome; the system of self-government must be replaced by a system of salaried officials. Moreover, since the entire system was to be reformed, it was impossible to tinker with details or employ optional methods as Sturges Bourne had done. A vast work of administrative specialization and centralization must be accomplished *en bloc* and must embrace the entire country in its scope. Bentham's disciples were obviously the men for the task.

On the Commission of Inquiry appointed in February, 1832, there was only one member of the group, W. Coulson, a barrister and a journalist who had been Bentham's secretary. But when assistant commissioners were appointed to conduct local inquiries in the provinces and report the results to the Central Board an invitation was addressed—perhaps on Coulson's recommendation—to several of Bentham's disciples: John Wilson, Charles Hay Cameron, and Edwin Chadwick. Wilson's report is devoid of interest[1]. Cameron's report on the other hand is most illuminating.[2] He proposed that the 'unsystematical' methods traditional in England should be given up, also the system of optional laws which the local authorities were free to apply or not to apply at their pleasure. He suggested the establishment in London of a central board to administer a national fund for poor relief, and the appointment of a sufficient number of local salaried officials. These must be bound to the rigid observance of certain rules. His suggestions were too dogmatic, too remote from reality to be convincing. The report presented by Chadwick, who accepted the same principles but sought to adapt them to the facts of the situation and therefore reached more moderate conclusions,

[1] Poor Law Appendix (A), pp. 119A sqq. Perhaps this is to say too little. It is difficult to resist the impression that in drawing up this strange report, extremely meagre in its information and entirely negative in its conclusions, John Wilson was deliberately doing his best to betray the confidence of the group to whom he owed his place on the commission.

[2] Poor Law Appendix (A), pp. 151A sqq. Report by C. H. Cameron and John Wrottesley, Esq. Cameron had been James Mill's candidate for the chair of philosophy at University College (A. Bain, *James Mill: a biography*, p. 263). He accompanied Macaulay to India and helped him to draw up a penal code in conformity with Bentham's principles (Leslie Stephen, *English Utilitarians*, vol. ii, p. 36). N.B.—The new Poor Law was passed after the Factory Act, but Edwin Chadwick took part in the Commission of Inquiry into the Poor Laws before he joined the commission which investigated child labour.

carried more weight.[1] He was given a seat on the central commission, and is generally believed to have drawn up the final report. Nassau Senior was the official mouthpiece of the commission in its relations with the Government. But Chadwick did the work.[2]

The system of poor relief established by the new law in conformity with the suggestions of the Benthamites was as follows. 'The Administration of Relief to the Poor throughout England and Wales' was entrusted to 'the Direction and Control' of a body of three commissioners. They were 'authorized to make and issue all rules, orders and regulations for the management of the Poor, and for the government of workhouses' and 'were empowered to order workhouses to be built, hired, altered, or enlarged where the present accommodation was insufficient'.[3] Such extensive powers had been unknown hitherto to English law and were regarded as unconstitutional by many members of Parliament, even by certain of the Ministers. Nevertheless, Nassau Senior and Chadwick carried the day. Minor concessions were made to the opponents of these bureaucratic innovations. Any administrative regulations of a general character the commissioners might make were to be submitted to the Cabinet for approval and that the Government might have sufficient time to consider them, would not come into force until forty days had expired. A limit was fixed to the expenditure the commissioners might sanction to provide workhouse accommodation in any one locality. Moreover, the powers conferred upon the commissioners were granted only for a period of five years. In 1839 Parliament would have an opportunity to decide whether they should be abolished, modified or maintained in their present form. But this was the utmost the opposition could obtain.[4]

In Chadwick's intention the purpose of the regulations to be made by the commissioners was to restrict the grant of relief. For they must make the conditions of life in the workhouse such as would repel instead of attracting the able-bodied pauper. But the commissioners were not content with this merely negative procedure. In collaboration with the local authorities they under-

[1] Poor Law. Appendix (A), pp. 11 and 111 sqq. Evidence collected by E. Chadwick Rural Questions.
[2] Thomas Mackay, *A History of the English Poor Law*, vol. iii. From 1834 to the present time. Being a supplementary volume to *A History of the Poor Laws* by Sir George Nicholls 1899. The author has made use of Nassau Senior's papers. (See especially pp. 117 sqq.
[3] 4 and 5 Will. IV, cap. 76, ss. 1 to 15, 26, 28 to 37, 42 to 51.
[4] T. Mackay, *Hist. of the English Poor Law*, vol. iii, pp. 118-19, 122-3.

took to organize the emigration of labourers from districts where the labour market was glutted, and thus reduce the surplus population of the southern counties to the advantage of public order and increase the population of the manufacturing districts of the north in the interest of production.[1] They even attempted on a small scale to carry out a scheme cherished by the followers of Bentham and organize emigration to the colonies.[2] Moreover, the statute entrusted them with the duty of making provision for the education and apprenticeship of pauper children.[3] The Poor Law Amendment Act of 1834 therefore as well as the Factory Act of 1833 could be employed to do something—this time at the cost of the State—for the education of the poor.

Another important task fell to the commissioners in virtue of the new statute, to divide the country into new administrative areas for the purposes of the poor law. Under the existing system the administrative unit was everywhere the parish. But the parishes were of very unequal size and usually very small. Of the 15,535 parishes, 737 contained less than 50 inhabitants; 1,907 less than 100; 6,681 less than 300; and 12,034 less than 800. If the overseers were to be freed from the direct pressure of paupers living at their doors and shielded in administering relief from the influence of pity or fear, the administrative areas must be enlarged. The reform was also necessary if the workhouses were to be organized scientifically, and provided with special wards for the different classes of paupers. In the workhouse of a tiny parish the aged and the sick, men and women, children old enough to receive education, and infants in arms were mingled indiscriminately. Nor could it possibly be otherwise. A clause, suggested by an old statute which bore the name of Gilbert, invested the three commissioners with full powers to group the parishes for the administration of poor relief in unions covering a wider area.[4]

The next step was to appoint the local authorities by whom these unions would be administered. Here the legislators of 1834 followed a precedent of recent date. In October, 1831, after long years of effort[5] Hobhouse had carried a measure which rendered

---

[1] T. Mackay, *Hist. of the English Poor Law*, vol. iii, pp. 213 sqq.
[2] Ibid., vol. iii, pp. 227–8.
[3] 4 and 5 Will. IV, cap. 15. The clause extended to the entire kingdom a provision of 7 Geo. III, cap. 39, applicable only to London and no doubt very badly observed.
[4] 4 and 5 Will. IV, cap. 76, ss. 26 sqq.
[5] H. of C., Dec. 16, 1830: Hobhouse's speech (*Parliamentary Debates*, 3rd Series, vol. i, pp. 1206 sqq.).

the constitution of the vestries democratic.[1] Thus on the threshold of the Poor Law of 1834, as on the threshold of the Factory Act of 1833, we meet Hobhouse. The Act to which his name was attached gave the inhabitants of a parish the right, if they expressed the desire to make use of it, to elect the members of their vestry in accordance with a definite procedure. What qualifications were attached to the right conferred by the new statute? When it was passed the political crisis which had begun in 1830 had reached its most acute stage.[2] To satisfy the London Radicals Hobhouse's Act introduced into the constitution of the new vestries, universal, or at least household suffrage, every rate-payer possessing a vote, the ballot, though its employment was made optional, and annual election, though the ratepayers were to elect only one-third of the vestry each year.[3] In 1834 the legis-lature extended the machinery of the act to the entire country.[4] Every 'union' of parishes was to be administered by 'a board of guardians of the poor', to be elected by all the ratepayers, though according to a method far less democratic than that prescribed by Hobhouse's Act. A return was made to the method of Sturges Bourne, the plural vote. Resident ratepayers and absentee land-lords received a number of votes determined by the amount of their contribution to the rates. It was the duty of the boards of guardians to apply to individual cases the regulations laid down by the commissioners. They also enjoyed the right to appoint the local Poor Law officials, subject to the commissioners' right to revoke the appointment. The origin of this vast system half elective, half bureaucratic, is easy to recognize: it is the system which Bentham had sketched in his 'Constitutional Code'. In 1833, his disciple Roebuck had failed in his attempt to set up a system of

[1] 1 and 2 Will. IV, cap. 60.

[2] H. of C., Sept. 30: Hume's speech (*Parliamentary Debates*, 3rd Series, vol. vii, p. 883): . . . the people were anxiously watching the Vestry Bill. He could assure the House that it caused a great sensation among the people, more than any other subject except the Reform Bill itself. See, on the other hand, the letter in which Wellington expresses his alarm to Lord Kenyon, November 19, 1831: '. . . it appears to me that we are upon some points gone one stage beyond the Reform Bill. I cannot give a stronger proof of this fact than our recent vote upon the Parish Vestries Bill, by which we have laid the foundation for leaving the property of every man at the disposition of the rabble of his parish, par-ticularly in the towns' (*Wellington, Despatches, Cont.*, vol. viii, p. 215).

[3] H. of C., June 30, 1831 (*Parl. Deb.*, 3rd Series, vol. iv, pp. 501-2); July 25, 1831 (ibid., vol. v, pp. 300-1); September 15, 1831 (ibid., vol. vii, pp. 51-2); above all, Sep-tember 30, 1831 (ibid., pp. 879 sqq.).

[4] Such had been Hobhouse's original wish (H. of C., September 30, 1831: ibid., 3rd Series, vol. vii, p. 882).

national education embodying his master's principles. Now another disciple, Chadwick, had applied the same principles to the reform of the Poor Law. Might it not be expected, if the reform proved a success, that Bentham's system would very soon be applied universally? The task once accomplished which the Poor Law commissioners were preparing to undertake and England divided into a number of 'unions' sufficiently large and sufficiently equal, could not the boards set up in each union be used for other purposes, national education, the upkeep of the roads and public health. At no distant date the entire local government of the country would be transformed,[1] and a democratic England emerge from the traditional welter of aristocratic self-government.

Here the astonished reader may well ask: If the new statute was in fact pregnant with these revolutionary consequences, why had it been passed so rapidly, almost in a hurry, by a Parliament in which the country gentlemen were supreme? And how had the Benthamite programme of administrative centralization, opposed as it evidently was to the most tenacious and deep seated prejudices of the public, secured on this particular point the well-nigh unanimous assent of both Houses? The answer is simple. The country gentlemen had a direct interest in the reform.

They saw the poor rate growing heavier every year, and pessimists predicted that it would finally absorb the entire rent of the Kingdom. Very cleverly, though in perfect sincerity, the ministers presented the bill as a measure of 'agricultural relief'.[2] It had been

[1] See *London and Westminster Review*, January–April 1836, 'State of Politics in General' (vol. xxv, p. 273). Cf. 'Municipal Reform as required for the Metropolis' (vol. xxv, pp. 98 sqq.). Cf. a curious pamphlet, a manifesto of the Benthamite group, *Hints on the expediency of an improved divisional arrangement of England for administrative purposes*, 1834. It develops an entire scheme of administrative reorganization. See p. 14: 'In a well-arranged *representative* Government where the central power is in fact, but the general expression of the will of the several parts, the influence exercised by the machinery of centralization is merely the reflection of the wishes of the different members of the society, after having been combined and brought into unison and regularity, by their transmission through and digestion by the central organ.' Also p. 15: 'The two systems, the Municipal and the Central are therefore essentially connected. . . . Experience alone can point out where lies the happy mean between, for example, the inconvenient restraint of the French system of Centralization, under which a stone cannot be laid upon a road at the extremity of the Kingdom, without an order from Paris, and the equally inconvenient want of control of the existing English system, under which a road may remain unrepaired for years, unless some private individual will take on himself the odium and expense of an indictment at Quarter Sessions.' See also in *The Times*, May 20, 1835, extracts from another pamphlet issued by the same group and inspired by the same spirit: *The Principles of Delegated, Central, and Special Authority applied to the Poor Laws Amendment Bill*, 1834.

[2] H. of C., February 21, 1834: Lord Althorp's speech (*Parliamentary Debates*, 3rd Series, vol. xxi, p. 661). H. of C., February 8, 18, April 27, 1836: Lord John Russell's speech (ibid., 3rd Series, vol. xxxi, p. 1491).

impossible to concede the remission or even the reduction of the malt tax for which the landowners had asked; but they were now promised, if not the abolition of the poor rate, at least the end of that extravagant system of Poor Law administration which had prevailed hitherto. So long as the squire harassed by the importunate solicitation of his poor neighbours was at liberty to grant them all the relief they asked, it was foolish to hope that the burden could be lightened. He must be protected against himself by rigid regulations and the decisions of anonymous officials. To escape ruin the Justices of the Peace consented, nay asked, to be deprived of their authority to dispense poor relief.

In the House of Lords Wellington took the bold step of supporting with due qualifications the principle of the new legislation.[1] And though Peel did not speak in favour of the Government's bill,[2] he gave it the silent support of his vote. The Opposition never mustered more than fifty votes, and was usually reduced to twenty, a handful of extremists of either camp, ultra-Tories and extreme Radicals. The little group was led by its Radical members. But even they were divided. Nor were the Benthamites merely supporters of the bill; it was actually their work.

A further cause contributed to hasten the passage of the measure, its unpopularity. The debates leave the reader with the impression that Parliament hurried it through in order to present the country as soon as possible with a *fait accompli* and not allow time for an organized agitation against the bill. For meetings were already being held in London and in increasing numbers to protest against this enactment of a heartless middle class which sought to deprive paupers of their freedom. And the Press was very far from sharing the affection Parliament displayed for the bill. It was on this question that *The Times* broke with Brougham, if not as yet with the entire Cabinet. And the conservative *Standard* which had begun by expressing its hearty approval of

[1] H. of L., July 21, 1834 (*Parliamentary Debates*, 3rd Series, vol. xxv, pp. 268 sqq.). The bill in the form in which it reached the House of Lords provided that after June 1835 no relief should be given outside the workhouse. Wellington carried an amendment by which the commissioners were empowered to prolong on the advice of the boards of guardians for a period varying according to local conditions the system of indoor relief. Thus Wellington, to render the application of the law milder and more gradual, increased the discretionary powers of the commissioners.
[2] To judge from the Parliamentary Debates. See, however (H. of C., February 21, 1834), a speech in which he expressly invited the ministers to undertake the reform of the Poor Law (ibid., 3rd Series, vol. xxi, pp. 691-2).

the measure gradually changed its tone and finally adopted an attitude of virulent hostility. Why, it asked, did the Opposition let slip this opportunity to recover the support of public opinion by resisting the new Poor Law by every means at its disposal? Why, asked *The Times*, did the Cabinet make the mistake of alienating the sympathy of the poorer classes by raising this thorny question at a time when on other questions it was engaged in a hard struggle with its Conservative opponents. The victory which the ministers won when they carried the new Poor Law was a Parliamentary, not a popular success. And it may well have contributed to weaken still further the position of the Government, already seriously shaken by a controversy which engrossed men's thoughts and kindled their passions, the discussion of those other questions to which *The Times* alluded, and which we have now to study. They were religious questions, intimately bound up with the problem of Ireland.

CHAPTER III

The Religious Question and the Irish Question

I THE REFORM OF THE IRISH CHURCH

I

A CONDITION of sheer lawlessness prevailed in Ireland, and during the long political crisis through which England had just passed the state of the country had gone from bad to worse. According to the official figures 9,000 crimes had been committed during the year 1832, including 568 acts of incendiarism, 290 cases of cattle maiming, and 242 murders.[1] Not a week passed without the news of some outrage perpetrated by an armed band practically certain of impunity. For an Irishman to give information against the culprits was to sign his death warrant. And even if the law succeeded for once in laying hands on a criminal a further difficulty arose. The juries refused to convict.

Stanley, the Irish secretary, had declared open war upon O'Connell and his followers, and all his words and deeds manifested his determination to fight to the finish. He could not, he informed the Cabinet, undertake the responsibility of restoring order in Ireland, unless he were armed with extraordinary powers which would necessitate special legislation. His arguments convinced Lord Grey, who succeeded, not without considerable difficulty, in securing the consent of his more Liberal colleagues. A Peace Preservation and Coercion bill was introduced in the House of Lords on February 15, 1833, and finally passed on April 1, after debates in both Houses.[2] The new statute made it illegal to hold a meeting for the purpose of petitioning Parliament unless ten days' notice had been given and the sanction of the Lord Lieutenant obtained. Moreover, the Lord Lieutenant was empowered to proclaim any districts in which in his opinion the disorder was such as to require special measures of repression. In every district thus 'proclaimed' the inhabitants must abstain from meetings he had pronounced seditious and illegal, no one might

[1] H. of L., February 15, 1833: Lord Grey's speech (*Parliamentary Debates*, 3rd Series, vol. xv, p. 733). [2] 3 and 4 Will. IV, cap. 4.

leave his house at night unless he could show a satisfactory reason for his absence, the police were authorized to search private houses for concealed arms and he could substitute for the ordinary courts, courts martial whose composition, procedure, and powers were defined by the statute. Finally, the Habeas Corpus Act was suspended, and no person charged with a crime could demand his trial until three months had elapsed. The clauses which provided for the establishment of courts martial were the most bitterly attacked in the Commons and were passed only with very considerable modifications.[1] But even in its final form the measure was extremely stringent. An odd beginning for the first Reformed Parliament! Palmerston was not blind to the humour of the situation. 'You see,' he wrote to his brother, 'by what spanking majorities this reformed House of Commons is passing the most violent bill ever carried into a law . . . It is a real *tour de force* . . . Few absolute governments could by their own authority establish such a system of coercion as that which the freely chosen representatives of the people are placing at the command of the Government of this country. To be sure,' he added, 'it is to be followed by remedial measures and there is the difference between us and Metternich or the Pope.'[2] What were the reforms for which the Irish were just then clamouring?

In the first place the Irish, or rather O'Connell in their name, demanded the repeal of the Act of Union and the restoration of the Dublin Parliament and the Cabinet considered the question sufficiently urgent to require the insertion in the King's Speech of a protest against any attempt to undo the legislative union of the two countries. Indeed, the Repeal of the Union was the programme of O'Connell's latest organization, the association of 'Irish Volunteers'. But this association had nothing to do with the armed bands who were terrorizing the countryside. For the moment at any rate the Irish Volunteers made a point of obeying O'Connell's instructions by a scrupulous respect for the law and were even prepared, if necessary, to assist in maintaining order. The campaign waged by the peasantry pursued an entirely different object.

[1] These amendments were introduced by the Government when the bill had already passed the Lords and its clauses were to be debated in the Commons (H. of C., March 13, 1833: Lord Althorp's speech, *Parliamentary Debates*, 3rd Series, vol xvi, pp. 589–90).
[2] To William Temple, March 21, 1833 (Sir H. L. Bulwer, *Life of Lord Palmerston*, Book X, ed. 1870, vol. ii, p. 147).

O'Connell's chief complaint against Stanley's bill was that the sole object of that Draconian measure was to make the collection of the tithe possible in Ireland. Lord Althorp, who had little love for the bill, though obliged as leader in the Commons to assume the responsibility for it, denied that the sole fact of refusing the tithe was sufficient to constitute an offence against the new law,[1] and was even prepared to accept an amendment put forward during the debate, which explicitly sanctioned this interpretation.[2] Stanley was furious;[3] for it was precisely against the payment of tithe that the Irish peasants were in revolt. In 1833 as in 1829 the Irish question was a religious question. In the important speech which he delivered during the debate on the Royal Address and by which he opened the long series of his attacks upon the 'bloody, brutal, and unconstitutional' policy of the Government, O'Connell passed lightly over the question of repeal, and dwelt at length on the standing grievances the Irish Catholics entertained against the established Church. Liberal statesmen must therefore deal with the abuses of the Establishment, if they wished to give even a partial satisfaction to the demands of the Irish public. And not only of the Irish but of the English public also. We have already noticed the outbreak of anti-clerical agitation which preceded the passing of the Reform Bill.

2

Before we follow the course of events any further, we must define the programme, or rather the conflicting programmes of those who in England, Scotland or Ireland were demanding, when the first reformed Parliament met, the reform of ecclesiastical abuses.

There was first the noisy section with whom unqualified disestablishment of the Church was a dogma and who called for the complete separation of Church and State. On this point, as on so many others,[4] the English Radicals were ready with an answer to the charge of pursuing a Utopian dream. They were merely asking English democracy to copy the example set by the demo-

[1] H. of C., February 27, 1833 (*Parliamentary Debates*, 3rd Series, vol. xv, pp. 1, 226–7).
[2] H. of C., March 18, 1833 (ibid., 3rd Series, vol. xvi, pp. 758, 766).
[3] H. of C., March 18, 1833: '. . . certainly his opinion was that the clause would be better without the Amendment, and the Government agreed to it merely in deference to the opinion of one hon. gentleman' (ibid., 3rd Series, vol. xvi, pp. 767–8).
[4] H. of C., February 5, 1833 (ibid., 3rd Series, vol. xv, p. 148).

cracy of the United States. They maintained that from the moment when the Catholics had been admitted to full civil rights and the Dissenters released from the obligations prescribed by the Test Act the separation of Church and State had been practically accomplished. What further was required to make it complete? The Dissenters must be freed from the obligation to be baptized, married, and buried according to the Anglican service. The Church must be deprived of her monopoly of higher education and the Dissenters either allowed to found a University of their own or admitted to the colleges of Oxford and Cambridge. The clergy must cease to exercise the administrative functions which were still entrusted to their performance, and the House of Lords must no longer include the 'bench of bishops' so unpopular since 1831.

Other claims were made, inspired by considerations of a more material order. The tithe must be abolished with or without compensation to the present recipients. The question was acute alike in England, Ireland, and Scotland. The church rates must be abolished. They were a local tax chargeable upon every rate-payer whose amount was fixed annually by the parish vestries, and whose proceeds were devoted exclusively to the upkeep of the Anglican churches. The London parishes were in a state of open revolt against the payment of Church rates, and Hobhouse's Act of 1831 for the reform of the vestries had been the insurgents' first victory.[1] The statute was purely permissive, and moreover, had been hardly applied outside the capital. But in the provinces the old system, whether the vestry were an 'open' vestry at which all the ratepayers attended and voted, or a 'close' vestry if the Dissenters happened to possess an accidental majority, provided opportunities for what was nothing short of a rebellion against payment of the church rates.[2]

And even in England there were some who were not content with demanding the abolition of the tithes and the church rates. They desired the State to confiscate the possessions of the Anglican church, as in the sixteenth century the Anglican church had

[1] See the events which in London immediately preceded the passing of Hobhouse's Act and which no doubt contributed to secure its passage while paving the way for the subsequent revolt (*Political Register*, September 24, 1831, vol. lxxiii, pp. 779 sqq.). In 1833 the inhabitants of Lambeth were still obliged to petition against a vestry elected on the system of Sturges Bourne (ibid., January 12, 1833, vol. lxxix, pp. 84-5).

[2] See the facts, related by Sp. Walpole, *Hist. of England*, vol. v, p. 267, of Manchester (open vestry) and Braintree, Essex (close vestry).

confiscated the possessions of the Catholic. The proceeds could
be applied to the redemption of the National Debt—that was
Cobbett's suggestion[1]—or to poor relief or national education.

From what quarters did these demands proceed? First and foremost among the enemies of the Church were the Radicals, sworn
foes not only of the Church of England but of every Church,
indeed of religion in any form, and comprising on the one hand
the disciples of Bentham and James Mill, on the other the revolutionaries in the strict sense whose violence far exceeded that of the
Utilitarians. But in the campaign which they were now opening
against the Established Church the Radicals found allies even
among the Christians. They were the Protestant Nonconformists.
Their number was increasing every year, and it is certain that in
England alone they already exceeded 2,000,000.[2] Their organization was improving. The Independents, for example, overcoming
at last their deep-rooted prejudice in favour of congregational
autonomy, had acquired by the founding of the General Congregational Union a centralized organization.[3] And it now seemed
likely that the effect of the Reform of 1832 would be to give the
Nonconformist groups a preponderating influence in the urban
constituencies. As a result of the joint operation of these causes a

[1] *Political Register*, January 14, 1831 (vol. lxxv, pp. 129 sqq.).

[2] The number of Dissenters was the object about this time of heated discussion, too
heated, indeed, to admit of easy control. See above, p. 62 *n.*, the figures of the *Morning
Chronicle*, contested by the *Standard*, and especially the copious statistics furnished by
James Bennett (*History of Dissenters during the last thirty years from 1808 to 1838*, pp. 268 sqq.).
Joseph Hume (H. of C., May 5, 1834, *Parl. Deb.*, 3rd Series, vol. xxiii, p. 509), maintained
that the Dissenters constituted a majority of the entire nation. 'From returns in his possession, it appeared that in twenty-nine large manufacturing towns in England the members
of the Established Church formed only one-fifth of the population.' According to
O'Connell (H. of C., June 3, 1836, ibid., 3rd Series, vol. xxxiv, p. 79), the Dissenters
were 6,000,000 as against 8,000,000 Anglicans. Both estimates are obviously excessive,
if we confine the appellation of Dissenters to those who *practised* forms of religion other
than that of the National Church. The lower classes, however, contained a vast mass of
persons indifferent to religion whom the Established Church might claim on the ground
that they were married according to her ritual, and the Dissenters might also claim on
the ground that they went to church only to be married because the law compelled them
to do so and for the rest of their lives never entered a church. See the strangely conflicting
figures for Lancashire, given respectively by the *British Magazine*, the High Church
organ (vol. v, pp. 205, 477), and by Slaney, a Radical M.P. (H. of C., November 30,
1837, *Parl. Deb.*, 3rd Series, vol. xxxix, pp. 390–1). The most trustworthy estimate in
our opinion is 3,000,000. It was accepted officially by the Dissenters in 1828 (*Test Act
Reporter*, p. 442); by James Bennett in his *History of Dissenters*, p. 272; by Lord Henley
(*Plea of Church Reform*, 1832, p. 10); by Lord Grey and the Bishop of London (H. of L.,
July 17, 1833, *Parliamentary Debates*, 3rd Series, vol. xix, p. 739). This estimate includes the
Catholics as well as the Protestant Dissenters.

[3] *British Magazine*, September 1, 1833 (vol. iv, pp. 241 sqq.). *Congregational Magazine*,
October 1836 (vol. xii, p. 628 sqq.). J. Waddington, *Congregational History*, continuation
to 1850, pp. 686 sqq.

committee was formed in March 1833, entitled the United Committee, to consider and redress the grievances which affected Dissenters.[1] But its programme was extremely moderate. If it demanded that Dissenters should be placed on a footing of complete civil equality with Anglicans, it carefully refrained from putting forward the demand made by the extremists for the disestablishment of the Church.[2] And we have already remarked the apathy the Dissenters had displayed at the December election.

During the first six months of 1833 there was only one portion of the United Kingdom where disestablishment was the avowed programme of the Protestant Dissenters, and that was not England but Scotland. In Scotland the established Church was the Presbyterian. The groups who for the past half century had separated from the State Church on doctrinal grounds, now shifted their position and claimed to have discovered in the fact of its alliance with the State,[3] the true reason why that Church had succumbed to latitudinarianism and rationalism. The new agitation was initiated towards the close of 1832 by Marshall Ewing and Wardlaw. 'The system of national Christianity,' wrote Wardlaw, '*necessarily* involves corruption and precludes the possibility of purification.'[4] A Voluntary Church Association was founded to maintain and spread the conviction that in future the organization of the Christian Churches should be based not on compulsion but on the voluntary principle.[5] For in its promoters' view a state religion, or compulsory support of religious institutions 'was inconsistent with the nature of religion' . . . 'its tendency, as exhibited by its effects' was 'to secularize religion, promote

[1] *Christian Advocate*, May 1834. The Wesleyans and the Quakers refused their co-operation.

[2] *Ecclesiastical Review*, February 1832, 'The Church and the Dissenters' (3rd Series, vol. vii, p. 113). '. . . They have engaged in no warfare against the temporalities of the possessioned Church; rarely are they found declaiming against the Establishment, or even its abuses, and the conduct of the clergy; and when these subjects are adverted to, it is, nine times out of ten, in self-defence.'

[3] Ibid., July 1833, 'Controversy on Establishments' (3rd Series, vol. x, pp. 69 sqq.).

[4] *Civil Establishments of Christianity tried by their only authoritative test, the word of God*, 1833, p. 43.

[5] For the origin of the expression, see Paley, *Principles of Moral and Political Philosophy*, Book VI, ch. x: 'This maintenance [of the clergy] must either depend upon the voluntary contributions of their hearers or arise from revenues assigned by authority of law.' 'The difficulty with which congregations would be established and upheld upon the *voluntary* plan' (ed. 2, vol. ii, pp. 310, 312). Robert Hall, *An Apology for the Freedom of the Press*, 1773, p. 75: 'Turn a Christian society into an established Church, and it is no longer a voluntary assembly for the worship of God: it is a powerful corporation, full of such sentiments and passions as usually distinguish such bodies; a dread of innovation, an attachment to abuses, and propensity to tyranny and oppression.'

hypocrisy, perpetuate error, produce infidelity, destroy the unity and purity of the Church, and disturb the peace and order of civil society.'[1]

Even more violent were the sentiments of the 6,000,000 Catholics led by O'Connell. The latter, at once a disciple of Bentham and a pious Catholic, followed his master by declaring himself in favour of complete democracy, complete free trade, and the complete separation of Church and State. And indeed what portion of the United Kingdom furnished such powerful arguments in favour of disestablishment than Ireland? On what possible ground could this State Church equipped with a large body of ministers and provided with rich endowments be justified in a country where the immense majority of the population were Catholics, that is to say members of the Church which had been stripped of her property to enrich the existing Establishment? Would it be urged that the State Church was a church of missionaries lavishly endowed to labour for the conversion of Ireland? Surely the experience of two centuries was sufficient to prove that she had failed in her task. Moreover, since the State by emancipating the Catholics seemed to have formally declared her neutrality in the matter of religion, she could hardly make herself responsible for such an undertaking.

3

The Radical programme was met by the very dissimilar programme of Church Reform. Its advocates were alive to the peril in which the Church stood since the Emancipation Act and the repeal of the Test Act. But far from desiring to see her reduced to the position of one sect among many others they desired to reform her, and thus strengthen her position by removing the blemishes which tarnished her purity. Even among High Churchmen there were those who recognized the need for reform. In 1831 the Archbishop of Canterbury had taken the initiative by introducing in the House of Lords three bills to improve the system of tithe, raise in certain cases the stipends of the clergy and regulate pluralism.[2] But generally speaking the High Church party was

---

[1] Rev. W. Hanna, *Memoirs of Thomas Chalmers*, vol. iii, pp. 349–50.

[2] For the Tithe Bill (a permissive measure), see several details in Cobbett, *Pol. Reg.*, August 13, 1831 (vol. lxxiii, pp. 415 sqq.); also Rev. J. Miller, *A Letter to the Right Hon. the Earl Grey . . . on the origin and nature of church property, and the connection of tithes with the existing agricultural distress, and on improvements which may be safely adopted*

averse to the idea, almost to the very name, of reform. High Churchmen delighted to call attention to the fact that the abuses so bitterly denounced were due very largely to the ecclesiastical patronage which the constitution of the Anglican Church placed in the hands of the crown and the laity.[1] They laid stress upon the steps individual bishops had taken during the last few years to reform these abuses by the exercise of their episcopal authority.[2] Only let that authority be reinforced, and the Bishops chosen from the High Church party, as Lord Liverpool had chosen them throughout his long ministry, and the Church, they maintained, would be purified without the necessity for any further action.[3]

It was members of the Evangelical party, scantily represented among the dignitaries of the Church—in 1832 there was only one Evangelical Bishop—but increasingly active and numerous in the Church at large, who were zealous in the cause of reform. Alarmed by the spectacle of Nonconformity making converts every day, the Evangelicals sought to rival the piety of the sects without leaving the Church, and to emphasize her Protestant character which the High Church party was only too inclined to obscure. They demanded that the thirty-nine articles which constituted the Anglican profession of faith should be accepted wholeheartedly and the liturgy reformed in harmony with their doctrine. The interminable office of Matins must be abolished, the Athanasian creed disused, or at least its damnatory clauses, which doomed to everlasting punishment all who maintained certain theological opinions, and the rites of ordination, baptism, marriage, burial, and absolution revised so as to get rid of many formulae which were a stumbling-block to the orthodox Protestant, and still bore the impress of Roman superstition.[4] They also asked for the construction of new churches, and the multiplication of episcopal sees. Two new sees must be carved out of the diocese of York and two out of the diocese of Lincoln.[5] One reformer even proposed that the number of Bishops in England

without the introduction of a new principle, 1831, p. 60. For the bill dealing with pluralism (reinforcing the powers of the Chancellor and the Archbishop), see H. of L., August 25, September 13, 20, 26, 1831 (*Parliamentary Debates*, 3rd Series, vol. vi, pp. 854, 1372; vol. vii, pp. 229, 589).

[1] Rev. E. Burton, *Thoughts upon the Demand for Church Reform*, 1831, pp. 14–15, 22.
[2] *British Critic*, January 1832, vol. xi, pp. 172 sqq. (the Bishop of Durham's Charge).
[3] Ibid., January 1832, vol. x, p. 225.
[4] Rev. Robert Cox, *Liturgy Revised*, 1830. Rev. C. N. Wodehouse, *Petition to the House of Lords for Ecclesiastical Improvements*, 1832.
[5] Lord Henley, *Plan of Church Reform*, p. 43.

and Wales should be raised to ninety-four.[1] Nor should ecclesiastical appointments be left any longer to the caprice of politicians,
but the Government should make them on the advice of a joint
committee of Bishops and laymen.[2] The Evangelicals sincerely
desired to strengthen the Church, and render her at once purer and
more independent. In many respects their aims were identical
with those of the High Church party.[3] But since they knew that
they could not trust the reform of abuses to the apathetic conservatism of the High Churchmen, they sought the intervention
of the State.[4] In this they conformed to the tradition of national
Protestantism. In the sixteenth century the Church of England
had been the creation of Parliament.

In detail the Evangelicals of 1832 envisaged as follows the relations between Church and State. The State had no right to
confiscate the endowments of the Church. But these endowments
had been given to the Church for the performance of specific
spiritual functions, and the question therefore arose whether the
clergy were still carrying out the donors' intentions. The State
had the right to interfere to secure this object; and if necessary,
alter a contract which no longer answered the purposes for
which it had been concluded. To justify their plans the Church
Reformers regarded the Church as being, if not in the strict and
legal sense, at least in a wide sense a Corporation; and in their
opinion the State was entitled, not indeed to confiscate the
goods of that corporation, but to redistribute them in such a
way as to render the Church's proper task of evangelization more
effective.

This was the procedure advocated by men like Lord Henley[5]
and the Rev. John Acaster[6] to reform the most glaring abuses of
the Anglican Church, plurality and non-residence. The evil had
not appreciably diminished since the opening of the century, nor
could it, so long as the Bishops were given a discretionary power
to tolerate exceptions, and the stipends of the parochial clergy

[1] Series (T), *A Model of Non-Secular Episcopacy*, including reasons for the establishment
of ninety-four Bishopricks in England and Wales.
[2] Lord Henley, *Plan of Church Reform*, pp. 53 sqq.
[3] Rev. Edward Burton, *Sequel to Remarks upon Church Reform*, with observations upon
the plan proposed by Lord Henley, 1832.
[4] Rev. John Acaster, *Remedies for the Church in Danger, or Hints to the Legislature on
Church Reform*, 1830, Part IV.   [5] *Plan of Church Reform*, 1832.
[6] *The Church in Danger from herself: or the Causes of her present declining State explained*,
1829. *Remedies for the Church in Danger, or Hints to the Legislature on Church Reform*, 1830.

were raised. The reformers therefore demanded the unqualified abolition of pluralism. And they asked that a minimum stipend should be fixed for the clergy. The necessary funds for that purpose could be found by a drastic reform of the Cathedral chapters whose members were too numerous and far too well paid for doing nothing. In this way £300,000 would be saved. Lord Henley further proposed that the administration of the diocesan endowments should be entrusted to a legally constituted body, a corporation. In this way, he maintained, the funds would be better managed, and would be more productive, so that the effect of the reform would be not only a better distribution, but an actual increase of the revenue of the Church.[1]

But this solution of the problem of Church Reform which determined the rights of the State in the sense most favourable to the interests of the Church did not fail to arouse the apprehensions of the new majority in Parliament. The old Whigs detested the religious zeal of the Evangelicals and the aristocratic abuses which disfigured the Church found favour in their eyes, since their effect was to make the Church less fanatical. From the opposite standpoint, the young Radicals wished to diminish the endowments of the Church in order to weaken her influence. And in Ireland especially it would not be easy to accord even a partial satisfaction to O'Connell's followers so long as the Government refrained from touching the wealth of a Church equipped to provide for the spiritual needs of a population of eight millions, of whom six would have nothing to do with Anglican worship. Some Liberals were attracted by a system intermediate between the American system of voluntaryism and equality and the old corporate system of a national Church. They had in view the French system established by Napoleon by which the State treated the priests as government officials and paid them according to the importance of their functions without any question of vested rights.[2] To complete our survey we may mention the eccentric proposals made by Thomas Arnold and James Mill. Thomas Arnold wanted a State Church whose buildings would be at the disposal of the preachers of any and every form of

[1] For instances of the acceptance by politicians of this view of Church Reform, namely, the right of the State to control the distribution of her endowments, see H. of C., January 23, 1832: Stanley's speech (Parliamentary Debates, 3rd Series, vol. ix, p. 793); also H. of L., July 18, 1833: Lord Plunkett's speech (ibid., 3rd Series, vol. xix, pp. 857 sqq.).
[2] H. of C., May 27, 1834: Ward's speech (ibid., 3rd Series, vol. xxiii, pp. 1385-6).

Christianity.[1] James Mill asked for a ministry of laymen to be paid by the State who would instruct both children and adults in civic morality and applied science.[2]

These were utopias which had no effect whatsoever on public opinion, and shocked even the friends of the two thinkers who put them forward. They are mentioned here only to give the reader a notion of the ferment of ideas which prevailed at this time. Napoleon's system of several religions all supported by the State was scarcely more popular. If a handful of English Statesmen entertained the notion of paying other ministers than those of the Anglican church, for example the Catholic priests and the Presbyterian ministers in Ireland,[3] the plan was never seriously considered, for it ran counter to the invincible opposition, both of the Irish Catholics who were far from disposed to accept the tutelage of the British Government, and of the English Protestants even less disposed to endow the Church of Rome. But at least the principle might be affirmed that the State possessed the right not only to control the administration of the endowments of the Church, but to determine their amount and could therefore confiscate endowments it considered excessive, and apply the proceeds to such purposes of public utility as Parliament might decide. Joseph Hume and O'Connell himself though partisans of total disestablishment accepted this compromise as a provisional measure. It was on its merits that the great controversy on the reform of the Irish Church turned in the years 1833 and 1834.

4

The Royal Address admitted that while the disorder in Ireland must be suppressed, the abuses from which the Irish Church was suffering must at the same time be reformed. On February 12, 1833, two days before the Coercion Bill was introduced in the Lords, a bill for the reform of the Church of Ireland was introduced in the Commons.

It began by dealing with the scandal of the excessive number of

[1] *Principles of Church Reform*, 1833.
[2] *London Review*, July 1835, 'The Church and its Reform' (vol. i, pp. 257 sqq.).
[3] *Memorandum by Lord John Russell on Irish Policy*, October 18, 1833: 'There are three principal religions in Ireland: the Establishment, few in numbers, but strong in landed property: the Roman Catholics, numerous and containing nearly all the very poor class: the Presbyterians, considerable in number, and remarkable for intelligence and commercial industry. All three ought to be provided for by the State' (*Early Correspondence of Lord John Russell*, vol. ii, p. 43).

clergy. Of the twenty-two Irish sees, ten were suppressed—or in the euphemistic language of the bill, for a term which smacked so strongly of revolution as *suppression* was carefully avoided—were 'united' with other sees. All chapters were abolished to which no cure of souls was attached. The income of the primate of Ireland was reduced by about a third. And finally in every parish where it was proved that no religious service had been performed within the last three years a body of commissioners set up by the act— six ecclesiastics and five laymen[1]—were empowered to suspend the appointment of an incumbent or curate.

In the second place the bill abolished the church cess, a local impost equivalent to the English church rate, which was applied to the upkeep of the churches and the cost of the services. According to the official calculation the church cess yielded a revenue of some £70,000. The Government proposed to replace it by a graduated tax to be levied on the stipends of the clergy and rising from five to fifteen per cent. The return from the proposed tax was estimated at £69,000.[2] It was hoped, moreover, that better management would reduce the expenditure for which the church cess provided at present, and therefore that there would be an eventual surplus available for improving the stipends of the poorer clergy or building new churches. This scheme of a graduated tax on clerical incomes had been conceived in those Evangelical circles which desired to reform the Church to strengthen her position.[3] But the Opposition, led by Peel, saw in the proposal an attempt to give legislative sanction to the Radical principle of a graduated income tax.[4] And indeed the Cabinet may have been glad of the opportunity to give this satisfaction to the Radicals

[1] Two of the six clerical commissioners (the Primate of Ireland and the Archbishop of Dublin) held their seats *ex officio*, the remaining four Irish archbishops or bishops in virtue of a royal warrant. Of the five lay commissioners, two sat on the commission *ex officio* (the Chancellor of Ireland and the Chief Justice of Ireland). Two were appointed by warrant and one by the Primate. In the original draft of the bill all three were to be appointed by the Government. It was Wellington who proposed (H. of L., July 22, 1833, *Parliamentary Debates*, 3rd Series, vol. xix, p. 1046) and carried an amendment providing that one of the three should be a nominee of the Primate.

[2] The bill presented the change under a somewhat different aspect. It began by abolishing the first fruits, that is to say, the income of a benefice during the first year, and it was to compensate for the consequent loss that a graduated tax was imposed on clerical stipends. But since the first fruits were a mere name (they were calculated on a basis dating from 1290), the new tax yielded in reality a very considerable revenue, which in turn made possible the abolition of the church cess.

[3] Rev. E. Burton, *Thoughts upon the Demand for Church Reform*, pp. 25–6. Lord Henley, *Plan of Church Reform*, pp. 19–20.

[4] H. of C., June 25, 1833 (*Parl. Deb.*, 3rd Series, vol. xviii, p. 1235).

and advanced Liberals at the very moment when they were resisting their demands in the matter of Church Reform.

In October, when the bill for the Reform of the Church of Ireland was under discussion by the Cabinet, Lord John Russell had asked all parishes in which the members of the Established Church were non-existent or a mere handful, should be suppressed, and the funds thus obtained employed to promote popular education. He was supported by Lord Althorp and Lord Durham. But he had been defeated by the determined opposition of Stanley who was upheld by Lord Grey and the majority of the ministers. He had taken the defeat so much to heart, that he was on the verge of tendering his resignation on the eve of the General Election. In the end Lord Holland had persuaded him to remain in the Cabinet.[1] The King's Speech had set the seal upon his failure: there was to be no question of diminishing the endowments of the Church, but only of their 'more equitable and more judicious distribution'.

When, however, Lord Althorp ten days later explained the provisions of the bill, it was evident that the Conservatives and the Moderates had not yet won the day. Stanley had made an implicit concession to the advocates of partial disendowment.

Under the existing system the Bishops' income was partly derived from the lease of their estates. It was illegal to let these lands for a period of less than twenty-one years. But the clergy had devised means to evade the prohibition. All that need be done was to renew the twenty-one years lease in advance every seven or three years, or even annually on payment by the tenant of a fine which amounted to an increase of the rent.[2] The bill provided that any tenant might demand the substitution for his twenty-one years lease of a lease in perpetuity. Under the new lease the rent would of course be considerably raised. But the tenant would make no objection to this, for the increase would be the price at which he secured himself for all time against the financial requisitions of the Bishops. And on the other hand the State, while fully respecting the Bishops' property, could pay them the equivalent of the old rent and retain the surplus to be applied to such purposes as Parliament might think fit.

[1] Lord John Russell to Lord Grey, October 20, 25, 1832; Lord Grey to Lord John Russell, October 25, 1832; Lord Holland to Lord John Russell, October 26, 1832 (S. Walpole, *Life of Lord John Russell*, vol. i, pp. 188 sqq.).
[2] For these devices, see Wakefield, *Ireland*, vol. i, p. 244; vol. ii, p. 470.

It was on this clause—clause 147 of the bill—that the entire debate turned from the moment when, after a lengthy delay occasioned by questions of procedure, it finally opened on May 6. The Cabinet was equally embarrassed by the violence of the attack delivered by the Conservative Opposition and the enthusiastic support of the Radicals. Clause 147 was regarded as the first attempt to introduce into the legislation of the country a theory of taxation, based on Ricardo's doctrine of rent, which James Mill had expounded in the successive editions of his *Elements of Political Economy*. According to this theory, the State may confiscate every 'increase of' the 'net produce' of an estate when it is not the result of the landlord's or tenant's labour, but entirely the creation of society, without doing any injury to the tenant or giving the landlord any just cause to regard himself as wronged.[1] Peel declared himself unalterably opposed to 'a principle—dangerous to the security of all property, whether lay or ecclesiastical, corporate or individual'.[2]

The ministers, though certain of a majority in the Commons, dared not face on this question the majority of the Lords supported by the opposition of the Court. They seem to have spent the first fortnight of June seeking a new formula which would conciliate the more moderate defenders of the Church, and to have contemplated the insertion into the bill of an explicit provision that the surplus must be applied to 'religious or charitable purposes'.[3] But it might be interpreted to mean that a portion of the money would be used to pay the Catholic priests, perhaps even applied in relief of the poor rate. Finally, on June 21, clause 147 was sacrificed. Infuriated by a diatribe of O'Connell, Lord John Russell with equal inconsistency and impolicy uttered during the speech in which he announced the abandonment of the clause words which must effect a breach between the Government and the advanced Liberals, and came strangely from the lips of a man who only six months earlier had almost caused a Cabinet crisis by upholding on

[1] *Elements of Political Economy*, ch. IV; 5, V. For the attention which this theory attracted when the book was first published, see *Morning Chronicle*, August 22, 27, 1825; also during the debates on the Reform Bill, H. of C., March 21, 1831 (Sir R. Vyvyan's speech, *Parliamentary Debates*, 3rd Series, vol. iii, p. 637).
[2] H. of C., May 6, 1833 (ibid., 3rd Series, vol. xvii, p. 1005).
[3] Sir Robert Peel to Goulburn, June 19, 1833 (C. S. Parker, *Sir Robert Peel*, vol. ii, p. 222). Creevey (to Miss Ord, June 20, 1833) appears to have believed that direct negotiations had taken place between the Cabinet and the Opposition (*Creevey Papers*, vol. ii, pp. 255–6); Peel's letter proves that Creevey's suspicions were unfounded.

this very question of the Irish Church the position of the advanced Liberals against the Moderates. 'This country,' he said, 'could not stand a revolution once a year. . . . They were all bound to make sacrifices to preserve and promote tranquillity.'[1]

The concession once secured, Wellington in the Lords judged it advisable to accept the bill without substantial alteration.[2] The House of Lords was content with introducing a few amendments, of which only one was important. It provided that the Irish clergy should not be liable to the tax on benefices they already held when the act came into force. It would be levied on benefices only from the next vacancy. Otherwise the Conservative party followed the advice given by their two leaders, and the Bishops of London, Bath and Wells, and Hereford explained the reasons of political expediency for which they voted for the bill.[3] Lord Grey and his colleagues might therefore fairly claim during these early days of August that by carrying their two Irish bills they had won two important victories. But these victories were after all dearly bought. The Cabinet had made enemies in every quarter. The Coercion Bill was hateful to O'Connell and the Radicals; yet it had been scarcely passed before the Conservatives were alarmed to see Lord Grey part with the two men who ever since the close of 1830 had been battling with O'Connell in Ireland. Stanley was transferred to the Colonial Office and was replaced as Irish Secretary by Littleton, Lord Anglesey was succeeded as Lord Lieutenant by Lord Wellesley. Moreover, the Church Reform Bill had been carried only at the price of an important amendment which abandoned one of the fundamental articles of the Radical creed, the right of the state to disendow the Church. Nevertheless, a measure which suppressed episcopal sees was an alarming attack upon the privileges of the established Church. It had scarcely been passed before it provoked a violent explosion of religious passion in England. The crisis lasted a year. It deserves detailed study, for it began the decline of the anti-clericalism which had so lately been transplanted to England under the disturbing influence of the Parisian Revolution.

[1] H. of C., June 21, 1833 (*Parliamentary Debates*, 3rd Series, vol. xviii, p. 1096).
[2] H. of L., July 19, 1833 (ibid., 3rd Series, vol. xix, pp. 948 sqq.). 3 and 4 Will. IV, cap. 37.
[3] H. of L., July 19, 1833 (ibid., 3rd Series, vol. xix, pp. 924 sqq., 975).

II REVOLT OF THE ESTABLISHED CHURCH AND THE SECTS

I

During the closing days of July while the Irish Church bill was being passed through its final stages in the House of Commons, three young fellows of Oxford, members of the High Church party, William Palmer, Arthur Perceval, and Richard Hurrell Froude, visited in his parish of Hadleigh the Rev. Hugh James Rose, a Cambridge theologian, who for the past two or three years had been conducting, with the full support of the Arch-bishop of Canterbury, a campaign on behalf of the principles of that party.[1] Rose had interested himself in the plan which a number of clergymen had conceived of forming an association of Churchmen, for the defence of the traditional creed.[2] It was he who had founded the *British Magazine*, a weighty review of theology and spirituality. And it was he who had founded the Theological Library to restore in England the tradition of the primitive church and revive a taste for patristic studies. In his search for collaborators in this series he had visited Oxford in 1832,[3] and it was during this visit that he had made the acquaintance of the young men who had now come to discuss with him what were the best measures to take in this emergency to defend the Church of England against the danger with which she was threatened.

These young men however, were content to regard themselves as the representatives of two Oxford men who were not present at Hadleigh. One of these, already forty years old, was famous throughout the religious world. He was John Keble, who with the hope of doing for the High Church what Wesley had formerly done for Evangelical pietism by bestowing upon it the consecra-tion of poetry and investing it with the glamour of romantic emotion, had published in 1827 a collection of sacred poems, the *Christian Year*, which had enjoyed a very great success; already by

---

[1] Rev. William Palmer, *A Narrative of Events connected with the publication of the Tracts for the Times, with reflections on existing Tendencies to Romanism*, 1843, pp. 5–6. H. P. Liddon, *Life of Edward Bouverie Pusey*, vol. i, p. 267. The group to which H. J. Rose then belonged was known as the 'Canterbury Party' (W. N. Molesworth, *History of the Church of England from 1660*, p. 317). [2] Rev. William Palmer, ibid., p. 6 n.
[3] T. Mozley, *Reminiscences chiefly of Oriel College and the Oxford Movement*, vol. i, p. 308. *Letters and Correspondence of J. H. Newman during his life in the English Church*, ed. Anne Mozley, vol. i, pp. 260–1.

1833 it had reached the fourth edition. It was only a few days since Keble had launched a thunderbolt by the sermon he had preached at Saint Mary's, Oxford, denouncing the Irish Church Bill as a 'direct disavowal of the sovereignty of God' and an act of 'national apostasy'.[1] The other, John Henry Newman, though nine years younger than Keble and still unknown to the general public, had already more than once caused a sensation at Oxford by his reckless pugnacity as a controversialist. Educated in the straightest school of Evangelical piety, he had begun his career as a theologian among the intelligentsia of Oriel College, the group of fellows known as the 'Noetics', and Whately and his colleagues had shaken his confidence in the pietist doctrines without converting him to their latitudinarianism. When in 1829 the University of Oxford was asked to re-elect Peel who had just committed his great act of treason on the question of Catholic emancipation, Newman had distinguished himself among the fellows by the more ardent zeal with which he had fought the renegade Tory. From that time we can watch him during the troublous years which followed the passage of the Emancipation Bill, inclining more and more towards the High Church and alarming his superiors and friends by the audacity of his conduct.[2] He was among those whom Rose had asked to collaborate in his Theological Library. Exhausted by the composition of a work dealing with 'The Arians of the Fourth Century' he had taken a holiday in Italy in the company of his friend Froude who was a consumptive. He had just returned to England, stirred to the depths of his being by the humiliating condition to which his Church was reduced. His temperament was feverish, restless, self-tormenting. He thirsted impatiently for action—he must be speaking, writing, arguing, fighting. 'If times are troublous,' he had written to his sister two years earlier when the entire country was in revolt against the Anglican clergy, 'Oxford will want hot headed men, and such I mean to be, and I am in my place.'[3]

The conspirators spent the month of August elaborating the programme decided at Hadleigh. Their original plan was to found an association of 'Friends of the Church' for the defence of her doctrine, ritual, and discipline. Perceval drew up a programme

[1] R. W. Church, *The Oxford Movement. Twelve Years, 1833–1845*, p. 83.
[2] *Affair of the Church Missionary Society*, 1830; see on the subject, Newman, *Letters and Correspondence*, vol. i, pp. 215, 223, 225; also *Via Media*, vol. ii, pp. 1–17.
[3] *Letters and Correspondence*, vol. i, p. 250.

which was circulated among the clergy and devout laity.[1] The project attracted considerable support and local societies were formed in several provincial towns. But objections were raised. The proposed association contradicted the principles of the men who wished to found it; for the genuine High Churchman there was only one association to which he had a right to belong, namely the Church herself.[2] And on the other hand it seemed likely to prove embarrassing to young innovators who were not prepared to submit their theological publications to the censorship of a committee.[3] Newman refused point blank. At bottom the two objections were contradictory. Nevertheless, each reenforced the other and the project of an association was abandoned. When on September 9 the members of the group began the publication of a series of tracts, each was responsible for his own contribution. The *Tracts for the Times* were pamphlets of various sizes, though usually quite short, and published at irregular but frequent intervals which their authors worked hard to circulate in large numbers throughout England. Newman and Keble were the most active collaborators. At the end of December, an Oxford theologian, already celebrated for his works of Hebrew scholarship, Pusey, published what was nothing short of a treatise on the practice of fasting.

What was the doctrine common to all the members of this group? In 1833 the problems of the hour compelled the young theologians of Oxford to make a definite stand on two points. In the first place the centre of the Christian religion is the Eucharist, and its celebration has been committed by God to the Bishops and their delegates the priests. The episcopate therefore is of Divine Institution. To suppress bishoprics as Parliament had just done was to outrage the dogma of the apostolic succession and usurp the prerogative of God. In the second place the details of Anglican worship were fixed by the Book of Common Prayer. The reformers, comparing the Anglican liturgy with the thirty-nine Articles, claimed that on certain points the liturgical formulae contradicted the doctrine of the articles and shewed vestiges of Romanism. They, therefore, demanded that the liturgy should be revised. There was no justification for this. On the contrary the doctrine

[1] Rev. William Palmer, *A Narrative* . . ., pp. 8 sqq. Hon. Arthur Philip Perceval, *A Collection of Papers* connected with the Theological Movement of 1833, 1842, p. 17.
[2] That was Froude's opinion (R. W. Church, *Oxford Movement*, p. 94).
[3] Rev. William Palmer, *A Narrative* . . ., p. 20.

of the Church should be determined by a careful study of her liturgy. It would then appear that the Church of England was the Catholic Church in her pure state, as opposed on the one hand to the Church of Rome, corrupt since the Council of Trent, and on the other to the Protestant sects equally corrupt and doomed sooner or later to fall a prey to Socinianism.

In short Keble, Newman, and their fellows were taking up from the opposite standpoint the work begun a century earlier by the Evangelical party in the church. The Evangelicals had sought to revive the Church by appealing to the emotions aroused in a pious soul by the dogma of justification by faith. They had failed and their attempt had served only to swell the numbers and increase the power of the sects who were now turning their might against the Church and threatened to destroy her. The 'apostolicals'—the young theologians had borrowed the title from the Spanish absolutists, the Carlists,[1]—were endeavouring to revive[2] the Church by appealing to the equally intense emotions aroused by the Eucharistic rite, by participation in the drama of the Divine Sacrifice renewed in every church. After a lull of a century and a half the war was renewed between the Christianity founded upon the mystery of grace and the Christianity founded upon the mystery of the Eucharist, the former colder, more austere, more virile, the latter more dramatic, more emotional, more feminine. Newman and his friends it is true did not immediately turn their attention to the question of the Eucharist.[3] The Oxford Movement was a sequel of the political movements of the day. The Government's Irish policy had raised the question of the existence of the Church as a Church, not a mere department of the State, and it was the object of the Oxford

[1] R. W. Church, *Oxford Movement*, p. 52. The appellation had been invented by Richard Hurrell Froude.

[2] Was it a mere accident that the word *revival* appears in the opening sentence of the preface prefixed in 1834 to the first volume of the Tracts: 'The following Tracts are published with the object of contributing something towards the practical revival of doctrines, which, although held by the great divines of our Church, at present have become obsolete with the majority of her members'?

[3] The Tract writers expressly repudiate the dogma of Transubstantiation (Tract No. 36). They reprinted the *History of the Popish Transubstantiation*, by John Cosin, Bishop of Durham, which maintained that the language used by Jesus and the Apostle Paul must be understood in 'a sacramental and mystical', not in 'a gross and carnal' sense. When Keble, on September 6, 1833, affirmed 'that the only way of salvation is the partaking of the body and blood of our sacrificed Redeemer' (*Perceval Collection*, p. 15), he adopted an explanation intermediate between the denial of the Real Presence and the literal interpretation of the Catholics.

theologians to combat the individualism of the Nonconformists by reviving together with the doctrine of the apostolic succession what we may term the ecclesiastical spirit, 'the mind of the Church'.

The High Churchmen, however, were not content with disseminating the Tracts in which they expounded their theological views. They did not abandon the project of a collective demonstration. When they gave up the plan of an association of Friends of the Church, they tried another. They collected signatures among the clergy to an address to the Archbishop of Canterbury, in which he was assured of the hearty co-operation of his clergy in all measures 'that may tend to revive the discipline of ancient times; to strengthen the connexion between the bishops, clergy, and people and to promote the purity, the efficiency and the unity of the Church'. This project also wore a disquieting aspect in the eyes of the Bishops. Like the original scheme, it did not, they considered, sufficiently respect ecclesiastical authority. Nevertheless, it was carried out and was as successful as its promoters could have hoped. Seven thousand signatures were received.[1]

Encouraged by their initial success the High Churchmen drew up a second address to be signed exclusively by laymen and presented by them to the Archbishop. A committee of laymen in London collected signatures. The organizers dared not hold a single public meeting. They were still timid and unable to forget the riots of 1831. But the response was overwhelming; in four months 230,000 signatures were received. And the response was even more remarkable because the signatures had been subjected to the most rigorous control, a procedure often neglected on such occasions. Only genuine householders, that is to say heads of families, were allowed to sign the address.[2]

2

Nor were the sects idle. The Nonconformists reproached themselves for the apathy they had displayed at the general election, the blind trust they had reposed in the Whig government. How had their patience been rewarded? Throughout the entire course of its first session the reformed Parliament had totally neglected

[1] Rev. William Palmer, *A Narrative . . .*, pp. 11, 12; he gives the text of the address. Cf. Newman to Froude, November 7, 1833; to S. Rickards, November 22, 1833 (*Letters and Correspondence*, vol. i, pp. 476, 488).
[2] Rev. William Palmer, ibid., pp. 13 sqq. *Annual Register*, 1834, p. 71. *British Magazine*, March 1, 1834 (vol. v, p. 346).

their claims and Irish affairs had engrossed its entire attention. And now they saw the High Church give the signal for a movement of agitation and propaganda, form in fact a sort of independent organization within the Establishment. At this critical moment their discontent was exasperated by a blunder committed by the Anglican clergy. The date was at hand, fixed by a recent statute,[1] after which the clergy could no longer claim the full payment of their tithes, and the clergy who were naturally unwilling to let their rights lapse appealed *en masse* to the courts. It was said that as many as 10,000, even 50,000 summonses had been issued.[2] The anti-clericalism of the small farmer and agricultural labourer which had shown no sign of life since 1831 revived. On September 5, contemporaneously with the first appearance of the *Tracts for the Times*, a group of Dissenters, pastors and laymen, met in Sussex and invited the United Committee of Deputies to summon in London, before Parliament met, a 'convention' of delegates from the Nonconformist congregations to present their grievances and demand instant redress from the Government. The United Committee replied that it was unable to take a step of such magnitude at the request of a single county, but advised the Dissenters to petition Parliament. In these petitions they must in the first place demand 'the removal of the grievances under which Dissenters still labour; but they must also assert . . . the great principle of the unjust and unscriptural union of Church and State, however it may be modified.'[3] The challenge was made.

The gauntlet was indeed thrown down in a fashion which impressed the entire Nonconformist world by the sermon preached by the Rev. T. Binney, a Congregationalist minister, when laying the foundation stone of a chapel in Southwark. 'It is with me,' declared the preacher, 'a matter of deep, serious, and religious conviction that the Established Church is a great national evil; that it is an obstacle to the progress of truth and godliness in the land; and that therefore its end is most devoutly to be wished by every lover of God and man.'[4] A certain Beverley, who had left the Anglican body, and whose pamphlet published in 1831

---

[1] 2 and 3 Will. IV, cap. 100.

[2] *Political Register*, September 7, 1833 (vol. viii, p. 609). *Edinburgh Review*, January 1834, 'The Church of England' (vol. lxxxi, pp. 501-2).

[3] *Christian Advocate*, December 9, 1833.

[4] *An Address delivered on laying the first stone of the new King's Weigh House* . . . 1833, Appendix, p. 20. For Binney himself, see the account given by J. Grant, *The Metropolitan Pulpit*, 1839, vol. ii, pp. 257 sqq.

on the corrupt state of the Established church[1] had achieved a huge success, became a Nonconformist worthy. The Congregationalists received him into their sect and made him a minister.[2] The numerous pamphlets in defence of the voluntary principle which had appeared in Scotland during the last year or two enjoyed an extensive sale in England.

In the large provincial towns meetings were held to draw up the petition Nonconformists would be invited to sign for presentation to Parliament. Manchester led the way; but the most imposing demonstration took place at Leeds, on December 3. The demonstrators were advised to concentrate their demands upon five points—release for Dissenters from any sort of obligation to contribute towards the cost of Anglican worship, their right to be buried in the churchyards by their own minister—free access to the Universities, the right to be married in their own chapels, a secular state observing neutrality towards all creeds. These were the five practical grievances of Dissent. The discussion had scarcely begun when one of the assistants, a minister, carried a resolution in favour of disestablishment.[3] The same claim was made by the Nottingham meeting in January, and by all the numerous meetings held in the Midlands, in Lancashire and in the Glasgow district. The time had come to carry out the plan the Sussex Dissenters had proposed in September. At a public meeting held on May 8, the United Committee gave a formal reception to more than four hundred delegations from every part of Great Britain, and an amendment to the original resolution demanding disestablishment was carried almost unanimously, only three votes being given against it.[4] It was obvious that the moderates who composed the United Committee were being pushed forward by the host of Dissenters from the provinces.[5] They were an imposing

[1] *A Letter to . . . the Archbishop of York, on the present corrupt state of the Church of England*, 1831. The work passed through twelve editions in the first year. By 1834 it had reached the seventeenth. Also, *A Second Letter to his Grace the Archbishop of York on the present corrupt state of the Church of England*, 1832.

[2] L.S.E. (Michael Augustus Gathercole), *Letters to a Dissenting Minister of the Congregational Independent Denomination, containing remarks on the principles of that sect, and the author's reasons for leaving it and conforming to the Church of England*, 1834, p. 27.

[3] *Morning Chronicle*, December 4, 10, 1833.   [4] Ibid., May 9, 1834.

[5] *Eclectic Review*, May 1834, 'Established and Voluntary Churches' (vol. xi, p. 320): 'The revolution which has taken place in the public mind within the last few years, nay within the last few months, upon the subjects to which these publications relate, is unexampled in its suddenness and rapidity. . . . Those who were foremost in the polemic fight, now overtaken by a whole army of voluntaries, are now reproached for caution and that most hated of all virtues, moderation.'

body, if we may trust the statistical inquiries which had been carried out during the past four months in Nonconformist circles with the object of proving that in the manufacturing districts of the north, in all the large towns, possibly even in the country as a whole the number of Dissenters exceeded the number of Anglicans.[1] Under these circumstances the Radical members of Parliament deemed it advisable to take command of this host and place disestablishment in the forefront of their programme. On May 12, Joseph Hume took the chair at a meeting, held in the London Tavern, of 'the friends of civil and religious liberty' at which O'Connell spoke in favour of disestablishment.[2]

3

The two armies were now arrayed for mutual combat and ready to come to blows. 'God forbid,' wrote Greville in his diary, 'that we should have two parties established upon the principles of a religious opposition to each other; it would be the worst of evils, and yet the times appear to threaten something of the sort.'[3] This was actually the case in France, and was perhaps the fundamental cause of the revolutionary character which marked French history. But England was not France; and it betrayed a strange blindness to the innate complexity, nay the innate confusion of British institutions to be deceived by superficial appearances. We are told that Coleridge shortly before his death, as he watched the attack made upon the Church of England by an alliance of so many diverse and powerful foes—Catholics, Protestants, Free-thinkers—pronounced her doomed by the vast mass of hostility she had aroused and in so many different quarters. Like Greville he was mistaken. He should have perceived that the mutual incompatibility of the parties to this alliance against the Church would prove her salvation.

In the front rank of the hostile combination were the Irish Catholics, and that was itself sufficient to render the movement suspect in the eyes of the British public. For the English entertained for the Irish nothing but hatred and contempt. Nor was this

---

[1] *The Times*, May 14, 1834. See the encouragement which Macaulay gave the agitators in his essay on Walpole which appeared in the *Edinburgh Review* in October 1833: 'If the Dissenters had been turbulent, he [Walpole] would probably have relieved them; but while he apprehended no danger from them, he would not run the slightest risk for their sake (vol. lviii, p. 245). [2] *Morning Chronicle*, May 13, 1834.
[3] *Greville Memoirs*, June 7, 1834.

attitude confined to the middle class. The proletariat could not forgive the Irish labourer for competing with themselves on the farms of the south and in the factories of the north, and thus reducing the rate of wages. We have already seen that the agrarian disorder of 1830 began by a rising of the labourers of Kent against the Irish immigrants. In the north incidents of this kind were of almost daily occurrence. For a time this anti-Irish agitation was absorbed in the wider movement and may indeed, by aggravating the disorder, have contributed to hasten the passage of the Reform Bill. But the crisis once over, O'Connell's alliance with the English Radicals had become a source of weakness to the latter. During the entire session of 1833 the question of Church Reform had been presented to the public as an Irish rather than an English question. Consequently the British public lost interest in it, and even conceived an inarticulate hostility towards ideas which lately had been far from unpalatable. If the party in favour of disestablishment and disendowment was the party of the low Irish, the cause of the Church was once more the cause of the nation. Only let the Church have the prudence to accept a minimum of inevitable reform, and her position will be again secure.

In their struggle against the Establishment, the Irish Catholics found allies in the Protestant Nonconformists. Such an alliance was a misfit, and the day was bound to come when the allies would realize that their common hatred of the Church was due to entirely different motives. But that was not all. The Protestant sects themselves did not present a solid front. On the question of disestablishment they were divided. There was a section of Nonconformity which witnessed with dismay the growth of Liberal and democratic ideas. The Wesleyan Methodists had always objected to being classified with the Dissenters. A branch detached from the Low Church, yet the High Church of Nonconformity, they ostentatiously adopted a position of neutrality as between the Church and the sects and aimed at infusing into both, by the influence of their preaching, a new spirit of Evangelical religion. In 1829 Conference had not had the opportunity of making any official pronouncement on the question of Catholic Emancipation. For the bill had been rushed through Parliament in the interval between two annual Conferences. But it was common knowledge that the majority of Wesleyans were opposed to Emancipation. Shortly afterwards Conference refused to concern itself with the question of Parliamentary reform, and was content to exhort the faithful not to neglect the salvation of their souls from an overzealous concern with the political issues of the day.[1] Possibly the majority of the Wesleyans were Tories. Had not their leading representative, the Rev. Jabez Bunting, declared that 'Methodism was as much opposed to democracy as to sin.'[2] And Conference had expressly forbidden Wesleyans to become members of the trade unions or, to use the language of Conference of 'associations which are subversive of the principles of true and proper liberty, employing unlawful oaths, and threats, and force to acquire new members and to accomplish purposes which would tend to destroy the very framework of civil society'.[3] Now when disestablishment was the issue, the Conference adopted the same attitude of unfriendly neutrality towards the new agitation. It deplored 'the high controversies . . . on foot, both as to civil and ecclesiastical affairs', declared forms of Church Government 'unessential' and warned the faithful of 'the danger of listening with too warm an interest to such debates'.[4]

This attitude was by no means acceptable to some members of the local congregations. But Bunting and the Conference braved their opposition and overcame it. A Wesleyan minister in Lancashire, the Rev. Joseph Rayner Stephens, without referring the matter to his superior, accepted the position of secretary of a Church Separation society. He was suspended from the ministry as having offended against 'the peaceable and anti-sectarian spirit' of Wesleyanism.[5] This was the signal for the revolt which

[1] Address of the Conference of 1831: 'We live in times of great political ferment and agitation. Take heed to yourselves, brethren, "lest your hearts be overcharged with cares of this life". Let not worldly politics engross too much of your time and attention.' Address of the Conference of 1832: '. . . it . . . seems probable that many of you may, in a short time, be required to take part in contests for the representation of your respective towns and counties in Parliament, to whom such strife will be new, and the moral effect of them upon your minds untried and unanticipated. We remind you that the Kingdom which you seek "is not of this world". You may innocently exercise the privileges which belong to you as members of civil society; . . . but can you, with perfect security to your religious character and your peace of heart, become the ardent agents of political parties?' (*Minutes of Conference*, vol. vii, p. 74, 1831–2).

[2] T. P. Bunting, *The Life of Jabez Bunting*, vol. i, p. 112.

[3] *Address of the Conference of 1833* (*Minutes*, vol. vii, p. 306).

[4] Ibid. (*Minutes*, vol. vii, pp. 305–6).

[5] For the Stephens affair, see *Minutes*, vol. vii, pp. 417–19. John Wilkes, the only member of Parliament who belonged to the Methodist body, was excommunicated by the Wesleyans in 1834. As an advanced Liberal he was under suspicion, and among other offences was charged with having made a speech of dubious morality at a banquet given in honour of the Radical Duncombe (*British Magazine*, September 1, 1834, vol. vi, pp. 196–8, 318–9).

broke out among the Lancashire Methodists. A considerable body
of laymen led by a minister named Warren took possession of the
local chapels and refused to obey the authority of their superintendent.[1] Conference fought the matter through the courts and
won its case. A judgment delivered by the Vice-Chancellor and
confirmed by the Chancellor gave Conference for the first time a
species of legal status as the central organ of Wesleyanism.[2] The
same year the entire organization of the Methodist body was
revised so as to give the lay members a limited control over the
chapel funds, but on the other hand to preserve unimpaired the
spiritual authority and the exclusively clerical character of
Conference.[3]

The Conservatives began to do justice to so unsectarian a sect.
The *Quarterly Review* pronounced a panegyric of the Wesleyans.[4]
In the House of Lords the Archbishop of Canterbury publicly
thanked them for the attitude they had adopted in the contest
between the Church and the sects.[5] In one of his charges, Phill-
potts, the Bishop of Exeter, celebrated for the ardour of his
churchmanship and his Toryism, pleaded with them in the most
friendly terms to return to the bosom of the Church,[6] and a
persistent rumour was current to the effect that negotiations were
taking place between Bunting and himself for a reunion between
the Wesleyans and Anglicans.[7] And it was significant that these
reciprocal advances made by the Wesleyans to the clergy of the
Establishment and by the latter to the Wesleyans, did not seriously

[1] A. Stevens, *History of . . . Methodism*, vol. iii, pp. 368–9 (*Minutes*, vol. vii, pp. 542 sqq.).
[2] See, in A. Stevens, ibid., vol. iii, pp. 368–9, the praise lavished by the Vice-Chancellor
on the Connexion: 'It is my firm belief that to that body we are indebted for a large
portion of the religious feeling which exists among the general body of the community,
not only of this country, but throughout a great portion of the civilized world besides.'
[3] For the details of the new constitution, see *Minutes*, vol. vii, pp. 548 sqq., 573 sqq.
[4] *Quarterly Review*, February 1835, 'The Church and the Voluntary System', vol. liii,
p. 193 *n.*, p. 197.
[5] H. of L., August 1, 1834 (*Parliamentary Debates*, 3rd Series, vol. xxv, p. 860).
[6] A. Stevens, *History of . . . Methodism*, vol. iii, pp. 290 sqq.
[7] *Christian Advocate*, September 16, 1833. Cf. Pusey to the Rev. R. W. Jelf, February
16, 1834: 'I hope yet some means may be devised by which the Wesleyans at least may
be reunited to the Church' (H. P. Liddon, *Life of E. B. Pusey*, vol. i, p. 286); also the
comic dialogue in Disraeli's *Coningsby* (Book II, ch. ii) between Lord FitzBooby and the
chief agent of the Conservative party. 'The Wesleyans,' said Tadpole, 'we never counted
on the Wesleyans.' 'I am told these Wesleyans are really a very respectable body,' said
Lord FitzBooby, 'I believe there is no very material difference between their tenets and
those of the Establishment. I never heard of them much till lately. We have too long
confounded them with the mass of the Dissenters, but their conduct at several of the
latter elections proves that they are far from being unreasonable and disloyal individuals.
When we come in, something should be done for the Wesleyans, eh, Rigby?'

damage the Wesleyans in the eyes of the public. Only during the four years of the crisis caused by the Warrenites did their number remain almost stationary at about 290,000. Then the upward movement began again. Their number rose in England and Wales from 248,592 in 1830 to 323,178 in 1840.[1]

The attitude of the Wesleyan Methodists was by no means that of the sects which had separated from the parent body, for the very reason that they found the spirit which animated Wesley's 'Connexion' insufficiently democratic. The members of the 'New Methodist Connexion'; the Primitive Methodists, the Bible Christians, the Protestant Methodists, and those who under Warren's leadership had just founded a body known as the Associated Methodists supported the Congregationalists and Baptists in their demand for a democratic and secular State. In England these groups formed together the main body of the host arrayed against Anglicanism. But if the right wing of this army was weakened by the hostility of the orthodox section represented by the Wesleyans, its left wing was simultaneously weakened by the desertion of the Socinians and Latitudinarians. The former maintained that the democratic Protestants, the Political Dissenters,[2] damaged the Christian faith by their attempt to damage the Church, and while they mingled in party strife forgot heaven and thought only of earth. The latter brought the contrary charge; for them the Political Dissenters were religious fanatics hide-bound by dogma. Thus the intellectual liberalism of which they boasted produced an unexpected result. It made them after all indulgent towards the Established Church.

The Nonconformist press was divided. Neither the *Eclectic Review*, the traditional organ of the Nonconformist middle-class, nor the *Congregational Magazine* was in favour of disestablishment. And if the *Christian Advocate* demanded the separation of Church and State, the *Patriot* hesitated and wavered. The attitude of the Unitarians is particularly instructive. Since they rejected the doctrine of the Divinity of Jesus Christ and throughout the early years of the century had professed almost without disguise a

[1] See the annual statistics: 1830, 248,592; 1831, 249,119 (the political crisis exerted a retarding effect); 1832, 256,272; 1833, 279,970; 1834, 291,939; 1835, 290,988; 1836 293,132; 1837, 292,693; 1838, 296,801; 1839, 307,068; 1840, 323,178.

[2] The expression appears to date from this period. It was soon to be the current designation of those Dissenters who meddled in politics. See the *Congregational Magazine* for November 1835: the individuals who are denominated in certain quarters, Political Dissenters (vol. xi, New Series, p. 687).

species of secularism, they had little claim to be regarded as Christians. They were united by close ties of friendship with the Benthamites. The Unitarian Bowring had won the confidence of the aged leader, John Stuart Mill was a contributor to the organ of the sect, *Fox's Monthly Repository*, and collaborated with the Unitarians in founding the *London Review*. And on the other hand, the Unitarians were at open war with the Congregationalists and Baptists who were doing their utmost to expel them from the old Committee of the Three Denominations and even to deprive them of their chapels, which, they maintained, had been founded for Trinitarian teaching and therefore must not be left in the hands of ministers who violated their founders' intention. The Unitarians, however, far from sharing the Radicalism of the more orthodox sects, refused to support their extreme demands, disestablishment and the expulsion of the Bishops from the House of Lords. Their ministers were educated men who frequented the company of statesmen, advocated a policy of compromise, and blamed the Congregationalist 'fanatics' for jeopardizing by their impracticable programme the legitimate objects for which they were contending. 'I was summoned,' wrote a minister, 'to the *United Committee* (but read *dis*-united) to-day and refused to attend . . . The state of the Dissenters is deplorable. No common understanding, no confidence, disowned almost by the Government . . . In such a condition, men that value sterling principles and entertain a sense of honour, have no other course than to keep aloof.'[1]

The intellectual leaders of the party victorious in 1832, Radicals or advanced Liberals displayed no greater zeal against the Church. Rejecting as they did the Christian creed they had always disliked the Evangelicals, both Anglican and Nonconformist, and among the Nonconformists both those who wished to maintain an established church and those who clamoured for disestablishment. And although the Protestant sects constituted the nucleus of their majorities in the country they could not refrain from irritating them by gratuitous insults. Brougham giving evidence before a committee of the House of Lords ascribed the growth of crime to the antinomian teaching of the Protestant fanatics.[2] Speaking at a public meeting Roebuck styled a Nonconformist 'book of'

[1] Rev. Robert Aspland to Rev. R. Brook Aspland, March 17, 1834 (Brook Aspland, *Memoirs of . . . the Rev. Robert Aspland*, 1850, p. 535).
[2] J. Waddington, *Congregational History Continuation to 1850*, pp. 389-90.

religious 'instruction' 'wretched farrago'.[1] Two or three years later the defeats suffered by a number of important Radicals at the election of 1837 will be universally attributed to the abstention of Puritans unwilling to vote for these too liberal moralists.[2] All the members of this group continued to make formal declarations in favour of disestablishment, but it is by no means so certain that their heart was in the cause. Certain High Churchmen were beginning to regard disestablishment as preferable to an establishment which involved the enslavement of the Church to a sceptical and unchristian state. The Liberals on the other hand were beginning to value an establishment which enabled Whig ministers to place over the Church Bishops free from fanaticism. Were the Church disestablished, Whately would not be Archbishop of Dublin. Nor must we forget the disillusionment which about this time affected several members of the intelligentsia. John Stuart Mill, educated from infancy by his father to be the future head of the Utilitarian school, has related in his classic autobiography the crisis through which he passed. His friends, Maurice and Sterling, came under the influence of Coleridge and German philosophy, and in turn entered the Anglican priesthood. Mill, though unable to follow their example, experienced the same intellectual distress they had suffered before their conversion, and felt keenly the failure of Utilitarianism to satisfy the heart, the need to complete it by borrowing from some external source, and called in Coleridge to supply the deficiencies of Bentham. Chance brought him into contact with two disciples of Saint Simon, missionaries of their sect who had come from Paris to confront Irving's millennium and Owen's with the millennium of Bazard and Enfantin, and he believed that in the religion of Saint Simon he had found the new faith which without forcing him back to the outworn dogmas of the past, would fill the void in his soul. Carlyle, now his intimate friend, felt the same influence. For two or three years the youthful Carlyle and the still younger Mill subscribed to a common philosophy, and held communion with each other in Saint Simon. Both regarded the Church as doomed sooner or later to dissolution, but they were unconcerned with the vicissitudes of a battle they regarded as already won. In the language of their Saint Simonian teachers they were attempting to forecast the positive system which would

---

[1] *British Magazine*, February 1, 1834 (vol. v, p. 224 *n.*).   [2] See below, p. 163, *n.* 3.

be set up after the inevitable demolition had been accomplished, and in tracing the programme of the era of re-organization which must follow the era of destructive criticism inaugurated by the revolutions of 1789 and 1830.[1] Mill's attitude was by no means reactionary nor strictly speaking was Carlyle's, but it was not aggressive.

4

The preceding analysis has shewn the elements which composed the main body of the forces hostile to the Church. They were the Irish Catholics on the one hand, on the other the Protestant Non-conformists with the exception of the Wesleyans—that is to say foreigners and Dissenters. At any moment this ill-assorted alliance might arouse public indignation. On the other hand the growth of a party of ultra-clericals might alarm the nation and weaken the Church by the civil strife of warring parties. This, however, did not in fact happen in 1833. The first effect of the High Church revival was to unite in a close bond all the friends of the Church, however diverse their doctrinal tendencies might be.

We must be on our guard against a mistake natural to those who study the origins of the Oxford movement at the distance of well-nigh a century. Since as everyone knows Newman was later converted to Roman Catholicism, the student is liable to conclude that already in 1833 he felt an irresistible attraction drawing him towards that form of Christianity. In fact when in 1833 Newman and his friends joined forces in a common effort, it was to make war upon the Church of Rome. Was it not the Irish Catholics who, under O'Connell's leadership, had just obtained from the British Parliament the suppression of the ten sees by allying themselves with the bitterest foes of Christianity? Was not the Irish Church Bill the direct result of Cathlic Emancipation which Newman had fought so strenuously four years earlier in clear prevision of its consequences? All the Catholics returned for English constituencies during the last election were Whigs,[2] and it was among the Liberals that Catholicism aroused

[1] J. S. Mill to John Sterling, October 20-22, 1831; to Gustave d'Eichthal, November 30, 1831; to Thomas Carlyle, July 17, 1832, March 9, 1833, April 11-12, 1833 (*Letters of John Stuart Mill*, vol. i, pp. 3, 20, 32, 37, 42).
[2] Election of 1830: five Catholics returned, of whom only one was a Tory; election of 1831: eight Catholics, one Tory; election of 1833: nine Catholics, all Whigs (B. Ward, *Eve of Catholic Emancipation*, vol. iii, pp. 276 sqq.). In the House of Lords in October 1831 only one of the nine Catholic peers voted against the Reform Bill (Lord Shrewsbury's letter to the *Sun*, quoted by Cobbett), *Political Register*, Oct. 29, 1831, vol. lxxiv, pp. 305-6.

sympathy and made converts.[1] Lord Althorp's brother, George Spencer, who had become a zealous Catholic and taken up his residence in Rome, encouraged Wiseman to undertake the conversion of his native country. Thomas Moore, who came of an Irish Catholic stock, an advanced Liberal, and Byron's friend and biographer, wrote in collaboration with a learned English free thinker a novel favourable to Catholicism, his *Travels of an Irish Gentleman in Search of a Religion*.[2] In the intention of Newman and his friends to revive the Church of England by making her once more conscious of her apostolic character was to put her in a condition to resist the assault of the Catholic Liberal alliance. Nor can it be maintained that Newman's judgment of Catholicism would have been more favourable had his acquaintance with that religion extended to French or Italian Catholicism instead of being confined to O'Connell's ochlocracy. For he had just visited Italy, where he had found an ignorant populace and a nobility and middle class free thinking and morally corrupt.[3] And in his opinion the Church of Rome was powerless to resist the 'hellish plague' of the Revolution.[4] On the other hand he had heard a rumour that the orthodox pastors and Lutheran Bishops of Prussia were about to apply for Anglican ordination. The Church of England was the only Church which had passed uninjured through the crisis of the last half century. Now indeed she was menaced in her turn by the spread of the Continental infection. But perhaps, Newman hoped, she would yet have time to

---

[1] See *The Times* of December 15, 1838, for a list of the Catholic converts in the Whig and Liberal party. Besides Lord Spencer's brother, *The Times* mentions Mr. Lisle Philips, Mr. Roche, M.P. for Cork County, Mr. Charles Wolseley, Mr. Bennett, son of the member of Parliament, and Sir Bourchier Wray. *The Times* comments: 'And are there not a hundred more in the ranks of the Liberal party who applaud Lord Morpeth in repeating the words of Pilate, "What is truth?"' For the Protestant orthodoxy of *The Times*, scepticism and Catholicism were the same thing.

[2] *Travels of an Irish Gentleman in search of a Religion*, with notes and illustrations, 1835: The hero, a Catholic, wished to turn Protestant to obtain the hand of Miss . . . and with it an Anglican *living*. But to his disappointment he found himself forced to recognize that Catholicism was in entire conformity with the Primitive Church, whereas Calvinism was a revival of Gnosticism and Manichaeanism. He visited Germany, followed the lectures of Professor Scratchenbach at Göttingen and found German Lutheranism in a state of dissolution. There was nothing for it, a Catholic he must remain.

[3] See his reflections on Papal Rome (characteristically entitled, *Home Thoughts Abroad*) in the *British Magazine*, January 1, 1834 (vol. v, pp. 1 sqq.). See especially on pp. 124–5 a discussion of the question 'How to avoid Popery without giving up the Church'; also Newman to Pusey, Rome, March 19, 1833 (H. P. Liddon, *Life of Edward Bouverie Pusey*, vol. i, pp. 284 sqq.).

[4] Newman to his sister Jemima, March 20, 1833 (*Letters and Correspondence*, vol. i, p. 377).

CHARLES, 2nd. EARL GREY
Sir Thomas Lawrence, P.R.A.
(National Portrait Gallery)

combat it successfully. The prospect flattered his patriotic pride.[1]

Thus the young 'residents of Oxford' when they began the publication of the *Tracts for the Times* towards the close of 1833 were not yet, as we might be inclined at first sight to think, the more or less conscious champions of Catholic belief and practice. Nor is there any reason to assume that the 7,000 clergymen and the 250,000 laymen who signed the addresses to the Archbishop of Canterbury accepted in their entirety the doctrines taught in the Tracts. No doubt the great majority of the signatories had never read them and, if there were any who had read them and disliked their teaching, they did not think it wise to break with the eccentric young thinkers whose alliance was valuable against the common foe. There existed at this time in the Establishment an entire movement favourable to the principles of the High Church which sought to emphasize the ritual and liturgical character of Anglican worship, but had no liking for the doctrinal subtleties of the Oxford theology.[2] Moreover, the two parties, High Church and Low Church, were drawing together under the common danger from the alliance of Catholics and unbelievers.[3] In the Church of Ireland, which had borne the brunt of the first attack,

[1] To his mother, February 28, 1833: 'I begin to hope that England after all is to be the "Land of the Saints" in this dark hour and her Church the salt of the earth' (*Letters and Correspondence*, vol. i, p. 310).

[2] Newman to the Rev. R. H. Froude, November 7, 1833: 'The tracts are spreading and the Evangelicals join us, but deprecate them' (ibid., vol. i, p. 419).

[3] Pusey to the Rev. R. W. Jelf, February 16 1834: 'A strong expression of love for the Church has been called forth by the violence of her enemies, a great union of parties among the clergy; members have withdrawn from the religious societies in which they used to act with Dissenters; and now that the Branch for Foreign Bibles is being formed within the Christian Knowledge Society, I trust that the occasion of confounding Churchmen with Dissenters and disuniting the Church will be removed' (H. P. Liddon, *Life of E. B. Pusey*, vol. i, pp. 285–6). Cf. the letter of a Unitarian minister, Robert Aspland, March 17, 1834 (*Memoirs*, p. 535): 'We have contrived, by our violence and folly, to force into union the hostile parties within the Church and to strengthen the Conservative Party.' *Westminster Review*, January 1836, 'The Fudges in England' (vol. xxiv, p. 79): 'The Orangeman was now a Saint; the clergyman was now an Evangelical. . . . Then did the pious Peeress nominate her moral agent. Then did holiness divide with hyson the attractions of the tea-table. Then did the prayer meeting grow into fashion and the sale of polyglots become a distinct commercial speculation. Then did the clergyman appear in the Sunday School, and the visage of the Tory lawyer show itself where the missionaries were gathered together.' Rev. R. Vaughan, *Thoughts on . . . Religious Parties*, 1838, p. 87: 'The Evangelical Clergy of the present day, while holding the same theological opinions with their devout predecessors who were expelled from the pulpits of the Establishment in 1662, were characterized by a singular absence of sympathy with those conscientious and holy men in their objections to many things in the discipline and worship of the Established Church and in their ardent attachment to the principle of free government.' J. Grant (*Travels in Town*, 1839, vol. ii, p. 108), deplores the unsympathetic attitude of the Anglican Evangelicals towards the Dissenters. They had founded a 'Pastoral Aid Society' in opposition to the City Mission.

the Low Church Party was supreme, and on the other side of St. George's Channel the rivalry between 'Church' and 'Chapel' was unknown. In 1832 the Orange Associations were reorganized on the model of the Irish secret societies, and constituted a vast system of freemasonry at once ultra Protestant and ultra Tory of which the King's brother, the Duke of Cumberland, was president, which established its 'lodges' all over the United Kingdom, and even found entrance into the Army.[1] The promoters of the Factory Bill of 1833, Oastler, Sadler, and Lord Ashley, were all three Evangelicals and all three Tories. Indeed, it was during this critical year, a few months after the passage of the Reform Bill, that English Evangelicalism may be said to have reached its apogee. It constituted the essence of Methodist preaching, and in their hatred of Catholics and Latitudinarians, the Wesleyans were drawing closer to the Church from which they were sprung. It had become predominant in the sects hostile to the Establishment, and its supremacy had produced the unexpected result of cooling the ardour with which Latitudinarians and free thinkers had hitherto attacked the Anglican Church. And within the Church the influence of the Evangelicals was growing stronger every day. The number of clergymen who had given their formal adherence to the party was estimated at between two and three thousand.[2] The parochial clergy were no longer the keen hunters and hard drinkers they had been a few years earlier. By their preaching and example the Evangelicals had enforced a stricter observance of decorum, and a more obvious regard for the dignity of their vocation. And in the last resort it is to their influence that we must attribute the moral reform which Thomas Arnold and several others were effecting at this time with enormous success in the Anglican public schools. Among the aristocracy which governed the country the Evangelicals were bringing the duel into discredit.[3] Among the lower classes they were attacking the

[1] For the Orange Lodges, see H. of C., February 23, 1836 (*Parliamentary Debates*, 3rd Series, vol. lxxxi, pp. 779 sqq.), also *London and Westminster Review*, January–April 1836, 'Orange Conspiracy' (vol. iii and xxv, pp. 181 sqq.).

[2] Robert Vaughan, *Thoughts on the Past and Present State of Religious Parties in England*, 1838, pp. 86–7: some thousands. J. Grant (*Travels in Town*, 1839, vol. ii, p. 105): 'I should suppose there could not have been' [twenty years before] 'one Evangelical clergyman for fifteen or twenty of an opposite class. Now, perhaps, the Evangelical clergy may be in the proportion of one to five of those who are merely moral preachers.' He speaks of a demonstration attended by 3,000 Evangelical clergymen.

[3] For the decline of duelling, see the entertaining account in Sp. Walpole's *History of England*, vol. iv. The total disappearance of the duel belongs to a slightly later period.

use of intoxicating liquors: the first Temperance Societies had just been founded in imitation of an American model,[1] and the House of Commons was shortly to appoint a committee to consider the advisability of passing legislation to diminish drunkenness.[2] The credit of the two great humanitarian measures passed by the new Parliament, the emancipation of the slaves and the protection of child labour in factories, belongs, as we have seen, to the Evangelicals even more than to the Radicals. Sir Andrew Agnew introduced annually a bill to prohibit Sunday work in any form whatsoever. He was always defeated, but the number of votes recorded in favour of his Sabbatarian bill increased every year, and every year the habits of the people, steeped ever more completely in Evangelical piety, rendered more superfluous the legal enactment of a rule everyone freely obeyed.[3]

Men of letters disliked the Evangelicals for their narrow Puritanism, men of science for their intellectual weakness. Nevertheless, during the nineteenth century their religion was the moral cement of English society. Their influence invested the British aristocracy with an almost Stoic dignity, restrained the plutocrats

[1] For the foundation of the British and Foreign Temperance Society, see the documents quoted in the *British Magazine*, March 1, 1832 (vol. i, pp. 54 sqq.). *The Gentleman's Magazine*, January 1836, p. 60, mentions two journals devoted to the cause of temperance, the *British and Foreign Temperance Advocate* and the *British and Foreign Temperance Herald*.

[2] *Abstract of Evidence before the Select Committee appointed by Parliament to inquire into the Extent, Causes, and Consequences of the Prevailing Vice of Intoxication, and to ascertain whether any legislative measure can be desired to prevent the further spread of so great a National Evil*, 1835. It is interesting to observe that it was only after considerable hesitation that the *Eclectic Review*, the traditional organ of Dissent, in an article commenting on this publication (October 1835, 'Claim of Temperance Societies', vol. xiv, p. 283), decided in favour of legislative interference. The budget of 1834, four years after the budget of 1830, shows the first sign of a change in public opinion. If the tax on spirits was still further reduced, the cost of licences was raised (*Annual Register*, 1834, p. 291).

[3] H. of C., July 3, 1832 (*Parliamentary Debates*, 3rd Series, vol. xiv, pp. 50 sqq.); March 20, 1833 (ibid., vol. xvi, pp. 898 sqq.); May 16, 1833 (ibid., vol. xvii, pp. 1325 sqq.); July 9, 1833 (ibid., vol. xix, pp. 384 sqq.); March 11, 1834 (ibid., vol. xxii, pp. 54 sqq.); April 30, May 6, 7, 21 (ibid., vol. xxiii, pp. 514, 587, 746, 1176); June 26, July 2, 7, 1834 (ibid., vol. xxiv, pp. 850, 1094, 1286). *The Patriot*, a Nonconformist organ, December 4, 1833, mentions three societies founded to secure the strict observance of the Sabbath: Sunday Trading Suppression Society, Sabbath Protection Society, Sabbath Observance Society. According to Plumptree (H. of C., March 21, 1838, *Parl. Deb.*, vol. xii, p. 1177), petitions bearing 280,000 signatures were sent up to Parliament during 1836. The opposition of Roebuck and several of his Radical friends to this Sabbatarianism cost them their seats at the General Election of 1837. See Roebuck's speech, H. of C., May 17 and 19, 1837, on the question of permitting Sunday travel on the railways, and June 7, 1837, on the general question of Sunday observance (*Parl. Deb.*, 3rd Series, vol. xxxviii, pp. 856 sqq., 898 sqq., 1229 sqq.). Cf. *Greville Memoirs*, May 23, 1834, and for a general account of Sir Andrew Agnew's bill, *Random Recollections of the House of Commons* (J. Grant), 1836, pp. 372-3.

who had newly risen from the masses from debauchery and vulgar ostentation and placed over the proletariat a select body of workmen enamoured of virtue and capable of self-restraint. Evangelicalism was thus the conservative force which restored in England the balance momentarily destroyed by the explosion of the revolutionary forces. Before many months it was evident that the agitation in favour of disestablishment had received a decisive check.

III VICTORY OF THE CHURCH
FALL OF THE WHIG ADMINISTRATION

I

In Scotland, where, as we have seen, the movement in favour of disestablishment had its birth, it suddenly assumed a different character. The reform of the Parliamentary franchise of 1832 had been followed in 1833 by a reform of the municipal corporations, which ceased to be close corporations, recruited by co-optation, and were henceforward elected by the ten-pound householders, that is to say, by a large number of the lower middle class, the class in which the Dissenters and the Voluntary Church Associations were most largely represented. But according to the constitution of the Presbyterian Church of Scotland every municipal corporation sent a representative to the General Assembly of the Church. Accordingly these Dissenters and advocates of disestablishment suddenly found themselves responsible for the government of the Church which hitherto they had attacked from without. The change had a decisive effect on the history of the national Church. If there were Evangelicals in Scotland who looked to the voluntary system to safeguard the integrity of the Christian faith, endangered in the national Church by the system of lay patronage, there were others, for example Dr. Thomson of Glasgow, and Dr. Chalmers at Edinburgh, who were members of the Church and did not despair of bringing her back to the purity of her original institution.[1] At the Assembly of 1834 they were in a majority. To compete with the Dissenters and make provisions for the spiritual needs of the growing population of

---

[1] Rev. W. Hanna, *Memoirs of . . . Thomas Chalmers*, vol. iii, pp. 341 sqq.

the large towns they had founded chapels by voluntary subscription. On their demand the General Assembly granted seats in their body to the ministers of these chapels, and at the same time they carried a statute which explicitly exempted the chapels from the right of nomination claimed by the lay patron of the parish in whose territory they had been built.[1] They were further successful in obtaining from the Assembly a decision of far greater importance. By a majority of forty-six and conditionally upon ratification by the majority of Presbyteries, the Assembly granted for the first time to a majority of the parishioners duly enrolled a right of veto on the presentation made by the local patron.[2] The decision embittered a struggle which for years to come would afflict Scottish Presbyterianism. But for the moment at least the ground of the conflict had changed. The malcontents no longer demanded the separation of Church and State, but the reform of the Church, that the Church should be rendered democratic rather than the State secular.

In England the setback was even more evident. It soon became clear that if the agitation against the Establishment was noisy it was not dangerous. The Political Dissenters and a handful of Radicals demanded disestablishment, but the London shopkeepers were agitating simultaneously for the abolition of the assessed taxes, and the Lancashire workers for a ten-hour day, and the variety of these demands weakened the agitation. The Dissenters, moreover, were dismayed by the success of the Anglican counter-demonstration organized from Oxford, which indeed surprised even its promoters, following, as it did, so closely the riots of November 1831 and the burning of the Bishop's palace at Bristol. It strengthened the partisans of order, and first and foremost the Whig ministers, in their determination not to lay hands on the Establishment. Lord Grey gave a chilling reception to the delegates who came to present a petition in favour of disestablishment,[3] and replied by a panegyric of the Established Church. During the session of 1833 Faithfull, the Radical member for Brighton, had moved resolutions of a revolutionary character affirming that an Established Church was of no benefit to the

---

[1] 4 and 5 Will. IV, cap. 41. Rev. W. Hanna, *Memoirs of . . . Thomas Chalmers*, vol. iii, pp. 446 sqq.
[2] Rev. W. Hanna, ibid., vol. iii, pp. 360-1. *Annual Register*, 1834 p. 220. *Quarterly Review*, December 1840, 'Affairs of the Church of Scotland' (vol. lxvii, pp. 203 sqq.).
[3] *Morning Chronicle*, April 30, 1834.

country and that Parliament had the right to apply to purposes of national utility the greater part, if not the whole, of her endowments. Cobbett had supported him. But the two stood entirely alone; no other voice was raised in their support.[1] In 1834, no motion was brought forward in favour of disestablishment. If Faithfull had been willing to renew last year's attempt, it is very doubtful if he would have had the support even of Cobbett. For before he died in June 1835 Cobbett had begun to return by imperceptible degrees to his original Toryism. A born demagogue, it would be unfair to say that he watched the movements of popular feeling in order to conform his views to the momentary whim of the rabble, it would be truer to say that he shared its whims himself. No longer as in 1831 was he forward with the cry 'Down with the Bishops'. No doubt he would have been far more pleased to raise the cry 'Down with the Irish'. A motion was indeed made in favour of excluding the Bishops from the House of Lords. But it was a mere formality, and secured only fifty-eight votes.[2]

2

An alternative to disestablishment was to reform the Church. One day Brougham suddenly introduced two measures of Church Reform,[3] the first dealing with pluralism, the second with non-residence. It was an empty gesture. Nothing further was heard of either bill. But at least the Cabinet could attempt to satisfy the more moderate and more pressing demands of the Dissenters and their allies in the campaign against the Church. They made the attempt, but it failed.

The Government began with the question of the Church rates. They amounted for the whole of England to about £550,000 a year, of which £250,000 went to keep the buildings in repair. The Government now proposed to allocate the annual sum of £250,000 to the Church. But it would no longer be raised by local rates. It would be included in the budget as a first charge on the proceeds of the land tax. The proposal proved equally objectionable to both parties, Dissenters and Churchmen. What

[1] H. of C., April 16, 1833 (*Parliamentary Debates*, 3rd Series, vol. xvii, pp. 178 sqq.).
[2] H. of C., March 13, 1834 (ibid., 3rd Series, vol. xxii, pp. 131 sqq.).
[3] H. of L., May 16, 1834 (ibid., vol. xxiii, pp. 1103 sqq.). Brougham's introduction of the bills appears to have been out of order. See the debate on this point, H. of L., May 23, 1834 (ibid., 3rd Series, vol. xxiii, pp. 1103 sqq., 1250 sqq.).

did the Dissenters care whether the sum paid to the Church were a tax or a rate? A boon forsooth to the tax-payer! Did the Government mean to make fun of them? What they wanted was the complete and unqualified abolition of the Church rates. This was what the Irish had just obtained, and they had already devised a method of obtaining it in every parish in England, a strike of the vestry. The compromise put forward by the Government failed. On April 21, Lord Althorp's motion was lost by a majority of 256 to 140 votes.[1] The matter was dropped.

The Government also attempted to settle the question of the tithe. It was an annual charge on English agriculture of over £4,000,000 a year, four-fifths of which was received by the Church.[2] And the burden was the more intolerable because the amount of the tithe depended on the amount of produce. The more labour therefore the cultivator bestowed upon his land, the more tithe he must pay. Every year he must haggle over the sum due, and fight it out with the clergy. On April 15, Lord Althorp proposed another system.[3] The tithe would be determined on a new principle. In each county an average would be struck between the amount of the tithe and the amount of the rent and the figure thus determined would be taken as the basis on which to calculate the tithe, which would therefore vary with the rental, instead of with the annual produce of the soil. And the tithe payer would be allowed to redeem his tithe by an easy and equitable method on payment of a sum equal to twenty-five years' tithe. The bill met with the approval of all parties in the Commons. Peel, however, raised certain objections of detail, which won the assent of the House. The proposal was dropped for the session.

The Dissenters complained of the matrimonial monopoly possessed by the Established Church. With the exception of the Jews and Quakers for whose benefit special legislation had been passed, everyone was obliged to be married by an Anglican clergyman. More than any others the Unitarians were bent on removing this grievance; for in the course of the marriage ceremony they were obliged to commit perjury by affirming the doctrine of the Trinity. Indeed, it was for this reason that they had displayed such annoyance at the agitation lately set on foot

[1] H. of C., April 21, 1834 (*Parliamentary Debates*, 3rd Series, vol. xxii, pp. 1012 sqq.).
[2] A. L. Lowell, *The Government of England*, vol. ii, p. 375.
[3] H. of C., April 15, 1834 (*Parl. Deb.*, 3rd Series, vol. xxii, pp. 818 sqq.).

by the Congregationalists in favour of disestablishment. Such an extreme demand would, they feared, injure the prospects of the reform on which they had set their heart. Lord Holland undertook to plead their cause with the ministers, and the latter promised to give them satisfaction.[1] But the bill to this effect introduced by Lord John Russell still required that the banns should be published in the parish Church,[2] and he was defeated by the uncompromising attitude of the Dissenters. On February 28, Sir John Campbell, who had just been made Attorney General, stood for re-election for the borough of Dudley. He was defeated and the Dissenters boasted that they had refused him their vote to teach the Whigs a lesson. The bill was withdrawn.

The Dissenters also demanded that Parliament should complete the work begun by the repeal of the Test Act and Catholic Emancipation by granting them the right, from which they were still debarred, to obtain university degrees in England. Having failed in the attempt to satisfy their wishes in regard to marriage the Government tackled this further problem. Two solutions were possible.

The first was to found in addition to the two Anglican universities of Oxford and Cambridge a new University which would be invested with the legal right to confer degrees and would be open to students of every denomination. The undenominational University whose foundation in London ten years earlier we have already related, petitioned for a charter of incorporation, and the ministers left to themselves might well have granted the request. But they dared not face on the floor of the House the opposition of the Universities of Oxford and Cambridge, armed as they were with knotty objections on technical points of law. The question was submitted for examination to the Privy Council, that is to say it was shelved.[3]

The other possible solution, the solution best adapted to gratify the Dissenters' impatience, was to grant them by Act of Parliament the right to obtain degrees at the old Universities. At the end of March a petition to that effect signed by sixty-three members of the University of Cambridge was presented in the

[1] R. Brook Aspland, *Memoirs of . . . the Rev. Robert Aspland*, pp. 534-5.
[2] H. of C., February 25, 1834 (*Parliamentary Debates*, 3rd Series, vol. xxi, pp. 776 sqq.).
[3] H. of C., February 27, 1834 (ibid., 3rd Series, vol. xxi, pp. 875-6). *Quarterly Review*, June 1834, 'Revolutions of 1688 and 1831' (vol. li, p. 516). *Greville Memoirs*, April 25, May 11, 1834.

House of Commons by Spring Rice,[1] and in the House of Lords by Lord Grey himself,[2] and a member of the Commons brought in a bill giving effect to the petition which received the unanimous support of the Cabinet. But the opposition was determined.

It was argued, Parliament had no right to pass such an enactment. The colleges were corporations and an Act of Parliament could not equitably set aside the terms of the foundations originally made in their favour. It was even alleged that the union between Church and State would be imperilled by the reform. The colleges of Oxford and Cambridge were the expression of that union in its intellectual aspect. They were destined to educate side by side the ruling aristocracy and the clergy of a Christian nation. It was therefore most important that they should retain their Anglican atmosphere. Peel, who on other questions favoured a policy of moderate concessions to the Nonconformist demands, delivered on the University question a speech warmly supporting the clerical position.[3] The bill, which passed the Commons by an overwhelming majority, was as everybody expected thrown out by the Lords at the first reading after the Prime Minister and the Lord Chancellor had defended it in a very half-hearted fashion.[4]

3

All these hasty and inconsistent attempts to satisfy the Nonconformists betrayed the anxiety of the Government. The ministers knew that if their candidates were to be returned, they could not dispense with the Nonconformist vote. But they also knew that while the political Dissenters were strong enough to make their support indispensable to the Whigs throughout the country, they were not strong enough to win the majority of the nation to their views. Their policy therefore was necessarily awkward and hesitating. But we must not imagine that the discussion of these questions had engaged to any considerable extent the attention of Parliament, the only question debated at all thoroughly being the opening of the Universities to those who were not members of the Anglican church. As in 1833 the Irish question was in the forefront. Such was O'Connell's will, to which the ministers were

[1] H. of C., March 24, 1834 (*Parliamentary Debates*, 3rd Series, vol. xxii, pp. 569 sqq.).
[2] H. of L., March 21, 1834 (ibid., 3rd Series, vol. xxii, pp. 497 sqq.).
[3] H. of C., June 20, 1834 (ibid., 3rd Series, vol. xxiv, pp. 697 sqq.).
[4] H. of L., August 1, 1834 (ibid., 3rd Series, vol. xxv, pp. 840 sqq., 861 sqq.).

obliged to submit, to the delight of the Conservatives who enjoyed witnessing the bondage of their Whig opponents. Every day the prestige of the Government was lowered by the disclosure of some new Irish scandal followed by a clumsy attempt to deny the damaging facts, a row in the House, calls to order by the Speaker, and challenges to a duel. The English had emancipated the Catholics and reformed the franchise; their reward was the degradation of their parliamentary government to the level of Irish mob rule.

O'Connell raised the question of repealing the Act of Union for the first time during the debate on the address, into which the Cabinet had decided to introduce an explicit repudiation of Irish Home Rule, two months later in the form of a motion made by himself. He spoke for five hours on end.[1] But O'Connell, whose political methods were tortuous and indirect, did not expect any practical result from this demonstration of eloquence. His sole aim was to irritate and intimidate the British public.

Far more pressing was the question of the tithe which came before Parliament on February 20. Indeed, it was scarcely possible to avoid dealing with the matter when once the state had intervened between the clergy and the farmers and by a statute passed in 1833[2] had undertaken to receive the Irish tithe on behalf of the Church. And in 1833 the Government had even issued Exchequer Bonds to the amount of £1,000,000 to advance to those to whom Irish tithe was owing the sums due for the years 1831, 1832 and 1833.[3] Either the State must now contrive to collect the amount they had advanced or the English tax-payer would be saddled with a permanent obligation to pay the Irish clergy the tithe the Irish peasants refused. In 1834 to settle the question finally Littleton introduced a bill modelled directly upon the bill Stanley had introduced in 1832.[4] It is unnecessary to set out the details of a measure which never became law. It need only be said that he proposed to commute the tithe into a land tax payable, not by the actual cultivator but by the landlord, to authorize redemption, and to hand over the entire proceeds of the tax to a body of

---

[1] H. of C., April 22, 1834 (*Parliamentary Debates*, 3rd Series, vol. xxii, pp. 1092 sqq.).

[2] H. of C., June 12, 1833: Lord Althorp's speech (ibid., 3rd Series, vol. xviii, p. 659; 3 and 4 Will. IV, cap. 100.

[3] H. of C., February 20, 1834 (ibid., 3rd Series, vol. xxi, p. 572 sqq.).

[4] 2 and 3 Will. IV, cap. 119. Cf. H. of C., July 5, 1832: Stanley's speech (ibid., 3rd Series, vol. xiv, pp. 95 sqq.).

ecclesiastical commissioners for distribution among the Irish Clergy.

Once again the Government implicitly refused to admit that the Irish clergy were overpaid and that the State had the right to apply a portion of their endowments to purposes of public utility. To the vehement protests of O'Connell and Sheil, Stanley replied on May 6 with his usual brutality and refused point blank to yield an inch. Thereupon, Lord John Russell believed himself released from the undertaking he had scrupulously observed for the past year and free at last to speak out. He therefore declared that in his opinion 'the Revenues of the Church of Ireland were larger than necessary for the religious and moral instruction of the persons belonging to that Church and for the stability of the Church itself'.[1] He was aware, he said, that this declaration would bring him into conflict with men who were his dear friends, and whom he held in high esteem, but he had a sacred duty to perform towards Ireland. Thus all the efforts made for the past year to preserve the unity of the Cabinet were rendered fruitless. The dreaded split had come. The English Radicals now took the field. Henry George Ward announced his intention to move a resolution in the Commons that the endowments of the Irish Church must be reduced. He was acting, it was said, as the mouthpiece of Lord Durham who had resigned from the Cabinet a year earlier and was apparently preparing to put himself forward as the popular leader in opposition to the Government. On the 27th the debate opened with an important speech by Ward who was supported by Grote, and before Lord Althorp could reply he received, while the House was sitting, an official intimation from Lord Grey that four ministers, Stanley, Graham, Lord Ripon, and the Duke of Richmond, had resigned. He moved the immediate adjournment of the House.

It was a victory for Peel. Ever since 1832 Peel had been at war with Wellington,[2] and their relations had never been so embittered as during the previous winter. For Wellington had been elected Chancellor of Oxford University, a position which many of his friends had wished to secure for Peel and Peel felt considerable chagrin at his disappointment.[3] Wellington now made over-

[1] H. of C., May 6, 1834 (*Parliamentary Debates*, 3rd Series, vol. xxiii, p. 666).
[2] Note by Sir Robert Peel, May 10, 1834 (C. S. Parker, *Sir Robert Peel*, vol. ii, p. 236 sqq.).
[3] C. S. Parker, ibid., vol. ii, pp. 227 sqq. *Greville Memoirs*, June 15, 1834.

tures to Peel and informed him that, in the event of the King inviting the Conservatives to take office, he was prepared to take the second place and serve under him.[1] On the day following Stanley's and Graham's resignation King William, receiving on his birthday a body of delegates from the Irish clergy, made a declaration, marked by his characteristic volubility and prolixity,[2] of attachment to the Church and hostility to her foes. And in the welcome with which his speech was greeted by public opinion, Peel and those who shared his views discovered a good omen for their cause. On the whole events had worked out as Peel had hoped and foretold for the past two years. On the double question of Ireland and the Church the Government was yielding to Radical pressure, and its compliance was forcing the moderate Whigs into the arms of a revived Tory party led by Sir Robert. The Cabinet was plainly doomed in the near future. For the moment it contrived to make good its losses without increasing the representation of the advanced Liberals. For the Government could not afford to offend Lord Lansdowne, who seems to have actually sent in his resignation,[3] and Lord Grey himself, who was weary of office. Lord Durham was kept out of office and four Whigs chosen. Lord Conyngham replaced the Duke of Richmond as Postmaster General, Lord Auckland succeeded Graham at the Admiralty, Lord Carlile became Lord Privy Seal in place of Lord Ripon, and Spring Rice Colonial Secretary instead of Stanley. Three peers and only one member of the Lower House! The Government was afraid to submit the new ministers to the test of a by-election. Spring Rice, however, who alone of the four was obliged to stand for re-election, managed to secure his return for Cambridge. His majority consisted of no more than a few votes and he owed it to Nonconformist support. In Parliament the Government contrived to play off a device first conceived by Brougham,[4] and prevent the defection of Stanley and Graham by appointing a committee of inquiry to examine whether the endowments of the Church were really excessive.[5]

[1] Arbuthnot to Sir Robert Peel, May 12, 1834 (C. S. Parker, *Sir Robert Peel*, vol. ii, pp. 240 sqq.). [2] *Annual Register*, 1834, pp. 43 sqq. [3] Sir D. L. Marchant, *Memoir of Lord Althorp*, pp. 488–9. *The Times*, June 2, 1839, remarks that 'Lord Auckland and Mr. Spring Rice are supposed to be mere echoes of Lord Lansdowne's sentiments'. [4] Lord John Russell, *Recollections and Suggestions*, p. 122. [5] H. of C., June 2, 1834: Lord Althorp's speech (*Parliamentary Debates*, 3rd Series, vol. xxiv, pp. 11 sqq.).

Ward's motion was thus shelved by a step which was tantamount to raising the previous question. At the same time the Government introduced into the Tithes Bill a series of extremely complicated amendments all of which were concessions to Radical and Irish demands and were bitterly contested by Stanley.[1] But while the debates pursued their course amid excitement and confusion, the existence of the Cabinet was suddenly jeopardized by another incident. If this time the Church was not concerned, Ireland was.

The Coercion Act was an annual measure and expired on April 1. There could be no doubt of its success. Statistics showed a rapid decrease in the amount of crime in every district where it had been put into force. The Government decided to continue its provisions while relaxing their severity. The clauses which set up courts martial for the trial of Irish offences were removed. But two days later, on July 1, when Lord Grey explained the new Coercion Bill in the House of Lords, O'Connell came forward in the Commons with revelations which threw the ministerial ranks into confusion. It became known that the advanced section of the Cabinet, disappointed with the spirit which had governed its reconstruction, had entered into a direct intrigue with O'Connell behind Lord Grey's back. The original idea was Brougham's. Lord Althorp had sanctioned the negotiations, which Littleton, the Irish Secretary, had conducted in person, and the agreement reached had been approved by Lord Wellesley, the Viceroy of Ireland. Littleton had promised O'Connell that he would not ask for the renewal of the Coercion Act, and under no circumstances would he propose to renew the clause forbidding public meetings. O'Connell on his part had revoked the orders he had just given for a political agitation on a large scale to be carried on both in Ireland and in Great Britain. He now declared himself betrayed.

4

On July 7, Lord Althorp resigned. After the revelations just made he did not consider himself in a position to defend the Coercion Bill in the Commons. On the 8th Lord Grey also resigned. Deprived of Lord Althorp's support in the Lower House he felt himself unequal to sustain the burden of office. On the 9th both resignations were made public and the Government found

---

[1] H. of C., July 4, 1834 (*Parliamentary Debates*, 3rd Series, vol. xxiv, pp. 1146 sqq.).

itself without a leader in either House. Had it ceased to exist? Not yet. The King sent for the Home Secretary, Lord Melbourne, the most conservative member of the Cabinet who two years before had accepted the Reform Bill only with reluctance. He asked him to attempt to form a Coalition Government with the support of Wellington, Peel, and Stanley. Melbourne explained that the suggestion was impracticable. Wellington, Peel, and Stanley could not join the Cabinet without repudiating every principle for which they had been contending during the past month.[1] Meanwhile, he was doing his utmost to persuade Lord Althorp to remain in the Cabinet. Lord Althorp was anxious to be quit of office, and held out for a time. A report spread that Lord Melbourne would resign and the King send for Wellington and Peel. In the end, however, Lord Althorp gave way and the Cabinet remained as it was with Melbourne as Prime Minister.[2] Lord Grey alone had departed.

Melbourne wound up the business of the session. The Coercion Bill, modified to satisfy O'Connell, was passed by the Commons and accepted by the Lords. The Tithe Bill, already drastically amended in May and June, underwent further alteration to satisfy his demands. It was, however, thrown out by the Lords. The discussion of the Poor Law Amendment Bill was wound up. Thus, when Parliament adjourned for tne holidays the intrigue hatched in June had apparently succeeded. First Stanley and his friends, then Lord Grey had been got rid of and the conspirators, Brougham, Lord Althorp, Littleton, and Lord Wellesley had kept their places. But it had been conducted so clumsily and with such fiction and hesitation that their success reflected little honour on the plotters. The real victor of the crisis was O'Connell.

Returning to Ireland as soon as Parliament adjourned he once more adopted an attitude of irreconcilable hostility to the British Government. He suggested an alliance between the Irish Catholics and the English Radicals with the object of replacing the House of Lords by an elective second Chamber. He advised the Irish peasants that when the tithe became due in November to meet the clergy with passive resistance. He continued nevertheless to

---

[1] *Lord Melbourne's Papers*, pp. 203–4. Greville's account, July 17, is incorrect.

[2] Lord Melbourne took the Treasury and left the Home Office to Lord Duncannon, who was raised to the peerage (of England) 'in consequence', as the *Annual Register* explains (1834, p. 124), 'of a rule that not more than two of the principal secretaries of state should be in the House of Commons'.

fight on a double front by employing constitutional as well as revolutionary methods, and he wrote to the Government to ask that the personnel of the Irish Executive should be changed so as to meet the wishes of the Irish Catholics.[1] In the Cabinet Lord John Russell now advocated the adoption of a bold policy. A special session of Parliament should be called before November when O'Connell had arranged to open his campaign of passive resistance. Parliament should then be asked to pass a Tithe Bill to reimburse the Treasury from the endowments of the Church the entire amount advanced to the tithe owners. It should also be invited to carry further the reform of the Irish Church by suppressing every benefice in which the number of churchmen did not amount to a tenth of the inhabitants.[2] Lord Melbourne was as hostile as the King himself to Lord John's proposal and his attitude had the support of the majority of his Cabinet and no doubt, though that was not so certain, of the majority of his party. Was he not liable nevertheless to find himself one day under the necessity of adopting a policy so distasteful? He began to long for a crisis which would transfer, temporarily at least, the burden of office to the shoulders of the Opposition.

Providentially an event occurred which released Melbourne from his difficult situation. Lord Spencer died. His son, Lord Althorp, succeeded to his father's title and thus went to the Upper House.[3] His position as Chancellor of the Exchequer and leader of the Commons was vacant. Should he be replaced by a second-rate politician, for example Spring Rice or Abercromby? The honour of the party would suffer from so mediocre a choice. Everything seemed to point to Lord John Russell. He bore an important name, famous in the annals of the party. For the last four years he had acted as Lord Althorp's lieutenant. But we know what his attitude had been during the past six months and

---

[1] O'Connell to Lord Duncannon, September 2, 6, 1834 (*Correspondence of O'Connell*, vol. i, pp. 473, 477). Sp. Walpole, *The Life of Lord John Russell*, vol. i, pp. 206–7).

[2] Lord John Russell to Lord Melbourne, September 22, 1834 (*Early Correspondence of Lord John Russell*, vol. ii, pp. 46–7).

[3] This death and its consequence would appear to have been long expected with impatience by the Protestant party. See Lord Kenyon's letter of August 13, 1833, quoted by Harris, H. of C., February 23, 1836: 'I am glad to hear that several persons of judgment think we might have a Government with which the House of Commons would act. If so, it is a pity that the Hero of Waterloo and others would not act so as to have obtained such a Ministry during the existing session. When Parliament is prorogued, it is well known nothing can be done, unless some death of importance occurs.' (*Parliamentary Debates*, 3rd Series, vol. xxxi, p. 800.)

his demands during the past month. He would no doubt exact conditions. Possibly Lord Lansdowne and Spring Rice would refuse to accept them and leave the Government as Lord Stanley had done in May and Lord Grey in July. Then for the third time the Government would be faced with the difficulty it had managed to elude on the two previous occasions. How could the Whig administration be reconstructed without admitting Radicals into the Cabinet?

The King objected to making the Government Radical. Lord Melbourne was equally opposed to the step. To gain his point he had only to explain to the King the situation such as we have just described it. He professed himself ready to retain office under these difficult circumstances. But he earnestly begged that no personal consideration for himself should keep His Majesty from taking any other course he might deem advisable. The King summoned him to Brighton and informed him that after careful consideration he did not consider he would be acting fairly towards him if he asked him to continue in a position 'so precarious', and had decided to send for Wellington. Melbourne, who had arranged to drive back to London, undertook to deliver at Apsley House the letter in which the King invited Wellington to take office.[1]

Melbourne had wished in vain to resign. He had succeeded in getting himself dismissed. But to the general public, which had no knowledge of the circumstances that led up to his dismissal, it appeared a *coup d'état* effected by the King. It saw in it the caprice of a despot and suspected the Queen of having a hand in bringing it about. But the greater the misapprehension as to the facts of the case, the more characteristic was the *sangfroid* with which this imagined exercise of arbitrary power was received. Lord Melbourne, who at first had felt somewhat anxious as to the consequences of his intrigue, was speedily reassured, and communicated his satisfaction to his confidant Lord Grey. 'Everything,' he wrote,

[1] *Lord Melbourne's Papers*, pp. 219 sqq. *Memoirs of Baron Stockmar*, vol. i, pp. 307 sqq. (Lord Palmerston's note). Raikes in his diary for February 8, 1836, embroiders the facts a little, but gives on the whole a truthful statement of Lord Melbourne's attitude. See in the same sense *Quarterly Review*, November 1834, *Postscript* (vol. lii, pp. 570–1), also *Greville Memoirs*, December 1, 1834. The article in the *Quarterly Review* was reprinted in *The Times* of November 27, and hotly disputed by the *Morning Chronicle*, November 28 and December 1. Nevertheless, neither the articles in the *Morning Chronicle* nor Lord Melbourne's denial (speech at Derby, December 1, see *The Times*, December 5; *Morning Chronicle*, December 6, 1834) can be regarded as convincing.

'appears to me likely to pass off quietly, as I am sure I wish it to do. The efforts made to raise a flame in London seem to me quite contemptible and to proceed from the lowest quarters.'[1] The Press, which two years before had been almost unanimous in supporting the Liberal administration, now changed to some extent its attitude. *The Times*, which for months had been at war with the Cabinet on the question of the Poor Law, passed over with a flourish of trumpets to the opposite camp.[2]

5

The Duke of Wellington accepted the responsibility of office. He even took over the interim administration of all the departments pending the definite constitution of a Cabinet. The Liberal Press charged him with attempting a dictatorship. But the Duke informed the King without delay that he could not accept the position of Prime Minister. Since the Commons would be the scene of the battles the future Government would have to fight, the Prime Minister must be a member of the Lower House and he asked the King to send for Peel. Peel, who was just then travelling in Italy, was hurriedly recalled and at once accepted the task of forming an administration. At the very outset he met with a rebuff. Stanley and Graham refused to enter his Cabinet. Nevertheless, he persevered in the attempt and within a few days the ministry was complete. Peel became Chancellor of the Exchequer, Lord Lyndhurst Lord Chancellor, Wellington Foreign Secretary, Goulburn Home Secretary, Lord Aberdeen Colonial Secretary, Baring President of the Board of Trade, and Herries went to the War Office. A seat in the Cabinet was found for Sir Edward Knatchbull. This was an advance to the Ultra Tories. It was not a very brilliant Cabinet, but the Whig administration at the end had hardly been superior. Its composition was less aristocratic than the Cabinet which passed the Reform Bill as it had been originally constituted in 1830. Lord John Russell made merry over the spectacle of Wellington presiding over a Cabinet which contained financiers. 'There stands his Grace between two Bank Directors.'[3]

[1] Lord Melbourne to Lord Grey, November 17, 1834 (*Melbourne Papers*, p. 228).
[2] For the negotiations between the Government and *The Times* conducted through the channel of Lord Greville and Lord Lyndhurst, see *Greville Memoirs*, November 17, 19, 23 and December 2, 5, 1834.
[3] Speech at Totnes, December 2, 1834 (*The Times*, December 8, 1834).

It was obviously impossible for the new Government to face the House of Commons elected in 1832. Parliament was therefore dissolved. And to make his political views known to the nation Peel adopted a method which to his contemporaries appeared almost revolutionary.[1] He drew up in concert with his colleagues a manifesto addressed to the electorate and communicated for publication to the leading London newspapers. From this celebrated document, the *Tamworth Manifesto*,[2] the note of reaction was entirely absent. Peel disclaimed any desire to tamper with the Reform Bill, which he regarded as 'a final and irrevocable settlement of a great constitutional question'. If he had no wish to see the nation condemned to live 'in a perpetual vortex of agitation' he was, as his entire conduct in the past abundantly proved, very far from averse to reform. He recognized that the reform of the franchise involved as its necessary corollary a reform of the municipal corporations. The commission which the late government had appointed to examine the question would continue its labours.

He concluded by dealing at length with the vital question of the Church. A fortnight before the publication of the *Tamworth Manifesto*, Lord Melbourne had made a violent attack upon the Dissenters. He charged them with dividing and weakening the ministerialists and complained that their attitude of hostility towards the Church had driven the timid and the waverers into the Conservative ranks.[3] To rally these waverers to the aid of the Church in her hour of peril was the strategy the circumstances dictated to Peel. In his manifesto, however, he declared his

[1] *Quarterly Review*, April 1835, 'Sir Robert Peel's Address': 'When before did a Prime Minister think it expedient to announce to the *People*, not only his acceptance of office, but the principles and even the details of the measures which he intended to produce, and to solicit—not from Parliament, but from the people—that they would so far maintain the prerogative of the King as to give the ministers of his choice not indeed an implicit confidence, but a fair trial' (vol. liii, p. 265). For the circumstances in which it was composed, submitted to the approval of a Cabinet council and communicated to *The Times*, the *Herald* and the *Post*, and for the sensation it produced, see *Greville Memoirs*, December 20, 1834.

[2] See the poll text, *Annual Register*, 1834, App. to Chron., p. 339.

[3] Speech at Derby, December 1, 1834: '. . . The violent and abusive opinions which have been declared, and particularly the bitter hostility and ulterior designs against the Established Church which have been openly avowed by several classes and bodies of Dissenters. . . . These sentiments and this conduct occasioned great alarm in high and powerful quarters; they terrified the timid, they rallied men around the institutions which they conceived to be attacked; and they gave life and spirit and courage to our political adversaries, whom you will recollect after all form a very large and powerful party in this country—a party powerful in numbers, powerful in property, powerful in rank and station' (*Morning Chronicle*, December 6, 1834).

intention to save the Church by the same method of prudent reform he had consistently pursued since he had joined Lord Liverpool's Cabinet in 1822. He reminded the Dissenters that although he had opposed the bill admitting them to the Universities he had supported the measures brought forward by Lord Althorp and Lord John Russell to release them from the obligations of paying the church rates and being married by the Anglican clergy. Though uncompromisingly hostile to any confiscation of Church property whether in Ireland or in England—this was the issue on which the dispute between the parties turned—he had no objection to a better distribution of her endowments if the step would tend to strengthen her legitimate influence. In England he proposed a commutation of tithes. He was prepared to consider such a reform of ecclesiastical abuses as the Evangelicals desired and the interest of the Church demanded. And without waiting for the result of the election, he took the initiative and appointed a royal commission to examine the question of Church Reform.

The election was held in January in an atmosphere of unruffled calm. At the election of 1832, 160 boroughs were contested in England and Scotland, at the present election only 145. Sixty-seven county seats were then contested, now only forty-seven. If the Conservatives had expected a victory, they were mistaken. The Liberals kept their majority. But there is good reason to doubt that Peel had entertained the illusion. From the moment Stanley refused his support he knew that he was fighting under most unfavourable conditions. And although the Conservatives remained a minority in Parliament the result of the election was after all far from disappointing.

In the first place the Liberal majority was very considerably reduced. Before Parliament met it was calculated that the Conservatives had gained at least 100 seats, and the Liberal majority been reduced to forty, possibly to twenty votes. And when Parliament met that majority seemed even more dubious. When the speaker was chosen, the Liberals mustered no more than 316 as against 306 votes, and at the debate on the Address only 309 against 302. How different was their present position from what it had been in 1833! Then the Conservatives were almost astonished to find themselves still in existence, and were an obscure group lost in the vast crowd of ministerialists. But the days of revolution were past. Once more elections were held under normal conditions. And two parties almost equal in number faced each other across the floor of the House.

Moreover, the composition of the majority which the Whigs still retained must be analysed. If they had lost a large number of seats to their Conservative opponents, they had lost an almost equal number to their Radical opponents. The Radicals, if we include under that term the Radicals of Great Britain and O'Connell's followers, had doubled their representation, and mustered some 160 votes in the Parliament of 1835. From this point of view the result of the London elections was sensational. Not only did the Conservatives fail to gain a single seat in the metropolitan area, almost all the seats were won by the Radicals. Their success placed Lord Melbourne in an extremely difficult position.

He had precipitated the November crisis to render his Radical allies more amenable; he had now good reason to fear that they had returned to Parliament in 1835 in a mood even more uncompromising than that which they had displayed in 1834. The decrease in the Liberal majority and the increase in their own representation had made their support indispensable if the Liberals were to have a majority.[1] Peel therefore, if only the Ultra Tories would accept his leadership and refuse to ally themselves with the revolutionaries, was in a position to continue the policy which had proved so successful during the past two years. Either the Liberals would maintain a coalition with the Radicals, and the moderate Liberals would be driven sooner or later into the Conservative party. Or they would attempt to break with the Radicals and would be dependent on the support of Peel. In what respect

[1] See two contemporary estimates of the numerical composition of the reformers. Estimate of the conservative *Annual Register*: 80 Radicals, English and Irish, 100 Liberals, 152 Whigs, total 332; by Sir John Walsh, *Chapters of Contemporary History*, 1836, p. 184: 170 Radicals (in place of 100 in the Parliament of 1833), 180 Ministerials, total 350. If these figures are so uncertain it is because there was no clear-cut demarcation between Whigs and Liberals, Liberals and Radicals. Each group was divided from its neighbour by indefinable shades of opinion. And if we regard the ministerialists as already the main body of the Liberal party, it is by a deliberate anachronism and for the sake of convenience. In reality the Liberals were at present only ministerialists too advanced to be classified as Whigs, but not sufficiently advanced to be classified as Radicals. As a party the ministerialists were called and called themselves Reformers. The designation signified either the party which in the past had carried out the Reform of 1832 or the party whose programme for the future was a programme of reform. It was still the official designation of the party at the General Election of 1837 and 1841, although in newspaper articles the term Liberal tended to supplant the term Reformer. But the designation was not adopted officially until the election of 1847.

indeed did their policy differ from his own? In the end both parties would be fused in the great party of moderate reform, which it was Peel's ambition to erect in opposition to the Radicals upon the ruins of the two traditional parties.

From another point of view the composition of the new Liberal majority requires analysis. When in February the two parties contested the choice of a speaker, it was remarked that the majority of English members voted for the Conservative candidate, the retiring speaker, Sir Charles Manners Sutton. As the division revealed, the majority of the county members were Conservatives, eighty-eight as against fifty-three. The price of corn was falling and Lord Chandos had taken advantage of the farmers' discontent to organize an agrarian party to defend the Conservative interest in the rural districts. In the boroughs to be sure the Liberals were still a majority; 171 borough members voted for Abercromby as against 159 who voted for Manners Sutton. But such a majority was clearly very small and in the urban as well as in the rural constituencies the Conservatives had secured many gains. Both members for Bristol were Conservatives, at Liverpool a Conservative headed the poll, and the Conservatives won seats at York, Leeds, Newcastle, Exeter, Hull, and Halifax. To prepare for the next election they had founded in every constituency, whether urban or rural, under the powerful stimulus communicated by the Carlton Club of London, active 'Conservative Associations'.[1] They had taken full advantage of the influence which a system of public voting placed in the hands of the wealthy and had made use of the complicated qualifications of the new franchise to establish a vigilant control over the annual composition of the registers. At present when the revolutionary movement had spent its force, trade was prosperous and hatred of Ireland was proving more potent than the passions of party strife, they were reaping the fruit of their hard work.

Of the English votes Manners Sutton received 247 as against 224. And even when the Scottish votes were added the Conservative candidate for the position of speaker still possessed a majority of ten votes from the representatives of Great Britain. It was Ireland with a Liberal majority of twenty votes which turned the

[1] *Edinburgh Review*, October 1835, 'Tory and Reform Associations' (vol. lxii, pp. 167 sqq.). M. Ostrogorski, *La Démocratie et l'Organisation des Partis Politiques* (vol. i, pp. 234–5).

scale against him.[1] The party led by Peel had been known hitherto as the party of the Crown and the Peerage. It was now also the party of England. In that character it stood opposed to a combination of heterogeneous groups in which the English Radicals and Dissenters were dependent even for their slight and precarious majority upon the support of the Scotch Presbyterians and the Irish Catholics. The Church, so unpopular only two years before, was now in the eyes of the nation the symbol of its order and its unity.

[1] *Annual Register*, 1835, p. 35. Cf. *Greville Memoirs*, February 20, 1835; *Quarterly Review*, 'Sir Robert Peel': 'In the question of the speaker there were of *English* members for Sir Charles Sutton 248, against him 228; but this majority of *English* members was overthrown by a majority of 30 Scotch and Irish who, voting for a *Scotchman* at the nod of an *Irishman*, have left England in the strange predicament of giving its title and supplying in a tenfold its resources to a government in which it is the insulted minority' (vol. liii, p. 564).

PART II

THE YEARS OF LORD MELBOURNE
(1835-1841)

CHAPTER I

Home and Foreign Policy

I THE PARTIES AND THEIR LEADERS

I

EVEN after the House of Commons had shown its hostility towards the Conservative government by electing a Whig Speaker, Peel considered himself justified in retaining office. He saw how small and how heterogeneous was the majority which had just elected Abercromby. And what after all was the grievance brought against him by this weak and disunited body? That he had accepted office in November under conditions alleged to be unconstitutional since the King had taken upon himself to dismiss a Cabinet which enjoyed the confidence of the Commons and replace it by a Cabinet of his personal choice? In that case let the Opposition have the courage to attempt a formal vote of no confidence in his administration! He refused to consider as such an amendment to the address drawn up by the Opposition leaders in terms purposely vague and passed by the insignificant majority of seven votes.[1] Or was it his policy that was disliked? Let his critics wait until they knew what it was. He asked for nothing more than a fair trial.

He began with the ecclesiastical question. On March 17 the Royal Commission appointed in December produced its first report,[2] in which the commissioners recommended the creation of two new bishoprics at Manchester and Ripon, the suppression of two existing sees, an alteration of the boundaries of several dioceses, the reduction of episcopal incomes, and the division of parishes at present too large. The stipends of the new parish incumbents were to be obtained by reducing the Cathedral Chapters. Peel proposed at the same time to settle the question of Nonconformist marriages by introducing civil marriage of which anyone who desired could make use.[3] He introduced a bill

[1] H. of C., February 26, 1835 (Parliamentary Debates, 3rd Series, vol. xxvi, p. 410).
[2] First Report from the Church Commission, as finally settled, March 17 (Annual Register, 1835, Public Documents, pp. 302 sqq.).
[3] H. of C., March 17, 1835: Sir Robert Peel's speech (Parl. Deb., 3rd Series, vol. xxvi, pp. 1073 sqq.).

to reform the ecclesiastical courts; four hundred of these were to be replaced by one whose jurisdiction moreover was narrowly circumscribed.[1] He proposed a complete system of tithe commutation in England, optional, however, not compulsory.[2] The Irish question remained to be dealt with. The Government adopted a scheme for the commutation of tithes in Ireland which both in its general principle and in its details closely resembled the bill introduced the year before by the Liberal Government.[3]

Thus the question of 'appropriation', in other words of applying to secular purposes a portion of the endowments of the Irish Church was again brought forward. The previous year Ward as the mouthpiece of the Radicals had used it as a weapon against the Whigs in the Cabinet. Now Lord John Russell, who had become the official leader of the Liberal Opposition, took the proposal out of Ward's hands and used it as a weapon against the Conservative administration. Without waiting for the report of the committee which the Liberals had appointed in 1834 to inquire into the endowments of the Church of Ireland, he invited the Commons on March 30 to 'consider the Temporalities of the Church of Ireland and to lay down the principle that any surplus which may remain after fully providing for the spiritual instruction of the members of the Established Church in Ireland ought to be applied locally to the general education of all classes of Christians.'[4] On its first introduction his motion obtained a majority of thirty-three votes,[5] reintroduced a few days later a majority of twenty-five.[6] When in spite of this defeat Peel was preparing to ask the House to continue the discussion of his bill for the commutation of tithe in Ireland, Lord John formally moved a further resolution which categorically declared that no proposal dealing with the tithe in Ireland could be considered a final or satisfactory solution which did not accept the principle of 'appropriation'. The Government was again defeated, by 285 votes against 258, that is

[1] H. of C., March 12, 1835: Sir David Pollock's speech (*Parliamentary Debates*, 3rd Series, vol. xxvi, pp. 908 sqq.).
[2] H. of C., March 24, 1835: Sir Robert Peel's speech (ibid., 3rd Series, vol. xxvii, pp. 170 sqq.).
[3] H. of C., March 20, 1835: Sir Henry Hardinge's speech (ibid., 3rd Series, vol. xxvii, pp. 13 sqq.).
[4] H. of C., March 30, 1835: Lord John Russell's speech (ibid., 3rd Series, vol. xxvii, pp. 361 sqq.).
[5] H of C April 2, 1835 (ibid., 3rd Series, vol. xxvii, pp. 770 sqq.). There was a majority of nine English members against the motion (*Annual Register*, 1835, p. 221).
[6] H. of C. April 7, 1835 (*Parl. Deb.*, 3rd Series, vol. xxvii, p. 861).

THE PARTIES AND THEIR LEADERS

to say was in a minority of twenty-seven.[1] At last Peel resigned.

It was with no light heart that the leaders of the Whig party prepared to resume office. From the very outset of the session Lord Stanley had acted as the leader of an independent group— in contemporary parlance a 'section'[2]—which comprised some forty members and was the potential nucleus of a centre party, sufficiently strong to govern the country after the fall of the Conservative Cabinet without the support of the Tories or Radicals. Lord Melbourne and Lord Grey were probably in favour of Lord Stanley's project,[3] for they loathed the alliance with the Radicals and O'Connell. Lord Grey's son, Lord Howick, whenever he was obliged by party discipline to vote against the Government was careful to state that his vote was not due to any desire to overthrow Peel.[4] And there were many members of the party who shared the sentiments of Lord Melbourne, Lord Grey, and Lord Howick.

But the Russells and their friends adopted a far more aggressive policy. When O'Connell made overtures to Lord John he was received with open arms.[5] Invited to a meeting of the Liberals held on March 18 at Lord Lichfield's, the Irish leader attended with his followers and offered his unreserved allegiance to the leaders of the party. And when a few days later a banquet was given to celebrate Lord John's appointment as leader of the Opposition, O'Connell was again present and declared at his departure, 'it was the most delightful evening he ever passed in his life'.[6] Those who recollected the abuse with which he had so lately loaded the Whig ministers were amused or indignant at this recantation. They were soon to discover behind the exterior of a noisy demagogue a past master of political intrigue. O'Connell's advances left the Liberal leaders defenceless against the Radicals. Lord Stanley's section melted away and Lord Stanley himself and Sir James Graham, soon the sole members of their group, were

[1] H. of C., April 7, 1835 (*Parliamentary Debates*, 3rd Series, vol. xxvii, p. 969).
[2] [J. Grant] *Random Recollections of the House of Commons*, pp. 152–3.
[3] There is even reason to believe that negotiations took place about this time between Lord Melbourne and Sir Robert Peel himself (W. F. Monypenny, *Life of Disraeli*, vol. i, pp. 278–9).
[4] H. of C., February 26, March 30, 1835 (*Parl. Deb.*, 3rd Series, vol. xxvi, pp. 375 sqq.; vol. xxvii, pp. 454–5).
[5] O'Connell to Lord John Russell, February 13, 1835; Lord John Russell to O'Connell, February 20, 1835; Lord Grey to Lord John Russell, February 23, March 11, 1835 (*Early Correspondence of Lord John Russell*, vol. ii, pp. 92, 97, 98, 103).
[6] *Greville Memoirs*, March 31, 1835.

187

thrust gradually into the ranks of the official Conservatives. The Liberal combination was reconstituted; it comprised the great Whig families, the Nonconformists, the Radicals, and O'Connell's Irish party.

Lord Melbourne reconstructed the administration whose fall he had himself so skilfully manoeuvred: for he was the only Liberal Prime Minister whom William IV would accept. There were two Whig leaders whose collaboration he desired, namely Lord Grey and Lord Althorp, now Lord Spencer. Both however refused and made it plain that they had retired for ever from active politics. There were two statesmen with whom Melbourne and with him the entire Whig aristocracy were anxious to dispense. One of these was Brougham who had sinned beyond pardon by his intrigue of the previous June and by the incredible eccentricity of his language and behaviour during a tour he had made two months later in Scotland. The other was Palmerston.[1] In August 1834, immediately after the signature of the final articles appended to the Treaty of the Quadruple Alliance, Talleyrand had asked for a holiday and the rumour immediately spread that he would never return since he did not wish to have anything further to do with Palmerston. Thus the entire diplomatic body, not only the representatives of Russia, Austria, and Prussia but the ambassador of Liberal France had so to speak gone on strike against him, as a dangerous mischief-maker. But if Melbourne managed to get rid of Brougham, Lord Grey's refusal[2] compelled him to put up once more with Palmerston. By his success in forcing himself on his recalcitrant colleagues, Palmerston began to justify the confidence reposed in him by a small group of admirers, who in spite of his unpopularity with the Press and the public appear to have already divined his future greatness.[3]

[1] Ellice to Lord Durham, March 21, 1836: 'We did all we could to throw over both the worthies . . . at least, to oblige them to change characters, for the unpopularity of the one and the indolence and indecision of the other were admitted on all hands and they have not hitherto changed their habits' (St. Reid, *Life of Lord Durham*, vol. i, p. 111). Lord Melbourne to Lord John Russell, April 12, 1835: 'The questions of Brougham and Palmerston are of the utmost importance, fully as much as any question of principle can be' (*Early Correspondence of Lord John Russell*, vol. ii, p. 108).

[2] Ibid., vol. ii, pp. 107-8.

[3] William Russell to Lord John Russell, April 24, 1835: 'Whatever you do, let me beg of you not to ask Palmerston for anything for me neither directly nor indirectly, don't even name me to him. He has his own corps of favourites to which I don't aspire to belong' (ibid., vol. ii, pp. 108-9). Greville, who on January 20 had written, 'Palmerston is beaten in Hants, at which everybody rejoices, for he is marvellously unpopular, they would have liked to illuminate the Foreign Office', wrote on February 17: 'The other

Spring Rice replaced Lord Althorp at the Exchequer; Charles Grant, now Lord Glenelg, succeeded Spring Rice at the Colonial Office and Grant's place at the Board of Control was taken by Sir John Hobhouse. Lord John Russell became Home Secretary with the leadership of the Commons. Lord Lansdowne and Lord Holland returned to their former positions. Lord Duncannon as Lord Privy Seal was deputed to maintain relations with O'Connell; Lord Howick at the War Office with Lord Grey. Poulett Thomson once more, as during the previous year, President of the Board of Trade, had a seat in the Cabinet and Sir Henry Parnell at last entered the Government. On the whole the ministry of 1834 returned to office without any considerable change of personnel.

2

When these ministers returned to power did they feel that they had achieved a decisive victory or that their return was merely a halt in the decline of their party? In the House of Commons they disposed only of a little over half the votes and even this on sufferance of Irish support, and the by-elections which were often defeats rendered their position more precarious every month. The Tories were still supreme in the Church and the Army. According to constitutional custom military promotions were made by the Commander in Chief, who was immediately responsible to the Crown, not by the Secretary of State for War, a member of the Cabinet and responsible to Parliament. It was in vain that Lord Melbourne's Government attempted in 1837 to take advantage of the accession of a new Sovereign to reform this abuse. They were obliged to abandon the project before it was even debated in Parliament, and after, as before, 1837, a recommendation from the War Office damaged an officer's prospects at the Horse Guards.[1] In Parliament the coming men, Gladstone since 1833 and

night I met some clerks in the Foreign Office to whom the very name of Palmerston is hateful, but I was surprised to hear them (Mellish particularly, who can judge both from capacity and opportunity) give ample testimony to his abilities,' etc.

[1] For this question, see H. of C., April 5, 6, 1837 (*Parliamentary Debates*, 3rd Series, vol. xxxvii, pp. 791 sqq., 813 sqq.). Lord John Russell to Lord Melbourne, October 8, 1837 (*Early Correspondence of Lord John Russell*, vol. ii, p. 205). September 13, 1839 (ibid., vol. ii, p. 266). Queen Victoria's Diary, January 4, 9, 1838 (*Girlhood of Queen Victoria*, vol. ii, pp. 252, 254). *The Times*, February 8, 1838: 'Turn over the Horse Guards to Lord Howick and we know whose cousins, to the tenth degree, will fill each successive promotion.' Cf. February 10, 1838, Queen Victoria to Lord Melbourne, December 29, 1837; Lord Melbourne to Queen Victoria, December 30, 31, 1837; February 10, 1839 (*The Letters of Queen Victoria, a selection from Her Majesty's Correspondence between the years* 1837 *and* 1861, vol. i, pp .128-9 184).

Disraeli since 1837, called themselves Conservatives, and even that title was not sufficiently Tory for their sentiments. The numbers of the Whig gentry were decreasing. If the father was loyal to the old family tradition, his sons were deserting it. Even the urban middle class was beginning at last to take alarm at the Radicals, and detested O'Connell. Moreover, the Conservative leader was the very man to win their sympathy, for Peel was the son of a cotton manufacturer, whose wealth almost vied with the enormous revenues enjoyed by the leaders of the British aristocracy.[1]

It was Peel who in spite of his defeat in Parliament was the true conqueror. He had scarcely resigned when he began to receive petitions despatched by hundreds from every part of the Kingdom, alike from the agricultural districts of the south and from the manufacturing towns of the north, assuring him that he possessed the confidence of the nation; and when a little later the University of Glasgow elected him Chancellor, the demonstrations were renewed. Several municipalities sent him addresses, and when the municipality of Glasgow refused to confer upon him the freedom of the City 3,000 working men of the district combined to purchase it for him.[2] He was a man of strangely tempered character, cold and disdainful, yet with a morbid sensibility to affronts real or imagined, ready at the least provocation to send a challenge or demand an apology, consistently presenting an appearance of philosophic detachment, but all the while devoured by ambition. By imperceptible degrees until the autumn of 1834, then blazing out with a sudden splendour during his hundred days in office, he had achieved a position of wellnigh incredible importance. Suspected for many a weary year of trickery and duplicity, he was now the object of universal respect. His stature dominated the statesmen of his party, indeed of all parties.

He styled himself a 'Conservative', and it was under his guidance that the Tories had abandoned their old designation in

---

[1] The seventh wealthiest man in England (C. S. Parker, *Sir Robert Peel*, vol. i, p. 371). He was believed to possess an income of £40,000, half of which was derived from real estate, half from investments (Lord Broughton's *Recollections*, May 14, 1830. Croker to Lord Hertford, January 19, 1831; *Croker Papers*, vol. ii, p. 101). According to Greville (*Memoirs*, March 5, 1831) his father, the first baronet, who had begun his career without a halfpenny, with two partners who possessed between them a capital of £6,000, left at his death £250,000 to each of his younger sons, £60,000 each to his three daughters, and to Sir Robert, his eldest son, real estate which produced an income of £22,000 and £450,000 in personal estate.

[2] Graham to Stanley, January 15, 1837 (C. S. Parker, *Sir James Graham*, vol. i, p. 251). Cf. C. S. Parker, *Life of Sir Robert Peel*, vol. ii, pp. 327 sqq.)

favour of this new name: 'Conservative', but not 'reactionary' nor even 'opposed to change'. For he believed that in a society in process of continuous change the traditional institutions of the country, monarchy, aristocracy, an established Church, could be 'conserved' only if they were continually adapted to a changing society and therefore continually reformed.

At this price and by the unremitting application of this maxim of government the Radical party, whose progress excited such alarm, could be isolated and paralysed. This extraordinary Conservative was therefore an innovator and moreover, an innovator, not only on principle, but by temperament. He had begun his political career by the restoration of specie payment, and had proceeded to reform the penal code. He had then committed a disastrous blunder. To justify his refusal to serve under Canning he had pleaded an uncompromising hostility to Catholic emancipation. For four or five years he paid the penalty of his mistake. He got no thanks for carrying through the Commons in 1829 the measure he had condemned two years earlier, and his reputation suffered so seriously that he was unable to take charge of the movement which led to the reform of the franchise. The credit of that measure therefore fell to the Whig aristocracy. But conditions were now more favourable and he declared himself ready to reform, to perfect, every national institution in a conservative spirit and assisted by moderate men of all parties with the sole exception of the democrats and the revolutionaries. His programme encountered an obstacle in the ranks of his own party. Those who persisted in calling themselves Tories and whom the public termed Ultra-Tories were ready to employ any means to overthrow the Liberal administration. They therefore attempted an alliance with the Radicals against the Whigs and, though Peel was not prepared to purchase office at such a price, the interest of his party compelled him from time to time to gratify their wishes. On the questions of the Poor Law for example and Factory Acts the Tories were able to carry with them besides the revolutionaries the main body of the Conservatives. Nor did the Ultra-Tories shrink from contemplating wilder projects. Incredible though it may seem, there can be little doubt that their leader, the Duke of Cumberland, the King's brother, believed it possible to set aside by a military *coup d'état* his little niece the Princess Victoria, who was a devoted Whig, and seize the succession of

William IV.[1] It was no light task for Peel to keep a firm hand on these wild men among his own followers and extenuate the scandal caused by their antics. Fortunately, in a country where parliamentary traditions were rooted so deeply this faction was weak and unable to equip itself with a definite organization. In the Commons it had not a single leader worthy of the name. In the Upper House Lord Lyndhurst, who had been Lord Chancellor in Peel's administration, attempted a few intrigues, but he was far too small a man for the task. The Tories it is true appeared to possess in the House of Lords the leader of whom they were in search, namely Wellington. Since he had fought the Reform Bill so energetically they had forgiven him the apostasy of 1829 and he was once more their idol. But he turned a deaf ear to their offers.

The old nobleman and old soldier for whom the age of conquests whether in love or war had gone by had determined to retire from public life. He had received too many insults, had been exposed too often to the hoots of the mob in 1831 and 1832 and in spite of the modesty he had shown when he yielded the first place to Peel and withdrew into the background, he had nevertheless been compelled at the close of 1834 to endure more innuendos and further suspicion. He now adopted a new attitude, the attitude of the sage and the counsellor; he would no longer be Achilles but Nestor, would belong in future not to a party but to the entire nation. And he had the pleasure of seeing his programme successful. In clubs and drawing-rooms the young men thronged and pressed around the aged hero to listen to the story of his battles, and, as he rode through the streets, the crowd saluted and cheered. Moreover, since the passage of the Reform Bill he had become a convinced pessimist. He did not believe it possible to govern the country under the new system. But that was another reason to shrink from office. He was delighted to leave the responsibility of government to the Whigs, ready to support them in their resistance to the demands of the Radicals and do all he could to retard what he regarded as the inevitable march of the nation towards the pit of democratic anarchy. His pessimism therefore produced the same line of action as had Peel's optimism. Wellington smoothed the path of the ministry because he believed the days of a Conservative administration had gone by for ever,

[1] Clare Jerrold, *The Early Court of Queen Victoria*, p. 114.

Peel because he was convinced that, if he could only persuade his party to adopt for a sufficient period his cautious strategy, the day would infallibly come when office would fall into his lap like a ripe fruit.

3

It was only the consideration shown by the two Conservative leaders which enabled the administration of Lord Melbourne and Lord John Russell to survive. For although those two statesmen differed so widely in character and endowments, neither possessed the qualities necessary to arouse the enthusiasm of the country for the Liberal cause.

All contemporary witnesses combine to give the impression that in 1835 the Liberal Prime Minister was an old man. In reality Lord Melbourne was only fifty-five. But if not yet old in years, he was and always had been temperamentally old. Sceptical and disillusioned he was convinced that life is short, statecraft difficult, human nature unchangeable. To this strange leader of the re-formers reform of any kind seemed impossible or dangerous. Intellectually, as all his ecclesiastical appointments prove, he was extremely Liberal. But politically he was an aristocrat and a Conservative. So long as William IV lived, he contrived by his unyielding opposition to prevent the creation of new peerages to strengthen his own party in the Lords, and in consequence of his attitude, for four years the Upper House tended to return to the eighteenth century ideal and become once more an exclusive aristocratic club.[1] He brought himself, however, to endure the

[1] Lord John Russell to Lord Melbourne, 1836 (*Lord Melbourne's Papers*, p. 495). On October 7, 1835, Lord John Russell had expressed his approval of this conservative policy. 'The Pitt party,' he wrote, 'has been weakened, not strengthened, by making so many dull country gentlemen, duller peers . . . Two or three now and then may be useful, but I should regret any large creation. The best stuff would be Liberal Irishmen' (Sp. Walpole, *Life of Lord John Russell*, vol. i, p. 250). Ten months later he had changed his mind: 'It appears to me . . . that this opportunity should be taken for the creation of eight, ten, or twelve peers, and that the Ministry be prepared to advise a similar creation whenever it is provoked' (to Lord Melbourne, June 5, 1836: Sp. Walpole, *Life of Lord John Russell*, vol. i, p. 266). But he was defeated by Lord Melbourne's opposition. The following is a list of the peerages *created* during the eleven years during which the Liberals were in power. (No account is taken of promotions *within* the peerage, promotions of Irish or Scotch peers to peerages of the United Kingdom, or the summons to the Lords of eldest sons before their normal succession.) 1831: thirteen peerages, of which eight were made at the Coronation, also the bestowal of a peerage on an illegitimate son of the King, who became Earl of Munster; 1832: one peerage; 1833: one peerage; 1834: one peerage (Chief Justice Denman); 1835: three peerages made by Peel's government (two of the new peers, Scarlett and Pratt, were law lords), also four peerages made by the Whigs on their return to office; 1836: two law lords; 1837: four peerages; 1838: four Coronation

alliance of the Radicals and the Irish in the belief that under the circumstances he had only one duty to perform, to do his utmost to render the coalition as far as possible innocuous, until the inevitable and no doubt desirable day came when he could restore to the Conservatives the trust committed to his charge. As far as it lay in his power he was determined to restore it intact. 'I like,' he said, 'what is tranquil and stable.'[1]

Lord John Russell was a man of very different stamp. He was a man of principles, the doctrinaire principles of Whig liberalism. His convictions were quite as much an ancestral heirloom as a personal possession: the honour of the family demanded that the Russells should remain what they had been for the past century and a half, leaders of the popular party. Though he was a writer of mediocre ability, and his oratory lacked brilliance, he enjoyed an increasing popularity in Parliament. The explanation is simple. For we love those who love us and the Commons could not help feeling gratitude towards a man who took seriously all the forms and fictions of Parliamentary procedure and party government. Nevertheless, his position was not easy. Inveterately opposed to any reconciliation with the Tories, even as regenerate under their new appellation of Conservatives, and convinced that there was no salvation for the country save in the rule of the great Whig families and no salvation for those families unless they kept in touch with the groups which represented Liberal opinion, he was soon to feel the difficulty of devising a programme which would

peerages; 1839: ten peerages; 1840: one peerage; 1841: six peerages (of these one peer was a law lord and four were created by the Whigs on quitting office). All these new peers belonged to the gentry, with the exception of the law lords and C. Poulett Thomson, who was created Baron Sydenham in 1840 on his appointment as Governor-General of Canada. On this occasion the insistence of Lord John Russell overcame, for the first and only time, Lord Melbourne's repugnance to the step (*Greville Memoirs*, August 24, 1840). Wealth was also required as a qualification for a peerage. See ibid., March 25, 1834: 'Denman's peerage is much abused: it is entirely the Chancellor's doing. Denman has no fortune and a feeble son to succeed him.' Lord John Russell to Lord Melbourne, September 30, 1838: '. . . Pepys is, I believe, rich, and so far would be a good new peer' (*Early Correspondence of Lord John Russell*, vol. ii, p. 126). Edward Bulwer Lytton, *England and the English*, vol. ii, p. 193 *n*.: 'The sordid and commercial spirit of our aristocracy may be remarked in the disposition of its honours. It is likely enough that there will soon be a numerous creation of peers; in France, such a creation would be rendered popular and respectable, by selecting the most distinguished men of the necessary politics;—here neither the minister nor the public would ever dream of such a thing; we shall choose the *richest men*.' For Lord Melbourne's determination to create as few peers as possible, see Queen Victoria's Diary, May 31, 1838 (*Girlhood of Queen Victoria*, vol. ii, p. 334). For the creation of thirty-eight baronets in 1838 at the Coronation, see a letter from Disraeli to his sister, July 4 (W. F. Monypenny, *Life of Disraeli*, vol. ii, p. 33); also an article in *The Times*, July 13.

[1] Queen Victoria's Diary, September 28, 1838 (*Girlhood of Queen Victoria*, vol. ii, p. 35).

express this coalition between the Whigs and their more advanced allies. He had accepted the responsibility for the Reform Bill, he urged that the municipal corporations should be transformed into democratic bodies, and his schemes of Irish Church reform procured him the support of the Radicals on his return to office in the spring of 1835. Nevertheless, he was neither a Radical nor, strictly speaking, a democrat. And in his capacity as leader he was constantly obliged to impose moderation on the Radicals. But a doctrinaire is ill adapted to play the part of an opportunist. His uncompromising language irritated those whom it was important to appease. Rightly or wrongly he gave the impression that he lacked Peel's sense of the plasticity of political institutions, and his language seemed at times to imply that on slight provocation he would maintain after the Reform Bill what Wellington had maintained in 1830, that if the constitution of Great Britain in its actual form were not already perfect it wanted very little to achieve perfection.

The great problem which both the sceptic and the doctrinaire, alike cautious though from different motives, must solve if they wished to remain in office was the management of the Radicals. The general election of 1835 had doubled their strength in the Commons, and if they continued to progress at the same rate and won, if not all, at least the majority of the English boroughs, the moderate section of the Liberal party would be placed in the precarious position of a centre party threatened on either flank. Many prophets foretold this fate, and as we have just pointed out, Peel, who shared this belief, was awaiting the day when the present distribution of the Liberal forces would be upset to the advantage of the Radicals, and the Conservatives would again become the normal government of the country. The forecast however, was mistaken. At the election of 1837 the Radicals made no progress and even lost many important seats. Indeed, the account we have given of the first reformed Parliament should enable the reader to discern the reason of their weakness.

They were a hybrid party which professed religious neutrality and a liberal code of morals, yet were obliged to rely in every constituency on the support of the lower middle class which was everywhere Nonconformist, pietist, and puritan. From another point of view they were also a hybrid party, composed of Englishmen yet voting in the House with O'Connell's Irish followers, and therefore condemned to share to the full the unpopularity of the Irish. And from yet another standpoint they were a hybrid party. Among their members were the humanitarian Radicals, who were led solely by their dictates of the heart, were ready to accept without criticism every popular claim, lamented the harshness of the new Poor Law, and asked for a minimum wage fixed by law for the cotton weavers, and a ten-hours day for every class of worker in the factories. Among these were Fielden, the manufacturer, and Duncombe, the eccentric man of fashion. But it was also among the Radicals that the Government found allies against this group. They were the more practical and the more intellectual Radicals, disciples of Bentham, the authors of the new Poor Law, men who were opposed to legal protection of adult labour, boasted that they were no demagogues and even appeared to take a positive delight in preaching to the working classes with a self-satisfied assurance the most unpalatable truths.

The natural result of this internal disunion was that the Radicals never succeeded either in the constituencies or in Parliament in becoming a definite party with a distinctive organization. Within the ministerial party there was a gradual progress from the moderate Whigs to the ordinary Liberals, from the ordinary to the advanced Liberals, from the advanced Liberals to the philosophic Radicals, and from the philosophic Radicals to the Ultra-Radicals. But the groups were distinguished by shades of opinion so fine as to be scarcely perceptible. Nor did any great man come forward to unite under his personal ascendancy the scattered fragments of the democratic party. Roebuck and Sir William Molesworth in the Commons were theorists of too narrow a cast to assume such a position. Brougham and Lord Durham in the Lords were too hot headed and too eccentric. Moreover, the House of Lords was not the field for a Radical leader. And if in a sense the English Radicals may be said to have possessed a leader in Parliament, that leader unfortunately for them was O'Connell, who was neither a genuine Radical nor an Englishman.

4

We have remarked O'Connell's efforts for the return of the Whigs to power. The Conservatives maintained, that at the meeting of March 18, a formal pact had been concluded between

O'Connell and the Liberal ministers, the so-called Lichfield Confederacy. O'Connell and the ministers disclaimed any such pact, but there can be no doubt that an alliance existed, whether formal or tacit matters little. O'Connell was no longer a revolutionary. The General Association, which he founded in 1836, was a perfectly legal organization whose object was the same as that of the Conservative associations, to prepare for elections by superintending the composition of the registers. The Society of Precursors, founded for the repeal of the Act of Union, became dormant and showed only an occasional sign of life by a demonstration in support of the Whig ministers. In the matter of reform O'Connell became the most opportunist of politicians. His new attitude did not lack its reward. The Cabinet left the Government of Ireland in his hands. The Lord Lieutenant systematically asked his advice on all matters concerned with the policing of the country and on all appointments. On two or three occasions he was within an ace of receiving himself a high administrative position as Master of the Rolls for Ireland. But he was too prudent to commit the Government to a rash step, and contented himself with securing the appointment of a Catholic barrister, a friend and political ally, David Richard Pigot, first as legal adviser to the Irish government, then as Solicitor General and finally as Attorney General for Ireland.

How did this new policy affect the condition of Ireland? The statistics which should answer the question are not easy to interpret. Agitation which can be termed in the strict sense revolutionary ceased altogether. But it is not so certain that the number of agrarian outrages decreased to any appreciable extent. The ministers asserted that this was the case and adduced statistics to support their contention;[1] but the Opposition speakers disputed their figures not without weighty arguments[2] and with considerable bitterness and pertinacity. Irish questions continued to occupy the greater part of every session, and the Protestant gentry refused to accept this new system by which Ireland was governed against their interest by agreement with the Catholics. The mysterious assassination of Lord Norbury, at the beginning of January 1839, occasioned such an outburst of indignation that Lord Mulgrave, now Lord Normanby, judged it prudent to hand over to a

[1] H. of C., February 7, 1837: Lord John Russell's speech (*Parliamentary Debates*, 3rd Series, vol. xxxvi, p. 220). H. of L., March 21, 1839: Lord Normanby's speech (ibid., 3rd Series, vol. xlvi, p. 1007).

[2] H. of C., February 7, 1837: Jackson's speech (ibid., 3rd Series, vol. xxxvi, pp. 246 sqq.).

successor his position of Lord Lieutenant. He went to the Home Office and his place was taken by Lord Ebrington, who, however, continued to follow the same policy of co-operation with O'Connell. It was indeed inevitable; for the very existence of the Government depended on the support of the Irish members.

In the House of Commons O'Connell most successfully tamed and curbed the Radicals. If they introduced a motion calculated to endanger the Government O'Connell himself with two or three of his friends voted for it. In this way appearances were saved, for he still professed himself a Radical. But he ordered the rest of his followers to vote against it, as his new opportunist tactics of co-operation with the Government demanded. His power in Parliament continued to increase. At the election of 1837, when the English Radicals suffered so many defeats, O'Connell's Irish phalanx doubled its numbers, and when Joseph Hume was defeated in Middlesex O'Connell made him a present of an Irish seat. In the long run this intimate alliance with the Irish demagogue tended to discredit the Cabinet. It undoubtedly lowered the level of English politics since every question was reduced to a question of patronage.[1] But it suited the immediate parliamentary interests of the Liberal party and it kept the Conservatives in awe; for they knew that the moment the Liberals quitted office, O'Connell would return to his old part, would be once again the 'agitator' he had been until 1834 and raise the standard of revolution. Thus a curious spectacle was witnessed in the House; the three leaders of the Commons, Lord John Russell, Peel, and O'Connell, all parading as moderates. Protected by Peel against the Ultra-Tories and by O'Connell against the Ultra-Radicals the Government survived.

It survived for six years. At first it attempted numerous and important measures of legislation. The ministry had scarcely taken office before two bills were introduced, one to reform the municipal corporations in England, the other to solve the question of tithes in Ireland. But at this juncture Peel intervened, and while expressing himself prepared to accept the first in an amended form, condemned the second unconditionally since its fundamental provision was the famous appropriation clause. In consequence the first bill was carried, the second after it had passed the

[1] *The Times*, March 16, 1838: 'It was to be "Government without Patronage" forsooth! Its proper name is "Patronage without Government", for they do *not* govern the Kingdom.'

Commons was dropped. Within a few weeks of his fall, Peel was arbiter of Parliament.

In 1836 important reforms were effected by agreement between the parties. The Church of England was reformed, and the questions of English tithe and Nonconformist marriages settled. During the four years following the Irish question to the great discredit of the ministry absorbed the attention of Parliament and paralysed its activity. Ireland was given a Poor Law copied from the English model. The question of municipal corporations and the question of the tithe were debated at great length and once more Peel imposed his will. He permitted the passing of an act to reform the municipal corporations on condition the Government abandoned the attempt to settle the tithe question on Radical lines by a partial confiscation of the endowments of the Church. Thus two men led Parliament, the Irishman O'Connell and the Conservative Peel. Meanwhile the Liberal Cabinet dragged out a humiliating existence. We do not propose to relate, year after year, the tedious story of this Parliamentary bargaining. It will suffice to give an account of the measures which had been passed before the six years of Liberal government came to an end in 1841.

II ECCLESIASTICAL QUESTIONS

I

The first question to be settled was the question of the Church both in England and in Ireland. We have seen how powerful, in appearance at least, had been the anti-clerical movement in Britain at the beginning of 1832. We have also seen how soon the real weakness of anti-clericalism had been revealed and how by compromising the Liberal party it had contributed to its decline. Now when the crisis had passed it was once more possible to settle the practical questions which demanded solution in a spirit not of war but of compromise, and in accordance with the programme which Peel had formulated when he was Prime Minister but had lacked the time to carry out.

The Dissenters obtained access to University degrees. The Liberal Cabinet revived the plan which had been suggested and postponed in 1834, and which Peel had just attempted with considerable hesitation and without success to postpone still further, the foundation of a new undenominational University furnished with the right to confer degrees. But the privilege was not granted as had been originally intended in 1834 to the University of London, founded by Bentham and his friends. Two charters of incorporation were simultaneously conferred in 1837, one upon this University which under the title University College was to be a teaching body without the right of granting degrees, the other upon a University of London which was not a teaching body but a mere jury empowered to grant degrees to the students of University College and such other teaching bodies as might hereafter be set up. The charters were temporary and were made permanent in 1838 after the accession of a new sovereign. It was in vain that the Protestant party attempted to make the University of London a denominational body or even to permit it to assume a denominational character at the choice of its members.[1] In London the question was settled as the Liberals desired. In future there would be a University in the capital open to all 'without distinction', to quote the language of the charter of 1838 and free to compete with Oxford and Cambridge. But although the solution seemed to satisfy everybody, it was nevertheless only a half-measure, a compromise. For in the two great historic Universities the Established Church kept her monopoly of degrees and fellowships.[2]

The Dissenters were also released from the necessity of being married in Anglican churches. There was a simple method of solving a problem, which for years had proved a stumbling-block to the English legislator, to copy the French model and institute a civil marriage, which any one who chose might complete by a religious ceremony but which alone would possess legal validity. This solution might have been expected to have been less offensive to Christian sentiment in a Protestant than in a Catholic country, since Protestants do not regard marriage as a sacrament. Nevertheless, English public opinion was hostile to the idea. When Lord John Russell made the suggestion in 1834 to Lord Melbourne, the latter took alarm. What would the Wesleyans say?[3] Accordingly

[1] Harriett Martineau, *History of the Thirty Years' Peace*, Book V, chap. i.

[2] Lord Melbourne to Lord John Russell, December 15, 1836: 'Rice tells me that you want a bill for the admission of Dissenters to the universities. Is this absolutely necessary? Is not the charter of the new London University enough for the present? If it is not absolutely necessary, I am sure that it is not prudent to stir this question. There is none upon which prejudice is stronger and more violent. Many of our own friends are in their hearts against it' (Spencer Walpole, *Life of Lord John Russell*, vol. i, p. 260).

[3] Lord Melbourne to Lord John Russell, August 16, 1834 (*Lord Melbourne's Papers*, p. 209).

although an approach was made towards the French solution it was indirect and complicated and accompanied by constant disclaimers that the Government intended anything of the kind.

Peel had proposed to permit all who did not wish to be married by an Anglican clergyman to contract a civil marriage before a Justice of the Peace. But the banns must always be published in the parish church and the rector or vicar of the parish would continue to have charge of the register in which every marriage, Anglican or otherwise, would be entered. Lord John Russell adopted and extended Peel's proposal.[1] A civil register of births, deaths, and marriages was introduced for the whole of England.[2] For the celebration of marriages the following provisions were adopted. The civil officials, the registrars, were empowered to receive the preliminary notice of all who intended to be married, twenty-one days before the marriage was celebrated. This notice was optional in the case of Anglicans (it dispensed them from the publication of the banns), obligatory for all who were not Anglicans. Three methods of marriage were permitted. Marriage in church before a clergyman of the Establishment, in which case the old usages were retained but the officiating clergyman would in future be obliged to transmit to the civil registrar a duplicate of the entry in the marriage register. Marriage in a place of worship other than an Anglican Church, which was duly licensed for the celebration of marriages, in which case the presence of the registrar was required. And finally as a provision for exceptional cases civil marriage before the registrar.[3]

By a statute of 1836[4] the question of the tithes was settled as far as England was concerned. In this matter it would appear at first sight that the initiative lay with the Liberal ministers. For the bill which Peel had introduced in March 1835 was content to lay down rules for the commutation of tithe, whereas Lord John Russell's bill prescribed compulsory commutation. But on closer inspection the difference between the two measures appears less considerable. In many respects the Act of 1836 followed the bill of 1835.

[1] H. of C., February 12, 1836: Lord John Russell's speech (*Parliamentary Debates*, 3rd Series, vol. xxxi, pp. 367 sqq.).
[2] 6 and 7 Will. IV, cap. 86.   [3] 6 and 7 Will. IV, cap. 85.
[4] 6 and 7 Will. IV, cap. 71. Cf. 5 and 6 Will. IV, cap. 84 (for the more easy recovery of tithes), cap. 85 (for the amendment of the law as to the tithing of turnips in certain cases), 1 Vict., cap. 69 (Act to amend the Act passed the previous session). For the explanation of the Government's measure, see H. of C., February 9, 1836: Lord John Russell's speech (*Parl. Deb.*, 3rd Series, vol. xxxi, pp. 185 sqq.).

In 1835 Peel proposed to follow the example set by the Poor Law Amendment Act and establish in London a central 'commission' for tithe commutation to consist of four members, a cleric, the Archbishop of Canterbury and two laymen appointed by the Crown. The commissioners were to appoint assistant commissioners to represent them in the provinces. This provision was incorporated in the statute of 1836. Though Peel desired commutation to be a matter of private arrangement between the parties concerned, he proposed to lay down definite rules according to which it should be effected. The tithe instead of being an annual toll of the year's crops would in future be a money payment, an addition to the rent, that is to say a rent charge whose amount would be calculated upon the average price of corn during the previous seven years. On this matter Lord John copied Peel's bill, with the further provision that the amount of the tithe after commutation should never exceed seventy-five per cent, nor fall below sixty per cent of the value of the tithe before commutation. Peel had provided that whenever one or more tithe-payers the value of whose tithe was not less than two-thirds of the tithe of the parish concluded an agreement with a tithe owner the agreement, if sanctioned by the central commissioners, should be binding upon all the tithe-payers of the parish. The Act of 1836 preserved this provision, or at least contained a provision to the same effect, to be operative for one year after the Act came into force. After the expiration of that period the commissioners were authorized on the request of even a single tithe-payer to enforce the commutation of the entire tithe of any parish in the Kingdom. This was an obvious departure from the bill of 1835. Nevertheless the statute of 1836 did not make commutation altogether compulsory, since the commissioners could take action only at the request of a tithe-payer, and on the other hand the bill of 1835 did not leave commutation purely optional since it obliged the minority in a parish to accept the decision of the majority. Moreover, the Act of 1836 effected by a quicker method the same object and embodied the same principle as the bill of the previous year. Peel was fully justified when in opening the debate he claimed that he had inspired the Government's bill.[1] The statute was a Conservative measure. It proved

[1] H. of C., February 9, 1836: Sir Robert Peel's speech (*Parliamentary Debates*, 3rd Series, vol. xxxi, pp. 192 sqq.).

successful. Soon nothing more was heard of the Radical demand for the abolition of tithe.

In Ireland the tithe question was far harder to solve. For this was an issue which the two parties had contested in the spring of 1835, and it was because he had refused to yield to the Liberal demands as formulated by Lord John himself that Peel had found himself obliged to resign. That is to say if the Liberal ministers wished to settle the problem amicably in agreement with the Conservatives they must give way on the matter of 'appropriation', which the Radicals demanded so insistently. They gave way, and Peel won a further success.

In December 1836 O'Connell, in pursuance of his new policy of opportunism, informed the English Radicals that he was not prepared to endanger the existence of the Cabinet for the sake of the appropriation clause.[1] After this Lord John was in no position to resist the King on the one hand,[2] and Melbourne on the other when they pressed him to abandon it; nor could he afford to neglect the lesson he was soon to be taught by the Radical losses at the election of 1837. The Irish Tithes Act of 1838[3] without appropriating a possible surplus to secular purposes, commuted the tithe from a toll upon the annual produce to a rent charge whose amount was fixed and guaranteed by the state at 75 per cent of the value of the uncommuted tithe. For all practical purposes it was the same measure which Peel's Cabinet had introduced in 1835. Lord John explained to his constituents that he had been obliged to adopt the course he had taken in view of the fact that the Government possessed a very weak majority in the House, that the English public was hostile to appropriation, and the Irish indifferent.[4] Possibly he was right. But in that case why had he driven Peel from office in 1835?

[1] O'Connell to Warburton, December 29, 1836: 'I wish with all my heart that the Ministry were decently freed from that dilemma. If there were a proper deduction from the tithe, there would for the present be no surplus, and it is really too bad to risk on such a point a Ministry who are for the first time in history conquering the anti-Saxon spirit of Ireland and adding 8,000,000 to the King's subjects' (Sp. Walpole, *Life of Lord John Russell*, vol. i, p. 273).

[2] Sir H. Taylor to Lord John Russell, January 2, 1837 (ibid., vol. i, p. 274).

[3] 1 and 2 Vict., cap. 107.

[4] *Letter to the Electors of Stroud on the Principles of the Reform Act*, 1839, ed. 2, p. 42. See especially pp. 30–1: '. . . The efforts of the Clergy to persuade the country that the measures of the present Ministry respecting the Church of Ireland and respecting Church Rates would shake and ultimately destroy Church property have had a considerable effect on the public mind.'

2

The measures of which we have just spoken may be regarded as steps in the direction of the purely secular State and the disestablishment of the Church.[1] But they went a very little way. If the Church wished to put a final end to the Radical campaign and once more make the Establishment popular, she must have the courage to undertake that work of Church Reform which was the desire of all her worthiest sons. Important steps were taken in this direction during these five years, and once more it was Peel who took the initiative. The new Government desired the commission he had appointed to continue its labours. The Conservative ministers serving on the commission were replaced by their Liberal successors: but in other respects the commission was for all practical purposes the same body. It issued three further reports during the first six months of 1836,[2] and three important measures of reform were passed, in 1836, in 1838, and in 1840. They gave effect to the recommendations of a commission on which the ecclesiastical element predominated.

The act of 1836[3] altered the diocesan boundaries and redistributed the income of the episcopate. Six sees were united into three but on the other hand a new see was created at Ripon to provide for the recent growth of population in Yorkshire. That the translations which for years past had caused such scandal and protest might lose their former attraction, the glaring inequality of episcopal incomes was considerably reduced. The Archbishop of Canterbury was to receive an income of £15,000, the Archbishop of York an income of £10,000 a year; the Bishop of London £10,000, the Bishop of Durham £8,000 and the Bishop of Winchester £7,000. The other bishops were to be paid between £5,000-£4,500 a year. If the new scale of incomes diminished in some cases the income of an archbishop or bishop, it raised the income of other sees. In future no bishop could plead

[1] For the sake of completeness mention must be made of certain statutes restricting the jurisdiction of the ecclesiastical courts over the laity, 6 and 7 Will. IV, cap. 19. An Act for separating the Palatine Jurisdiction of the County Palatine of Durham from the Bishoprick of Durham, 6 and 7 Will. IV, cap. 87. An Act for extinguishing the Secular Jurisdiction of the Archbishop of York and the Bishop of Ely in certain liberties in the counties of York, Nottingham and Cambridge.

[2] *Second, Third, Fourth Reports of Commissioners on the State of the Established Church with reference to Duties and Revenues*, May 4, 13, June 24, 1836. A fifth and final report appeared 1837-8.

[3] 6 and 7 Will. IV, cap. 77 (Established Church Bill).

the insufficiency of his income as an excuse for holding a number of benefices in conjunction with his bishopric. The practice was indeed expressly forbidden by a statute of 1836[1] which thus paved the way for the Act of 1838 which dealt with the entire question of pluralism.[2] Members of chapters were forbidden to hold more than one benefice or to belong to more than one chapter and it became illegal to hold two benefices if they were more than ten miles apart, if the population of either benefice was above 3,000 or the combined stipends exceeded £1,000.

Finally the statute of 1840[3] settled the question of the cathedral chapters. The number of canons was limited to six at Canterbury, Durham, Ely, and Westminster, five at Winchester and Exeter, two at Llandaff and Saint David's, four everywhere else. The reduction was considerable and was expected to save £130,000 a year. This sum was to be utilized to raise the stipends of the poorer clergy. A minimum stipend was fixed for all livings in the gift of the Crown. When the number of parishioners was less than 1,000 it was £180, and rose with the increase in their number until it reached the sum of £400 when the number of parishioners exceeded 5,000.

These drastic reforms aroused the protest of several High Churchmen, for example, Sir Robert Inglis in the Commons and the Bishop of Exeter in the Lords.[4] They maintained that the State as represented by Parliament had no right to treat the possessions of the Church as a fund it could distribute at its pleasure. Every bishop, every chapter, every dean, every canon, and every incumbent possessed an income it was not entitled to touch. Otherwise a priest would become a government official paid by the State and the entire constitution of the Church be destroyed.

---

[1] 6 and 7 Will. IV, cap. 77, sec. 19.   [2] 1 and 2 Vict., cap. 106.

[3] 3 and 4 Vict., cap. 113 (Ecclesiastical Commissioners Act). This Act, on which the leaders of both parties were agreed, was passed amidst universal indifference. (See Baron Bunsen, *Memoirs*, vol. i, pp. 509–10: letter of February 27, 1839.) Two 'stalls' were added to the chapter of Christ Church College, Oxford, to be attached respectively to the chair of ecclesiastical history and the chair of 'Biblical criticism' (H. of C., April 6, 1839; *Parliamentary Debates*, 3rd Series, vol. liii, p. 59). For the establishment of these stalls, see Bunsen's letter to his wife, April 16, 1839 (*Memoirs*, vol. i, p. 517). Alternative plans were proposed by Sydney Smith (see *Second Letter to Archdeacon Singleton, sub finem*), and by a committee representative of the cathedral chapters (H. of C., April 6, 1839, *Parl. Deb.*, 3rd Series, vol. liii, pp. 590 sqq.). On November 25 Peel showed impatience and warned Goulburn that unless the chapters proposed an acceptable scheme without further delay, he should act independently (C. S. Parker, *Sir Robert Peel*, vol. ii, pp. 411–2).

[4] See especially H. of C., March 10, 1836: Sir Robert Inglis' speech (*Parl. Deb.*, 3rd Series, vol. xxxii, pp. 162–3). H. of L., July 29, 1836: the Bishop of Exeter's speech (ibid., 3rd Series, vol. xxxv, pp. 661–3).

They also protested against the machinery set up to execute the act of 1836. They objected to this permanent 'corporation' of 'ecclesiastical commissioners', in which the two Archbishops and the Bishop of London sat with a majority of laymen for the purposes of confiscating the surplus income of stipends they considered excessive, granting a subsidy to poorly paid sees or benefices and drawing up regulations which when approved by the Crown and published in the *Gazette* came into force without even the sanction of Parliament.

No doubt the legislature had endeavoured to allay the anxiety of the High Church Party. The administration of the revenues of his see remained in the hands of the bishop, who was merely obliged to declare the amount of his income to the commissioners and in certain cases hand over to them the sum prescribed by the Act. The following year, however, to settle the complicated question of the Church Rates the Government attempted a further step.[1] It proposed to place the administration of the entire endowments of the Church in the commissioners' hands. They would administer the possessions of the Church more competently than the clergy, would pay the latter their usual stipends, and employ the surplus for the upkeep of the churches. The Church Rates being thus rendered superfluous could be abolished; it was in this fashion that the church cess had been abolished in Ireland in 1833. The plan failed. England was not Ireland and since 1833 the Church had realized her power. The outcry of the clergy against this disguised confiscation was so violent that the Cabinet retreated, shelved the bill, and contented itself with instituting an inquiry into the present management of ecclesiastical property. It was not until 1840 that the bill for the reform of the chapters adopted—but this time explicitly—the principle of entrusting the administration of church property—the income of the suppressed canonries—to the 'commission', a body which was admittedly a creation of Parliament and the State. Were not the fears of the High Churchmen justified? If the measure was not the separation of Church and State, was it not at least the subordination of Church to State?

Despite appearances this was not yet the case. The composition

[1] H. of C., March 3, 1837: Spring Rice's speech (*Parliamentary Debates*, 3rd Series, vol. xxxvi, pp. 1207 sqq.). For the protests of the clergy who regarded Spring Rice's proposal as a breach of faith with themselves, see Sp. Walpole, *Life of Lord John Russell*, vol. i, p. 278 *n*.

of the body of commissioners, which had originally contained more laymen than ecclesiastics was radically changed in 1840 when its competence was extended. In future all the bishops would be members of the commission, which therefore would be in the strict sense a clerical body entrusted with the administration of the temporalities of the Church. And in any case the proposal to reduce the endowments of the Church was explicitly abandoned by the new statute; it was simply a question of redistributing property whose amount was left untouched. The Government did not even dare to make the income of the bishops contribute to the stipends of the poorer clergy, and the Act of 1836 had not only left a considerable inequality between the incomes of different sees, it had also maintained them at a high figure. This is not surprising; for in accordance with the method of reform devised by Peel the ecclesiastical legislation was actually the work of the episcopate. And for the same reason the effect of reforms against which the more intransigent clergy protested so loudly was to strengthen the bishops' authority. The Act of 1836 extended the bishop's power to dispense an incumbent from the obligation of residence.[1] The Act of 1840 placed the appointment of the canons in his hands whereas the chapters had hitherto been chosen by co-optation. And a Church Discipline Bill passed the same year strengthened the control of the bishops over their clergy.[2]

3

In short the same thing happened again now which had happened when the Church Reform Bill was passed in 1817.[3] The Evangelical party had initiated the movement for reform, the High Church had benefited by it. But it would be truer to say that on this occasion a compact had been concluded between the two parties against the unholy alliance of Catholics and infidels. It bore fruit. The Church manifested her vitality by reforming herself and by reforming herself grew stronger. Her position had never seemed more powerful than on the morrow of the election of 1837 when for the first time since 1830 the progress of the Radicals was definitely checked.

To be sure the success won by the Church of England shortly

[1] In its original form the bill had extended still further the authority of the bishops, but its provisions were modified during the debates. See S. Smith, *Third Letter to Archdeacon Singleton* (*Works*, vol. ii, p. 287). [2] 3 and 4 Vict., cap. 86. [3] See vol. i., pp. 390-401.

before 1840 was not a final victory which achieved permanent results. The sciences continued their irresistible progress, and gave birth to a new view of the origins of the world more difficult every day to reconcile with the biblical cosmogony. Geology in particular had for the past decade caused grave difficulties to orthodox Christians, and when geological questions were discussed at the annual summer meeting of the British Association, the wrath of the religious press broke out anew. And even inside the Church the zeal of the Evangelicals and High Churchmen was held in check by the Liberalism of the statesmen. Melbourne 'liberalized' the episcopate by a series of appointments which scandalized the orthodox, Maltby to Chichester and later to Durham, Whately to Dublin, Butler to Lichfield, Stanley to Norwich, and Thirlwall to St. Davids. The appointment of Hampden in 1836 as Regius Professor of Theology at Oxford provoked a rebellion among the clergy memorable in the history of the Church. Nor was it only Whig statesmen who made a point of using their patronage to restrain the excesses of Anglican orthodoxy. Peel during his brief tenure of office had taken Milman, the historian of the Jews, who was held suspect by the orthodox, under his protection, and made him a Canon of Westminster. But when all this has been said and due account taken of the extremely complicated and indefinite character of British institutions, it remains true that the period we are now studying witnessed a marked revival of orthodox Christianity in its most uncompromising form.

The blasphemous anti-Christian propaganda which had enjoyed a superficial vogue in the period immediately following 1815 seemed altogether discredited. To perceive this we have only to compare the tone in which Owen conducted his propaganda on behalf of a purely secular society, with the language of Bentham, Hone, Carlile, and even Byron fifteen or twenty years earlier. When Bowring published his edition of Bentham's complete works, he entirely omitted his attacks upon Christianity. German criticism was very little known and regarded with suspicion. Strauss' *Life of Jesus* which had already been translated several times into French still awaited an English translator. The attacks made about 1832 against the Anglican liturgy had been defeated. The Church had reformed her organization and retained her creed in its integrity.

As has just been pointed out this victory of the Church was in many respects precarious, and threatened by many dangers. Under the leadership of Wiseman, a skilled controversialist, the Catholics were making numerous converts, and before many years had passed the adherents of the Oxford movement would join them in large numbers. But at present Newman had no inkling of his destiny and it was in reply to Wiseman that he published at the beginning of 1837 his book on 'The Prophetical Office of the Church viewed relatively to Romanism and Popular Protestantism'.[1] It remains to this day the classical defence of the Church of England as the Via Media between Catholicism and the Protestant sects. Moreover, the Scottish Evangelicals disgusted by their failure to effect that reform of the national Church which in 1834 they had regarded as assured would shortly decide under the leadership of Chalmers to separate from her communion and form a schismatic body. But at present Chalmers was still a supporter of establishment and had just come to London to defend the Established Church in a series of lectures which created no little stir.[2] The youthful Gladstone published a treatise on the relations between Church and State, and the fact that the book seems a poor performance to-day only makes its success when it first appeared the more significant.[3] Sydney Smith, now a Canon of St. Paul's, disappointed of the bishopric he had expected from his Whig friends, took his revenge by coming forward in defence of the Cathedral Chapters threatened by the bill which was to become law in 1840. Never had his vein been richer or his manner more youthful than in his three 'Letters to Archdeacon Singleton'.[4] Even the Dissenters or at least their most prominent representatives, Baines in the House of Commons[5] and Vaughan

[1] In 1836 Wiseman published his Lectures on the doctrines of Catholicism. But Newman appears to have begun as early as 1834 the book which he published in 1837 (*Apologia pro Vita Sua*, Part IV, ed. 1913, p. 164).

[2] Rev. W. Hanna, *Memoirs of Thomas Chalmers*, vol. iv, pp. 345 sqq. John Morley, *Life of W. E. Gladstone*, vol. i, pp. 177 sqq.

[3] *The State in its Relations with the Church*, 1839 [1838]. See Macaulay's article on Gladstone's book in the *Edinburgh Review*, April 1839, 'Church and State' (vol. lxix, pp. 231 sqq.). Cf. Bunsen to his wife, December 13, 1838: 'Last night at eleven, when I came from the Duke, Gladstone's book was on my table. . . . It is the book of the time, a great event. . . . The first book since Burke that goes to the bottom of the vital question, far above his party and his time. . . . Gladstone is the first man in England as to intellectual power' (*Memoirs of Baron Bunsen*, vol. i, pp. 489–90).

[4] *First Letter to Archdeacon Singleton on the Ecclesiastical Commission*, 1837. *Second Letter* . . 1838. *Third Letter* . . . 1839 (*Works*, vol. ii, pp. 255 sqq.).

[5] H. of C., May 22, 1837 (*Parliamentary Debates*, 3rd Series, vol. xxxviii, p. 232).

in print,[1] disclaimed any wish to attack the principle of establishment. All alike—Newman and Chalmers, Gladstone and Sydney Smith, Baines, and Vaughan—were zealous in defence of the Church.

III ADMINISTRATIVE QUESTIONS

I

While the question of Church Reform was thus settled by agreement between the two parties and in concert with the Bishops, what was the fate of those comprehensive measures of administrative reform conceived by Bentham and his disciples whose adoption seemed the logical consequence of the Reform of the franchise in 1832? The Poor Law Amendment Act of 1834 had been the first victory of the Benthamites, and the Liberal Government now took the paradoxical step of introducing the Poor Law into Ireland where hitherto there had been no system of poor relief. It was paradoxical because it had been Michael Thomas Sadler and the Tory publicists who had originally proposed to extend the English Poor Law to Ireland whereas the orthodox Liberals had declared themselves opposed in principle to the step. And even when their reform of the English system of poor relief had reconciled them to a law which they could now regard as their own work, the difficulty was not at an end. The Cabinet governed Ireland in concert with O'Connell, and O'Connell, an uncompromising disciple of Ricardo, was opposed to a Poor Law in any shape or form.[2] They appointed a commission to examine the question of poverty in Ireland, and the commission, which included Whately, an ardent Malthusian, reported against any grant of relief to able-bodied paupers. Nevertheless,

---

[1] R. Vaughan, *Thoughts on the Past and Present State of Religious Parties in England*, 1838, p. xvi: 'It may be strictly lawful that there should be no Established Church; but in the state of society existing in England it may be far from expedient. The whole question, though truly one of principle, is also one to be determined in a great degree by circumstances. While the social system of England shall be what it is, and while the prevalent feeling in favour of an Established Church shall be what it is, there ought, as I conceive, to be such a Church.' P. xviii: 'My own conviction, in regard to the Church of England and that, as I believe, of Dissenters generally, is not that she should be demolished or despoiled, but that she should be regarded as pertaining to the religion of the majority, according to the real state of things in England.'

[2] H. of C., February 13, 1837 (*Parliamentary Debates*, 3rd Series, vol. xxxvi, pp. 485 sqq.); April 28, 1837 (ibid., 3rd Series, vol. xxxviii, pp. 360 sqq.); February 9, 1838 (ibid., 3rd Series, vol. xxxviii, pp. 947 sqq.); April 30, 1838 (ibid., 3rd Series, vol. xlii, pp. 681 sqq.).

it was imperative to provide relief for the Irish poor in their own country, otherwise the influx of Irish immigrants into England would be a source of constantly increasing disorder.

The Government then sent to Ireland one of the three Poor Law commissioners, George Nicholls, with instructions which amounted to orders. After travelling about the country for six weeks he drew up a report in which he recommended that the principle of the new Poor Law should be applied to Ireland. Relief must be given only in workhouses, and the system administered by the ratepayers under the supreme control of the three commissioners in London. His recommendations were embodied in a bill introduced in 1837 and finally passed in 1838.[1] Thus the principle which the Whig ministers under the influence of the Benthamites had introduced four years before into the administration of England won a further triumph. It seemed only logical to extend to the other branches of local government the new system whose application to the Poor Law had received the sanction of Parliament. Such was the desire of the philosophic Radicals. But insurmountable difficulties stood in the way.

In the first place, as was only to be expected, when public opinion became once more favourable to the Church, it became at the same time favourable to the entire body of local traditions of which the Church was in a sense the symbol. The upheaval of 1832 once passed, not alone in the province of religion, but in all matters whatsoever England had ceased to be revolutionary. And on the other hand the Poor Law which might have served as the foundation of an entire edifice of local administration was the object of a formidable movement of popular hostility. We must return later to the agitation against the construction of workhouses which, springing up about this date among the lower classes in the manufacturing districts, presented a further obstacle to the reformers of local government. The fashion in which they had dealt with the Poor Law had made their principles suspect. Only one attempt was made by the Government to utilize for other purposes the machinery set up by the new system of poor relief. When in order to settle the question of Nonconformist marriages a civil register was set up, the framework of the Poor Law was employed. The three Poor Law commissioners were to appoint in every union registrars who were to be co-ordinated

[1] 1 and 2 Vict., cap. 56.

by a central board for every county (district) and these in turn would be under the control of a national board. The scheme was excellent and destined in the long run to prove successful. Indeed Chadwick even secured a provision by which the new officials would register not only deaths but their causes, a provision which paved the way for the ultimate adoption of that service of public health which Southwood Smith and himself never ceased to advocate.[1] But it was some time before the new system could function in some districts of the north. The populace regarded it as an indirect method of forcing upon them the hated Poor Law.[2] The politicians took the warning. They abandoned the idea of consolidating local government on the basis of the Poor Law. They were content to tinker at the old system by piecemeal reforms introduced from time to time, gradually replace the old anarchy which prevailed in local government by a new system equally chaotic and continue as in the past to trust the working of the administrative machine to public spirit rather than legal enactment.

2

The first obstacle to be overcome, if the centralized system so dear to the Benthamites was to be introduced, was the traditional separation between the towns and the rural districts, the boroughs and the counties. Even in that more unstable period when the franchise was reformed, the reformers had not dared to abolish an arrangement hallowed by immemorial antiquity. It was therefore out of the question to contemplate the abandonment of the dual system when the storm had been succeeded by calm and even by apathy. Separate legislation was therefore introduced for the boroughs and the counties.

The reform of the Scottish corporations had been effected quietly and almost without debate by the first reformed Parliament in 1833.[3] The commission appointed the same year to

---

[1] *The Health of Nations. A Review of the Works of Edwin Chadwick. With a biographical dissertation* by Benjamin Ward Richardson, 1887, vol. i, pp. xliii-xlv. For the use which Chadwick made of the commissioners in 1839 to prepare by the provision of the necessary statistics for the final introduction of a service of public health, see Gilbert Slater, *The Making of Modern England*, pp. 165-6. It need hardly be said that it was upon the registrars that the task devolved in 1841 of carrying out the census and the Registrars' Districts provided the necessary framework.

[2] See especially in the Appendix to *Third Annual Report of the Commissioners under the Poor Law Amendment Act* 1837, the Report from the Commissioners to the Right Honourable Lord John Russell relative to proceedings in the Huddersfield Union, June 21, 1837 (pp. 71 sqq.).   [3] 3 and 4 Will. IV, cap. 76, 77.

advise upon the reform of the English Corporations issued its report in 1835.[1] Lord Melbourne's Cabinet had barely returned to office when it decided to give effect to the report. The bill, whose first reading was passed by the Commons on June 5, finally became law on September 9.[2] It had involved serious conflict with the House of Lords which at one moment had believed that by introducing amendments which restricted very considerably the scope of the measure they had succeeded in making it unacceptable to the Liberals and had thus secured its abandonment. But Peel had found a way out of the impasse. The Irish Corporations were still to be reformed. It was a heavy task which occupied the attention of Parliament during five successive sessions.[3] And the bill which was finally passed in 1840[4] after lengthy debates contained many concessions to the objections and prejudices of the Conservative and Protestant party. A reform of some kind had now been effected throughout the United Kingdom. In what did it consist?

To discover the general character of the reform we will examine the most important of the three statutes, the Act passed in 1835 for England and Wales. Before the passing of the Act there had existed 184 'close' corporations, appointed by co-optation, citadels of nepotism and religious intolerance, whose principal function was to administer a number of charitable or pious foundations. These were suppressed and replaced by the same number of elected bodies. The competence of these new corporations was minutely prescribed by law and narrowly restricted. On the one hand they lost the right to administer the religious trusts. But on the other hand they received powers to provide for the lighting and safety of the streets on the lines laid down by the Lighting and Watching Acts which during the past half century Parliament had been in the habit of passing from time to time in favour of a particular locality. The revenue which had belonged to the old corporations was handed over to their successors to meet the local expenditure and, if that expenditure should exceed the revenue thus provided, they were empowered to levy a rate

---

[1] *First Report of the Commissioners appointed to inquire into the Municipal Corporations in England and Wales*, 1835, followed the same year by an Appendix consisting of five parts dealing respectively with the different 'circuits' into which the Commissioners had divided the country.   [2] 5 and 6 Will. IV, cap. 76.

[3] *Annual Register*, 1836, pp. 21 sqq.; 1837, pp. 40 sqq.; 1838, pp. 126 sqq.; 1839, pp. 81 sqq.; 1840, pp. 105 sqq.   [4] 3 and 4 Vict., cap. 108.

on the inhabitants of the borough, a rate which those who passed the statute of 1835 no doubt expected would in all cases be very moderate. The corporations were to be elected by all the householders of the borough who were liable for poor rate, and a third part of the council was to be elected annually. These provisions were a partial realization of the double programme of the Radicals: universal suffrage and annual elections. The Conservatives were obliged to be content with securing several provisions of a less democratic character. To qualify for the vote three years' residence was required. No one was eligible who did not possess a certain income. And a body of aldermen was added to the councils, equal in number to a third of the entire body and elected by the councils themselves for a term of six years. Moreover, the statute only applied to corporations already in existence. Such important towns as Manchester and Birmingham which returned members to Parliament did not receive the right to elect a municipal council because hitherto they had not possessed a corporation. The sole concession made by the Act was that householders might petition for a council and the Crown if it thought fit was empowered to grant their petition.

We shall understand the new statute better if we compare it with the Scottish and Irish Acts.

The Scottish Act began by bestowing an elected council on all the royal burghs with the exception of nine whose size was regarded as too insignificant. And a council was also granted to thirteen other towns which had not been royal burghs but which had received the parliamentary franchise in 1832. In this respect therefore, the Scottish measure was more liberal than the English statute of 1835. But on the other hand it restricted the municipal vote to those inhabitants who already possessed the parliamentary vote, that is to say to the occupiers of a tenement whose rental value was £10. Since it was the intention of the statute to bring the municipal franchise into harmony with the parliamentary, it could not be more democratic than the Reform Bill of 1832. In this respect the English Act was the more liberal.[1]

The Irish Act of 1840 was in every respect more Conservative

---

[1] A bill introduced by Brougham in the House of Lords during the session of 1833 to reform the English municipalities proposed a system akin to that which was actually adopted the same year for the Scotch burghs. (H. of C., February 27, 1835: Peel's speech, *Parliamentary Debates*, 3rd Series, vol. xxvi, p. 424. *The Reform Ministry and the Reformed Parliament*, 1833, p. 75.)

than the Scottish and English. The Tories resigned themselves to
the unqualified suppression of the old corporations constituted by
co-optation; for the scandal of corporations restricted to Protestants in a Catholic country was too glaring to be any longer
endurable. But they resisted the proposal to replace them by
elective councils on which the Catholics would always have an
overwhelming majority. Their opposition was partly successful.
Of the forty-eight corporations suppressed, only ten were replaced
by elective councils. They also demanded that in the new municipalities the franchise should be restricted within the narrowest
possible limits. Finally a qualification of £10 was adopted—that
is to say, apparently the same qualification as in Scotland, but
which would in reality produce a far narrower franchise. For the
country was far poorer.[1]

Thus were formed in Scotland and even in Ireland, but above
all in England, what were nothing less than islands of representative democracy. Three months after the English Act of 1835
came into force the first municipal elections under the new
statute took place. They were a victory for the cause of reform.
They amounted in fact to a social revolution. In the local government of the boroughs the clients of the nobility were replaced by
merchants and shopkeepers. And to a religious revolution also,
for the Dissenters were strongly represented on all the new
councils, sometimes were actually in the majority. In some towns
the Mayor was a Nonconformist.[2] The Liberals drew a favourable
presage from these elections. Their position in Parliament, which
had been extremely precarious during the first six months after
their return to office, had improved. They even ventured to hope
—they were disappointed by the event—that the new general
election would compensate them for their poor success at the
election of 1835. O'Connell declared that the new municipal
councils would be 'normal schools' for democratic agitators.

[1] The thirty-eight boroughs which were deprived of corporations by the statute of 1840
could manage their local affairs under the system set up by the General Lighting and
Watching (Ireland) Act of 1828 (9 Geo. IV, cap. 82). By a statute passed in 1842 they
received the right, in common with every Irish borough, of petitioning for a charter of
incorporation. The procedure to be followed in making a petition was subjected to complicated regulations, more complicated than the similar regulations prescribed for English
towns by the Act of 1835 (3 and 4 Vict., cap. 108, s. 14).
[2] See especially Bunce, *History of Birmingham*, vol. i, pp. 153 sqq. Clause 50 of the
Statute of 1835 imposed on municipal councillors the oath prescribed by 9 Geo. IV,
cap. 17. For the difficulties felt by Dissenters in regard to the oath, see E. Baines, *Life
of Edward Baines*, p. 223.

In addition to its direct operation, the Municipal Corporations Act affected indirectly the local government of the country. In its original form the bill had proposed to place the appointment of the magistrates in the hands of the municipal councils. The House of Lords rejected a provision which revolutionized the national institutions. But to persuade the Radicals to accept the amendment Lord John had promised that in the appointment of magistrates for the boroughs he would take account of the council's recommendations.[1] The Liberal party finally came to regard this verbal undertaking as a statutory provision, and Lord John considered that he was carrying out the spirit, if not the letter of the law, by systematically appointing the Justices of the Peace on the recommendation of the new councils. In this he did but carry further the practice he had already adopted in his appointments of neglecting to consult the lord-lieutenants. Since the Justices of the Peace were always taken from the gentry and the clergy, it necessarily followed that they were all or almost all Tories. To restore the balance Lord John appointed Whigs on his own initiative.

There were, therefore, towns in which the established tradition was reversed and all or almost all the magistrates were Whigs. And even in the country districts, to Lord Melbourne's disgust, Dissenters and manufacturers found places on the bench.[2] Two

[1] H. of C., September 1, 7, 1835 (*Parliamentary Debates*, 3rd Series, vol. xxx, pp. 1221 sqq., 1405-6). Clause 98 of the Act of 1835 provided for the appointment of an indeterminate number of magistrates in every borough 'to which His Majesty may be pleased upon the Petition of the Council thereof to grant a Commission of the Peace'. This power conferred upon the borough councils to ask for magistrates without the specification of any person in particular seems to have been interpreted by the Liberals as empowering them to recommend individuals by name (*Morning Chronicle*, December 28, 1835). Cf. *Greville Memoirs*, July 22, December 31, 1839; also H. of L., February 9, 1836: Lord Salisbury's motion (*Parl. Deb.*, 3rd Series, vol. xxxi, pp. 177 sqq.).

[2] Lord Melbourne to Lord John Russell, October 6, 1835: '. . . It is certainly true that I always admitted a man's being a Trader to be an objection to his becoming a Magistrate, and I believe it is upon this principle that the commissions have been constituted generally, and particularly in the manufacturing Counties. The notion was that Manufacturers would not be considered impartial Judges in cases between the workmen and their employers. You may certainly say the same with respect to country gentlemen in disputes between farmers and their men, and also upon the Game Laws, but after all country gentlemen have held, and do hold, a higher character than Master Manufacturers. . . . You must also bear in mind that the majority of Master Manufacturers are Tories, particularly, for instance, in this very town of Wolverhampton . . .' (*Early Correspondence of Lord John Russell*, vol. ii, pp. 138-9). Lord John Russell to Lord Melbourne, October 9, 1835: '. . . You must recollect the power of a Magistrate does not begin and end with sending a sheep-stealer to jail. The county purse is in a great degree under his control, roads are turned, bridges made, the poor relieved by his decisions, and in this county our Whig magistrates have reduced the expenses 50 per cent by economy and honesty. The landed gentry are very respectable, and I have always found them kind and humane, but they

lord-lieutenants resigned rather than countenance what they considered a usurpation of their functions.[1] The scandal reached its climax when there was an outbreak of rioting, and it became known that two notorious agitators were or had been Lord John's magistrates. Not only in the towns, but in the country also, a silent revolution had occurred in the appointment of the men entrusted with the local government.[2] Was it an adequate solution of the question? Or would the ministry dare to take the step which logically followed the reform of the borough corporations, and reform the administration of the country districts by abolishing the aristocratic method of co-optation in favour of the principle of election? For a measure so revolutionary Lord Melbourne's Cabinet possessed neither the courage nor the power.

3

A commission which had been appointed to inquire into the management of the county finances[3] issued a first report in

are certainly the class in this country most ignorant, prejudiced, and narrow-minded of any. The uneducated labourers beat them hollow in intelligence' (ibid., pp. 143–4). The Liberal party chafed at the consideration for the Tories which the Government had displayed between 1830 and 1834. See *Morning Chronicle*, May 5, 1834: 'What can be expected when Tories are not only continued in every office of power and authority, but when they share equally with the Liberals in all vacant patronage. General Jackson's sweep is preferable to this silly game of attempting to catch enemies by putting salt on their tails.'

[1] The Duke of Newcastle in Nottinghamshire (see *Greville Memoirs*, May 2, 1839): he would not accept the appointment of a Nonconformist Radical, and the Marquis of Queensberry in Dumfriesshire 'from feeling it incompatible with his sense of honour to continue to the Lord Melbourne Ministry the benefit of His Lordship's support' (*The Times*, July 4, 1838). To judge by Lord Melbourne's letter to Lord John Russell of January 20, 1839, some Liberals seem to have urged the ministers to go further and dismiss Tory lord-lieutenants who proved recalcitrant (the letter is, however, concerned with Ireland): '. . . There is nothing so bad as a bad precedent. Everybody condemned the dismissal of the Duke of Norfolk and Lord Fitzwilliam, and yet everybody has it always running in his head to do the same. I know that, if we continue in office, I shall be overruled and made *volens nolens* a party to some folly of this kind' (*Lord Melbourne's Papers*, p. 390).

[2] H. of L., February 9, 1836: Lord Salisbury's motion (*Parliamentary Debates*, 3rd Series, vol. xxxi, pp. 177 sqq.); July 5, 1838: Lord Harewood's motion (ibid., 3rd Series, vol. xliii, pp. 1267 sqq.); July 17, 1838: Lord Wharncliffe's motion (ibid., 3rd Series, vol. xliv, pp. 1122 sqq.). Cf. *The Times*, August 31, 1838. Unfortunately, the three returns published in 1836 give only the names of the magistrates with no indication of their profession, and are therefore useless to the historian. Of greater interest are the returns published on August 16, 1833, of the magistrates appointed since January 1, 1831, 'and distinguishing the Number of Clerical and Lay Justices, and those who have qualified'. But it is earlier than the period with which we are concerned.

[3] It was the country gentlemen who, alarmed by the increase of the rates, sought a remedy from Parliament and thus had a very large part in initiating the reform of the county administration. This was equally true of the reform of the Poor Law in 1834. See Lord Chandos's speech, May 25, 1835 (*Parl. Deb.*, 3rd Series, vol. xxviii, p. 86); April 27, 1836 (ibid., 3rd Series, vol. xxxii, pp. 337–8). Cf. *First and Second Reports from the Select Committee of the House of Lords to inquire into the Charges of the County Rates in England and Wales*, 1834; also H. of C., *Report from the Select Committee on County Rates with Minutes*

August 1835 and a second in June, 1836.[1] Joseph Hume came forward in the Commons to demand that the magistrates should be deprived of their financial functions retaining only the judicial. The counties also must participate in the reform which the statute of 1835 had effected for the towns and the ratepayers be given control over local administration.

Hume did not follow those who proposed to confer on the Poor Law Guardians the right to determine, collect, and administer the County Rate. He disliked the system by which the Guardians were elected, since the number of votes possessed by each elector was determined by his wealth.[2] He proposed that in every county a County Board should be set up, elected by every ratepayer with the same procedure and franchise with which the urban ratepayers had just elected their municipal councillors in the 184 English boroughs. The bill was accepted by the Government and passed the first reading, but at the second reading it was opposed by the county members and thrown out. It was in vain that Hume renewed the attempt in 1839.[3] Each time he was thwarted by the opposition of the gentry and the apathy of the Government.

of Evidence, 1834. The Poor Law Amendment Act of 1834 was not only a measure of administrative centralization, but also a measure of financial relief to the agriculturalists. Nevertheless, the most powerful motive with the country gentlemen was the desire to retain their control of local government. It is of interest to recall that in 1829 Peel had introduced an important bill for the reform of the county administration to which he seems to have attached considerable weight, but had finally been content to consolidate in one statute all the existing statutes respecting the Justices of the Peace, extend while more accurately defining their authority, and make it more difficult to join the bench by raising the qualification from £100 to £300 (H. of C., March 25, 1829, Parliamentary Debates, N.S., vol. xx, pp.1445 sqq.).

[1] Preliminary Report of the Commissioners appointed to inquire respecting County Rates, August 12, 1835. Report of the Commissioners for inquiring into County Rates, and other matters connected therewith, June 16, 1836. The Report recommends a mixed system of financial administration in the counties: '. . . no reason is apparent why persons elected by boards of guardians should not satisfactorily conduct the affairs of the county in conjunction with a limited number of magistrates' (p. 50).

[2] Hume brought other objections against the proposal to entrust the administration of the counties to the Boards of Guardians. The area of the Unions was too small, one Union often belonged to two counties, and the Poor Law had hitherto been enforced only in about one-half of the kingdom. These reasons do not appear to have been unanswerable, since before the year had ended the framework of the Poor Law was employed for another purpose and co-ordinated with the county organization. See Hume's speech, H. of C., June 21, 1826 (Parl. Deb., 3rd Series, vol. xxxiv, pp. 680 sqq.).

[3] H. of C., August 21, 1839 (ibid., 3rd Series, vol. l, pp. 465, 471). An opponent objected to Hume's bill on the ground 'that the existence of boards of guardians . . . rendered the formation of such bodies as these councils unnecessary' (ibid., 3rd Series, vol. l, pp. 465-6). It was on this occasion that the term 'County Councils' appears to have been employed for the first time (cf. Report of Commissioners on County Rates, p. 51). In 1836 Hume spoke of 'County Boards'.

If, with a caution pardonable under the circumstances, the Cabinet shrank from adopting Hume's proposal to deal with the administration of the counties as a whole, it could hardly avoid dealing with special problems which clamoured urgently for solution. What solution would the ministers adopt since they were afraid of that proposed by the Radicals? The administration of the roads was sheer chaos. There were turnpike roads controlled by trusts, corporations which enjoyed the legal right to levy a toll on those who made use of the road. But since the introduction of railways had dealt a fatal blow to the stage-coaches and had thus deprived the turnpike trusts of the most productive source of their revenue, they were all bankrupt.[1] Besides these there were a host of by-roads left to the uncontrolled and unco-ordinated management of the parochial authorities, and therefore in a disgraceful condition. The Cabinet proposed to settle the question of the turnpike trusts by abolishing them entirely and to replace them by a special department to operate throughout the country under the supreme control of a board sitting in London. But the private interests threatened by the reform were too powerful, and found it an easy task to intimidate the Government by declaiming against the danger of a centralized bureaucracy.[2] The remaining roads, however, were dealt with by the Highway Bill of 1835.[3] It was a voluminous enactment whose 119 clauses gave it the appearance of a complete code. But on detailed examination, it proves a feeble measure. The parishes were to elect a surveyor annually. If they refused to do so the magistrates were empowered to interfere and appoint one themselves. But this merely optional sanction was the sole sanction imposed. The parishes were further empowered to call upon the magistrates to unite them in groups each of which would be placed under a district surveyor. But within the district, were it ever formed, the financial independence of each parish was jealously safeguarded. The district must be re-erected every three years and any parish might withdraw from its district by giving a year's notice. Thus the Parish and the Justices of the Peace remained the sole permanent administrative authorities recognized by a law which was throughout

[1] For the ruin of the Turnpike Trusts, see S. and B. Webb, *The Story of the King's Highway*, pp. 215 sqq.
[2] H. of C., March 2, 1837 (*Parliamentary Debates*, 3rd Series, vol. xxxvi, pp. 1196–8); May 10, 1837 (ibid., 3rd Series, vol. xxxviii, p. 789); June 11, 1839 (ibid., 3rd Series, vol. xlviii, pp. 149 sqq.)   [3] 5 and 6 Will. IV, cap. 50.

merely optional. Indeed, the bill was so ineffective that the Government attempted to replace it by a far more drastic measure. It proposed to identify the districts throughout the country with the Poor Law Unions and place them under the jurisdiction of the Boards of Guardians.[1] But the bill was dropped in the course of debate.

Another problem which had long demanded solution became urgent in 1839. That year the entire north of England was the scene of riots against which in the absence of a local police force the supporters of order had no other resource than to call out the troops. How should the necessary police be provided? Should a national force be instituted, under the exclusive control of a central department in London? In 1829, Peel had established a force of this kind in the metropolis, but a Tory government could afford a step too daring for a Liberal administration. Were they then to wait until the County Boards urged by Hume and his friends had been set up and entrust them with the control of the country police? It was impossible to adjourn to the fulfilment of that Utopia the solution of a problem so pressing. Lord John decided to place the local police force under the control of the Justices of the Peace, the Home Secretary reserving only the right to prescribe uniform regulations for the management of the police throughout the Kingdom.[2] The Justices received the right to increase or reduce at their discretion the number of constables, the right to appoint the chief constables—one for every county or constituency—who in turn should have full power to appoint or dismiss the constables under his authority. The effect of the statute was no doubt to centralize local government and it was violently opposed by Disraeli, Fielden, Attwood, and a handful of extreme Radicals.[3] But the centralization was confined to the county areas and unlike the Poor Law was not effected at the expense of the country gentlemen. On the contrary it operated to their advantage and was carried out under their control. After

---

[1] H. of C., March 6, 1839. The bill had already been amended—the Board of Highways was no longer the Board of Guardians (*Parliamentary Debates*, 3rd Series, vol. xlv, pp. 1319 sqq.); also April 24, 1839 (ibid., 3rd Series, vol. xlvii, pp. 499 sqq.).

[2] 2 and 3 Vict., cap. 93. The title of the statute is characteristic, 'An Act for the establishment of County and District Constables by the Authority of Justices of the Peace'. A statute had been previously passed (5 and 6 Will. IV, cap. 43) 'for enlarging the powers of magistrates in the appointment of special constables'.

[3] H. of C., July 24, 1839 (*Parl. Deb.*, 3rd Series, vol. xlix, pp. 731, 738; August 7, 1839, vol. l, p. 6; August 8, 1839, vol. i, p. 116).

nine years of Whig rule the aristocrat Justices of the Peace had actually strengthened their hold upon the government of the country districts.[1]

4

There was, however, in the programme of reform, an article on which the Radicals could not honourably retreat from the position they had taken up. The question of public education raised by Roebuck in the first Reformed Parliament could hardly remain in suspense. The system of grants in aid which had been inaugurated in 1834 had failed to satisfy the Dissenters, for after the first year, it had become evident that on the system by which the grants were allotted, not only would the Catholics receive nothing, but the Anglican schools, the schools founded by the National Society would be automatically favoured to the detriment of the Nonconformist schools, founded by the British and Foreign School Society. But unfortunately whenever the Radicals raised a protest against the practical monopoly of popular education enjoyed by the Church of England the same conflict always arose between the Evangelical Protestants of the sects who were ardent supporters of religious instruction and the free thinkers who, faithful to the doctrine of Bentham, demanded a purely secular system of education. After 1835 Roebuck ceased to put forward his programme of compulsory education on the American or Prussian model.[2] Moreover, he was not returned in 1837, and his place was taken by an Irish Catholic, Thomas Wyse, who had taken the initiative in setting up the Irish system of national education[3] and was conducting by means of the Central Society for Education a campaign for the establishment of a similar system in England. He also thought it more prudent to limit his demands in view of the fact that the popularity of the Church was plainly increasing. He therefore decided to support[4] the more moderate scheme which in December 1837 Brougham put forward in the House of Lords.[5]

[1] The statute was amended in 1840 (3 and 4 Vict., cap. 88). The debates on the new bill afford interesting information as to the application of the Act of 1839 (H. of C., February 18, March 24, 30, June 18, 26, July 16, 1840, *Parliamentary Debates*, 3rd Series, vol. lii, pp. 387 sqq.; vol. iii, pp. 19 sqq., 50 sqq.; vol. liv, pp. 1269 sqq.; vol. lv, pp. 109, 762 sqq.).

[2] H. of C., March 3, 1835 (ibid., 3rd Series, vol. xxvi, pp. 495 sqq.).

[3] H. of C., February 12, 1839 (ibid., 3rd Series, vol. xlv, p. 289).

[4] H. of C., June 14, 1838 (ibid., 3rd Series, vol. xliii, pp. 710 sqq.); February 12, 1839 (ibid., 3rd Series, vol. xlv, pp. 289 sqq.).

[5] H. of L., December 1, 1837: Lord Brougham's speech (ibid., 3rd Series, vol. xxxix, p. 432). Cf. *A Letter on National Education to the Duke of Bedford from Lord Brougham*, 1835.

In the first place Brougham proposed that a department of public education should be set up in the form of a board consisting of two of the principal secretaries of state together with three members appointed for life. It would control the allocation of grants to the schools founded by private charity. It would also control the management of the numerous religious foundations of extremely ancient origin, which were at present administered with a laxity shocking to the radical reformer, who was convinced that if they were well managed under state control their revenues might possibly suffice to provide for the entire education of the poorer classes. And it would be empowered to take more direct measures and found schools wherever private enterprise proved inadequate. Brougham disclaimed, as he had disclaimed all along, any desire to introduce into British legislation the tyrannical and Prussian principle of compulsory education.[1] He did not even suggest that the State should compel the provision of a school in every locality, he merely proposed that the inhabitants should have the right to obtain a school, if they made the request according to specified legal forms. It was frequently suggested that the framework of the Poor Law should be utilized for the organization of this voluntary system. Brougham, however, rejected the suggestion. He did not wish to involve his schools in the unpopularity which rightly or wrongly attached to the new system of poor relief.[2] He proposed that the local administration of his education bill should be entrusted to the new municipalities wherever they existed, and elsewhere to local committees elected on a very broad franchise. Not only would every ratepayer vote

This is the place to mention the suggestion made by Peel in 1841 to utilize the machinery of the Poor Law for the furtherance of popular education. He proposed to make use of certain schools set up under the Act of 1834—those which were attached to a workhouse —to educate the children of the neighbourhood on payment of a trifling fee. A member urged that the scheme should be extended to all the workhouses of the kingdom. 'In each workhouse a school must be maintained, and by adopting the right hon. Baronet's suggestions, this school might be rendered available for the education of the independent poor of the neighbourhood. This arrangement would at once give to the country the advantage of schools of the best kind in about six hundred unions' (H. of C., April 6, 1841: W. S. O'Brien's speech, *Parliamentary Debates*, 3rd Series, vol. lvii, p. 946).

[1] H. of L., November 27, 1837: He did not believe that the conduct of the German princes would be recommended for imitation in this country, with reference to education by the Central Society (*Parl. Deb.*, 3rd Series, vol. xxxix, p. 211).

[2] H. of L., December 1, 1837, Lord Brougham's speech (ibid., 3rd Series, vol. xxxix, p. 452): He might be asked, as he had been frequently asked out of doors and once or twice asked by one for whom he had the greatest possible regard—he meant a noble friend in the other House of Parliament—he might be asked why he did not take the machinery that was in existence, 'You have, it is said, the machinery of the new Poor Law.' Who was the friend to whom Lord Brougham referred? Lord Milton? Or Lord Morpeth?

but everyone who could prove that he had received even an elementary education. In these schools the reading of the Bible would be compulsory except for Jews and Catholics.

Brougham's bill passed the first reading for form's sake, but nothing further was heard of it. Nevertheless, a heated controversy continued between the Anglicans and their opponents. The former urged on behalf of the existing system the fact that their enterprise had, with the assistance of the Government grants, provided for the education of more than 1,000,000 children. 'What of the 3,000,000 children,' was the reply, 'who need to be taught to read and write?'[1] In the matter of primary education England took the last place among the Protestant countries. In 1839 the Cabinet yielded. But it lost credit by pursuing the tortuous and timid methods characteristic of Lord Melbourne's administration.

Lord John[2] proposed the nomination of a board closely resembling that for which Brougham had asked. It would be a committee of the privy council and be composed of five councillors and the president of the council. Its functions would be to allocate the grants and establish a 'normal school' (training college). This was very little when compared with Brougham's scheme which was itself a modification of Roebuck's original project. But it was sufficient to alarm the supporters of the Church and denominational education.[3]

When the committee which was appointed by an Order in Council began its work, it protested at once against the proposed foundation of a training college. For the normal school which was planned on the pattern of the normal schools already set up in Ireland would be a model school, where future teachers would learn their profession by actual practice in teaching and the

[1] *The Report from the Select Committee on Education of the Poorer Classes in England and Wales*, 1838, contains the following estimate: 'Recent statistics proved that the number of children between five and fifteen years of age amounted to a quarter of the entire population: roughly speaking, that figure could be taken to represent the number of children in need of primary education. Deduct the children in easy circumstances for whom no provision was necessary and the children working in factories who from the age of nine were employed for eight hours a day. It would follow that an eighth part of the population ought to be attending school. But at Westminster only a fourteenth part were receiving education, at Bethnal Green a twentieth, and in five other metropolitan parishes a twenty-seventh. At Leeds, Birmingham and Manchester respectively, a forty-first, a thirty-eighth, and a thirty-fifth part.'

[2] H. of C., February 12, 1839 (*Parliamentary Debates*, 3rd Series, vol. xlv, pp. 273 sqq.).

[3] See the debates, H. of C., April 30, 1839, Lord Stanley's question; June 4, 14, 19, 20, 24, 27, 1839 (ibid., 3rd Series, vol. xlvii, pp. 680, 1378; vol. xlviii, pp. 227 sqq., 529 sqq. and 578 sqq., 731 sqq., 967 sqq.); H. of L., July 5, 1839 (ibid., 3rd Series, vol. xlviii, pp. 1234 sqq.).

instruction given would be undenominational.[1] The Cabinet gave way and abandoned the project of founding a normal school under State control. Then the new committee claimed the right to depart from the rules which had been followed during the previous five years in allocating grants. Moreover, they declared their intention to apply a portion of the funds at their disposal to setting up a body of inspectors, and announced that in future no school would receive a grant which refused to conform to the rules laid down by the committee and accept the permanent control of the State inspectors. In terms of contemporary legislation the Cabinet no longer sought a model in the Poor Law of 1834, but turned instead to the Factory Act of 1833—that is to say, abandoned the principle of direct intervention for the principle of inspection and control.[2] Even this was too much for the clericals. Once again the Government was made to feel the power of the Church. The alliance concluded in 1834 between the Evangelicals and the High Churchmen was drawn closer. The Wesleyans placed their powerful organization at the service of the anti-liberal propaganda.[3] Over 3,000 petitions against these new measures were received by Parliament and when the question was debated in the Commons the Government's majority was so weak that an agreement with the Bishops became inevitable. They were to be consulted in the appointment of inspectors, and the inspectors were to report to them as well as to the committee of the privy council.

[1] *Education Commission*, 1861. Appendix. *Minutes of Evidence*: evidence of Sir J. K. Shuttleworth, January 26, 1860 (vol. vi, pp. 300–1). Finally, in 1841 three training colleges were opened, but they were all denominational (ibid., p. 304).

[2] The same principle had been applied to the reform of the prisons. See 5 and 6 Will. IV, cap. 36, 38: An Act for effecting greater Uniformity of Practice in the Government of the several Prisons in England and Wales and for appointing inspectors of Prisons in Great Britain. Introducing on February 11, 1839, a bill 'for the better ordering of Prisons' (2 and 3 Vict., cap. 56), Lord John explained as follows the rejection of that very measure by the Lords in 1838, 'he could only suppose that it was on account of some misconception on the part of their Lordships as to the nature of the powers proposed by the bill to be given to the Secretary of State which might have been imagined to have been powers for enforcing rules for the separate confinement of prisoners'. In fact the powers of the Justices of the Peace were not touched. To remove all doubt on the point, the clause to which exception had been taken was redraughted (*Parliamentary Debates*, 3rd Series, vol. xlv, p. 220).

[3] *Minutes of the Methodist Conferences*, vol. viii, pp. 514–5 (Liverpool Conference, July 31, 1839). The attitude of the Conference is pre-eminently anti-Catholic. 'The attempt to allow the introduction of the Roman Catholic Version of the Scriptures into the Normal School . . . could not but appear eminently calculated to afford facilities and means for the . . . propagation of the . . . tyrannical system of Popery.' The *Christian Advocate* accuses the Wesleyans of a design to lay hands on a portion of the property of the Canadian clergy, possibly even become a state-endowed church.

IV COLONIAL QUESTIONS

I

All this work of reform, whether the reform of the Church or of local government occasioned lengthy debates in Parliament. But nobody was really anxious as to the result, not even the members who kept the debate going. For the vast majority both of Parliament and the country without distinction of party agreed in approving the compromise which was always adopted in the end, and the conservative spirit in which the reforms were effected: Melbourne and Lord John merely carried out Peel's programme. If during these six years the existence of the ministry was several times imperilled, it was when altogether different questions were under discussion. England was beginning to awake to the fact that she was a colonial power and her colonies nothing less than a new world in process of birth, and she often found herself in difficulties when faced by the novel and complicated problems involved in the government of these subordinate States.

It is not our intention to undertake a detailed history of the British colonies. For the object of our study is not that vast Anglo-Saxon world in which perhaps Great Britain is destined one day to be absorbed, but simply Great Britain. Nevertheless, a brief account of colonial history is indispensable in so far as it was bound up with the history of the mother country and influenced its course. At this date, the morrow of the election of 1835 and a critical moment in the history of the British colonies, we must once more study the doctrine of the Radicals of Bentham's school. To that doctrine indeed we must constantly return, for it was the standard with reference to which every British party must be described whether as accepting, modifying or rejecting it. What then was their view of the colonial question? For on this as on every other they possessed a fixed and clearly defined belief.

It was this. Two distinct systems of government prevailed in the British possessions overseas. In some a handful of British officials governed as despotic lords in the name of the home Government. The extreme instance of this was British India with a native population of 100,000,000, in which the British Government had taken the place of the Great Mogul.[1] In others the

[1] We must, of course, bear in mind that since British India was governed by an important company under the control of a special department, the Board of Control, it was not in the technical sense a colony.

colonists formed an independent society democratically governed. They thus approximated to the extreme case of the United States of America which had broken away from the empire and formed with its 10,000,000 inhabitants a powerful nation, noisy, hard-working, prosperous, and animated by an aggressive hostility towards the mother country.[1] For the philosophic Radical the American Republic was the ideal British colony. It fulfilled the two essential purposes of a colony. It absorbed the surplus population and the surplus products of the mother country.[2] And if America were hostile to England, it was because she had been compelled to seize by armed revolt an independence which should have been freely given as her right. And if she erected a tariff wall against British goods, it was by way of reprisals because Britain refused to admit the produce of American agriculture. Let England take the advice of Bentham[3], James Mill, and Joseph Hume, emancipate her colonies and at the same time introduce a system of complete free trade. The colonies would cease to be a burden when they ceased to be dependencies. Instead, they would become so many free and friendly nations.

The doctrine aroused no opposition from a party of enthusiastic imperialists. During the years which followed the Reform Bill there were very few in England who dared to dream of empire. Empires were too expensive and too uncertain: Spain and Portugal had just lost their colonies, and old men still retained vivid

[1] H. of C., March 6, 1838: Sir William Molesworth's speech: 'The saying "Emancipate your colonies" means with those who employ it, most emphatically, a great deal more than the mere words convey. . . . What! are we to repent of having planted the thirteen English colonies of North America, which have expanded into one of the greatest, most prosperous, and happiest nations that the world ever saw' (*Parliamentary Debates*, 3rd Series, pp. 476 sqq.). The entire speech is devoted to a criticism of the colonial administration and therefore gives an excellent picture of the colonial empire at this date. It may be found among the *Selected Speeches of Sir William Molesworth* on questions relating to Colonial Policy, ed. H. E. Egerton, 1903. For another picture of the empire sketched in the same spirit by another Radical writer, see *Westminster Review*, January 1836, 'The Colonial Expenditure' (vol. xxiv, pp. 1 sqq.). A detached statement of facts which, moreover, is concerned only with legal matters, will be found in Clark (Charles), *A Summary of Colonial Law, the practice of the court of appeals from the Plantations and of the laws and their administrations in all the colonies; with Charters of Justice, Orders in Council, etc.*, 1834.

[2] H. of C., January 25, 1838: Warburton's speech: 'It was not to our colonies that emigration was chiefly directed. . . . At present the amount of emigration to the whole of our North American colonies was not more than 30,000 persons annually: whereas the emigration to New York alone exceeded 60,000. So that in the event of our emancipating the North American colonies, there would be no diminution, but, on the contrary, a considerable increase of emigration' (*Parl. Deb.*, 3rd Series, vol. xl, pp. 481–2).

[3] *Emancipate your Colonies! addressed to the National Convention of France, Anno* 1793. *Showing the uselessness and mischievousness of distant dependencies to an European State* (*Works*, ed. Bowring, vol. iv, pp. 407 sqq.).

memories of the loss of the American colonies, so soon after the victory which concluded the Seven Years War.[1] But it was too blankly negative, too 'radical' to please moderate opinion. Nor did even the Radicals venture to push it to its logical consequences. They admitted that their programme of emancipation was not applicable to all the colonies. Indeed, at this very time an entire group of Bentham's disciples was putting forward a positive programme of organized emigration and colonization and thus assisting the growth of the British Empire.

2

In Asia, England was extending her sphere of influence. Alarmed by the attempt of the Russian Emperor to establish a joint Russian and Persian protectorate in Afghanistan, the Governor General, Lord Auckland, despatched an expedition across the Himalayas under the command of Sir John Kean, which marched to Kabul and set up a new Amir. In 1840 it seemed that Afghanistan had become another dependency of the Indian Government, and on its march the expedition had finally established British rule throughout the entire Indus valley. Aden, the gate of the Red Sea, was occupied in January 1839. Moreover, when the Chinese Government forbade the English merchants to import opium into China, they appealed for help to the Indian government and demanded that reparation should be exacted from the Chinese for the humiliations they had suffered at their hands. A fleet was despatched in consequence to Chinese waters, which

[1] A French publicist, the Abbé de Pradt, was perhaps the first to foretell at the opening of the nineteenth century the future importance of what contemporary Englishmen love to call 'the British Commonwealth of Nations'. But what Englishman entertained such thoughts, out of harmony with an age in which imperialism was so discredited, when in 1823 M. de Pradt published his *Parallèle de la Puissance anglaise et russe relativement a l'Europe*? See the curious chapter (X) entitled 'The Six Englands'. These are England properly so called, the United States of America, Canada and British North America, the Cape of Good Hope, British India, and New Holland. It is plain, wrote M. de Pradt, that England by the multiplication of her family, the manner in which she is scattered over the entire face of the globe, the attraction of her perfect institutions, is destined without force of arms to impart a new aspect to the world. In the course of the debate on the Reform Bill, Hume expounded in detail a scheme for the parliamentary representation of the colonies (H. of C., August 16, 1831, *Parliamentary Debates*, 3rd Series, vol. vi, pp. 110 sqq.), and a Conservative speaker could complain a little later that the new franchise had proved detrimental to the 'virtual or indirect' representation the colonists had possessed under the old franchise through their ability to purchase rotten boroughs (H. of C., May 30, 1833, Sir Richard Vyvyan's speech, ibid., 3rd Series, vol. xviii, p. 113). But Hume's scheme was too inconsistent with his own colonial policy. His aim was not to tighten the bond which united the colonies with the mother country, but on the contrary to relax it.

twice occupied the Chusan islands, anchored in the gulf of
Pe-tchi-li and from there sailed to Canton where tne British flag
was hoisted in January 1841. For all these military undertakings
the Government of Calcutta was responsible. We might therefoɪe
have expected that the Radical opponents of colonial expansion
would have attacked the evil at its source. On the contrary their
organ, the *Westminster Review*, that severe critic of all established
institutions, was careful not to offend the susceptibilities of the
East India Company, indeed even spoke in its praise.[1]

Their attitude is explained by the fact that the disciples of
Bentham were all powerful in the Company's offices. James Mill,
who had entered its service in 1819 through the influence of
Ricardo, was receiving a salary of £2,000 a year when he died in
1836,[2] and his son John Stuart Mill, who worked with him,
continued in the Company's service after his father's death.[3]
When at the end of 1827 Lord William Bentinck left London to
become Governor General in India he went to receive Bentham's
philosophic blessing. 'I am going to British India,' he told the old
man, 'but I shall not be Governor General. It is you that will be
Governor General.'[4] And when at James Mill's advice the
government of India was committed to a legislative council of
four members, he persuaded the directors to appoint Macaulay
legal adviser. Indeed, two currents of influence converged to make
the appointment. Charles Grant, the President of the Board of
Control, was an Evangelical and although Macaulay's creed was
distinctly latitudinarian, he belonged to an Evangelical family. He
had, it is true, attracted attention by the lively criticism of the
Utilitarian philosophy he had published in the *Edinburgh Review*.
But James Mill had sufficient insight to perceive the close affinities
which united him with the Utilitarians. Before embarking for
India Macaulay was a frequent visitor at the house of the man who
was at once the oracle of the Utilitarians and the acknowledged
authority on Indian affairs. At a moment when his head was full

---

[1] *London and Westminster Review*, January 1837, 'Fallacies on Poor Laws' (vol. xxvi,
p. 367): 'The offices of the Poor Law Commission and of the India House are the only
exceptions with which we are acquainted where a large proportion of the officials seem
to have anything to do beyond giving trouble to every person requiring information or
other service at their hand.' Cf. Bentham, *Emancipate your Colonies, post scriptum of June
24, 1829* (*Works*, ed. Bowring, vol. iv, p. 418).

[2] A. Bain, *James Mill*, p. 185.

[3] A. Bain, ibid., p. 207; *John Stuart Mill Autobiography*, pp. 81-2.

[4] Bentham to Col. Young, December 28, 1817 (*Works*, ed. Bowring, vol. x, p. 577).

of schemes for Indian legislation, James Mill was lavish of his counsel. 'Keep,' was his emphatic advice, 'to the line of an honest politician.'[1]

Macaulay was able to do useful work in a position which might have been a well paid sinecure. His sojourn in India was marked by reforms. Freedom of the Press. Equal treatment of Englishmen and natives in the Indian courts of law. Encouragement of education by the foundation of schools. The success of his educational policy was direct and speedy, and might be regarded from the Evangelical standpoint as a victory of the Christian religion or from the standpoint of the Utilitarian Enlightenment as a victory of western rationalism. 'No Hindoo,' wrote Macaulay, 'who has received an English education ever remains sincerely attached to his religion.'[2] His work was crowned by the compilation of a penal code based, as he explained in the language of unadulterated Utilita ianism 'on two great principles—the principle of suppressing crime with the smallest possible amount of suffering, the principle of ascertaining truth at the smallest possible cost of time and money.'[3] The code, completed by 1837, abolished the death penalty except for 'aggravated treason' and 'wilful murder', tended indirectly to get rid of every Indian institution which bore a taint of slavery, and was free from legal jargon, written from beginning to end in the language of every-day life. Thus the codification which Bentham had desired in vain for England and the republics of America was fully carried out[4] by the Government of Calcutta. How could the Benthamites do otherwise than wink at the faults of the instrument by which their ideas were put into practice? 'I am convinced,' declared Sir William Molesworth, 'that the form of government which a colony should possess must depend upon the special circumstances of the case. . . . Certain colonies absolutely require a despotic authority . . . our Government of 100,000,000 of people in India . . . is anything but democratic. Yet I know not if a better could be devised for the people who are subject to it.'[5]

[1] A. Bain, *James Mill*, pp. 369, 370.
[2] Macaulay to Zachary Macaulay, October 12, 1836 (Sir G. O. Trevelyan, *Life and Letters of Lord Macaulay*, Popular Edition, 1901, p. 329).
[3] Sir G. O. Trevelyan, ibid., Popular Edition, 1901, p. 299.
[4] But not immediately applied. Since James Mill was dead, the Directors hesitated for over twenty years before they enforced the new code (Bain, *James Mill*, p. 356).
[5] H. of C., March 6, 1838 (*Parliamentary Debates*, 3rd Series, vol. xli, p. 484).

3

To the south of British India a group of colonies surrounded the southern Pacific. To the north were the colonies of the Australian continent,[1] to the south-east New Zealand, to the south-west Cape Colony. All alike could be colonized and cultivated by Europeans. A governor appointed by the Crown was assisted by a legislative council, whose members were also appointed by the Crown. Would the Colonists submit much longer to this despotism?

Australia, discovered by Captain Cook in 1770, had taken the place of the lost American colonies as a convict settlement to which English criminals were transported. There was a lack of women and to restore the balance of the sexes the Government raided the London streets and despatched batches of prostitutes to the Antipodes. Gradually, however, the convicts were joined by free emigrants, and the former, who were placed under conditions which differed according to their offences, could themselves become free citizens on the expiration of their sentences.[2] Even under these circumstances New South Wales, favoured by the excellent climate which was admirably adapted to the raising of sheep, became rich by exporting wool; and as her commercial prosperity increased a semblance of civic life came into existence, and the wealthier colonists began to demand political rights. But on what basis should they be granted? To refuse or to grant civil rights to the ex-convicts, the 'emancipists', was equally difficult. Even the London Radicals though disposed to adopt an extremely

[1] New South Wales; 27 Geo. II, cap. 2; 4 Geo. IV, cap. 96; 9 Geo. IV, cap. 83. Van Diemen's Land, 4 Geo. IV, cap. 96; 9 Geo. IV, cap. 83. Western Australia, 10 Geo. IV, cap. 22; 5 and 6 Will. IV, cap. 14; 6 and 7 Will. IV, cap. 68; 1 and 2 Vict., cap. 46. South Australia, 4 and 5 Will. IV, cap. 95.
[2] Some figures will give a more definite idea of the society which occupied the colony at this period. Porter gives the following immigration statistics for the years preceding 1834. Transported convicts: 1825, 1,916; 1826, 1,815; 1827, 2,587; 1828, 2,712; 1829, 3,664; 1830, 3,225; 1831, 2,633; 1832, 3,119; 1833, 4,151; 1834, 3,161; Free immigrants: 1829, 546; 1830, 309; 1831, 457; 1832, 2,006; 1833, 2,585; 1834, 1,564 (*Porter's Tables*, Supplement to Part V, *Colonies*—1834). The *Annual Register* (1837, p. 251) gives the results of the census of 1837: 77,096 inhabitants, of whom 27,831 were convicts; Free colonists—males over twelve years of age, 23,121; females over twelve years of age: 11,973. Protestants: 54,621; Catholics (in other words Irish): 21,898. Then the proportions changed. In 1838 and 1839 Canada passed through a period of disturbance and emigrants went to Australia instead of America. In 1838 and 1839, according to the calculation of Ch. Buller (H. of C., May 5, 1840, *Parliamentary Debates*, 3rd Series, vol. liii, p. 1301), there were 10,000 free emigrants to 5,000 convicts. For the social conditions obtaining in New South Wales, see an excellent article in the *Quarterly Review*, October 1838, 'New South Wales' (vol. lxii, pp. 475 sqq.).

indulgent attitude towards the emancipists considered the problem in this form insoluble. They condemned the entire system of Australian colonization as fundamentally vicious.

They demanded that the transportation of criminals should cease. Bentham, indeed, had never ceased to attack the system from its first introduction. But since in Australia the harm was already done, they urged that measures should be taken to swamp the criminal population in a vast mass of free immigrants. Edward Gibbon Wakefield, a Quaker by birth, who had been sentenced to imprisonment for abduction, employed his three years of enforced idleness in Newgate to elaborate an entire scheme of systematic emigration and colonization. Land societies, furnished with a government Charter should put up to sale the unoccupied land and thus obtain sufficient funds to finance the immigration of the labour needed to cultivate this virgin soil.[1] Bentham approved the scheme.[2] The opinion of his disciples was divided. The section represented by the *Westminster Review* condemned it[3] and not without reason. For if in the intention of their founder Wakefield's colonies were to become in the long run independent democracies after the American pattern, that did not alter the fact that they could begin their career only under the control and protection of the State. But James Mill, John Stuart Mill, and Sir William Molesworth, in short the entire group which in 1833 founded the *London Review* in opposition to the *Westminster* were keen supporters of Wakefield.

In this way the philosophic Radicals contributed directly to the growth of Britain's colonial empire. It was on their initiative, if not altogether in conformity with their ideas, that the colony of South Australia was founded in 1834 between the older colonies of New South Wales and Van Diemen's Land.[4] And it was also at their initiative that the Government made up its mind to a further step. Some 1,200 miles to the south-east of Australia the English had discovered a group of islands which enjoyed a very

[1] R. Garnett, *Edward Gibbon Wakefield, The Colonization of South Australia and New Zealand*, chaps. iii and iv, pp. 50 sqq. R. C. Mills, *The Colonization of Australia, 1829–1842*, 1915.

[2] See my *Formation du Radicalisme Philosophique*, vol. iii, pp. 380–1, also the note to p. 484: A Proposal for the formation of a joint stock Company by the name of the Colonization Company on an entirely new principle: The Vicinity-maximizing or Dispersion-preventing principle, August 11, 1831.

[3] See especially *Westminster Review*, October 1834, 'New South Australian Colony' (vol. xxi, pp. 441 sqq.).

[4] 4 and 5 Will. IV, cap. 95, amended by 1 and 2 Vict., cap. 60.

favourable climate, delightfully tempered by the surrounding sea, yet free from fogs. A British resident had been sent to New Zealand in 1832. But the step had been taken only to guard against the danger of French annexation, and the home Government was so afraid of being involved in a colonial enterprise that the resident was expressly forbidden to exercise judicial authority over British subjects. New Zealand therefore remained for several years a den of pirates among whom were many convicts who had escaped from Australia. Then the philosophic Radicals, Sir William Molesworth and Wakefield, took action and in despair of overcoming official apathy formed in 1839 without a charter from the Government a 'New Zealand Colonization Company'. A ship was chartered and Sir William's brother joined the expedition. In 1840 the Cabinet at length decided to appoint a Governor and the colony of New Zealand was founded.[1]

To complete our account of the group of southern colonies, we must speak of South Africa, where entirely different problems awaited solution. Here the philosophic Radicals counted for nothing, it was the Evangelicals and emancipationists who pressed the Government to extend its control. Officially the Cape Colony consisted only of the town and harbour at the Cape itself, which was a useful port of call on the route to India. In reality the Colony, before its conquest by Great Britain a portion of the former colonial empire of Holland,[2] was something entirely different, an enormous pastoral territory settled by the Boers. Since the close of the Napoleonic war, and especially during the long crisis of unemployment which followed it, the Government had encouraged British immigration to the Cape. In consequence there were now in the colony two hostile communities, one speaking Dutch, the other English. The English colonists among whom were a large number of Evangelical ministers denounced the harsh treatment of the natives, the Hottentots and the Kaffirs, by the Boers. Fowell Buxton championed their cause and secured an order in council emancipating the slaves. Whereupon the Boers trekked *en masse* towards the interior to escape British

[1] H. of C., June 20, 1838 (*Parliamentary Debates*, 3rd Series, vol. xliii, pp. 871 sqq.). *Annual Register*, 1839, Chron., p. 162. R. Garnett, *Edward Gibbon Wakefield*, pp. 142 sqq.

[2] Since the Colony had been obtained by conquest its status was that of a 'Crown Colony'. Other Crown Colonies at this date were British Guiana, Mauritius, Ceylon, Gibraltar, Malta, and Heligoland (C. Clark, *A Summary of Colonial Law* . . . 1834, p. 23). The title was apparently regarded in certain quarters as unconstitutional (*Reflections on . . . policy of Great Britain. By a British Merchant*, 1833, pp. 113–14).

rule.[1] The Evangelicals at once demanded that the trekkers be pursued and thus prevented from abusing their independence to enslave the native population a second time. For the moment the Government returned an uncompromising refusal. The poor success of the establishment of Sierra Leone, which philanthropic motives had founded somewhat earlier on the West African coast, as an asylum for the negro, did not encourage a second experiment. There was no telling where the Government would be led if once it began to pursue a policy of this nature. For Fowell Buxton invited Great Britain to strengthen her fleet on the African coast, employ steamers to ascend the great rivers into the heart of the continent, and conclude treaties with the negro chiefs both on the coast and in the interior until finally the whole of Africa had become one vast British dominion cultivated by the free labour of the native inhabitants.[2]

4

We must not however imagine that the birth of this new world on the coasts of the Pacific engaged to any considerable extent the attention of Parliament. Nor was any more time bestowed on the tiny dependencies sprinkled over the seas of the world, Gibraltar, Malta, Heligoland, the Ionian Islands, St. Helena, and Mauritius. There were many who wished to see the Ionian Islands handed over to Greece. And in regard to the others, which were mere military stations, the sole complaint raised was that their government was too costly since the aristocracy, it was alleged, too often made use of them to give employment to relatives and dependants. We may pass to the consideration of the long-established colonies in North America and the West Indies, which were further developed than the colonies newly born in the South Seas but where just on that account the problem of home rule was far more urgent. In North America, Nova Scotia, New Brunswick,

[1] H. of C., March 6, 1838: Sir W. Molesworth's speech (*Parliamentary Debates*, 3rd Series, vol. xli, pp. 498 sqq.). H. M. Egerton, *A Short History of British Colonial Policy*, pp. 336 sqq.
[2] T. F. Buxton, *The African Slave Trade*, 1839, p. 240: 'It is earnestly to be desired that all Christian powers should unite in one great confederacy, for the purpose of calling into action the dormant energies of Africa; but if this unanimity is not to be obtained, there are abundant reasons to induce this nation alone, if it must so be, to undertake the task.' *The Remedy being a Sequel to the African Slave Trade*, 1840, pp. 5, 171, 236. *The African Slave Trade and its Remedy*, 1840, fused the two preceding volumes in a single work. Cf. the alarmed letter from Lord Melbourne to Lord John Russell, September 3, 1838 (*Lord Melbourne's Papers*, pp. 376–7).

Newfoundland, Upper and Lower Canada, not to mention the small colony of the Bermudas, were governed by a system of partial home rule. A Governor appointed by the Crown and assisted by his executive council nominated the members of a legislative council which ruled the country in conjunction with a legislative assembly elected by the inhabitants on a franchise usually very wide.[1] The character of these constitutions was disputed. Did they reproduce the three elements of the British Parliamentary System—King, Lords, and Commons? In that case the Governor was an irresponsible monarch and his executive council a ministry in the true sense of the term responsible to the council and the assembly. Or was he a Prime Minister presiding over his executive council, as over a Cabinet, and himself responsible to the Parliament of the Colony? The Governor accepted neither view. He regarded himself as responsible, but only to the King who had appointed him.

Since the constitution of the legislative council, which was composed entirely of the Governor's nominees made it easy for the latter with the support of the council to resist a less pliable assembly, the colonists demanded that the council should be made elective and elected on the same franchise as the assembly. The effect of the change would be to assimilate the constitution of the colony to that of the United States. This was another reason why both the governors and the ministers at home were opposed to the reform. For the United States was in a position to exercise a dangerous fascination over the colonial malcontents. Moreover, the attitude of the States towards Great Britain was brutally insolent. For years past a frontier dispute had raged between the State of Maine and the Colony of New Brunswick, and American obstinacy had always postponed the settlement the British Cabinet wished to reach. Would not the dispute be settled at some future date by incorporating the British colonies on the continent of America into a vast federal republic? There were 10,000,000 American citizens, and scarcely 1,000,000 British; and the latter were faced with the unwelcome fact that the development of

---

[1] Electoral qualification in Canada: the occupation of land of the annual value of forty shillings, or in the towns, of a tenement of the annual value of £5 or at a rental of £10 a year (*Annual Register*, 1831, p. 3). In Newfoundland, since 1832, the franchise belonged to any male inhabitant who had occupied a tenement of whatever value for at least a year before the election (Royal Proclamation, July 26, 1832; C. Clark, *A Summary of Colonial Law*, 1834, p. 449).

their own territory was almost at a standstill, whereas the resources of the United States were increasing by leaps and bounds.

The difficulties we have described were practically the same in all the English colonies in North America, but they came to a head in the two Canadas, and finally in Lower Canada. These provinces demanded that their Parliaments should be given complete financial control, and when in 1831 restrictions were attached to the concession[1] Lower Canada refused every year to pass the budget. Upper Canada asked that the revenues of the Anglican Church should be applied to national education of an undenominational character. Lower Canada protested against the use the Government made of the revenue obtained many years before by confiscating the property of the Jesuits. Upper Canada asked for a responsible Cabinet, Lower Canada for the election of the legislative council. During Lord Grey's administration, when Lord Stanley was Colonial Secretary, his harsh government welded the discontent in both provinces into one solid body of opposition. But under Lord Melbourne's second administration, Lord Glenelg's more adaptable, or perhaps merely weaker, methods revealed the gulf which divided the agitation in Upper from the agitation in Lower Canada. When in 1837 an armed rebellion broke out in Lower Canada it was evidently not a rising of the British colonists against refusal of their constitutional rights, but of the French 'habitants' against British rule, in other words, a national conflict. The French Canadians numbered some 450,000, the British 150,000.[2] The French complained that they were oppressed by a minority. The neighbouring colonies reconciled with the home Government by their fear of the French peril, made haste to settle their differences with the mother country by accepting a temporary compromise,[3] and in Upper Canada the Governor, Sir Francis Head, after putting down, without the least difficulty, an insignificant attempt at insurrection which lasted only a few hours, was able to dispatch all tne troops at his disposal to the assistance of Sir John Colbourne, the Governor of Lower Canada. He trusted the patriotism of the civil population to repel the American raids on the southern frontier.

[1] 1 and 2 Will. IV, cap. 23.   [2] Lord Durham's Report, ed. Lucas, vol. ii, p. 397.
[3] *Annual Register*, 1838, pp. 338–9 (New Brunswick, Nova Scotia).

5

To cope with the situation in Lower Canada, now the sole seat of dissaffection, the Cabinet called upon Parliament to suspend its constitution and despatch a high commissioner to govern the province and take all the measures necessary to restore order throughout the North American Colonies. To conciliate Liberal opinion, liable to take alarm at these dictatorial methods, the Cabinet chose Lord Durham to fill the post of high commissioner.[1] He took with him an official staff which included two philosophic Radicals, a member of Parliament named Charles Buller, and Edward Gibbon Wakefield. The report he drew up in collaboration with Charles Buller and published in 1839 on his return to England, is still esteemed a classic.[2] To settle the problem presented by French Canada, he proposed the repeal of the statute of 1791, which had constituted Upper and Lower Canada separate provinces. If there were only one Canada, the French Canadians would be a minority in the United Canada, 450,000 to 500,000. And that were minority would be further reduced if Wakefield's method applied and British immigration to Canada systematically fostered.[3] On the other hand, he proposed a radical solution of the constitutional question, to recognize the principle of ministerial responsibility. It was definitely incorporated in the measure which Lord John Russell introduced in 1839, and which was passed in 1840.[4] It was as colonial secretary that Lord John introduced the bill and the fact that the leader of the Commons

[1] It was the choice of Lord Durham which won Lord John Russell's consent to the suspension of the constitution. See his Memorandum on Canada of January 1838, also his letter to Lord Melbourne of October 25, 1838 (*Early Correspondence of Lord John Russell*, vol. ii, pp. 215, 232).

[2] Lord Durham's report has recently been the subject of a monograph: *Lord Durham's Report on the Affairs of British North America*, edited with an introduction by Sir C. P. Lucas, 3 vols., 1912.

[3] For the undisguised hostility towards the French Canadians which everywhere inspires Lord Durham's proposals, see *Report*, ed. Lucas, vol. ii, pp. 63 sqq., 288 sqq. See especially pp. 288 sqq.: '. . . it must henceforth be the first and steady purpose of the British Government to establish an English population, with English laws and language, in this Province and to trust its government to none but a decidedly English Legislative.' Also p. 292: 'The language, the laws, the character of the North American Continent are English: and every race but the English (I apply this to all who speak the English language) appears there in a condition of inferiority. It is to elevate them from that inferiority that I desire to give to the Canadians our English character.' See further, p. 299, an appeal to the example provided by Louisiana. The act of 1840 provided that English should be the sole language used in Parliamentary documents, and the clause was only repealed in 1848: 11 and 12 Vict., cap. 56 (Bourinot, *A Manual of the Constitutional History of Canada*, p. 36).

[4] 3 and 4 Vict., cap. 35.

thought it incumbent upon him to assume that office, shows the anxiety which the problem of colonial administration caused the Government at this time.

The concession to the legislative assembly of Canada of full control over the administration of the colony was undoubtedly a triumph for the disciples of Bentham. During the two years, however, which preceded the passage of the bill, the Utilitarians had by no means smoothed the path of the Cabinet and its agent, Lord Durham. If the latter had hoped to win their support by taking with him one of their number in the person of Charles Buller, he was quickly undeceived. For he was violently attacked in Parliament by Leader, who was supported by Grote and Hume. Roebuck, a Canadian by birth and the paid advocate of the French Canadians, was not then a member of Parliament. But he supplied his political friends with information, warned them of the sinister design which lurked in the suspension of an assembly, whose rights they had so long defended against the colonial office in London, and put them on their guard against a policy whose manifest aim was to destroy the liberty of French Canada. It mattered nothing that these Radical malcontents were a mere handful, for the defection of four or five members sufficed to transform into a minority the precarious majority which kept in office the Government represented in Canada by Lord Durham.

The Conservatives were alive to their opportunity and delivered a frontal attack upon the Government. After three years' temporizing Peel began to envisage the possibility of defeating the ministry and taking office himself. In the House of Lords he found an invaluable ally in Brougham, a liberal freelance, who bore a grudge against the Cabinet, against the freetraders, and against Lord Durham, whose overthrow he made it his object to bring about. Peel demanded that the high commissioner's powers should be strictly defined and the Government was compelled to accept his amendments.[1] Besides Wakefield, Lord Durham had taken with him to Canada a man named Turton, who, like Wakefield, had formerly been found guilty of abduction, and the choice occasioned lively incidents in the House. On his arrival, he surrounded himself with royal state, and behaved as though

[1] H. of C., January 17, 1838: Sir Robert Peel's speech (*Parliamentary Debates*, 3rd Series, vol. xl, pp. 149 sqq.); January 26, 1838: Lord John Russell's speech and Sir Robert Peel's reply (ibid., 3rd Series, vol. xl, pp. 543 sqq.).

invested with sovereign power. He issued an ordinance in which he condemned to death without trial those rebels for whose arrest a writ had been issued but who had not yet been captured. Those already in prison he transported to the Bermudas. The Bermudas, however, had not been included in his jurisdiction, and he was plainly exceeding his powers.[1] The ordinance was attacked in the Lords by Brougham, and when Lord Melbourne was placed in a minority on the question, he announced on the following day that the Cabinet had decided to cancel it.[2] On October 9, 1838, Lord Durham published the cancellation in Canada. But at the same time he issued a proclamation which was nothing short of a diatribe against the British Government.[3] To close his theatrical career by an impressive gesture, he had already notified his resignation. He sailed on November 1, landed at Plymouth on the 26th and at once plunged into a campaign of public speeches in the towns of the south-west. Since he had quarrelled with the Cabinet, the Radicals rallied to his support. Sir William Molesworth came to meet him.[4] John Stuart Mill pronounced his panegyric in a lengthy article in the *London and Westminster Review*, of which[5] he was editor. At this juncture the provinces were the scene of disturbances which recalled 1816 and 1819. During these critical months Lord Durham seemed disposed to come forward as a popular leader. Though his proposals would be adopted and prove successful, his administration had been a complete failure. He had failed to restore order in Canada, where the rebellion had broken out afresh. He had not even strengthened the Cabinet against the Radical attack.

6

The breach with the Radicals was intensified when on April 6, 1839, the Government asked Parliament to suspend for five years the constitution of Jamaica. And in truth the colonial policy of this Whig Cabinet was, to say the least, disconcerting. It seemed as

[1] See the text of the ordinance dated June 28, 1838 (*Annual Register*, 1838, pp. 304 sqq.).
[2] H. of L., August 10, 1838 (*Parliamentary Debates*, 3rd Series, vol. xliv, pp. 1127 sqq.).
[3] See the full text of the proclamation (*Ann. Reg.*, 1838, pp. 311 sqq.).
[4] It was only with considerable reservations that he had associated himself with the protests of his Radical friends against Lord Durham's dictatorship. See his speech, H. of C., January 23, 1838 (*Parl. Deb.*, 3rd Series, vol. xl, p. 358).
[5] *London and Westminster Review*, December 1838, 'Lord Durham's Return' (vol. xxxii, pp. 241 sqq.). Cf. April 1839, 'Reorganization of the Reform Party' (vol. xxxii, pp. 475 sqq.).

though despotism had been erected into a principle of government. To suspend the constitution of some colony or other was an annual event.[1]

What was taking place in the West Indies?

The reader will recollect that when slavery was abolished, the West Indian negroes had been placed under a provisional system of 'apprenticeship' intermediate between freedom and slavery, to continue for a period of six years. The negroes bore this legal purgatory with impatience, and complained that the planters refused to carry out the rules laid down for their protection. They were supported by the governors, the Methodist and Baptist missionaries, and the magistrates to whom the mother country had committed the task of securing obedience to the statute. At home they were supported by the abolitionists whose power was always considerable. In 1838, the anti-slavery group in Parliament led by Brougham had proposed that emancipation should be conceded immediately without waiting until it fell due in 1840. When a motion to this effect was introduced in the Commons on May 22, the Government, in spite of Conservative support, was defeated by a majority of three votes. The matter was carried no further. But the colonists in the West Indies, the Windward Islands, the Leeward Islands, and British Guiana, understood the gravity of the warning. All these colonies possessed constitutions of the same type as those we have just described in the North American colonies, but far older, since they dated from the seventeenth century. The colonial 'assemblies' decided to wind up the situation and release the planters from the inextricable difficulties in which they would be involved if the negroes were kept two years longer in the state of apprenticeship. They proclaimed immediate emancipation.

This was the solution adopted by the large island of Jamaica, which, with its 30,000 British colonists and its 350,000 slaves, equalled in importance all the other West Indian colonies together. The planters hoped to be rid at this price of the interference of the mother country in their affairs; where there were no more slaves, the emancipationists would have no concern. But they were speedily undeceived. Though the House of Commons had not adopted the motion in favour of immediate emancipation, a

[1] H. of C., May 3, 1839: Sir Robert Peel's speech (*Parliamentary Debates*, 3rd Series, vol. xlvii, p. 766).

statute had been passed giving the colonial governors supreme control over the administration of the prisons.[1] And even after the Jamaica Assembly had accorded immediate emancipation, the Governor announced his intention to apply the new law, which had been passed to protect the negroes against the brutality of their former masters. Then the Assembly revolted. On October 30, it declared that the prison Act, since it had been put into operation without their consent, was illegal and infringed the rights of the colonists, whom it treated as 'British subjects', and decided to suspend the exercise of its functions until it had been repealed. In short it followed the example set by the Assembly of Lower Canada. Two alternatives were before Lord Melbourne. He might yield to the colonists and wait until the working of the constitution had given the negroes sufficient voting strength to assert their rights. Or he might resist them and set up a dictatorship over the recalcitrant island. He chose the latter course. A bill was introduced in the Commons suspending the constitution of Jamaica for five years. During that period the colony would be ruled by the governor with the assistance of a council on which a number of commissioners should sit appointed by the Home Government. When the difficulties attendant upon emancipation had been settled, the constitution would be restored 'with the necessary modifications'.

Like the Canadian troubles in 1838, the Jamaican crisis in 1839 came as a thunderbolt upon the Radicals. For if they were patrons of the slaves, they were also defenders of constitutional liberty. Charles Buller, Lord Durham's secretary, was the solitary Radical who supported the Jamaica Bill. On the opposite side of the House the Conservatives under Peel's leadership opened an attack upon the ministry. They hoped either to compel the ministers to alter the bill in accordance with their wishes, as they had consented to do with the Canada Bill the previous year, or defeat them if they refused to give way. Peel without expressly espousing the cause of the colonists objected to the harsh character of the measures proposed to be taken immediately against them and urged that the bill should make provision for a final attempt to conciliate the Assembly before the dictatorship came into force. On May 6, the defection of ten Radicals reduced the Government majority to five. Lord Melbourne and Lord John Russell decided

[1] I and 2 Vict., cap. 67.

that under these circumstances they could not honourably remain in office and the Cabinet resigned. But Sir Robert's hour had not yet struck. Once more the Liberal party was saved, in curious circumstances, by what amounted to a court intrigue.

V QUEEN VICTORIA

I

Two years earlier King William IV had died. He had been succeeded by a young girl, his niece Victoria, who scarcely a month before her accession had been proclaimed of age on reaching her eighteenth birthday. A daughter of the Duchess of Kent, she had spent her childhood at Kensington Palace in a circle more German than English, which was at open war with the Court of St. James, and professed Liberal opinions. It was therefore a little devotee of Whiggery, who became Queen of England for the greater good of the Liberal party. Lord Melbourne attached himself to the young Queen. Since the distant period— so distant that it was all but forgotten—of his unhappy marriage, he had lived in town the life of a gay bachelor moving constantly in society, free in speech and morals. The Queen's friendship made him a changed man. He became her elderly friend, her careful guardian. The world saw him give up his life of pleasure, spend entire days at Windsor, and submit to the tiresome etiquette of the Court, delighted to have a place always reserved, whether at the dining-table or in the drawing-room, at the right hand of this little princess, who to the charm of youth added a precocious gravity which was not a little entertaining and an admirable commonsense, though she was narrow minded and wholly uncultivated.[1]

The Whigs made the most of this revolution at Court. Constitutional custom required that the accession of a new sovereign should be followed by a general election, and during the campaign they made free use of the Queen's name to win the favour of the electorate. They accused the Tories of conspiring to place on the throne the former Duke of Cumberland, now King of Hanover. They accused Peel of having threatened the young Queen with the fate of Marie Antoinette. Then the time came

---

[1] *Greville Memoirs*, September 12, December 15, 1838. Creevey to Miss Ord, October 9, 1839 (*Creevey Papers*, vol. ii, p. 323).

to arrange the Coronation festivities, and the Liberal Cabinet decided to alter the traditional usage. The Whitehall banquet to which it had been the custom to invite a few guests, the princes of the blood royal, and a certain number of Peers, was replaced by a popular demonstration. The Queen drove in procession from Buckingham Palace to Westminster Abbey along a route of two miles before the gaze of a million spectators. The Tories now began to speak in insulting terms of the Court and professed alarm at this 'alliance' between the Crown and Democracy,[1] which, they complained, had destroyed the balance of the Constitution. Radical orators, on the other hand, displayed an unusual attachment to the throne, and in his professions of loyalty O'Connell was louder than the rest.

The young Queen, however, was by no means her minister's captive, nor, as the Tories maintained, had Lord Melbourne become a sort of mayor of the Palace.[2] She had a will of iron, and no sooner had she ascended the throne than she astonished everyone by the firm exercise of her authority. Her mother had been impatiently awaiting her accession, to govern England herself. She was treated with the affection and respect which were her due, but was strictly excluded from politics.[3] Her intimate friend and adviser, Sir John Conroy, expected the Garter and an Irish peerage; Victoria informed him he would have neither but must be content with a baronetcy and a pension.[4] Leopold, the King of the Belgians, who had taken the position of an adoptive father since her infancy, and by frequent letters had supervised from Brussels her political education, also hoped, through her, to influence English politics. The moment she became Queen she discouraged his advances and their correspondence slackened. Towards Lord Melbourne she did not act otherwise. She supported his policy because she was a Whig and so ardent a Whig that she often found the attachment of the Prime Minister to Whig principles too lukewarm for her taste.[5] But she kept a close

[1] Sir James Graham to Croker, May 22, 1839: 'The Crown in alliance with the Democracy baffles every calculation on the balance of power in our mixed form of Government. Aristocracy and Church cannot contend against Queen and people united' (*Croker Papers*, vol. ii, p. 356).

[2] Croker to Peel, August 15, 1837 (C. S. Parker, *Sir Robert Peel*, vol. ii, pp. 320-1). *Greville Memoirs*, June 29, 1837.

[3] *Greville Memoirs*, June 29, 30, 1837. S. Lee, *Queen Victoria*, pp. 66 and 81.

[4] *Greville Memoirs*, August 28, 30, 1837. Creevey to Miss Ord, January 3, 1838 (*Creevey Papers*, vol. ii, p. 332). S. Lee, *Queen Victoria*, pp. 63-4.

[5] Diary, August 28, 1839: account of a conversation with Lord Melbourne. '... They

watch over all his actions, and called him to order whenever he presumed to take any decision without consulting her.[1] If, in May 1839, she kept Peel out of office she acted entirely on her own initiative, unasked by Melbourne, and in opposition to the wishes of several of his colleagues.

When Melbourne informed the weeping Queen[2] that his Cabinet had decided to resign, he gave her both verbally and in writing the advice for which she asked.[3] She must first send for Wellington and do her best to persuade him to become Prime Minister, or at least to join the Cabinet if Peel, that 'close stiff man',[4] were Premier. Melbourne shrank from the prospect of the encounter between Peel and the Queen, and counted on Wellington's diplomacy to smooth over many difficulties. Then the question of the Royal Household was raised.

On several occasions in the past the question had caused difficulty to the Whigs when the Court was Tory, and they had made it the custom to demand that those Gentlemen of the Household who were also members of Parliament should be asked to resign their posts. The Conservatives were now faced with the same difficulty when the Court was Whig. The position was rendered even more difficult by the fact that the sovereign was a Queen and her Household, Ladies. Should the Tories require the dismissal of those Ladies whose husbands were members of Parliament? It was possible by insisting upon a literal interpretation of the existing usage to maintain that there was no precedent for the demand. Nevertheless, it was amply justified. The government of Ireland, for example, was a permanent source of anxiety to the Conservatives. Would it be prudent to leave in immediate attendance on the Queen, Lady Normanby, the wife of the statesman who had just been governing Ireland by agreement with O'Connell, while the Conservative party was attempting to

(the Tories) ought to help and not to oppose every reasonable measure, as they had done, and not behave as they had done in the House of Lords. "They didn't behave so badly in the House of Lords," said Lord M. (This is admirable fairness), "they didn't throw out many bills." "But altered a good many," I said. "But I didn't know that those alterations didn't do them good," said Lord Melbourne' (*The Girlhood of Queen Victoria*, vol. ii, p. 242).

[1] The Queen to Lord Melbourne, August 26, 1839 (*The Letters of Queen Victoria*, vol. i, p. 233).

[2] Diary, May 7, 1839 (*The Girlhood of Queen Victoria*, vol. ii, pp. 159–60). The Queen believed she saw tears in Lord Melbourne's eyes also.

[3] Lord Melbourne to the Queen, May 7, 1839 (*The Letters of Queen Victoria*, vol. i, p. 195. Diary, May 7, 1839 (*The Girlhood of Queen Victoria*, vol. ii, p. 161).

[4] Diary, May 8, 1839 (ibid., vol. ii, p. 163).

govern by totally different methods? Melbourne advised the young Queen to make a strong stand for her rights in the matter but not to hold out obstinately; she must reserve her determination for the moment when Sir Robert would raise another question of far more serious political importance, and ask her to dissolve Parliament immediately.[1]

The Queen sent for Wellington, who referred her to Peel, then for Peel who never had the opportunity even to raise the question of dissolution. Was he too stiff, too formal? On the real issue, the question of the Ladies of the Bedchamber, the Queen did not allow him to explain his position. She began by telling him bluntly she 'could *not* give up any of her Ladies and never had imagined such a thing'. Peel asked her if she 'meant to retain *all*'. 'All,' was her answer. 'The Mistress of the Robes [Lady Normanby] and the Ladies of the Bedchamber?' 'All,' she replied.[2] An interview with Wellington failed to settle the difficulty. Melbourne was recalled. After a protracted discussion, his colleagues with the exception of two who, however, yielded to the opinion of the majority, gave their opinion in favour of supporting the Queen.[3] The Cabinet accordingly remained in office.

The immediate effect of the incident on public opinion was favourable to the Queen. Peel had claimed the right to impose conditions upon her, settle the details of her private life, and separate her from those whom she had chosen to be her daily companions. There was an outbreak of popular indignation

[1] Lord Melbourne to the Queen, May 9, 1839 (*The Letters of Queen Victoria*, vol. i, p. 201). Without wishing to enter into the details of this affair we must call attention to a point which unfortunately is involved in considerable obscurity. The letter we have just quoted was written by Melbourne after the Queen at her first interview with Wellington and Peel had already raised the question of the Ladies of the Bedchamber (the Queen to Lord Melbourne, May 8, 1839). What advice had Melbourne given before that first interview? Queen Victoria in her Diary for May 7 states that he presented to her a written note in which he advised her to request that none of her Ladies except those who had concerned themselves with politics should be dismissed (*The Girlhood of Queen Victoria*, vol. ii, p. 161). But the note, reproduced in *The Letters of Queen Victoria* (vol. i, p. 195), contains neither this advice nor any mention of the Queen's Household. The speech which Melbourne delivered in the House of Lords on May 14, 1839 (*Parliamentary Debates*, 3rd Series, vol. xlvii, pp. 10–13), adds to our perplexity. He there stated that 'he gave H.M. no advice whatever as to the Ladies of the Household, for he fairly declared that he did not expect, that he did not anticipate—that he could not conceive that this proposition could be made to H.M.'. But he is speaking of what passed on Wednesday, May 8, not of Tuesday, May 7, and he had, in fact, an interview with the Queen at eleven o'clock on Wednesday morning (Diary, May 8).

[2] Diary, May 9, 1839 (*The Girlhood of Queen Victoria*, vol. ii, p. 171).

[3] See the minutes of the Cabinet Council (*The Letters of Queen Victoria*, vol. ii, p. 215).

against his brutality, of sympathy with the young Queen so grossly insulted, and it was sedulously nursed by the Liberal politicians. The Queen was cheered when she went to Church on Sunday morning and the same evening at the Opera.[1] O'Connell was remarkable for the exuberant loyalty of his speeches. From Birmingham, where the working class was in a state of almost open rebellion, the Cabinet received information that preparations were being made to assassinate Peel if he dared to take office.[2]

But the truth was not long in coming to light, and well-informed persons changed their opinion. It was evident that the Queen had been very stupid and very obstinate, Melbourne very dishonourable or very weak, his colleagues too eager to resume office at any cost. Extenuating circumstances were pleaded for Peel's conduct. Perhaps he was a poor courtier. Possibly also his reputation as a man at once proud and shy had created a prejudice against him. But it could not be denied that Melbourne's resignation had placed him in an extremely awkward position and he could not reasonably be expected to take office under humiliating conditions. In any case his influence in the House was unimpaired. The position of the Liberal party which by a freak of fortune had become the court party was as precarious as ever. When in July the Jamaica Bill was reintroduced, it had undergone the drastic amendments for which Peel had asked in May and which the Government had then refused.[3] Things had always ended in this way since 1835.

2

Though she had come triumphantly through the late crisis the Queen had little joy of her victory. She detested the Tories more than ever and Melbourne was obliged to calm her by his paternal admonitions.[4] And it was no doubt at his instance, that in August an empty place in the Household was filled by her first Tory Lady-in-Waiting, Lady Sandwich, the wife of a Tory Peer.[5] But she felt less sure of herself than she had been during the first two years of her reign. The unfortunate business of Lady Flora Hastings, one of her maids of honour, who was accused of being

[1] Diary, May 12, 1839 (*The Girlhood of Queen Victoria*, vol. ii, p. 177).
[2] Lord John Russell to Sir Robert Peel, May 14, 1839 (C. S. Parker, *Sir Robert Peel*, vol. ii, p. 401). [3] 2 and 3 Vict., cap. 26.
[4] Diary, September 23, 1839 (*The Girlhood of Queen Victoria*, vol. ii, p. 253). Cf. *Greville Memoirs*, January 22, 1840. [5] *Greville Memoirs*, July 14, 1839.

pregnant, was compelled by the Queen to undergo the humiliation of a medical examination and had returned to her home to die of a cancer, was not just a passing vexation but left an enduring impression on the Queen.[1] She was depressed[2] and nervous. She clutched eagerly at every chance of amusement,[3] delighted to find herself in the company of young people and to remember that she was herself very young,[4] and alarmed on the morrow of a ball to find herself once more alone surrounded by aged statesmen.[5] Just then a letter arrived from the King of the Belgians announcing the visit of two young princes of Saxe-Coburg-Gotha. 'You wish them to come?' Melbourne asked the Queen, and when she expressed a desire that the visit should take place, 'he saw no objection'.[6]

The two princes were sons of the reigning Duke of Saxe-Coburg, and the Queen's first cousins. Ernest, the elder son, was heir apparent to the Duchy, and Leopold, their uncle, had long cherished the idea of marrying the younger son Albert to his niece Victoria. When in 1836 Albert had been presented to his cousin he had made a favourable impression on her by his faultless looks and distinguished manners. She had accepted him for her future husband in preference to a Prince of the House of Orange proposed by William IV. The King of the Belgians, acting in concert with Princess Victoria, had chosen, to complete the Prince's education, Baron Stockmar, a bizarre personage, well known both at the Court of Brussels and at Kensington Palace, Leopold's former doctor, a patriotic German and a devoted servant of the Coburg family.[7] He had taken Albert to Brussels to learn from Leopold the duties of a constitutional monarch, to Italy to visit the museums and the churches. He sent excellent reports of his pupil to London and Brussels, anxious only about Albert's weak health, indifference to politics, and coldness towards women. This precocious wisdom alarmed the old man, who had

[1] According to Sir Sidney Lee (*Queen Victoria*, pp. 93–4), Melbourne was responsible for this shocking blunder. This is difficult to believe. See, on the contrary, *Greville Memoirs*, March 2, 1839.
[2] Diary, June 12, 1839 (*The Girlhood of Queen Victoria*, vol. ii, p. 205).
[3] Ibid., May 29, 1839 (vol. ii, p. 189).
[4] Ibid., May 30, June 16, 1839 (vol. ii, pp. 191, 207).
[5] Ibid., September 26, 1839 (vol. ii, p. 256).
[6] Ibid., June 17, 1839 (vol. ii, p. 207).
[7] King Leopold to the Queen, June 30, 1837; the Queen to King Leopold, April 4, 1838; King Leopold to the Queen, April 13, 1838 (*Letters of Queen Victoria*, vol. i, pp. 105, 141). Cf. Sir Th. Martin, *Life of H.R.H. the Prince Consort*, vol. i, pp. 15 sqq.).

been a doctor before he became a courtier.[1] In June 1839 Albert returned to Coburg to be present at the celebration of his brother's majority, in which indeed he had a personal share, for in virtue of a special enactment his own majority had been anticipated by more than a year, and he was proclaimed of age the same day as his elder brother.[2] In other words he was officially declared of marriageable age.

On October 10, both princes arrived at Windsor, Albert, however, considerably out of temper. For he had received from his uncle a letter written at Victoria's request to prepare him to regard the engagement as broken off or at least postponed indefinitely.[3] Had the young Queen taken fright when she saw herself obliged to take the decisive step in the absence of the man chosen to be her husband? Did she feel that the proposed marriage was disliked by Melbourne and unpopular with her people? Or was it simply that this very self-willed young person revolted against a marriage arranged for her by others, and desired her marriage to be her personal choice, a genuine love match?

A love match it was. Albert was 'excessively handsome'.[4] He danced 'beautifully'.[5] Victoria was fascinated. Only four days after his arrival she told Melbourne that her mind was made up and Prince Albert became engaged to the Queen.[6] Immediately his troubles began. For two whole months he was exposed to the most ill-natured curiosity on the part of the British nobility.

Everything about him was made the object of their ridicule, his taste for literature and 'metaphysics', his good looks, his virtue. By every class of society, the aristocracy, the middle-class,

[1] *Stockmar Memoirs*, vol. ii, p. 7.

[2] Sir Th. Martin, *Life of H.R.H. the Prince Consort*, vol. i, p. 32.

[3] Prince Albert to the Prince of Loewenstein (Lieut.-General the Hon. Ch. Grey, *The Early Years of His Royal Highness the Prince Consort*, p. 246). The Queen to King Leopold, July 15, 1839 (*The Letters of Queen Victoria*, vol. i, p. 223).

[4] Diary, October 10, 11: '*Beautiful* . . . so excessively handsome' (*The Girlhood of Queen Victoria*, vol. i, pp. 262–3). The Queen to King Leopold, October 12, 1839: 'Albert's *beauty* is *most striking*, and he so amiable and unaffected—in short, very *fascinating*' (*The Letters of Queen Victoria*, vol. i, p. 237).

[5] Diary, October 11: 'I danced . . . with dearest Albert who dances beautifully' (*The Girlhood of Queen Victoria*, vol. i, p. 263).

[6] Ibid., October 13, 14, 15 (vol. i, pp. 264 sqq.). The Queen to King Leopold, October 15, 1839 (*The Letters of Queen Victoria*, vol. i, p. 238). In order to avoid summoning Parliament before the usual date, it was decided to keep the engagement secret. Only Lord John Russell was informed. And Melbourne and Lord John kept the secret so well that when the engagement was at length published it was believed at court that once more the Queen had acted entirely on her own initiative, and had become engaged without asking anyone's advice or informing anyone (*Greville Memoirs*, November 27, 1839).

and the people, this new Coburg was distrusted.[1] And it did indeed seem as though the chief occupation of the Coburg family was to make brilliant matches, in England, in Portugal, and in France. The Duke of Nemours had just become engaged to Princess Victoria of Saxe-Coburg. And the family factotum, the German Stockmar, was always to the fore arranging the marriage. As soon as Parliament met, Tories and Radicals united to persecute the Queen's future husband, while the Whigs and Liberals looked on with complete concern.

In the first place was he a Protestant? There seemed no doubt that he was. Yet what trust could be placed in the Protestantism of a family, two of whose members had made Catholic marriages in Belgium and in Portugal?[2] And if he was, why had the government omitted—deliberately omitted[3]—to mention the fact in the declarations the Queen read to the Privy Council and in Parliament? In the House of Lords, Wellington carried an amendment to add the word Protestant to the word Prince in drawing up the Address.[4] In the House of Commons Inglis and Sibthorpe provoked unpleasant incidents;[5] and to answer ridiculous questions of this kind, Palmerston found it necessary to ask Stockmar, 'whether Prince Albert belonged to any Protestant sect, the tenets of which could prevent him from partaking of the Lord's Supper according to the rites of the Church of England?'[6]

The dowry of £50,000 for which the Government asked was denounced as excessive. Joseph Hume proposed to reduce it to £21,000. He did not succeed. But Conservatives and Radicals

[1] *Greville Memoirs*, February 4, 1840: 'There is no great sympathy for the lucky Coburgs in this country.'

[2] Lord Melbourne to the Queen, November 27, 1839 (*The Letters of Queen Victoria*, vol. i, p. 251).

[3] Diary, December 6, 1839: '. . . Lord Melbourne said he left it out on purpose, *not* to attract attention, as else they would have said that wasn't true, and that many of the family had collapsed into Catholicism.' King Leopold also had severely blamed the omission (Sir Th. Martin, *Life of H.R.H. the Prince Consort*, vol. i, p. 57). It is interesting to recall that in December 1831 William IV, from a Tory scruple, to conform to what he believed to be the received usage, had omitted the word 'Protestant' in his speech from the Throne. See Sir Herbert Taylor to Earl Grey, December 3, 1831: '. . . Your Lordship will observe the proposed substitution of the word *Established* for *Protestant* Church, which occurred to H.M. from a belief that *established* has been the term generally used heretofore and that the change of it, upon this occasion, might attract notice. If, however, H.M. be mistaken in his recollection of former usages, his objection will of course fall to the ground' (*Correspondence of Earl Grey with William IV*, vol. ii, p. 13).

[4] H. of C., January 16, 1840 (*Parliamentary Debates*, 3rd Series, vol. li, pp. 11 sqq.).

[5] H. of C., January 16, 1840 (ibid., 3rd Series, vol. li, pp. 110, 114).

[6] *Stockmar Memoirs*, vol. ii, pp. 24–5.

combined under the conduct of Peel to reduce it to £30,000 by the large majority of 262 to 158 votes.[1]

Was it the correct procedure to give the Prince, as the Naturalization Bill proposed, precedence over everyone else, except the Queen, both in and out of Parliament? The Queen, who would have liked Albert to receive the title of King, like Philip and William in the sixteenth and seventeenth centuries, had the passage of this clause particularly at heart. She was defeated by the uncompromising opposition of the Lords. If the Queen died, ought the Prince Consort to take precedence over the heir to the throne? Wellington wished to give all the Princes of the Blood precedence over the Prince. Tired of the contest, the Government decided to omit all mention of precedence from the Naturalization Bill.[2]

The marriage was solemnized on February 10 amid general rejoicings. Four months later an attempt by a young madman on the Queen's life restored the popularity of the royal couple. The Queen became pregnant and Parliament passed without debate an Act appointing Albert regent in the event of the Queen's death. The Queen bestowed upon him by warrant the precedence the House of Lords had refused;[3] and when Parliament was adjourned the Prince presided seated in an armchair to the left of the throne. In this way the humiliation which noble cliques, political parties, and the jealous nationalism of the Press and public opinion, had combined to inflict upon Prince Albert, was in some degree removed. But in his own home he was still subject to humiliations of a different kind, less public but no less galling.

The young Queen, who loved ruling, had taken a husband that in the society of a young man of her own age she might find distraction from political cares. Never for a single moment did she dream, even when she desired the royal title for him, of

[1] H. of C., January 24, 27, 1840 (*Parliamentary Debates*, 3rd Series, vol. li, pp. 554 sqq., 584 sqq.). Cf. *Stockmar Memoirs*, vol. ii, p. 30: 'As I was leaving the Palace . . . Melbourne . . . used the following remarkable and true words . . . "The Prince will doubtless be very much irritated against the Tories. But it is not the Tories alone, whom the Prince has to thank for the curtailment of his appanage. It is the Tories, the Radicals, and *a good many of our own people.*" '

[2] H. of L., January 27, February 3, 1840 (*Parl. Deb.*, 3rd Series, vol. li, pp. 575 sqq., 1079 sqq.).

[3] Who first thought of settling the question of precedence by the use of the royal prerogative? Lord Melbourne? Or Greville himself? See on the point Queen Victoria's Diary, February 3, 1840 (*The Girlhood of Queen Victoria*, vol. ii, p. 313), also *Greville Memoirs*, January 31, February 13, 16, 1840. Stockmar had suggested an Order in Council (*Memoirs*, vol. ii, pp. 34–5).

making him her master or even her adviser. She refused the repeated request of the King of the Belgians, that she would give him a seat in the House of Lords.[1] She refused his personal request to be allowed to choose the Gentlemen of his own Household, and began by forcing upon him as Private Secretary an Englishman named George Anson, a tried servant of the Whigs and Melbourne's secretary.[2] He was not even allowed to set up a non-political salon according to the custom which prevailed in the German courts, at which he could receive men of learning, professors, and artists. 'The Queen,' wrote Anson, 'has no fancy to encourage such people. This arises from a feeling on her part that her education has not fitted her to take part in such conversations.'[3] In the end Anson took pity on the Prince and made representations to Melbourne and Stockmar, who argued the point with Victoria and persuaded her that she would not be unfaithful to her duty as Queen if she took Albert into her confidence in matters of State.[4] From August onwards we find the Prince taking an active part and to good purpose, so at least he believed,[5] in the serious problems of foreign policy which absorbed about this time the entire attention of British statesmen.

3

Relations between England and France caused grave anxiety. We have already spoken of the friction which almost unknown to the general public had taken place between the two Governments during the summer of 1834. Since that time Wellington had held the Foreign Office for three months. He had attempted without success to alter the line of action England had adopted in her Spanish policy and had offered to act as impartial arbiter between the factions contesting the rule of the Peninsula. He had offended Liberal opinion by sending as ambassador to Saint Petersburg

---

[1] The Queen to King Leopold, November 26, 1839; to Prince Albert, November 27, 1839 (*The Letters of Queen Victoria*, vol. i, pp. 250, 252).

[2] The Queen to Prince Albert, December 8, 1839 (ibid., vol. i, p. 254).

[3] Anson's Memorandum, January 15, 1841 (ibid., vol. i, p. 322).

[4] See Anson's Memorandum, May 28, 1840 (ibid., vol. i, p. 283). Anson remarks that in Stockmar's opinion the Queen's Lady-in-Waiting, Baroness Lehzen, was responsible for her attitude.

[5] To his father, August 1840: 'Victoria allows me to take an active part in Foreign Affairs, and I think I have done some good. I always commit my views to paper, then communicate them to Lord Melbourne. He seldom answers me, but I have the satisfaction of seeing him act entirely in accordance with what I have said' (Sir Th. Martin, *Life of H.R.H. the Prince Consort*, vol. i, p. 95 n.).

Lord Londonderry, the most aggressive of Tories. Would he have improved or rendered worse the relations between England and France? He had been turned out of office and Palmerston had returned. And there could be no doubt that ever since he became Foreign Secretary, British relations with France had gone steadily from bad to worse.

In every quarter of the globe conflicts had arisen between the two nations. In America the French were very active, and in Buenos Ayres and in Mexico in 1838 French admirals had defended the interests of French subjects by the threat of bombardment. In 1839 the French fleet had blockaded the Mexican coast and bombarded Vera Cruz, and when the Americans called upon Palmerston to protect their 'natural rights', the British Government had finally intervened between Mexico and France.[1] The position was the same in the Old World as in the New, though here the conflicts between France and England were in a sense more direct. Wherever there was civil war, one of the two contending parties was the French party, the other the English. This was the case in Greece, where France was accused by England of conducting revolutionary propaganda when the English party was in power, and the charge was returned when the French party had the upper hand.[2] And it was also the case in Spain, where opposition between French and English policy seemed to be the established tradition.

The British Government found it no easy matter to carry out the Quadruple Alliance. Article 3 of the Treaty bound the British Government to assist 'by the employment of her naval forces' to drive out the Carlist and Miguelist armies, and the further clauses added in August mentioned only arms, munitions, and warships. But of what possible use was the British fleet against the Carlist bands fighting in Navarre and the Basque country? And how could the Government hope to obtain the consent of Parliament to exceed the strict letter of the treaty and shoulder the cost of a regular expedition? Like Canning before him, Palmerston took refuge in half measures.

A number of marines, out of all proportion to the size of the fleet, were dispatched to Spanish waters. An Order in Council

[1] *Annual Register*, pp. 496–7.
[2] Duvergier de Hauranne, 'De l'alliance anglo-francaise et de l'ouverture du Parlement' (*Revue des Deux-Mondes*, February 15, 1841, vol. xlvii, pp. 474–5).

suspended the Foreign Enlistment Act and authorized 10,000 British volunteers supplied with arms by the Government to defend in Spain the cause of constitutional monarchy against Don Carlos.[1] De Lacy Evans, a Radical member of Parliament and a Colonel retired on half pay, took command of this band of adventurers, which, ill equipped and badly fed, decimated by disease and flung into the horrors of a Spanish civil war, went from one disaster to another.[2] The English Cabinet might employ another device by which to intervene in Spain without openly violating the principle of non-intervention, and encourage the intervention of a third power, in this case, France, a course which was in fact sanctioned by Article 4 of the Quadruple Alliance. But other difficulties stood in the way of this plan. The Constitutionalists in Spain were divided into two hostile factions. One of them, the moderate party whose programme resembled that known at Paris as the programme of resistance was led by Count Torreno and took its orders from the French ambassador. The other, more democratic and akin to the French party which went by the name of the party of movement, worked in harmony with Palmerston and his ambassador at Madrid. Therefore, when armed intervention by France in Spain was proposed, agreement between France and England proved impossible. If as happened in 1836 London asked Paris to intervene, Paris refused. If as in 1835 and 1840 a French Government proposed to dispatch an expedition, Palmerston threw cold water on the plan.

4

In such circumstances it might well seem that these clashes between the two leading naval powers were unavoidable and the understanding which had been reached between the two Governments necessarily artificial and insecure. It would, however, revive after 1840 and be transformed fifteen years later into an active military alliance. It must be admitted therefore that during the middle of the nineteenth century the understanding with France in spite of frequent disagreements met a persistent demand

[1] H. of C., February 26, 1836: Speeches by Lord Palmerston and Sir Robert Peel (*Parliamentary Debates*, 3rd Series, vol. xxxi, pp. 993 sqq., 1005 sqq.). H. of C., March 10, 1837: Lord Mahon's speech (ibid., 3rd Series, vol. xxxvii, pp. 223 sqq.).
[2] *Annual Register*, 1836, pp. 354, 399; 1837, p. 206. H. of C., April 17–18, 19, 1837; H. of L., April 21, 1837 (*Parl. Deb.*, 3rd Series, vol. xxxvii, pp. 1329 sqq., 1394 sqq.; vol. xxxviii, pp. 1 sqq., 21 sqq.).

of the situation, and that it was due only to accidental causes that it was shaken about the year 1840. The immediate cause of quarrel was indeed a conflict which ever since 1834 had been in progress between the self-esteem and vanity of two individuals, Louis Philippe and Palmerston.

Palmerston desired that in the agreement between France and England, of which he was the author, England should as far as possible take the first place, and that it should be made to appear as though, by concluding the agreement, she had taken French interests under her protection.[1] Talleyrand was by no means the man to bow to Palmerston's arrogance or flatter his conceit. He considered himself a person of sufficient importance to treat with monarchs on equal terms. He may even have cherished in secret the dream of repeating a second time his master stroke of 1815 and effecting an alliance between France, England, and Austria, a dream he could never hope to realize so long as the Whigs and Palmerston were in office. Hence the difficulties to which we have already alluded and his departure in September 1834. He had no difficulty in communicating to Louis Philippe the sentiments of distrust and dislike he entertained for Palmerston. Both on dynastic grounds and for other reasons the British alliance was distasteful to the French King. He was weary of patronizing, at Palmerston's beck and call, the revolutionaries who in Paris were threatening his throne. He would have liked to reach an understanding with the Northern Powers, and made advances to Austria which Metternich, delighted to see the concert between France and England weakening, was not slow to encourage. Palmerston was therefore anxious to prove to the King, since he was so blind to the advantages of British friendship, that he was pursuing a chimera if he believed it possible to substitute an understanding with Austria for the understanding with England or even to complete the latter by the former or balance one against the other.

He enforced the lesson with complete success. The memory of the revolutionary crisis through which the two great western

[1] Lord Palmerston to Lord Melbourne, March 1, 1836: '. . . When Ancillon and Metternich complain of the division of Europe into two camps, that which they really complain of is, not the existence of two camps, but the equality of the two camps. The plain English is that they want to have England on their side against France, that they may dictate to France, as they did in 1814 and 1815, and they are provoked beyond measure *at the steady protection which France has derived from us. But it is that protection which has preserved the peace of Europe*' (*Lord Melbourne's Papers*, pp. 339-40).

nations had passed in 1830 and the following years had begun to fade. The monarchy of Louis Philippe, which had now become reactionary, no longer evoked the same instinctive sympathy from British Liberals. England no longer absorbed by domestic problems, was showing signs of anxiety lest French competition should interfere with the growth of her commerce. As time went on, Palmerston came to love his work at the foreign office and threw himself into it with increasing zeal. In the Commons he renewed his rhetorical triumphs of 1829 and 1830 and Parliament, impressed by his imperturbable self-confidence, became accustomed to trust the foreign policy of the nation blindly to his conduct. It is not surprising that so many years elapsed before he entered upon the full exercise of his powers. In a democratic state to climb the ladder of office a politician is obliged to exert all his faculties at the beginning of his career. In an aristocratic state like the England of the early nineteenth century, fortuitous circumstances and the accident of birth have placed him from his youth at the head of a government department and the practice of office must be the school in which he learns the capacity to fill it. The moment had now come when Palmerston had at last completed his apprenticeship and mastered his profession. He was growing old. In 1839 'Cupid' took a wife. The age of amusement yielded to the age of hard political work and lofty ambitions.

The Belgian question gave him his first opportunity to teach Louis Philippe a lesson. The treaty of twenty-four articles of 1831, which guaranteed the independence of Belgium, left to Holland the greater part of Luxemburg, the greater part of Limburg, and the town of Maestricht. Leopold had accepted the treaty under protest, it was the King of Holland who had refused to sign. In 1838 the Dutch monarch suddenly changed his mind and demanded the full execution of the treaty. Leopold again protested, urging that the conditions were no longer the same as in 1831, since the King of Holland had allowed the treaty to lapse and for six years the Belgian Government had administered the disputed territory to the entire satisfaction of the inhabitants. He therefore claimed that the treaty should be revised and felt confident of success since Louis Philippe with the loud approval of the Parisian press had promised his support and his niece Victoria had just ascended the British throne. But Victoria refused to allow her uncle to dictate her policy[1] and Palmerston decided in favour of the Dutch claim, which was supported by the Northern Powers. The French Government, left completely isolated, finally gave way in December 1838.

Thus on the Belgian question, the very question whose settlement in 1831 had sealed the Anglo-French understanding, Palmerston separated himself from Louis Philippe and ostensibly supported the Northern Powers against him. It was a return to 1815, a triumph for the policy of the Holy Alliance and it was the work of a Whig administration. It was also the victory of the Protestant party in England over the Catholic. It was remarked that by some strange play of circumstance, all over the world, in Ireland, Belgium,[2] Poland, Canada, and Newfoundland,[3] the malcontents, the clients of the advanced Liberals, were Catholics. In Rhenish Prussia the Archbishop of Cologne was at open war with the King of Prussia, and there was a party in Belgium which advocated the formation of a Belgo-Rhenish Confederation which would have united in a single State the Belgian Catholics and the Catholics of the Rhineland.[4] Even in France the whites

[1] The King of the Belgians to Queen Victoria, November 24, 1838; Lord Melbourne to Queen Victoria, December 2, 1838; Queen Victoria to the King of the Belgians, December 5, 1838; Queen Victoria to the King of the Belgians, February 7, 1839, April 9, 1839; the King of the Belgians to Queen Victoria, April 19, 1839; Queen Victoria to the King of the Belgians, April 30, 1839 (*The Letters of Queen Victoria*, vol. i, pp. 170, 172, 183, 190, 192, 193).

[2] *The Times*, January 12, 1836: '. . . Well, here are the three great strongholds of Popery surrendered [Spain, Portugal, France]: the West of Continental Europe is free, save only Belgium, where the priestly tyranny has been kept alive, as in Ireland it has been reinforced and exalted. . . . Neither in Belgium nor in Ireland is the priest obstructed by the genius of military government, which in France, Prussia, and Austria keeps him to his good behaviour—it is a worthy rival to its sister tyranny. If we would promptly put down the evil, brute force is, in such cases, a not unfit teacher of brute intelligence.'

[3] For the situation in Newfoundland, see H. of C., December 12, 1837: Hume's speech (*Parliamentary Debates*, 3rd Series, vol. xxix, pp. 978 sqq.).

[4] O'Connell undertook the defence of the Catholics of the Rhineland, and the King of Prussia was so anxious as to the attitude British public opinion might adopt on the question that he sent a special envoy to London to open the eyes of the British Protestants. He was Baron von Bunsen, a man who united the theologian with the statesman (see his *Memoirs*, vol. i, pp. 465 sqq.). Bunsen inspired the two articles on the question which appeared respectively in the *Quarterly Review* of January 1839 ('Papal Conspiracy. Archbishop of Cologne', vol. lxiii, pp. 88 sqq.), an exceedingly clever article plentifully furnished with evidence, and in the *Foreign Quarterly Review* for January 1839 ('The Archbishop of Cologne, Prussia and Rome', vol. xxii, pp. 231 sqq.). See *Memoirs of Baron Bunsen*, vol. i, p. 499. Letter to his wife, undated, early in 1839: '. . . Lord Melbourne complained of me at Lord Holland's, saying, "Bunsen is setting up the country against us —his article in the *Quarterly* is in everybody's hands, and makes people mad." Bülow endeavoured to soothe him, saying "that *I* had not *written* it, that the article was good and true, and he, Melbourne, would ruin himself and his colleagues by opposing its cause." Melbourne thereupon softened and added, "All the young people are growing mad upon religion."' Cf. *Greville Memoirs*, May 11, 1838: 'Stanley thinks the peace of Europe will be

made common cause with the reds and in their hatred of Louis
Philippe worked together for the establishment of a democratic
Republic. In consequence, the English Conservative middle class
whose outlook was more accurately represented by Peel than by
any other statesman regarded Catholicism as at once popular and
reactionary, the religion of the ignorant and superstitious masses,
and Protestantism on the contrary as the religion of respectability,
reason, and moderation. And now the Whigs, who ever since the
century opened had been considered the 'Catholic' party, had
betrayed Poland, placed Lower Canada under martial law, and
returned the Catholics of Luxemburg and Limburg to a Calvinist
Government.

5

Louis Philippe had already received one warning. He was now
to be taught a harsher lesson in the East. The crisis began when on
April 21, 1839, the Turkish army crossed the Euphrates and
threatened to cut in the neighbourhood of Aleppo the land communications of Ibrahim Pasha's Egyptian army, then encamped
at Adana, on the southern shore of the bay of Alexandretta.

Sultan Mahmoud's declaration of war against the Pasha had
been made with the approval, indeed on the advice, of the British
ambassador, Lord Ponsonby. But we must not imagine that when
he encouraged Mahmoud to take the step, he had acted under
instructions from Palmerston. This eccentric diplomatist, at once
indolent and domineering to a degree wellnigh incredible and
regarded by the entire diplomatic service as three-parts mad, was
Lord Grey's brother-in-law and owed his appointment to the
insistence of Lord Grey and his following.[1] On the other hand

disturbed, and that speedily, by the great antagonistic forces of religion growing out of
the Prussian disputes between the Court of Berlin and Archbishop of Cologne; this he
told me the other day, and said people were little aware of what a religious storm was
brewing . . .' Cf. also Lord Stanhope, *Conversations with Wellington*, p. 179, October 7,
1839: 'Popery and Protestantism have changed sides as to their social relations. At the
outset Protestantism took the side of popular claims. Popery, on the other hand, ranked
itself with the monarchical institution—with the aristocratical institution—with the
institution, in short, of conservatism. The scene has now changed. . . . It is remarkable
that the Papal government which rejects democracy and the voluntary principle in its
own Italian States, readily encourages and avails itself of them elsewhere for the extension
of its influence and power.' Cf. the popular excitement aroused by Austrian persecution
of the Protestants of Zillerthal: *Annual Register*, 1838, pp. 468 sqq.; also *Quarterly Review*,
June 1839, 'Popish Persecution in the Tyrol—The Exiles of Zillerthal' (vol. lxiv, pp.
120 sqq.).

[1] *Greville Memoirs*, June 18, 1837. See another version, which, however, is by no means
reliable, in the *Reminiscences of William IV. Correspondence between Lord Ponsonby and Mr.
Urquhart*, 1813 to 1836, p. 4.

the First Secretary, Henry Bulwer, who had just given his warm
support to Lord Palmerston's Spanish policy, was on the whole in
favour of Mehemet Ali.[1] Palmerston, who had not made up his
own mind, accepted at first the French proposal of a joint intervention by England, France, Austria, and Prussia to maintain the
status quo in the Levant. To be sure there was already friction
between London and Paris. The British Foreign Office demanded
that Syria should be evacuated by the Egyptian army, if the Sultan
agreed to recognize the hereditary right of the Pasha and his
successors to the government of Egypt. The French on the other
hand wished the Egyptians to remain in permanent occupation of
Syria. For the moment, however, Palmerston did not insist, and
the policy which Talleyrand had always pursued and Louis
Philippe had resumed, the policy of friendship with Austria, had
apparently triumphed.

It was not long before a series of critical events alarmed the
statesmen of London and Paris. During July the news arrived,
first that Mahmoud had died, then that the Turkish army had been
annihilated at Nezib, finally that the entire Turkish fleet had
deserted to the Pasha. Palmerston hesitated, anxious as to the
attitude of Russia, whose armed intervention seemed inevitable.
For the three Governments of Paris, London, and Vienna one
step was now imperative, to make sure of the Czar's intentions.
What action did Nicholas contemplate?

Ever since 1815 British public opinion had been pulled in
different directions by two incompatible sentiments, hatred of
France and hatred of Russia. But since 1830 hatred of Russia had
been definitely predominant. While the Tory party remained
true to the traditional Gallophobia, the Liberals had affected to
ridicule its suspicions and fears until Russia reconciled both parties.
For the Conservatives dreaded Russian encroachment in the
Levant, Persia, and Afghanistan. And the Liberals dreaded the
permanent menace which Russian influence presented to the
Liberal cause throughout Europe. Everywhere the Russophobes
were raising the cry of danger and predicting the imminent outbreak of war. Dudley Stuart speaking in the House of Commons
had even depicted the Prussian Zollverein as a Russian plot to
extend her sway over the whole of Germany through the

[1] H. L. Bulwer to Lord Palmerston, August 28, 1838 (Sir H. L. Bulwer, *The Life of Lord Palmerston*, Book XII, ed. 1870, vol. ii, p. 282).

instrumentality of the Prussian Government.[1] The Court was animated by the same feelings and the aged King William hated France and Russia impartially. It is possible that David Urquhart, who had been dismissed from the diplomatic service, and had placed his talents as a publicist at the service of the enemies of Russia, was the King's confidential agent.[2]

Urquhart accused Palmerston of working in secret for an understanding with Russia and though his charges against the Government were extremely wild, they were not perhaps wholly devoid of foundation. In 1832, Palmerston in spite of the fact that Belgium had secured her independence had obtained the sanction of Parliament to the continued payment by England to Russia of her portion of the Russo-Dutch loan, had sent Lord Durham on a special mission to St. Petersburg to conclude if possible, an agreement with the Czar, and ever since had obviously pursued a conciliatory policy towards Nicholas in Poland,[3] in the Levant,[4] and even in Persia. His motive is not difficult to understand. England must not be in danger of diplomatic isolation should Louis Philippe decide to terminate the understanding between France and England, nor must Louis Philippe be allowed to imagine his friendship was as indispensable to Liberal England, as her friendship to him. The task, however, of arriving at an understanding with Russia was not easy in view of the hostile attitude of British public opinion, the strong personal dislike towards

[1] H. of C., February 19, 1836 (*Parliamentary Debates*, 3rd Series, vol. xxxi, pp. 614 sqq.). Cf. *The Portfolio* (by David Urquhart), vol. i, 1836: *Memoir on the means of maintaining tranquillity in the Interior of Germany in the event of War with the Exterior*, drawn up at the desire of the King of Prussia by Count Bernstorff, January 20, 1831, pp. 3 sqq. *Memoir on the State and Prospects of Germany*, drawn up under the Direction of a Minister at St. Petersburgh, confidentially communicated to several of the German Governments, pp. 57, 115; also Urquhart's comments on the *Memoir*, pp. 49 sqq., especially p. 55: 'Russia ... supports Prussia until the "Commercial League" is effected, but that league is to be in *a state of transition*. It must speedily pass into her Dictatorship of Germany, through the struggle of the two great Monarchies, she, through the German Diet, stepping into this intermediary position of supreme control and direction.' Cf. Cargill (Wm.), *An Examination of the Origin, Progress and Tendency of the Commercial Political Confederation against England and France called the 'Prussian League'*, 1840.

[2] See the *Reminiscences of William IV*, *Correspondence between Lord Ponsonby and Mr. Urquhart, 1833 to 1836*, pp. 71, 78-9, 86 sqq., for the relations between Urquhart and Sir Herbert Taylor.

[3] For Lord Palmerston's attitude towards the destruction of the Republic of Cracow, see H. of C., March 16, 1838 (*Parl. Deb.*, 3rd Series, vol. xxxii, pp. 403 sqq.).

[4] For the affair of *The Vixen*, a British merchantman, which made a considerable stir and brought Urquhart into collision with Palmerston, see H. of C., March 17, 1837 (ibid., 3rd Series, vol. xxxvii, pp. 621 sqq.), also *British Diplomacy illustrated in the affair of 'The Vixen'* addressed to the Commercial constituency of Great Britain by an old diplomatic servant, 2nd ed., 1838.

Palmerston entertained at the Russian Court, the Russian intrigues in Afghanistan and the pronounced Russian threat to Constantinople. No doubt the July Revolution had put an end to the danger of an open alliance between Russia and France. But if the French protégé, the Pasha of Egypt, established himself in Syria, and the Russian army occupied Turkey on the pretext of protecting her against Egypt, the situation in the Levant would be the same as though an actual Franco-Russian alliance existed and British interests and influence would correspondingly suffer.

Instead of approaching the Russian Government in concert with France, Palmerston to the great annoyance of the French Government[1] sent Lord Clanricarde to negotiate directly with M. de Nesselrode. His anxiety which had been very considerable was somewhat allayed when on August 17 the news was received that on July 27 the Russian agent at Constantinople had signed the joint note[2] and was still further relieved when on September 13, Baron Brunnow arrived in London charged with a special mission from the Czar to settle the Eastern question.[3] In December, Brunnow after a visit to St. Petersburg to obtain further instructions announced the unqualified acceptance by his Government of the British proposals. The Pasha was to hold Egypt and Syria as far as the fortress of Acre as his hereditary domain, and Russia would enter into a military convention with the other Powers to defend the Bosphorus. 'We may count upon the agreement of Austria, England, and even of Prussia . . . we hope that France will not adopt an attitude of isolation from the other Powers but will act in concert with them.'[4] Thus in January 1840, the old system of alliances was reversed. No longer did four Powers call upon Russia to abandon her protection of Turkish interests. On the contrary, four Powers—the allies of 1814 and 1815—invited France to unite herself with them and abandon the cause of the Pasha. Six months later, when Thiers was Prime Minister in

[1] *Guizot Mémoires*, vol. iv, pp. 483, 527.
[2] Ibid., vol. iv, p. 541.
[3] Ibid., vol. iv, p. 362.
[4] Sébastiani to Soult, January 5, 1840 (ibid., vol. iv, pp. 560–1). See further, Lord Palmerston to H. L. Bulwer, September 24, 1839: 'Brunnow says that the Emperor will entirely agree to our views as to the affairs of Turkey and Egypt, and will join in whatever measures may be necessary to carry those views into effect; that he will unite with us, Austria and Prussia, either with France or without her; and that though, politically speaking, he sees the advantage of having France of the party, he would be better pleased that she should be left out' (Sir H. L. Bulwer, *The Life of Lord Palmerston*, Book XIII, ed. 1870, vol. ii, p. 299).

France and Guizot his ambassador in London, Palmerston made the fact that Thiers had encouraged direct negotiations for peace between Constantinople and Cairo a pretext for maintaining that France had broken the convention of July 1839, and extorting the consent of his reluctant colleagues to a secret treaty concluded on July 15 between England, Austria, and Russia. It provided for the dispatch of an ultimatum to the Pasha of Egypt in which he was ordered to accept the conditions laid down by the allied Powers on pain of being deprived of the government of the pachalik of Acre, if he did not signify his acceptance within ten days, and of the hereditary government of Egypt, if his acceptance were not received within twenty. Palmerston refused to communicate the treaty to Parliament on the plea that it had not been ratified,[1] but he took care to conceal the fact that the signatories had agreed to carry out the military action it envisaged without waiting for its formal ratification. Immediately afterwards the session concluded and the foreign office was left to treat with the allied Powers in uncontrolled freedom at the very moment when the crisis must necessarily reach its most acute stage.

6

What were the sentiments of the British public at this juncture? There was no deep feeling of animosity towards France, it was Russia which was the object of popular suspicion. The English bore no grudge against the French for being defeated at Trafalgar and Waterloo and were genuinely surprised that the latter did not reciprocate their sentiments. The Londoners had given Marshal Soult a warm welcome when he came to represent France at the Queen's coronation. And during this month of August when the diplomatic situation was so strained, when Guizot, after a difficult crossing landed at Margate on his return from a visit to France, he was received on the pier not only by the local authorities but by almost the entire population, who greeted him with loud cheers.[2] The opinion of the Press was divided. Lord Palmerston was supported by the Whig newspapers, the *Globe*, the *Sun*, and the *Morning Chronicle*, to which indeed he was believed to be a contributor, and by the *Standard*, a Tory organ. But he was

[1] H. of C., July 24, August 6, 1840: Speeches by Joseph Hume and Lord Palmerston (*Parliamentary Debates*, 3rd Series, vol. lv, pp. 954 sqq., 1366 sqq.).
[2] *Guizot Mémoires*, p. 271.

opposed by the Radical papers, the *Spectator* and the *Examiner*; the Conservative Press headed by *The Times* was plainly in favour of an agreement with France, and only the violence of the Paris papers prevented their support of this policy from being as whole-hearted as it would otherwise have been.

One fact alone prevented this opposition from becoming really dangerous—London did not believe in war. This was obvious from the coolness with which the House of Commons during the final weeks of the session had received Hume's demands for an explanation of the Government's policy, and the ease with which Palmerston had managed to wind up the session, leaving the House in total ignorance of his intentions. But it was not the same in the provinces. Several districts showed signs of grave discontent with the attitude of the Government. The manu-facturing districts of the north, which for the past two years had been troubled by serious social disorders, were now in a ferment over the eastern question, and in Yorkshire and above all in Lancashire, there was an explosion of popular feeling against Palmerston's Russian policy. Urquhart had visited the north of England, and entered into relations with the Radicals and revolu-tionaries, who were very active in the manufacturing areas. He held meetings and founded 'committees for the examination of diplomatic documents' which he intended to be an instrument by which public opinion could exercise a check upon the policy of the Foreign Office.[1] He found an unexpected ally in the person of a young Manchester manufacturer, Richard Cobden. Cobden had begun his career as a publicist by combating Urquhart's propaganda in favour of war against Russia, refuting the theory of the European balance of power which he regarded as a hypo-critical excuse for wars of conquest and national aggrandizement, and proving that war always costs more than any possible gain from its success and he had placed the principle of non-interven-tion on a new basis by founding a thorough-going pacifism on the economic doctrine of free trade.[2] Now when there was a

[1] For this campaign of meetings and the speeches delivered at them, see *Quarterly Review*, vol. lxvii, pp. 261 sqq.

[2] In the Parliament of 1835 Cobden had made at least one convert. See the speech which Roebuck delivered on the Spanish question (H. of C., April 19, 1837): Mr. Roebuck 'professed to take very little interest in those questions: considering that they were treated by the respective leading parties in the House as mere implements for effecting their own particular objects'. On the conclusion of his speech he quitted the House by way of demonstrating his independent position (*Annual Register*, 1837, p. 202).

possibility that the Russian alliance might involve the country in a war with France, Urquhart's hatred of Russia suddenly converted him into an apostle of peace. Under the joint leadership of Urquhart and Cobden, Liberals and revolutionaries, manufacturers and workers, though at that very time ranged in opposite camps, united in a common hostility to Palmerston. One of the Stanleys who had just arrived in London from Lancashire told Greville in conversation 'that he had found at Manchester and elsewhere a strong public opinion of which he was sure Palmerston was not aware and would not believe in if told'.[1]

If Palmerston was perhaps ill-informed of the state of opinion in the north, he was certainly well aware of the obstacles which faced him in diplomatic circles, at Court and in the very Cabinet of which he was a member. Lord Granville, the British ambassador at Paris, openly expressed his disapproval of his chief's policy, and absented himself from his post throughout the entire month of September, leaving the conduct of business in the charge of his chief secretary, Henry Bulwer, more docile than himself towards the Home Government but who nevertheless deplored the treaty of July 15, as being a most unfortunate reply to the overtures which Thiers had made to England on taking office.[2]

It was reported that Metternich had told the British Ambassador in Vienna, Lord Beauvale, Melbourne's brother, that, 'if the treaty could quietly fall to the ground it would be a very good thing'.[3] The story no doubt represented accurately Metternich's sentiments. For Vienna and Berlin were also alarmed. They were not accustomed to take their instructions from Palmerston. Where did he wish to lead them? Into war? Ever since 1815 all the Govern-

Cobden did not sit in the House elected in 1837, but allusions by Macaulay at the beginning of his article in the *Edinburgh Review* (January 1841, 'France and the East', vol. lxxii, p. 529) and Brougham in his speech in the Lords, January 26, 1841 (*Parliamentary Debates*, 3rd Series, vol. lvi, p. 17) bear witness to the progress which Cobden's ideas had made. See also *Edin. Rev.*, January 1839, 'Foreign Relations of Great Britain' (vol. lviii, pp. 495 sqq.), especially p. 496: 'There cannot be a greater delusion than those labour under who entertain a jealousy of this country meddling with the affairs of the Continent. Many very worthy and enlightened men—men whose views are sound upon most other subjects—are persuaded that such connections lead to war. They probably might, if formed on bad principles: and they certainly would, if conducted in a meddling and encroaching spirit. But even then it would be difficult to conceive a state of things, involving us in hostilities, which would not also have existed and brought on the last of national calamities just as much [as] if we had kept aloof from all concern in European affairs.'

[1] *Greville Memoirs*, October 1, 1840.

[2] This is proved by Palmerston's letters to Bulwer of July 21 and 22, 1840 (Sir H. L. Bulwer, *The Life of Lord Palmerston*, Book XIII, ed. 1870, vol. ii, pp. 315, 318).

[3] *Greville Memoirs*, September 21, 1840.

ments who supported the *ancien régime* had a nervous horror of war, which they envisaged as a repetition of that revolutionary war France had declared in 1792. The Court of Windsor, which was as much a German as an English Court, shared their misgivings, and Prince Albert, whom the Queen at Melbourne's advice had just admitted to share secrets of State, supported the counsels of caution urged by the representatives of Austria and Prussia, who were far from pleased that the first effect of the new combination Palmerston had engineered had been to rekindle in Paris the flames of an aggressive republicanism. King Leopold happened to be on a visit to Windsor. Delighted to have at last an opportunity to interfere in British politics with his niece's consent, he became the intermediary through whom indirect communications were established between Windsor and the Tuileries.[1]

Within the Cabinet the opposition to Palmerston, which had been considerable from the outset, continued to increase throughout September and October. To be sure Lord Grey, the patriarch of Whig orthodoxy, was no longer a member of the Cabinet, and his son Lord Howick had resigned a year ago. Though furious to see the Whig doctrine of alliance with France thus endangered by Palmerston, he could make his influence felt only indirectly. His brother-in-law, Ellice, a personal friend of Thiers, went to and fro between Paris and London pouring oil on the troubled waters.[2] But the heads of Lansdowne House and Holland House were members of the Cabinet, and a tradition which dated from the Napoleonic War attached both families to a policy of friendship with France. Lord Clarendon, who had left the embassy at Madrid to become Lord Privy Seal, had from the beginning consistently opposed Palmerston's policy, not so much from any sympathy he felt towards France whose influence he had just been fighting in Spain, as from his distrust of Russia.

[1] The Queen took alarm when in September she believed that Lord John Russell would resign and the disruption of the Cabinet compel her once more to face Peel. See her letters to Melbourne and King Leopold of September 26 (*The Letters of Queen Victoria*, vol. i, p. 290). Also *Greville Memoirs*, October 1: 'She said that it was her wish that some attempt should be made to open communications with the French Government. If Palmerston chooses to give way, he may make her wishes the pretext for doing so, and yield to them what he refuses to everybody else.'

[2] Lord Palmerston to H. L. Bulwer, July 21, 1840: 'I am inclined to think that Thiers has been misled by Ellice and by Guizot.' To the same correspondent, July 22, 1840: 'It would never do to let Thiers bully us, as our friend Ellice, who has misled him, will no doubt advise him to try to do' (Sir H. L. Bulwer, *The Life of Lord Palmerston*, Book XIII, ed. 1870, vol. ii, pp. 315, 318).

At the beginning of the summer it was only by the threat of resignation that Palmerston had secured his colleagues' consent to the treaty of July 15. In September the news reached England that British warships were blockading Beyrout and others were at anchor off Alexandria before Mehemet Ali had had the time to make known his acceptance or refusal of the terms laid down by the Powers. It also became known that Palmerston had signed in concert with the plenipotentiaries of the Powers a protocol disclaiming all intentions of national aggrandizement. Though perfectly correct in itself the document had not been communicated to his colleagues, who had come to know of its existence only by accident through unofficial channels. This was too much for the great Whig families. At the instigation of the Duke of Bedford and Lord Spencer, Lord John Russell, who in July had supported Palmerston's policy,[1] revolted and demanded for the entire Cabinet its constitutional right of control over the foreign policy of the nation, which had been sacrificed to Palmerston's love of power and Melbourne's indolence. In his turn Lord John threatened to resign and forced an emergency meeting of the Cabinet.[2] Melbourne, who was himself in favour of a less warlike policy than Palmerston's, kept his head and his *sangfroid*, and just managed to prevent the Cabinet crisis which the diplomatic crisis threatened to produce.[3]

[1] Lord Palmerston to Lord John Russell, December 4, 1840: 'It was your support of the Treaty of July which chiefly induced the Cabinet to adopt it' (Sp. Walpole, *Life of Lord John Russell*, vol. i, p. 362). In his *Recollections and Suggestions*, a work of his old age (1875, pp. 223–5), Lord John, whose attitude was more hostile to the French than it had been in 1840, emphasized as a matter which reflected credit upon himself, the support he had given to Palmerston that July (Quadruple Treaty, Instructions to Admiral Stopford), and passed over without a word his subsequent quarrel with him.

[2] Sp. Walpole, *Life of Lord John Russell*, vol. i, pp. 349 sqq.

[3] See his letters to Lord John Russell, September 19, 26, 28, and 29 (*Lord Melbourne's Papers*, pp. 477 sqq.). Greville, who was a very active member of the group which opposed Palmerston, has left us in his *Memoirs* an amusing picture of Melbourne's attitude. It is, however, a caricature, and Thureau-Dangin was not entitled to accept it without control and without even indicating his source (*Histoire de la Monarchie de Juillet*, vol. iv, p. 294). In the Cabinet Palmerston was supported throughout by the new Secretary for War, Macaulay. He was an advanced Liberal, almost a Radical, but had returned from India what we should now call an Imperialist. See his speech of April 7, 1840 (*Parliamentary Debates*, 3rd Series, vol. liii, pp. 704 sqq., especially p. 719), on the situation in China, a speech which evidently inspired Palmerston's famous peroration of June 21, 1850. Macaulay was commissioned to write in the *Edinburgh Review* (January 1841, vol. lxxii, pp. 529 sqq.) the article dealing with the Egyptian crisis. According to Duvergier de Hauranne (*Revue des Deux-Mondes*, vol. xlvii, p. 480), the article 'bore the corrections of Palmerston himself, but also of Lord Clarendon and all the ministers most favourable to France since Lord Holland's death'.

7

Palmerston's confidence was unshaken. He refused to take seriously this revolt of the Whig aristocracy. At this season of the year those to whom Lord John must look for support were not thinking of politics. When in September, Guizot learnt of the first demonstrations by the British fleet, he went the round of the government departments in search of an explanation. It was time wasted. 'Not a minister in London, Lord Palmerston at Broadlands, Lord Melbourne and Lord John Russell at Windsor. They take life easily across the Channel.'[1] When Melbourne summoned the Cabinet, the ministers were still scattered in every part of the country. They were at a loss to explain the unexpected summons, and not a single minister guessed why his holidays had been interfered with. These wealthy noblemen regarded politics as a particularly honourable form of sport, played in accordance with strict rules. They were a narrow clique of powerful families whose members visited, dined, and hunted at each other's houses, and inter-married. Lord Grey was the very last man to censure Lord Ponsonby for damaging his country's interests by his bellicose policy, for Lord Ponsonby was his brother-in-law and owed his position at Constantinople to his influence. And Palmerston had just married Melbourne's sister. Therefore if Melbourne supported Lord John and his friends too warmly the Cabinet crisis would produce a family feud. At first sight the reform of 1832 might have been expected to alter the rules of the political game and put an end to this *dolce far niente*. Nothing of the sort. The middle class showed no desire to interfere with the easy-going ways of the aristocracy. There was not a trace in England of that fury with which in France the classes new to power stormed the citadel of government and when once installed in power disputed among themselves the precarious tenure of office.

Nor was Palmerston in the least disturbed by the attitude of the French Press. On the contrary he was delighted with a violence which made the position of the English supporters of France so difficult. And he was well aware that the Parisian newspapers by no means voiced the public opinion of their country, that the vast majority both of the nation as a whole and that portion which was represented in the Chamber wanted peace, and that

[1] *Guizot Mémoires*, vol. v, p. 309.

this would be evident as soon as the next session opened. He also knew that although Louis Philippe had appeared for once as the leader of the party favourable to hostilities and had encouraged Thiers' warlike attitude, he did not really wish to go to war.[1] Like every Frenchman he had a very high opinion of Mehemet Ali's military strength. He believed that even with the support of the British fleet the Turkish army would not be able to defeat him, that the Turks would be obliged to invoke the assistance of a Russian army and that the moment a Russian force passed through the Dardanelles at the invitation of an English government, Palmerston would be the most unpopular man in England. In short Louis Philippe was betting on Mehemet Ali and Palmerston against him. Events must very soon decide in favour of one or the other.

Throughout October the language of the French Press continued to be as violent as ever, but the Government inclined increasingly towards a policy of peace. Thiers made propositions of a conciliatory nature which Palmerston showed no great eagerness to accept. Then he again adopted a warlike attitude, whereupon Louis Philippe dismissed him and replaced him at the foreign office by Guizot, who left the British embassy with the good wishes of the Court. Immediately before his departure Guizot spent two days at Windsor and the formation of his Cabinet was preceded by conversations between the Tuileries and Brussels.[2] Encouraged by this success at Paris the peace party in England became more insistent than ever, and again Lord John called upon Melbourne to choose between Palmerston and himself. But on November 8 the news arrived of the annihilation of Ibrahim's army, and on the 27th of the capture of Acre. Louis Philippe had lost his wager and the whole of France had lost it with him.

Subsequent events made the Pasha's defeat, and therefore the indirect defeat of France, somewhat less complete than Palmerston

[1] See Louis Philippe's declarations to Count Apponyi in September, which were immediately transmitted to London (Lord Melbourne to Lord Palmerston, September 19, 1840, *Lord Melbourne's Papers*, p. 478).

[2] The Queen to King Leopold, October 16, 1840; King Leopold to the Queen, October 20, 1840; the Queen to King Leopold, October 23, 1840 (*The Letters of Queen Victoria*, vol. i, pp. 305, 307, 309). See especially the last of these letters written from Windsor: 'Guizot is here since Wednesday and goes this morning. Albert . . . has been talking to him and so have I, and he promised in return for my expressions of sincere anxiety to see matters *raccommodées*, to do all in his power to do so. *Je ne vais que pour cela*, he said.'

had hoped. For it was no longer a question for Palmerston and Lord Ponsonby of leaving Mehemet Ali in entire or only in partial possession of Syria. It was now Egypt itself of which they desired to deprive the Pasha, and the Sultan at Lord Ponsonby's instigation declared him deposed. But on November 25 Commodore Napier, who was in command of the fleet off Alexandria, concluded on his own authority, without consulting London or Constantinople, a treaty by which Mehemet kept the hereditary government of Egypt under Turkish Suzereignty. Palmerston yielded to the pressure of his allies, Austria, Prussia, and even Russia, and obtained the Sultan's ratification of Commodore Napier's agreement. It was a slight compensation to Guizot's Government in Paris, and the peace party in London. But it did not alter the fact that Palmerston had won.

He had triumphed over Louis Philippe. Indeed he even amused himself by goading French anger to exasperation so as to make the humiliation of France the more complete. And he had sacrificed no British interest to his new allies. The Czar lost the quasi-protectorate he had exercised at Constantinople in virtue of the treaty of Unkyar-Skelessi. And in December Lord Auckland, Governor of India, who was usually considered as a creature of Palmerston's, informed the Cabinet that Ghazni had fallen and Candahar and Kabul were occupied by British troops. Palmerston was now accepted as a great statesman, and gathered round him that floating mass which irrespective of party allegiance was enthusiastic for any person or policy that increased the national prestige. Prince Albert referred to him in jest as 'the Second',[1] 'The First' being Melbourne. Lord John now took the third place. Moreover, Melbourne though only five years older than Palmerston seemed a worn out old man, whereas Palmerston at the age of fifty-six wore the appearance of youth. Henceforward he represented in his person the honour and self-assertion of the country. He was John Bull in person.

Was Palmerston's victory also a victory for the Liberal Party? When that party took office ten years earlier, it had adopted a programme of peace and retrenchment to be made possible by means of a French alliance and to that policy for four or five years Palmerston had been faithful. Then he had suddenly reversed it,

[1] The Queen to Prince Albert, December 8, 1839 (*The Letters of Queen Victoria*, vol. i, p. 255).

and as a result of the new policy he had adopted England and France were now arming against each other. If there was no war, there was at least a heavy expenditure on armaments: the expression 'armed peace' dates from 1840.[1] Nevertheless if during the debate on the address the Radicals and Conservatives criticized Palmerston's foreign policy, their mild protests awoke no response. The debate languished. For more than a year the entire life of Parliament had languished.

No sooner had the alarm which had aroused them in 1830 passed away, than the great noble families sank back into the somnolent routine of government as it had been carried on in the eighteenth century. What should be the amount of the Prince Consort's dowry? What precedence should he occupy at processions and banquets? Should the Ladies of the Royal Bedchamber belong to the Whig or the Tory connexion? These were the questions which occupied the 'reformed' House of Commons. A dispute which broke out between the courts of law and Parliament in the case of Stockdale versus Hansard was still unsettled. The point at issue was the liability of the firm of Hansard for defamatory statements contained in an official publication printed by order of the House. It was difficult to regard a question of this kind as a grave issue in which the liberty of the nation was at stake. Nevertheless, it formed the subject of interminable debates in Parliament and the ludicrous turns the discussion took contributed to discredit still further a House of Commons whose prestige was already very small. That Palmerston's policy was inconsistent with the principles of 1832 mattered little. It had succeeded. And his victory had undeniably assisted his party. It had strengthened the position of this administration without a programme whose existence was endangered anew at the opening of every session. 'At present,' remarked Greville in his diary

---

[1] It was apparently coined by Thiers (*Thureau-Dangin Histoire de la Monarchie, de Juillet*, vol. iv, p. 241). Cf. Thiers to De Barante, August 22, 1840: 'Armed preparation is our policy' (ibid., vol. iv, p. 240). De Bourquency to Guizot, February 12, 1841: '. . . Then the question will arise of armed peace (*paix armée*)' (*Guizot Mémoires*, vol. vi, p. 80). The expression was soon naturalized in England. Raikes to Wellington, December 6, 1840: 'Her [France's] *paix armée* will entail upon all Europe the burdensome necessity of great standing armies, which will be worse than real war, because its termination can never be foreseen.' Wellington to Raikes, December 27, 1841: 'The armed peace, as it is called, is nonsense.' Wellington to Raikes, March 1, 1841: 'I have no confidence in the system of *isolement*. It does not answer in social life for individuals, nor in politics for nations. Man is a social animal. I have still less confidence in *paix armée*' (L. Raikes, *Private Correspondence with the Duke of Wellington and other distinguished contemporaries*, pp. 162–3, 202, 218).

for January 30, 'everything promises a very easy session and the Conservatives are confessedly reduced to look to the chapter of accidents for some event which may help them to turn out the Government and get hold of their places.'[1] The 'accident' occurred, and within a few weeks. It was the question of free trade. That this demand of the working and middle classes took by surprise even the more clear-sighted members of the ruling aristocracy reveals the degree to which the latter had lost touch with the nation. To understand the events which led up to the crisis, and prepared this second reform, a reform comparable in its significance for the historian of ideas and manners to the reform of 1832, of which it was at once the complement and the defeat, we must bid farewell to this nobility to which the indulgence of an easy-going public so readily entrusted the reins of government, descend into the workaday world, and regain contact with reality.

[1] *Greville Memoirs*, January 30, 1841.

CHAPTER II

Chartists and Free-Traders

I THE PROGRESS OF INDUSTRY
AND AGITATION AGAINST THE NEW POOR LAW

I

WHILE Parliament wasted its time with insignificant squabbles, England was hard at work. The industrial revolution pursued its silent course. The growth of large-scale industry had no doubt been interrupted since the restoration of peace by crises of an exceedingly serious nature, and political disorders had prolonged the crisis of 1825 until 1832. But a boom in trade had followed immediately.[1] The unrest among the working class in 1834, the agitation for an eight hours' day, and the monster demonstration by the Trade Unions in London were but the final peals of the departing storm. Never had the relations between masters and men been more satisfactory, never had greater optimism prevailed throughout the world of commerce and industry than during the two years which followed Melbourne's return to office. A series of books which appeared about this time witness to the new spirit which prevailed. Baines devoted an enormous monograph to the Cotton Industry.[2] Babbage published his *Economy of Manufacturers*,[3] Ure his *Philosophy of Manufacturers*.[4] G. R. Porter, the head of the statistical

[1] *Minutes of Evidence taken before the Select Committee appointed to inquire into the present state of Manufactures, Commerce and Shipping*, 1833; also for an excellent summary of the evidence, *Edinburgh Review*, October 1833, 'Present State of Manufactures, Trade and Shipping' (vol. lviii, pp. 40 sqq.).

[2] Baines (Sir Edward), *History of the Cotton Manufacture in Great Britain*, with a notice of its early history in the East . . . a description of the great mechanical inventions which have caused its extension in Britain; and a view of the present state of Manufacturers, 1836 [1835].

[3] Babbage (Charles), *On the Economy of Machinery and Manufactures*, 1832.

[4] Ure (Andrew), *The Philosophy of Manufactures, or, an exposition of the scientific, moral and commercial economy of the Factory System of Great Britain*, 1835. The two works by Babbage and Ure are of peculiar interest to the historian of ideas, for Karl Marx was greatly indebted to both. From Babbage he borrowed his theory of the division of labour, from Ure, among other things, his theory of machinery. In those passages of his work in which in a vein of serious irony he celebrates the panegyric of modern capitalism, Marx follows, often literally, the man whom he terms 'the Pindar of Manufactures'. 'Under the auspices of steam,' wrote Ure, 'and in obedience to Arkwright's policy, magnificent edifices, surpassing far in number, value, usefulness and ingenuity of construc-

department of the Board of Trade, published an account of the progress, by which of course he meant the economic progress, accomplished by the nation.[1] The titles of these works are a sufficient indication of their contents. They are no longer, like the works published during the lifetime of Malthus and Ricardo, expositions of economic theory. The economists have, so to speak, taken service with the captains of industry and are content to celebrate their triumphs.

2

The textile industry in its various branches was still the most important branch of British manufacture. Linen, wool, silk, cotton, all these manufactures had progressed. The linen manufacture was no longer confined to Ireland. Not only had the use of spinning machines spread so widely in the West Riding and in Scotland that Ireland now purchased from Great Britain a considerable proportion of her yarn,[2] but in certain districts, and especially at Dundee, machinery was employed in weaving the cloth.[3] The woollen manufacture was so extensive that England could no longer supply the raw material, and although sheep-farming at home had increased, wool must be imported from Germany, Spain, Australia, and Russia.[4] Since Huskisson had reformed the tariff to which it was subject, the silk industry had revived, not only at Spitalfields, where it had been on the verge of extinction, but in Lancashire where a new centre had come into existence. Nevertheless, neither the woollen nor the silk manufacture showed prospects of any considerable future development. The export of woollen goods was stationary, the amount of silk goods exported insignificant. It was British cotton goods which, produced every year in greater excess of the needs of the home market, were finding new markets in every quarter of the globe.

tion the boasted monuments of Asiatic, Egyptian, and Roman despotism, have risen up in this Kingdom' (ibid., p. 18). This is the original of a celebrated passage of the Communist Manifesto, S. 7: 'The bourgeoisie has shown, as no other power before, the achievement of which human activity is capable. It has accomplished marvels far greater than the pyramids of Egypt, the Roman aqueducts or the Gothic cathedrals.' See also the passages from Ure quoted below, pp. 289–90.

[1] Porter (George Richardson), *The Progress of the Nation in its various social and economical relations from the beginning of the nineteenth century to the present time*, 2 parts, 1836 (French trs., 1837).

[2] G. R. Porter (ibid., vol. i, pp. 266–7).

[3] Ure, *Philosophy of Manufactures*, pp. 208, 213, 216, 432.

[4] Ibid., p. 142.

The produce of the cotton manufacture, cotton yarn and piece-goods, accounted for one-nalf of the total exports,[1] and were by themselves equal to twice the total exports of the Russian empire.[2] The manufacture, which in 1815 consumed 77,175,000 pounds of raw cotton, consumed 257,985,000 pounds in 1832 and 330,750,000 pounds in 1835,[3] and there was every reason to expect a further increase. Doctor Kay, one of the Poor Law commissioners, in a statement he drew up in 1835 of the number of machines driven by steam either recently constructed or in process of construction, which within the next year or two would be in operation in the cotton factories of Lancashire and the surrounding districts, estimated that 169 manufacturers were installing these new machines whose power he calculated at 7,500 horse-power and which would provide employment for more than 43,000 persons.[4]

If the Lancashire cotton manufacturer had thus achieved the first place in the world market, though obliged to obtain his raw material from abroad and in spite of the exceptionally high wages paid, it was due to the excellence of the machinery with which the mills were equipped, and the manufacture of machinery, not only to supply the demands of the home market but for export, furnished the Lancashire industry with a further source of wealth.[5] To make the machinery iron was needed. To smelt the iron and drive the machinery coal was needed. This provided a further motive for exploiting the mineral wealth of Great Britain. 'To

[1] *Edinburgh Review*, July 1832, 'Recent Commercial Policy of Britain' (vol. lv, p. 428). R. Cobden, *Russia* (*Works*, vol. i, pp. 292–3).

[2] Ibid., vol. i, p. 196. See the figures given by G. R. Porter, *Progress of the Nation*, vol. i, pp. 208 sqq.

[3] Ibid., vol. i, p. 205.

[4] Ibid., vol. i, p. 239. The census returns made every ten years enable us to measure exactly the rapid growth—greater than that of the rest of the kingdom—of the population of Lancashire since the opening of the century. Figures for Great Britain, 1801: population, 10,472,048; 1811, 11,969,364 (increase 14.3 per cent); 1821, 14,072,331 (increase 17.6 per cent); 1831, 16,260,381 (increase 15.5 per cent); 1841, 18,535,786 (increase 12.9 per cent). For Lancashire: 1801, 672,731; 1811, 828,309 (increase 23 per cent); 1821, 1,052,859 (increase 27 per cent); 1831, 1,336,854 (increase 27 per cent); 1841, 1,667,064 (increase 24.7 per cent).

[5] The value of the machinery exported rose from £60,028 in 1831 to £387,097 in 1840 (H. of C., February 16, 1841: Mark Philips's speech, *Parliamentary Debates*, 3rd Series, vol. lvi, p. 674). Cf. A. Ure, *Philosophy of Manufactures*, p. 39: '. . . in the course of last year, Mr. Fairbanks equipped water wheels equivalent to 700 horses' power, from his engineer factory alone, independent of his millwright and steam-boiler establishment. Hence, whenever capital comes forward to take advantage of an improved demand for goods, the means of fructifying it are provided with such rapidity, that it may realize its own amount in profit, and an analogous factory could be set agoing in France, Belgium or Germany.'

appreciate the importance of iron,' wrote a French contemporary, 'you must visit England. The fact that the English are obliged to use it instead of the timber they do not possess has led them to invent cheap processes for its manufacture, and to put the metal to a large number of uses which we on the continent would never have believed possible. Iron and steel in every shape and form—you meet them at every step and under every conceivable guise—machinery, props, pillars of every dimension from two inches to four feet in diameter, water-pipes, gas-pipes, gutters, gratings, fences, bridges, floors, and roofs, even entire quays and railroads. Without pig iron and wrought iron those well-ventilated and well-lit constructions, apparently so light, yet able to bear enormous loads, for example the six storey warehouses at Saint Catherine's dock in London would be massive and dark prisons with clumsy and hideous wooden posts, and walls and buttresses of brick. The gas carried a distance of nine miles is brought by pipes of pig iron and distilled in iron gasometers. The slender bridges, the light footbridges over canals or between docks are all made of iron, as are the fluted columns which close the vista of Regent Street.'[1] But the great marvel in the eyes of the visitor from abroad was those iron railways over which carriages of iron drawn by locomotives were beginning to run throughout the length and breadth of the land.

3

The first successful experiment had been made in Durham in September 1825, when the line was opened from Stockton to Darlington. But it was in 1828 that the Lancashire capitalists put the movement under way by building a line from Manchester to Liverpool. When it was opened in 1830, Parliament showed great reluctance to grant the further concessions for which it was asked. The railway from London to Birmingham, to be continued by another line from Birmingham to Manchester which would establish rapid communications between the metropolis and the manufacturing districts of the north, though planned in 1830, did not receive the sanction of the House of Lords until 1833.[2] Nor was the public in a hurry to welcome the new railroads and

[1] Michel Chevalier, *Lettre sur L'Amérique du Nord*, vol. i, note 5, p. 325.
[2] *Edinburgh Review*, October 1834, 'Improvements in Inland Transport' (vol. lx, p. 107).

the shares of the London and Birmingham Railway Company remained for several years below par.[1] In 1835, Cobden contrasted the apathy of the British with the activity displayed by the Americans, who in less than seven years had built 995 miles of railway.[2] In 1836 the attitude of the public changed and the construction of railroads in Great Britain proceeded with a feverish haste. By 1837 there were nearly 400 miles of railway in actual use and nearly 450 miles under construction, and the list of new companies sanctioned every year by special acts of Parliament filled the bill sheet.[3]

The need for which the railway companies originally sought to provide was the rapid transport of passengers which the use of steam had made possible. It was not expected that for the economical transport of goods the railroad could compete with the excellent system of canals at the service of the British manufacturer.[4] But the invention of the locomotive produced a revolutionary effect in another sphere. The public clamoured for cheaper postage, and Rowland Hill, by his invention of the postage stamp sold at a uniform price and affixed to the letter by the sender, provided a practical method by which the demand could be satisfied.[5] The Conservatives urged as an objection to the proposal the enormous increase of correspondence which would follow, and the impossibility of dealing with it by the horse transport on which the post office was obliged to rely. The railways, 'moving post offices, proceeding at the rate of twenty-five or thirty miles an hour',[6] solved the difficulty.

At the ports the railways were linked with the shipping. The condition of the merchant service was far from creditable to the nation. During the first three years of this decade fewer and fewer

[1] T. Tooke, *Hist. of Prices*, vol. ii, p. 275.
[2] R. Cobden, *England, Ireland and America* (*Works*, vol. i, p. 116).
[3] G. R. Porter, *Progress of the Nation*, Fr. trs., 1837, translator's note p. 191. The most important lines open at the moment of writing were the following: Carlisle to Newcastle, 72 miles; Cromford to High Peak, 39 miles; Stockton to Darlington, 45 miles; and Liverpool to Manchester, 37½ miles. An anonymous work, *Railways of England*, 1839, p. 107, gives the following list of the Acts of Parliament sanctioning the construction of railways: 1801, 1; 1802, 2; 1803, 1; 1804, 1; 1808, 1; 1809, 2; 1810, 1; 1811, 3; 1812, 2; 1814, 1; 1815, 1; 1816, 1; 1817, 1; 1818, 1; 1819, 1; 1821, 1; 1823, 1; 1824, 2; 1825, 5; 1826, 6; 1827, 6; 1828, 11; 1829, 9; 1830, 8; 1831, 9; 1832, 8; 1833, 11; 1834, 14; 1835, 18; 1836, 35.
[4] Michel Chevalier, *Cours d'Economie Politique*, 1842, pp. 331-2.
[5] For this reform, see Sir Spencer Walpole's excellent account, *History of England*, vol. iv, pp. 188 sqq.
[6] H. of C., July 21, 1838: Graham's speech (*Parliamentary Debates*, 3rd Series, vol. xliv, p. 468).

British vessels entered and left the ports of the country, whereas the number of foreign vessels increased every year. During the next seven years the number of British vessels began once more to increase, but the number of foreign vessels increased even more rapidly.[1] The competition of the American merchant service seemed so menacing that many observers foresaw the day when the two English-speaking nations would dispute by armed force the supremacy of the seas. The obstacle which hampered the British shipbuilder was the excessive cost of timber. There were no forests in Great Britain and the complicated tariff which gave Canadian timber a preference over timber from the Baltic prevented the shipbuilders from obtaining it in the cheapest market. To neutralize the disadvantage, the English were exploring the possibility of using for ocean transport vessels built wholly of iron. The first would be launched in 1843.[2] For years past experiments had been made in steam navigation. Already a service of steamships plied regularly between England and the coast of France, and between England and the Rhineland cities as far as Coblenz. The establishment of a service between London and Paris via Brighton and Dieppe in the incredibly short space of twelve hours was in contemplation.[3] In 1825 and again in 1829 an English vessel navigated partly by steam and partly by sails had reached India.[4] In 1838 two vessels crossed the Atlantic for the first time without once using their sails. The Cunard Company, encouraged by the success of this double experiment, undertook in 1840 the construction of a fleet of steamships for the transatlantic service, and the same year the Peninsular Company was preparing to establish a regular service of steamers to Alexandria and Bombay interrupted only by the overland passage across the Isthmus of Suez.[5]

On what system were the lines of railways laid down which linked the inland towns with one another and the manufacturing

[1] Accounts relating to Trade and Navigation Customs Duties and Tonnage Duties and Tonnage of Vessels, 1842.

[2] E. Cressy, *A Brief Sketch of Social and Industrial History*, p. 146. For years experiments had been made in building iron ships; but, as late as 1840, no iron ships had yet been used except for river navigation. Cf. J. H. Clapham, *An Economic History of Modern History. The Early Railway Age*, 1820–1850, pp. 439–41.

[3] *The Times*, September 21, 1838.

[4] F. Bradshaw, *Social History of England*, p. 274. *Edinburgh Review*, January 1835, 'On Steam Navigation to India' (vol. ix, pp. 445 sqq.).

[5] W. Cunningham, *The Growth of English Industry and Commerce*, p. 817. E. Cressy, *A Brief Sketch of Social and Industrial History*, p. 146.

centres with the ports? If the Radicals had come into power at the election of 1834, a consistent and well-thought-out plan might perhaps have been adopted. The State might have undertaken the construction and operation of the railways, as the State of Pennsylvania had just done and Belgium was shortly to do.[1] Or if this extreme solution were not adopted the State could have laid down a co-ordinated plan of railway construction which the private companies would be obliged to follow. And by fixing fares it might have protected the public against the companies. The Parliaments returned in 1834 and 1837 preferred to leave everything to chance. The construction and working of the railways were left entirely to private enterprise. Only for Ireland where private enterprise was wanting did a parliamentary committee recommend a national system and the recommendation was finally rejected by the Commons. It ran counter to the dominant prejudice.[2] The State did not even take any steps to control the companies. The lines were laid down at haphazard as best suited the interests of those who wielded influence in the locality or in Parliament. It was not until 1840 that a statute vested in the Board of Trade a very general and vaguely defined control over the railways;[3] and wherever a tariff of railway fares was imposed on the companies it was a tariff of maximum fares which made no distinction between different classes of passengers and was so high that it was ineffective.

Notwithstanding its many deficiencies—the bad planning of several lines, excessive fares, and the undemocratic division of the passengers into three classes, the third class passengers being conveyed in open trucks like cattle—this system or rather want of system enabled Great Britain to outstrip in the development of her railways, if not the United States, at least all the continental nations. How was the necessary capital obtained? A wide field was opened to those joint stock companies which had been the object of such bitter attack during the crisis of 1825. These were

[1] *London and Westminster Review*, January 1836, 'Progress of Reform' (vol. xxv, p. 277). But it is not in the Radical magazine, but in the important Liberal organ, the *Edinburgh Review* that we must look for the most complete plan for the construction and ownership of the railways by the State. (April 1839, 'Commission on Irish Railways' (vol. lxix, pp. 173 sqq.).)

[2] H. of C., March 1, 1839 (*Parliamentary Debates*, vol. xlv, pp. 1051 sqq.).

[3] 3 and 4 Vict., cap. 97. See the curious debates which took place in the House of Commons in 1838 on the right of the State to use the railways for the postal service; H. of C., June 14, July 4, 21, 26, 1838 (*Parl. Deb.*, 3rd Series, vol. xliii, pp. 739 sqq.; also xliv, pp. 447 sqq., 698 sqq.).

not only the railway companies formed to raise directly the necessary capital for railway construction but the joint stock banks
which served as intermediaries between the general public and
the railway companies. Their number had slowly increased
during the years immediately following the statute of 1826 which
legalized their activities. In 1833 there were thirty in the provinces,
and three in Ireland. The renewal of the privilege of the Bank of
England under a modified form gave an enormous stimulus to
their growth. For they were now permitted to establish in London
itself banks for deposits and discount though not for the issue of
notes, and to draw upon their London agents bills to any value.
Between 1833 and the end of 1836, seventy-two banks were
founded in England and ten in Ireland. Fifty new companies
came into existence during the single year 1836.[1]

4

At first this multiplication of joint stock companies aroused no
protest. The House of Commons was only too ready to sanction
the foundation of the new railway companies. But it was not long
before the outcry raised ten years earlier was renewed, and an
attack launched against the joint stock companies and in particular
against the joint stock banks. In November 1836, the Agricultural
and Commercial Bank, the largest of the Irish banks, suspended
payment.[2] A few days later an important Manchester bank, the
Northern Central founded in 1834 with a capital of £700,000,
asked help from the Bank of England.[3] In February 1837, the
Bank of England was obliged to come to the assistance of three
American banks.[4] After this crisis the banks recovered, but only to
be again involved in difficulties in 1839.

Optimists minimized, and not altogether without reason, the
significance of these disorders. They pointed out that, when all
was said, the speculation of 1836 rested on a far more solid basis

[1] J. Horsley Palmer, *The Causes and the Consequences of the Pressure upon the Money Market*, 1837, p. 10. Cf. *An Account of the Number of Private and Joint Stock Banks registered in each year from 1820 to 1842; and of all Joint Stock Banks existing in England and Wales on the first day of January 1840, 1841, 1842 and 1843*. The number of Joint Stock Banks rose from 6 in 1827 to 7 in 1828, 11 in 1829, 15 in 1830, 19 in 1831, 25 in 1832, 35 in 1883, 47 in 1834, 65 in 1835, and 100 in 1836. The years of crisis followed and the rate of increase slackened: 107 Joint Stock Banks in 1837, 104 in 1838, 108 in 1839, 113 in 1840, 115 in 1841, and 118 in 1842.
[2] *Minutes of Evidence before Select Committee on Joint Stock Banks*, 1837, pp. 162 sqq
[3] Ibid., pp. 1 sqq.
[4] T. Tooke, *History of Prices*, vol. ii, p. 106.

than the speculation of 1825, on British railway enterprise not on some Eldorado overseas: that exports, after a temporary fall in 1837, exceeded in 1838 the level of 1836 and ever since had shewn a continuous increase until in 1840 they had reached an amount double that at which they had stood in the time of Canning.[1]

They further attempted to prove, that serious or not, the crisis was due to accidental and temporary causes. The Bank reserve which in October 1833 stood at the figure of £10,900,000 fell continuously until it was under £6,000,000 in May 1835, and again in September 1836. In 1838 it once more exceeded £10,000,000 but finally fell to £2,522,000 in 1839.[2] To what was this drainage of gold due? During the period which followed 1838 the primary cause was a series of bad harvests which necessitated a very large importation of foreign corn. Indeed, the drain on the gold reserve would have been more serious than it actually was, if profitable investments in foreign funds had not effected a partial compensation. A further cause—particularly operative during the two years of most serious crisis, namely 1836 and 1839 —was the disturbances which had taken place in the American money market and for which the commercial and financial system of Great Britain could not be held responsible. President Jackson's bank reform had created a sudden demand for European, and in particular for English gold, and its influx had occasioned in America a period of frantic speculation which in turn produced a further demand for gold. The crisis which began in 1836 was at its height in London in February 1837 when the American banks sought the assistance of the Bank of England. In May they renewed their request, were refused and failed. The same phenomenon was repeated in 1839 when the Bank of the United States, whose example was followed by several local banks, decided to make advances of credit to the cotton planters to enable them to postpone the moment of sale and thus raise the price of raw cotton to the Lancashire manufacturers. The latter replied to this attack by diminishing the output of their factories, which enabled them to reduce their orders for raw material. This gave rise to a further crisis, explicable like the crisis of 1836–1837 by the solidarity

---

[1] 1836, £85,220,000; 1837, £72,544,000; 1838, £92,454,000; 1839, £97,395,000; 1840, £102,707,000. Figures for 1825, £47,151,000; for 1827 (after the crisis), £52,222,000. W. Page, *Commerce and Industry. Tables of Statistics for the British Empire from* 1815, vol. ii, p. 71.

[2] T. Tooke, *History of Prices*, vol. ii, pp. 281, 300; vol. iii, p. 78.

which existed between the English and in particular the Lancashire market and the American.[1] If economic crises of a magnitude comparable to those which afflicted England were unknown in France, it was because a more agricultural and less industrialized country was not so liable to feel the effects of any disturbance which might occur at any point on the globe.[2]

Was it, however, possible to exonerate the policy of the Bank of England from all responsibility for the economic difficulties into which the country was once more plunged after four years of prosperity? The Bank was still exposed to the charge brought long ago by Grenfell and Ricardo; it could not be at the same time a banking company and an important department of the public service, a deposit and discount bank managed by a group of important financiers and a bank of issue entrusted with the regulation of the entire national currency. The enemies of the Bank asserted that during the boom which followed 1832 it had reckoned among its assets deposits which had been temporarily entrusted to its keeping, a deposit made by the East India Company, and the amount of the loan issued to indemnify the West Indian Planters for the emancipation of the slaves.[3] It had therefore permitted its gold reserve to be deplenished and had unduly inflated its note issue. It had made a loan in America to make it easier for American merchants to pay their debts in England. It had made loans in England below the current rate of interest. Having thus by an excessive issue of currency done everything in its power to cause a rise of prices and overproduction, it had found that the joint stock banks were surcharged with American notes, had suddenly refused to grant them credit, had raised the bank rate too suddenly and too late, and had thus, by provoking a panic, at least aggravated the crisis, if indeed it had not produced it.

With the stupidity shown by the Bank of England its critics contrasted the wisdom of the Bank of France. And they were enabled to rub in the contrast when further financial difficulties occurred two years later. When in 1838 specie was once more plentiful, the Bank of England was anxious to make use of it. Once more it lent money to America, and lowered the bank rate

[1] T. Tooke, *History of Prices*, vol. iii, p. 73.
[2] A. Ure, *Philosophy of Manufactures*, pp. 442–3.
[3] J. Horsley Palmer, *The Causes and the Consequences of the Pressure upon the Money Market*, 1837, pp. 11–12.

279

from 5 per cent to 4, 3½ and finally 3 per cent. As prosperity returned the demand for money increased and with it the rate of interest. The Bank did not follow the general movement and on several occasions the public could borrow on easier terms from the Bank than in the open market. Then as suddenly as in 1836 and, as then, after pursuing a course of action the exact contrary of that which it ought to have pursued if the public were to be warned against imprudent speculation, it raised the bank rate not merely to 5 but to 5½ per cent. In taking this step the Bank was making use of the power it had received in 1833, but this 'usurious' rate of 5½ per cent caused a sensation which turned to panic. On the verge of suspending payment, the Bank of England borrowed from the Bank of France £2,000,000 on the guarantee of twelve of the leading banks in Paris.[1]

But if the imprudence of the Bank of England was a legitimate subject of complaint, equally, indeed more culpable were the acts of imprudence committed by the joint-stock banks, which were of such recent origin, so inexperienced, and so often founded on grossly insufficient security. If the Bank of England had neglected to preserve the proper balance between its reserve and its note issue, at least the total value of the bank notes in circulation had remained the same or nearly the same. This was by no means the case with the joint stock banks. It was estimated that between the spring of 1834 and June 1836 the note issue in England, Wales and Ireland had increased by a quarter.[2] And this surely was the inevitable result of the system? When a host of rival bankers engaged in reckless competition for the patronage of the public, they were bound to offer their money cheap and produce this fall in the value of money to which indeed it had been the sole offence of the Bank of England to yield, and which in turn had given birth to the worst of all forms of overproduction, the excessive issue of paper currency?

The complaints brought against the Joint Stock Companies ten

---

[1] For a criticism of the Bank's policy, see C. S. Lloyd (Lord Overstone), *Reflections suggested by a perusal of Mr. J. Horsley Palmer's Pamphlet on the Causes and Consequences of the Pressure on the Money Market*, 1837.

[2] The value of the notes (other than those of the Bank of England) in circulation in England and Wales rose continuously from £10,152,104 on December 28, 1833, to £12,202,196 on June 25, 1836. And even these figures do not adequately represent the growth of the joint stock banks. For the issue of notes by private banks fell from £8,836,803 to £8,614,132; that is to say, had decreased in value; while the notes issued by the joint stock banks rose in value from £1,318,301 to £3,588,064. See *Report from the Committee on Joint Stock Banks*, 1836, p. ix.

years before once more arose on all sides.[1] The railway companies were denounced and the House of Commons took measures to strengthen its control over the formation of new companies. But they were not the sole object of attack. The heaviest onslaught was directed against the banking companies, which actually owed their origin to the crisis of 1825. They had been confidently expected to stabilize the national credit, and the crisis of 1836 had proved these hopes ill founded. Once more the principle of limited liability was called in question, and denounced as opposed to the spirit of English law. Complaints were made of the way in which the companies began operations before all their capital had been subscribed. The original subscribers lost no time in selling their shares to a third party at a high profit and left the unfortunate purchaser saddled with the responsibility for a rotten concern. The proposal was made that when a joint stock bank failed a first claim among its creditors should be given to the holders of its notes, which in consequence of the failure were now waste paper. Was not the Government responsible for their loss? By permitting these banks to issue what was nothing less than a paper currency, it had made them quasi-legal tender.[2]

It was easy to find a remedy for the ills which afflicted the economic life of the country, if they were in fact due to a vicious banking system. All that need be done was to withdraw from private hands the power to issue bank notes.

The Government might return to Ricardo's plan which was now being advocated by his son, and establish a National Bank for the exclusive purpose of issuing paper money to meet the demands of the public and without making any profit.[3] If, however, this suggestion seemed too bold, it could fall back on the

---

[1] See vol. ii, pp. 231–2, also *Edinburgh Review*, October 1833, 'Present State of Manufactures, Trade and Shipping' (vol. lviii, p. 64). The principle of limited liability had been introduced into Ireland (21 and 22 Geo. III, cap. 46 Irish), but does not appear to have produced the same effects as in France and America (*Report from Select Committee on Joint Stock Companies*, 1844, Appendix, pp. 258, 260).

[2] For the debates in which all these points were raised, see H. of C., March 12, 1836: W. Clay's speech (*Parliamentary Debates*, 3rd Series, vol. xxxiii, pp. 840 sqq.), published separately under the title: *Speech of William Clay, Esq., M.P., on moving for the appointment of a Committee to inquire into the operation of the act permitting the establishment of joint stock banks*. To which are added, *Reflections on limited liability, prices of capital, and publicity of accounts* . . . 2nd ed. 1837. Also H. of C., February 6, 1837: debates on the reappointment of the committee appointed the previous year (*Parl. Deb.*, 3rd Series, vol. xxxvi, pp. 155 sqq.). H. of C., March 10, 19, 1840 (ibid., 3rd Series, vol. lii, pp. 1112 sqq., 1245 sqq.).

[3] Samson Ricardo, *A National Bank, the remedy* . . ., 1838.

plan suggested by Torrens,[1] which had received considerable support, and without depriving the Bank of its privilege, establish a watertight division between the department concerned with the issue of notes and the other departments of the bank, and place the note issue under stringent legal regulation.

Any such remedy, however, must remain inefficacious, so long as the private and joint-stock banks were allowed to issue notes at their discretion. Therefore the proposal was again brought forward which the Government had contemplated and abandoned in 1818 to subject these banks to strict state control and thus secure the public from being victimized by their ill-advised operations. The present agitation sought to deprive them entirely of the right to issue notes, and events were evidently tending in this direction. The Bank of England had obtained the right to open branches in the provinces and was making use of them to gain control over the local banks, often refusing to open an account with them, unless they gave an undertaking not to circulate any notes except its own.[2] And in London itself the London and Westminster Bank, founded immediately after the Act of 1833, proved that a bank could prosper without issuing notes. Other banks were soon founded in London on the same model, the London Joint Stock Bank in 1836, the Union Bank and the London and County Bank in 1839, and the Commercial Bank in 1840. For a time their legal status was doubtful—for they were not protected either by the statute of 1826[3] or by the statute of 1838[4] which completed the act of 1826 by giving the joint stock banks the right to take legal proceedings against defaulting members. They prospered notwithstanding, and their prosperity presaged, the present crisis once passed, the opening of a new epoch in the history of banking companies.

[1] R. Torrens, *A Letter to the right honourable Lord Viscount Melbourne on the causes of the recent derangement in the Money Market and on Bank Reform*, 1837. Cf. George Warde Norman, *Remarks upon some prevalent errors with respect to currency and banking*, 1838. C. S. Lloyd (Lord Overstone), *Reflections suggested by a perusal of Mr. J. Horsley Palmer's Pamphlet on the Causes and Consequences of the Pressure on the Money Market*, 1837; also *Thoughts on the Separation of the Departments of the Bank of England*, 1844.

[2] Ellis T. Powell, *Evolution of the Money Market*, pp. 344–5.

[3] For the difficulties which attended their foundation, see M. D. Macleod, *Theory and Practice of Banking*, vol. ii, pp. 504 sqq., and Ellis T. Powell, *Evolution of the Money Market*, pp. 304 sqq.

[4] 1 and 2 Vict., cap. 96. A temporary measure renewed 2 and 3 Vict., cap. 68, 3 and 4 Vict., cap. 111, and finally made permanent 5 and 6 Vict., cap. 85.

5

But whatever the worth of these suggested reforms there could be no question of carrying them into execution until the privilege of the Bank of England expired in 1844, and the Parliamentary Committees appointed in 1836 and in 1840 to investigate the banking system, were therefore planning for a future still at some distance. Moreover, these controversies were too technical to arouse the feeling of the masses. The working class, which felt acutely the effects of these crises, unemployment, and the fall of wages, demanded remedies more immediate and more tangible than banking reform. A vast wave of popular discontent passed over the country. It seemed as though the Whig Liberalism of 1830 had failed where the Tory Liberalism of 1820 had succeeded. 1816 and 1819 had returned.

The opponents of the factory system who advocated the legal regulation of the conditions of labour had not abandoned their propaganda, and the language used by the panegyrists of the factory system was by no means calculated to allay their discontent. Ure, whose book appeared in 1836, uttered sentiments difficult to reconcile with Liberal principles. In his eyes Arkwright was a great man because, 'a man of Napoleon nerve and ambition',[1] he knew how to impose the discipline of the factory upon an unruly mob. If the industrial development of Great Britain had outstripped that of France, it was not because the British workman was more intelligent than the French or possessed more initiative; it was because he was more patient, more willing to endure the monotony of indefinitely repeating the same operation.[2] According to Ure, the introduction of machinery would make strikes impossible, the machine 'strangle the hydra of misrule'.[3] And he waxed eloquent in his praises of the 'Prussian' order which in the factory regulated every movement of man or machine. 'When capital enlists science in her service, the refractory hand of labour will always be taught docility.'[4]

The Factory Act was a concession to the opponents of the factory system though far too slight to satisfy their demands. But they suddenly found themselves thrown on the defensive, when at the beginning of 1835 the Tory administration was faced

[1] A. Ure, *Philosophy of Manufactures*, pp. 15–16.
[2] Ibid., p. 12.   [3] Ibid., p. 368.   [4] Ibid., p. 368.

with an organized attempt to prevent the enforcement of the statute.[1] And a year later, the date on which the Act would come into full operation, March 21, 1836, had barely arrived when the President of the Board of Trade, Poulett Thomson, attempted to induce Parliament to modify the law by allowing children over twelve years old to work twelve hours a day. In spite of Peel's support his majority at the second reading was so infinitesimal— only two votes—that he was obliged to withdraw the bill.[2] The Act, however, was very largely inoperative; for it rested with the Justices of the Peace to punish offenders against its provisions, and if not themselves manufacturers, they were very often their friends or relatives, and their sentences were glaringly inadequate.[3] Moreover, the executive possessed indirect means of evading the law. An official circular ordered the inspectors to take the children's legal papers as sufficient evidence of their age. The Cabinet stated that its motive in issuing the circulars was to protect the children against the false papers with which they were furnished by their parents. But were the ministers speaking the truth? Was it not rather their intention to make it easier for the manufacturers to set the children to work at the inspector's arbitrary decision?[4] But the disciples of Thomas Sadler no longer as in 1833 confined their attack to the factory, they attacked the workhouse at the same time. When the new Poor Law was debated in Parliament in 1834, it had been fought by a minority as violent as it was small. And even when the Act had been passed and enforced, that minority did not lay down its arms.

They accused the Poor Law Commissioners of forming unions far larger than the object of the new legislation required. One workhouse was provided for a union of thirty, forty, sometimes even fifty parishes. It seemed as though it were the Commissioners' deliberate aim to make it impossible for the pauper to obtain relief.[5] In the workhouse no distinction was made between the genuine worker who was the victim of unemployment, and the semi-criminal who made a profession of idleness. The law

[1] H. of C., March 4, 1835: Lord Morpeth's motion and Goulburn's reply (*Parliamentary Debates*, 3rd Series, vol. xxv, pp. 526 sqq.).
[2] H. of C., May 9, 1836 (ibid., 3rd Series, vol. xxxiii, pp. 737 sqq.).
[3] Alfred, *History of the Factory Movement*, vol. ii, pp. 83, 121.
[4] H. of C., July 21, 1838 (*Parl. Deb.*, 3rd Series, vol. xliv, pp. 394–6, 430–2).
[5] H. of L., March 17, 1833: the Duke of Buckingham's speech (ibid., 3rd Series, vol. xxvi, p. 1056); H. of C., August 7, 1838: Fielden's speech (ibid., 3rd Series, vol. xliv, pp. 1045 sqq.).

appeared to regard poverty as itself a crime. The paupers were deprived of sufficient bedding, warmth, and nourishment. Indeed, it was the avowed object of the regulations to make the conditions of life in the workhouse harder than those of the worst-paid labourer in the district. Moreover, both on moral and on economic grounds the poor who received relief in the workhouse were segregated according to age and sex. The opponents of the new Poor Law looked back with regret to the humanity of the old parochial system which had often allowed husband and wife to set up a joint establishment in the little poorhouse of their parish.[1] Once inside the workhouse no inmate could put foot outside its walls without immediately forfeiting the right to relief, and could not be re-admitted without submitting to a lengthy series of official formalities. Even on Sunday the paupers were not allowed to go to church; a chaplain visited the workhouse to conduct a service for its prisoners.[2] For the inmates were in very truth prisoners, confined under lock and key in these new 'Bastilles'. This then was the achievement of the new Liberalism which had conquered in 1832. If a labourer were willing to work, he must be imprisoned in a factory; if he found himself out of work, he could obtain relief only by entering another prison.

At first these complaints awoke little response outside the walls of Parliament. The enormous prosperity England had enjoyed since 1832, and which had apparently increased immediately after the passage of the new Poor Law, enabled the three Commissioners to accomplish their work of reorganization under the most promising conditions and within a short space of time. During the first year, boards of guardians were set up in 112 unions which together comprised 2,066 parishes, and during the second, in 239 unions comprising 5,800 parishes. In July 1837 of the 13,433 parishes of England there were only 1,300 to which the reform had not yet been applied, and the population of those 1,300 parishes was less than a quarter of the entire population of the Kingdom.[3]

Did the new system of poor relief produce the consequences its advocates expected? And in particular did it effect that reduction of the poor rate for which the ruling classes were so anxious? The

---

[1] H. of C., March 17, 1835: the Duke of Buckingham's speech (*Parliamentary Debates*, 3rd Series vol, xxvi, p. 1056); H. of C., May 13, 1835: Walter's speech (ibid., 3rd Series, vol. xxvii, p. 1052).
[2] H. of C., June 22, 1836: Maclean's speech (ibid., 3rd Series, vol. xxxiv, p. 720).
[3] *Annual Register*, 1837, p. 129.

statistics enable us to return an affirmative answer to the latter question, though it is not easy to determine how far the reduction was due to the operation of the new law and how far to the improvement of trade. If the Poor Rate fell from £6,317,000 in 1834 to £5,526,000 in 1835, £4,718,000 in 1836 and finally to £4,045,000 in 1837, it must be added that the fall began not in 1834 when the statute was passed but in 1832 when the boom in trade began. That year the Poor Rate stood at £7,037,000 and it had fallen the following year to £6,791,000. On the other hand were the opponents of the Act of 1834 justified when they maintained that the reduction of the Poor Rate proved that the working class was now treated more cruelly than before by the ruling class and its lot was harder than ever? According to the Commissioners' reports the effect of the new legislation upon the poorer classes had been to raise their moral standard and consequently to improve their economic position. The agricultural labourers were drinking less, and there had been a marked decrease in the number of public houses which had reached its height in 1830 and the years immediately following. More money was being placed in the savings-banks, and friendly societies were increasing their membership every year. And if in the southern counties the supply of labour was perhaps in excess of the demand, the statute of 1834 empowered the Commissioners to transport the superfluous labourers to districts where the demand was greater. They made use of their powers and sent unemployed agricultural labourers—certainly very few, some five thousand in all—to colonize Australia and New Zealand. They sent a far larger number to the Lancashire factories where they suddenly found themselves in receipt of wages, twice or thrice the amount they had been earning on the farms of Sussex or Devonshire.

6

The crisis of 1836 followed which was aggravated in 1837 and further prolonged by two severe winters. The local authorities requested that the discontent of the lower classes should be met by a return to the practice of outdoor relief. The Poor Law Commissioners returned an unqualified refusal. If the crisis could not be surmounted without violating the fundamental principle of the Poor Law, their work was a complete failure. But their refusal was the signal for the storm which had been gathering for the past two years to break in full fury upon their heads. Nothing short of an insurrection was organized against the three 'tyrants', the three 'Pashas'.

At this very moment the Commissioners, having set up unions throughout the south of England, were beginning the same work in the north. Here, however, when the boundaries of the unions had been drawn on paper and the time came to set about the actual construction of a workhouse, the popular opposition threatened to become dangerous.[1] At Todmorden, in Lancashire, Fielden, the Radical manufacturer, whose untiring efforts to promote factory legislation have been related above, opposed with the support of all his workmen the construction of a workhouse, and the authorities had the sense to give way.[2] Two leaders whose power and ability were by no means to be despised undertook to organize the agitation against the Poor Law, in Yorkshire, Oastler, and in Lancashire, James Rayner Stephens, like Oastler a Methodist, who as the reader may remember had quarrelled with the Wesleyan hierarchy and formed a little independent sect. Oastler and Stephens founded in every locality Anti-Poor Law Associations, which were finally federated in one Association.[3] They held mass meetings at which they inflamed the popular indignation against the double tyranny of the factory and the workhouse. 'You see,' exclaimed Stephens, 'yonder factory with its towering chimney, every brick in that chimney is cemented with the blood of women and little children.' 'Sooner,' declared the same speaker, 'than wife and husband and father and son should be sundered and dungeoned and fed on skillee—sooner than wife and daughter should wear the prison dress—Newcastle ought to be and should be—one blaze of fire with only one way to put it out, and that with the blood of all who supported this abominable measure.'[4] We must not mistake the character of this campaign. Stephens and Oastler never ceased to call themselves Tories, doctrinal 'reactionaries'. The abominations of the industrial system had made them in spite of themselves advocates of violence. They wished to turn their country 'back' to a time still innocent of the factory and the steam engine. They found, therefore, sympathizers among the Conservative Party.

[1] *Fifth Annual Report of the Poor Law Commissioners*, 1839, pp. 19–20.
[2] J. Holden, *A Short History of Todmorden*, pp. 190 sqq.
[3] *The Times*, February 8, 1838.
[4] R. G. Gammage, *History of the Chartist Movement*, pp. 56, 59

The Tory gentry had at first welcomed the new Poor Law. For it had been passed in their interest, to reduce the burden of rates which pressed so heavily upon them, and put an end to the agitation among the agricultural labourers which threatened them in the southern counties. But now when the peaceable application of the new system for two years had apparently effected a satisfactory settlement of the social problem in the south, and it was sought to introduce it in the north, and it was the manufacturers who were being attacked by its opponents, they were not slow to perceive that it was to their interest to ally themselves with the insurgents against the upstarts of the factory. In London John Walter made *The Times*, now an organ of the Conservative opposition, the official mouthpiece of the Anti-Poor-Law. This was perhaps the eccentricity of an ambitious journalist bent on the overthrow of the Whig administration who deemed any weapon which might serve his purpose legitimate.[1] But it does not alter the fact that his campaign possessed his readers' approval. They were only too pleased to sympathize with the alleged victims of the Liberal bureaucracy and enjoy the discredit brought upon their cruelty on a Government which pretended to represent the people. The best expression of this somewhat hazy humanitarianism is to be found in the works of a young novelist who became famous about this time. Charles Dickens, who had made his name by the publication of the *Pickwick Papers*, began the following year the series of his great social novels with *Oliver Twist*. An advocate of the poor against a middle class callous to their suffering, he dreamed of a return to those good old times when machinery and Utilitarianism were alike unknown, and England had never gone to school with Ricardo or Bentham. His hero, Oliver Twist, an ill-used child is brought up in a workhouse. These chapters of Dickens' novel introduced the Anti-Poor-Law propaganda into the homes of the middle class.

[1] The reader may be amused by the entertaining account given by the *Manchester and Salford Advertiser*, June 30, 1838, of the causes to which the Whigs ascribed the Tory campaign. Edwin Chadwick, 'the great Chadwick', had begun his career as a reporter on the staff of *The Times*, engaged under Walter's orders, in the most humble form of reporting. 'Here was the source of Mr. Walter's spite. His Berkshire neighbours were immersed in pauper-jobbing. His own parish received a severe visitation from the man who had so often made his early readers stare with astonishment at "dreadful fires", shocking accidents and enormities in the vegetable and animal world. Enough, Mr. Walter forthwith took a seat for Berkshire, and made war upon the new Poor Law. This is more monstrous than any of Chadwick's fictions, and yet the Whigs have put it about as a fact.'

I

The success achieved by the Anti-Poor-Law propaganda alarmed the supporters of the Government. They saw their party falling into ever deeper discredit, exposed as it was to the attack of two powerful forces, a large middle-class body, whom the dread of disorder was driving into the ranks of Peel's moderate Conservatives, and the hosts of a disaffected proletariat. The Radical members of Parliament, who gave the Government a merely conditional support were even more uneasy. They saw the constituencies a prey to forms of corruption scarcely less blatant than before the passage of the Reform Bill, and Parliament refuse to submit disputed elections to the judgment of an impartial tribunal. They saw the disappointment of 1832 produce among the working class a hearty distrust of political methods. The workers no longer gave ear to the Radical speakers, but to Oastler and Stephens, Tory free-lances, or Robert Owen, the 'Socialist' and the sworn foe of Radicalism. Surely there was no time to be lost, they must make the people understand that if the Reform of 1832 had proved so disappointing the fault lay not with the democrats, but the Whigs, that it had not been sufficiently demo-cratic and must therefore be completed by a further measure of reform. And in fact at the election of 1835 they made repeated attempts to revive in the nation at large the revolutionary spirit of 1830.

They opened their campaign with an attack on the House of Lords. They did not indeed demand its abolition; for they recog-nized the necessity of a Second Chamber, if the destinies of the nation were not to be at the hazard of a chance majority. But they asked that its powers should possess only a suspensive veto on measures passed by the Commons. They also demanded that its composition should no longer be hereditary, but should become wholly or in part elective.[1] O'Connell, who as we have already

---

[1] See the detailed proposals made by Roebuck. *Of What Use is the House of Lords, and the Evils of the House of Lords* (*Pamphlets for the People,* vol. i, 1835, also *Westminster Review,* October 1835, vol. xxiii, pp. 509 sqq.; January 1836, vol. xxiv, pp. 47 sqq.). The articles are from the pen of Macaulay, who would appear to have forecast the end of the House of Lords at no distant date. 'I am quite certain,' he wrote to Ellis from Calcutta, 'that in a few years the House of Lords must go after Old Sarum and Gatton. What is now passing is mere skirmishing and manoeuvring between two general actions. It seems to be of little consequence to the final result how these small operations turn out. When

seen had contemplated the adoption of this programme in 1834,
spent the summer of 1835 travelling about England and Scotland
to urge the reform of the Lords. But in 1836 he was obliged to
admit that the agitation had failed to mature.[1] It was impossible
to arouse the enthusiasm of the working class for the rights of an
assembly in whose election they had no share.

Another plank of the Radical programme was the introduction
of the ballot, a reform which had been rejected in 1832. Every
year Grote introduced a motion to that effect, and every year it
was defeated.[2] In 1838, however, the Cabinet could receive little
satisfaction from its victory. Grote's motion was indeed defeated
by 315 to 200 votes; but only sixty-five ministerialists voted with
the majority. That is to say the majority of the supporters of the
Government declared in favour of the ballot, and the ministry
could obtain its rejection only from a majority composed for the
most part of its political adversaries. Lord John, who had wished
to leave the question open, but in obedience to Melbourne's
orders had spoken vigorously against the motion, contemplated
resignation.[3] But there is no evidence that a debate which
occasioned a storm in the House had any appreciable effect on
public opinion outside. It was a favourite argument with the
opponents of the ballot that under a restricted franchise the
publicity of the vote was the only means by which the disfranchised masses could exercise any control over the electors.[4]
The plea was insincere. The real reason why the country gentlemen were in favour of public voting was that it enabled the upper
classes to put pressure upon tenants, tradesmen, and other

the grand battle comes to be fought, I have no doubt about the event' (Sir G. O. Trevelyan, *Life and Letters of Lord Macaulay*). Macaulay's belief was shared outside Radical
circles by Archbishop Whately (*Letter to Nassau Senior*, November 30, 1834; *Life*, by
E. J. Whately, vol. i, pp. 246–7).

[1] *Annual Register*, 1834, p. 333; 1835, p. 367; 1836, p. 299.

[2] H. of C., June 2, 1835 (*Parliamentary Debates*, 3rd Series, vol. xxviii, pp. 369 sqq.);
June 23, 1836 (ibid., 3rd Series, vol. xxxiv, pp. 780 sqq.); March 8, 1837 (ibid., 3rd Series,
vol. xxxvii, pp. 8 sqq.). Grote proposed that provision should be made for an optional
ballot in the new municipalities (H. of C., July 1, 1835, ibid., 3rd Series, vol. xxix,
pp. 159 sqq.).

[3] *Greville Memoirs*, February 18, 1838. Cf. Lord Melbourne to Lord John Russell,
September 15, 1837 (*Early Correspondence of Lord John Russell*, vol. ii, pp. 202–3). See also
Lord Francis Egerton to Arbuthnot, February 17, 1838: 'You will have heard of our
commencement de la fin in the shape of the division on the ballot. It is a fatal one, and I
see nothing but a coalition with the remnant of the sounder Whigs that can delay the
consummation' (C. S. Parker, *Sir Robert Peel*, vol. ii, pp. 359–60).

[4] *Edinburgh Review*, July 1837, 'Newspaper Literature' (vol. lxv, p. 213). The article
was written by Brougham.

dependants. Nevertheless, the argument was effective. The populace had no interest in safeguarding the exercise of their civic rights by a restricted electorate from which they were excluded.

In the end it was discovered that there was only one parliamentary reform for which it was possible to arouse the enthusiasm of the masses, namely the extension of the franchise. The Cabinet was hostile to the proposal and in the speech he delivered during a debate in November 1837, Lord John pronounced categorically against any further measure of Parliamentary Reform, since, in his opinion, the Reform of 1832 was a permanent and final achievement with which it would be most unwise to tamper.[1] What was the explanation of this blunt refusal to extend the franchise by a statesman who in 1831 had said the exact contrary?[2] It was just Lord John's way. At that very moment however, the Radical leaders acting in concert with the more moderate section of the workmen's associations were engaged in reviving the old programme of universal suffrage.

2

Two years earlier there had been formed in London a small association of workmen under the title of the London Working Men's Association. It was an association for reading and debate, whose members sought to promote popular education by means of schools, books, and newspapers. Its constitution is dated June 16, 1836. A month later the budget reduced the stamp tax on newspapers from 4d. to 1d. The object of the reduction, the Chancellor of the Exchequer explained, was to secure the revenue. For the newspapers which appeared without payment of the duty were now so numerous that the law was powerless to take action against them. Among the founders of the Working Men's Association were Hetherington the printer, John Cleave the bookseller, and James Watson, a workman, men who had acquired considerable popularity during the previous five or six years by the prominent part they took in circulating unstamped papers during the war between the Radical Press and the police. Now

[1] H. of C., November 15, 1837 (*Parliamentary Debates*, 3rd Series, vol. xl, p. 1192).
[2] H. of C., August 5, 1831 (ibid., 3rd Series, vol. v, p. 867). A few changes of detail were, however, made in 1836, the duration of the poll in the counties was reduced from two days to one, and the number of polling stations increased (6 and 7 Will. IV, cap. 102). Two years later the qualification was altered in favour of personal estate, the ownership or occupation of real property being no longer required (1 and 2 Vict., cap. 48).

the Government had yielded and they were free to continue their propaganda openly and legally.

What was its nature? Hetherington was a 'socialist', a disciple of Owen. And when the Association was founded, its founder, the cabinet maker, William Lovett, was also Owen's disciple.[1] But the Association received frequent visits from Francis Place, the Radical tailor of Charing Cross, the friend of James Mill and Joseph Hume. Its programme as we know it from Lovett's account was vague—no doubt intentionally—and unmistakably moderate. The Association proposed 'To seek by every legal means to place all classes of society in possession of their equal political and social rights'. A democratic franchise and the institution of a system of popular education were the points on which all the members were agreed.[2] That is to say the Association went back upon Owen's communism and returned more or less consciously to Bentham's programme. It is therefore not surprising that the Radical politicians tended to make common cause with Lovett and his friends. At a banquet given on February 15, 1837, by the Radical voters of Finsbury, in honour of their member Wakley, Joseph Hume and Daniel Whittle Harvey suggested that the moment was opportune to arouse public opinion and intimidate Parliament by combining in a single bill the various proposals which had been constantly brought forward ever since 1832 for the extension of the franchise, the ballot, the reduction of the life of Parliament, and the total abolition of the stamp duty on newspapers. Roebuck and O'Connell who were present, expressed their misgivings and pointed out the risk which in their opinion attached to the method of campaign proposed by the speakers.[3] In spite of their objections the London Working Men's Association adopted the suggestion, but enlarged the demand for an extended franchise into the demand for universal suffrage. Then Roebuck and O'Connell gave way and consented to sit on a joint committee of members of Parliament and members of the Association formed to draught a bill on these lines. It was Roebuck's aim to found on the frontier of the official Whig party an independent Radical party. O'Connell was by no means so ready to break with the Cabinet. His object was rather to assist

[1] See his article in *Hetherington's Twopenny Dispatch*, September 10, 1836. See also his article in *The Charter*, February 17, 1839.

[2] *Life and Struggles of William Lovett*, pp. 94 sqq.

[3] *Morning Chronicle*, February 16, 1837.

the Government and break the redoubtable agitation against the Poor Law by putting forward in revolutionary circles the alternative programme of parliamentary reform.[1]

The organization spread to the provinces. In February 'missionaries' left London to establish all over the country 'Working Men's Associations'. A hundred were founded before the close of the year, one hundred and fifty in 1838. But the most important success achieved by the London Working Men's Association during the campaign was the adhesion of the famous Political Union of Birmingham. It had been dormant since 1832, and when the new crisis arose, Attwood, as we should have expected, bestirred himself anew. It was an excellent opportunity for him to raise once more his old cry that England was suffering from the effects of Peel's preposterous bill of 1819, which had dealt a fatal blow to her prosperity by restoring specie payment with the general fall of prices which was the inevitable result. To save the country he continued to urge his old remedy, the raising of prices by the issue of paper money on an enormous scale. But within a few months he found himself swamped even in his own local Union, which became purely and simply a society for the promotion of universal suffrage.

3

At the beginning of 1838 the programme of the London and Birmingham Radicals, who had now joined forces, assumed a definite shape; and to understand this new brand of Radicalism, we must follow attentively the disputes which broke out within the London Working Men's Association. In June, a strike occurred in the Glasgow cotton mills, a certain John Smith was found during the strike murdered in the street, and the strikers were accused of the murder. An inquiry was held at the offices of the corporation, and eighteen workmen were arrested. At first the gravest charges were brought against the accused, incendiarism and murder. They were dropped later, and the men were accused only of 'conspiracy' to intimidate their comrades and secure higher wages. By an insignificant majority the jury returned a

[1] *Life and Struggles of William Lovett*, p. 102; M. Hovell, *The Chartist Movement*, pp. 69–71. Cf. Oastler's *Open Letter to Lord John Russell* (*The Times*, August 12, 1839). See also *The Times*, August 21, 1839. The details of Oastler's story do not bear investigation, but the part played by O'Connell is nevertheless unmistakable.

verdict of guilty and the prisoners were sentenced to transportation for seven years. The Trade Unions were up in arms. A petition bearing twenty thousand signatures was presented to Parliament. It was the affair of the Dorchester Labourers over again.[1]

At that very moment O'Connell broke with the Trade Unions. Difficulties had arisen with the Trade Unionists of Dublin, whose programme of class war cut across his programme of national emancipation. And his financial agents in Dublin were large-scale employers whose men were on strike. He therefore declared war against the Unions. His political opponents at Westminster enjoyed the treat of hearing him enumerate in accents of righteous indignation the criminal outrages committed by the Trade Unionists, denounce secret societies, and complain that the anarchy which prevailed in Ireland made it impossible for judges and juries to convict and punish the guilty. 'What a curious Actaeon-like fate,' wrote Whately, 'would it be, if O'Connell were to be murdered by a mob.'[2]

The members of the Working Men's Association were called upon to decide a very difficult question of tactics. They could not take the part of the workers without breaking with O'Connell. They could not break with O'Connell without losing their most powerful supporter in Parliament. To evade the difficulty they decided to ask Parliament, not to pardon the condemned strikers, but to open an inquiry into the conduct of the Glasgow Union, and to extend it to all the Trade Unions of the country.[3] If the trade unionists were innocent of the crimes laid to their charge, they had nothing to fear from it. But a revolutionary minority of the Association were in arms against the proposal and refused to accept the decision of a House of Commons entirely drawn from the wealthy classes, a House which the manifestoes issued by the Association stigmatized as 'the rotten House'.[4] A man named Harvey, a prominent figure among the London revolutionaries, was loud in his denunciations of O'Connell. Lovett and his friends charged Harvey with a breach of party discipline in

[1] *Life and Struggles of William Lovett*, pp. 158 sqq.
[2] To Nassau Senior, January 25, 1838 (*Life*, vol. i, p. 414).
[3] H. of C., February 13, 1834: Wakley's motion (*Parliamentary Debates*, 3rd Series, vol. xl, pp. 1059 sqq.). Cf. H. of C., January 25, 1838 (ibid., 3rd Series, vol. xl, pp. 473 sqq.).
[4] *Life and Struggles of William Lovett*, p. 100.

attacking O'Connell when they were endeavouring to concert with him a common programme of universal suffrage. Thereupon after a stormy meeting Harvey left the Association and founded a rival society which termed itself the 'Democratic Association'. He had the support of a demagogue far more formidable than himself. He was an Irishman named Feargus O'Connor, who in the Parliament of 1833 had been a member of O'Connell's 'tail'. In 1835 his election was invalidated because he did not fulfil the pecuniary qualifications prescribed by the law, and ever since he had pursued the career of an agitator outside Parliament, and in opposition to O'Connell, with whom he had quarrelled.[1] He betook himself to the north of England, where he organized Radical Associations. Towards the close of 1837 he took the initiative in founding at Leeds an important Radical weekly the *Northern Star*.[2] He conducted a campaign for universal suffrage. But he did not own allegiance to the Working Men's Association.

4

These were the difficulties with which the leaders had to contend, who during the early months of 1838 were working out in London the new Radical programme. It was published on May 8, and is famous under the name of the People's Charter.[3] It was a long and detailed Reform Bill drawn up by Lovett, revised and corrected by Francis Place, and approved by Roebuck. It demanded six alterations of the existing system—Manhood Suffrage—The Ballot—Payment of Members of Parliament—Abolition of the Property Qualification for Members—Equal Constituencies—Annual Elections. It had been originally intended to include a

---

[1] See a curious and extremely favourable description of Feargus O'Connor at the moment of his exclusion from Parliament in *Random Recollections of the House of Commons*, 1836, pp. 322–4; also a history of his life as an agitator from September 1835 to April 1838, related by O'Connor himself (*Northern Star*, December 15, 1838).

[2] *Life and Struggles of William Lovett*, p. 173 *n.*

[3] See the text of the People's Charter as revised in 1842 in the *Life and Struggles o, William Lovett*, pp. 449 sqq. The term appears for the first time in the *Northern Star*, July 21, 1838. But already on May 26 the same paper contained the following passage: 'Let every man be at his post and every banner fly in the breeze of hallowed liberty, upon that day when the new Charter of our Rights shall be proclaimed upon Hunslet Moor.' J. West (*History of the Chartist Movement*, p. 82) mentions an anonymous pamphlet which appeared in 1832 under the title of the *People's Charter*, and in which, he tells us, the programme of 1838 is already to be found. We are ignorant of the origin of the legend which relates that it was O'Connell who, at a meeting held in 1838, gave the movement its name (R. G. Gammage, *History of the Chartist Movement*, p. 6).

demand for women's suffrage, but it was finally decided that for such a proposal the time was not ripe.

Immediately the work of propaganda was set on foot. It took the forms traditional since 1826 and 1819. A body of delegates from Birmingham headed by Attwood in person, organized monster meetings which were often attended by more than 100,000 or even 200,000 persons. The first was held at Glasgow, and was followed by a series held in various Scottish towns. Meetings were then held at Newcastle, in the Yorkshire towns, at North-ampton, where the meeting was held on August 1, 'the anniver-sary of the emancipation of the slaves', and on August 6 at Birmingham. The London meeting held on September 17 proved disappointing. The organizers had expected an attendance of 100,000, and that to obtain sufficient room they would be obliged to transfer the meeting from Palace Yard to Hyde Park. According to the most favourable calculations not more than 30,000 attended, only 4,000 or 5,000 according to The Times.[1] But at the same time the movement in the provinces took a fresh start and until midwinter, meetings were held almost every day in Lancashire, Yorkshire, the Midlands and South Wales.

The object of these public meetings, as originally intended by Lovett and Attwood, was the same as it had been in 1816 and 1819, to sign a national petition to be presented solemnly to Parliament. A million, even two million signatures were expec-ted.[2] Then a new plan was broached at Birmingham, also copied from the procedure of 1819, the election at every meeting of delegates who in contrast to the members of Parliament returned by a restricted franchise, would be the genuine representatives of the people and would constitute in London the General Conven-tion of the Industrious Classes.[3] The scheme amounted to setting up Parliament against Parliament and was a departure from con-stitutional methods. If the petition were refused, what was to be the next step? Attwood brought forward a third plan, which

[1] The Times, September 18, 1838. When, at a meeting held a few days later at Colchester, a speaker maintained that 'as all other classes are represented in the House of Commons, some of the working classes ought to be seated in that House', The Times was indignant. To admit working men to Parliament would be to return 'to that state of savage nature in which the natural rights of men might be exercised by everyone who was strong enough to oppress his neighbour'.

[2] M. Hovell, Chartist Movement, p. 101.

[3] Ibid., p. 106.

dated not from 1819 but from 1833, a general strike.[1] Such a strike was in itself an act of violence against the possessing classes and moreover would inevitably lead to the employment of physical force. Feargus O'Connor, who from the outset had taken part in the mass meetings with the object of getting into his own hands the authority originally assumed by the Radicals of Birmingham and London, preached open sedition. He never, it is true, displayed the least desire to put himself at the head of a revolution, for he was a talker, not a man of action. But if he were to accomplish his programme he must, like O'Connell though in another sphere, inflame and command, for use against the constitutional Radicals of the south, the violent spirits of the north, who cherished dreams of class war, and in the first instance those who for months past had been agitating against the bondage of the factory and the workhouse.

We have already seen that O'Connell in 1837 regarded the agitation for universal suffrage as a useful diversion of the agitation against the new Poor Law. His attitude was shared by Francis Place, Roebuck, and all the Utilitarian Radicals; for the Poor Law was their own work. It is most probable that the members of the Working Men's Association shared from the outset, or very soon came to share, the hostility entertained by the Radical members of Parliament towards the agitators who were attacking the Poor Law to the profit of the Tories. And their attitude was also shared by the middle class in Birmingham which had contributed so largely to the Liberal victory of 1832, had just obtained for their city a charter of incorporation and having filled all the municipal offices openly patronized the alternative agitation. When the London Association several months later decided to arrange a meeting to demand universal suffrage, and wished to hold it in Palace Yard, the request for a permit to use the Yard was supported by the signatures of the most important inhabitants of Westminster.[2] And the original manifesto issued by the Radicals had in fact been couched in indirect language susceptible of different interpretations. 'Fellow men!' it ran, 'do not be led away by promises of repealing the detested Poor Law, or any of

---

[1] R. G. Gammage, *History of the Chartist Movement*, p. 143. For the publican Benbow, his pamphlet of 1832 entitled *Grand National Holiday and Congress of the Productive Classes*, and the first suggestion made about the same time of a general strike, see E. Dolléans, *Le Chartisme*, 1912, vol. i, pp. 122 sqq.

[2] *Life and Struggles of William Lovett*, pp. 172–3.

the other infamous laws which Whig and Tory have united to enact—unless the promise be accompanied by the Pledge of Universal Suffrage'.[1] But it was precisely this political diversion of the movement which Feargus O'Connor and his colleagues of the *Northern Star* wished to prevent.

Ever since its foundation the *Northern Star* had conducted a double campaign against the Poor Law and on behalf of universal suffrage. This was O'Connor's tactics—never to allow the first demand to be abandoned in the pursuit of the second. When Sir William Molesworth declared himself in favour both of Universal Suffrage and the Poor Law of 1834, the *Northern Star* loaded him with abuse.[2] And on the other hand the same paper supported a subscription which was being raised for Richard Oastler since he was an opponent of the Poor Law, although he had declared himself a convinced opponent of universal suffrage.[3] Bolder than Oastler, the other leader of the Anti-Poor-Law movement, Stephens, without explicitly adopting the six points of the People's Charter, took part in the Chartist meetings, those dramatic winter meetings often held after nightfall by the light of torches. O'Connor helped to introduce into the movement, which soon became known as Chartism, the language of 'physical force'. He openly incited his hearers to armed rebellion.[4]

5

Eighteen months earlier when Queen Victoria ascended the throne, certain Tories were already indulging in gloomy forecasts, but at the time the astute Greville did not take their fears seriously. 'The Tories,' he wrote in his diary, 'prognosticate all sorts of dismal consequences none of which of course will come to pass. *Nothing* will happen, because in this country *nothing* ever

[1] See also the remarkably conservative language of the Chartist Petition drawn up, Lovett tells us, by R. K. Douglas, a Birmingham journalist. 'We tell your Hon. House that the capital of the master must no longer be deprived of its due reward' (*Life and Struggles of William Lovett*, pp. 201, 469 sqq.). Cf. the letter from Lovett to Francis Place in which he insists that the Radicals must 'give up their various hobbies, of anti-poor-Laws, factory bills, wage protection bills, and various others, for the purpose of conjointly contending for the Charter' (M. Hovell, *Chartist Movement*, pp. 203–4). But this letter was written in 1840.
[2] *Northern Star*, August 4, 1838, an article entitled 'The man who endeavoured to please everybody, pleased nobody, and lost his ass into the bargain'.
[3] *Northern Star*, August 4, 1838.
[4] See his speech on Kersall Moor, September 24, 1838 (*Annual Register*, 1838, p. 311). Cf. *Life and Struggles of William Lovett*, pp. 172–3.

does.'[1] Now even Greville seemed affected by the general un-
easiness.[2] Without distinction of political allegiance the members
of the governing class were terrified by this underground agitation, the more alarming because it was carried on in quarters with
which they had no direct channels of communication. Once more
the memory of the French Revolution obsessed their imagination.
On the morrow of the Reform Bill, when the present crisis was
still in the future, a Radical, John Stuart Mill, and Carlyle, a
thinker who had deliberately severed himself from all ties of
party, had set themselves to write the story of the Revolution.
Mill had finally abandoned the undertaking, but Carlyle finished
the history he had planned, and in language inspired by the
Jewish prophets warned the wealthy in the concluding para-
graphs of his work of the dangers they ran, if they continued to
live 'indolent as Epicurus' gods, with the living chaos of ignorance
and hunger weltering uncared for at their feet'.[3] At present he
might well be thought a true prophet. The revolutionary movement in process of birth, was led by men such as Bronterre
O'Brien, the translator of *La Conspiration de Caius Gracchus
Babeuf* and the biographer of Robespierre, and Harvey, who
styled himself the British 'Marat'. The workmen who flocked to
the Radical meetings wore tricolour cockades and caps of liberty,
and were making preparations to summon in London the 'Convention' of the British proletariat.[4] Those torches which lit the
nocturnal meetings, what conflagrations they might yet kindle![5]

---

[1] *Greville Memoirs*, June 16, 1837.
[2] Ibid., December 31, 1839: 'Parties are violent, Government weak, everybody wonder-
ing what will happen, nobody seeing their way clearly before them.'
[3] *The French Revolution, a History*, Book VII, ch. vi. In his biography of John Sterling
(Part II, chap. vii) Carlyle quotes the following sentence which Sterling had written in
his Diary on March 6, 1839: 'English politics seem in a queer state, the Conservatives
creeping on, the Whigs losing ground; like combatants on the top of a breach, while
there is a social mine below, which will probably blow both parties into the air.' For
somewhat earlier expresssions of the same fear, see Sir James Graham to Sir Robert Peel,
July 1837: 'Surely these outrages' [certain acts of violence which had occurred during the
late election] 'fatally resemble the fiendish temper of the French Revolution' (C. S. Parker,
Sir Robert Peel, vol. ii, p. 349). *Greville Memoirs*, February 18, 1838: '. . . Parke, who was
an alarmist, had said shortly before that he had never doubted when the Reform Bill had
passed that England would become a republic; and when Brougham said that the Ballot
would be conceded in five years' time, Parke said: "And in five years from that we shall
have a republic." '
[4] *London Democrat*, N. 2, 1839: 'In the Democratic Association the Jacobin Club again
lives and flourishes, and the villainous tyrants shall find to their cost that England too has
her Marats, St. Justs, and Robespierres' (quoted by F. F. Rosenblatt, *The Social and
Economic Aspects of the Chartist Movement*, 1916).
[5] *Manchester Guardian*, December 12, 1838; *Morning Chronicle*, December 14, 1838.

The very night in fact that Stephens pronounced one of his most violent diatribes against the tyranny which prevailed in the factories, a factory was set on fire at Ashton.

Nevertheless, experienced politicians were not wanting among the Conservatives who refused to take so gloomy a view of the situation. The revolutionary agitation coincided with the annual revision of the registers, and they noticed that the results were most favourable to their party. Fear of revolution had evidently driven a considerable number of voters into the Tory ranks.[1] And they witnessed the dilemma in which the Whigs were placed, obliged either to tolerate the disturbances and offend all the supporters of order, or suppress them and incur an unpopularity as intense as that from which the Tories had suffered after Peterloo. In September, Lord John, speaking at Liverpool, had advocated a policy of unqualified toleration,[2] and the speech was widely blamed as an encouragement to disorder. In December he gave way to the pressure of the manufacturers, issued a proclamation forbidding the torchlight meetings and arrested Stephens.[3] At once The Times was up in arms. Why, it asked, should Stephens be persecuted when nothing whatever was done against O'Connell, who had incited the Irish to rebellion, or Hume, who defended the Canadian rebels?[4] Throughout the summer The Times had systematically ignored the demand for universal suffrage, and depicted the agitation in the north as exclusively an agitation against the Poor Law. By September, it had become alarmed by the serious nature of the revolutionary movement and suspended its campaign against the Act of 1834. In December it had recovered from its fears, once more treated the demand for universal suffrage as negligible and made common cause with Stephens.

On the whole when the New Year opened, it was clear that the tactics pursued by Oastler and Stephens had succeeded. They had taken their revenge upon the alliance of O'Connell, Roebuck, Lovett and Thomas Attwood. The Radical municipalities which the previous summer had tolerated and even patronized the popular demonstrations were now hostile to the movement.

[1] The Times, September 20, 1838. Cf. September 12 and 25, and October 4, 1838.

[2] R. G. Gammage, History of the Chartist Movement p. 92. See on this speech the passage of arms between Lord John Russell and Sir Robert Peel, H. of C., February 5, 1839 (Parliamentary Debates, 3rd Series, vol. xlv, pp. 108, 117).

[3] R. G. Gammage, History of the Chartist Movement, p. 98. Annual Register, 1838, Chron., pp. 168 sqq.   [4] The Times, January 1, 1838.

When the agitators asked for the use of a Town Hall for a meeting, it was nearly always refused.[1] O'Connell, whose language, if not his acts, knew no restraint, was now in full cry against the Chartists.[2] Roebuck and Francis Place, who had been appointed by the London meeting as their representatives in the Convention, resigned. These desertions weakened the moderate section of the Chartist movement, the section known as the party of moral force. In London indeed, the conduct of the movement remained in their hands, and the extremists found no followers except among the half-starved silk weavers of Spitalfields. In Edinburgh it was the same.[3] Everywhere else the party which O'Connor had christened the party of physical force was triumphant. Alike by his violent methods and his programme, O'Connor was the most serviceable tool of the Tory demagogues. In the opinion of the *Morning Chronicle* the Chartist agitation was simply the Anti-Poor-Law Agitation in disguise.[4]

III THE AGITATION AGAINST THE CORN LAW

I

Once more the Radical group in Parliament was compelled to devise some means of counteracting the agitation and regaining contact with the working class. It was clear from the reports of the Chartist mass meetings, that the demonstrators expected from a system of universal suffrage, not only the abolition of the workhouses and the factory system, but the provision of cheap bread by the removal of the duties on imported corn.[5] On this last point, it would seem, the programme of the Ultra-Radicals coincided with the Benthamites'. Might it not be possible to persuade the workmen that the free import of foodstuffs could be

[1] R. G. Gammage, *History of the Chartist Movement*, p. 94.
[2] *The Times*, November 28, 1838. See the letters addressed to O'Connell by Oastler and Stephens. *The Times*, December 4, 1838, January 3, 1839. *Life and Struggles o William Lovett*, p. 191.
[3] Ibid., p. 199. R. G. Gammage, *History of the Chartist Movement*, p. 84.
[4] Article by Sir Edward Lytton Bulwer reproduced by the *Northern Star*, October 13, 1838.
[5] Fielden's speech at the Manchester meeting of September 23, 1838 (R. G. Gammage, *History of the Chartist Movement*, p. 61). 'At the Birmingham Meeting of August 6, . . . a banner . . . was displayed in the hall, on which was represented the figures of three loaves of different sizes, but all marked at the same price. The English loaf was the smallest, the French loaf larger, but the Russian loaf was the largest of all. Underneath was inscribed "The effects of the corn laws" ' (ibid., p. 42).

secured without taking the roundabout route of parliamentary reform, to concentrate their attention on a programme, not political but economic, of complete free trade, and in this way compose conflict between the manufacturers and their men which seemed to threaten civil war, by uniting both parties against their common enemy, the landowner?

To be sure the agitation conducted by the free-traders for the reduction, or even the eventual removal of the duties on corn, was considerably anterior to the winter of 1838. It had already been carried on for two years. For two years ago, the balance of economic forces had once more been altered by one of those frequent shifts to which it was liable. When 1836 opened, trade and manufacture were prosperous, foodstuffs cheap, and agriculture depressed. In the House of Commons, Lord Chandos had moved that financial relief, of a nature not clearly specified, should be given to the agriculturists,[1] and both the Commons and the Lords had appointed a committee of inquiry into the agricultural distress. By the end of the year, however, conditions had changed. The price of wheat, which in January 1836 had been about 38s. the quarter, rose continuously until it reached 58s. It did not again fall below 53s., and in January 1837 was nearly 80s. The industrial depression could not be reasonably ascribed to a crisis on the Stock Exchange or the mismanagement of the Bank of England. No doubt it was possible to account in this way for the difficulties under which the commercial and financial relations between Great Britain and the United States laboured during the first half of 1837. But how was it that when the alleged causes of the depression had been removed it did not come to an end? The free-traders ascribed it to the high price of corn. So long as the price of corn remained high, the depression must continue. When at the end of 1836 the price of corn reached its earlier maximum, the first Anti-Corn-Law Association was founded in London.[2] The Radical members of Parliament, the disciples of Bentham and James Mill, Grote, Molesworth, Joseph Hume, and Roebuck were already preparing the ground for an agitation against the Corn Law, several weeks before they began to collaborate with the Working Men's Association in drawing up a programme of political reform. In March 1837, the Radical member for one of

[1] H. of C., April 27, 1836 (*Parliamentary Debates*, 3rd Series, vol. xxxiii, pp. 333 sqq.).
[2] A. Prentice, *History of the Anti-Corn-Law League*, vol. i, pp. 49–50.

the London suburbs, William Clay, invited the House of Commons to declare in favour of a fixed and moderate duty of 10s. a quarter on imported corn. His motion mustered only eighty-nine votes. But of these eighty-nine, ten were the votes of Ministers.[1]

Not London, however, but Lancashire was to be the headquarters of the campaign for free trade. For Lancashire provided the most favourable soil in which the doctrine of free trade could take root. It was a great exporting district. We have already seen what an enormous proportion of the British exports consisted of Lancashire goods. And the special conditions of the cotton manufacture were particularly favourable to the propaganda. The advocates of Protection were fond of insisting upon the danger to which in time of war a country was exposed which depended on foreign markets for its food supply. That argument did not touch the Lancashire manufacturers. For their industry was by its very nature dependent for its raw material on the foreigner; Lancashire must in any case obtain her cotton from America. Consequently when Cobden, in two pamphlets published in 1835 and 1836, expounded a new foreign policy, based on free trade and a thorough-going pacifism, he voiced the unspoken desires of the district from which he drew his wealth. For Lancashire was obliged to purchase abroad, not only her cotton, but also the corn, which was an essential ingredient of the real wage of her workmen, and therefore entered indirectly into the total cost of manufacture.

Poulett Thomson, to whom in 1830 the Liberals had given a seat in the Cabinet as the representative of the principle of free trade, had been returned in 1833 for the new borough of Manchester. In January 1834, a number of Manchester merchants and manufacturers had founded a committee to inquire into the best means of obtaining the repeal of the Corn Law of 1828. In 1835 Cobden in his influential pamphlet, *England, Ireland and America*, expressed the wish that a society might be founded to propagate the 'beneficent truths' of Adam Smith's philosophy.[2] Though he advocated free trade in every province, he devoted his chief attention to the campaign against agricultural protection. To defend their interests the agriculturalists had founded an Association in every county of England. Why, asked Cobden, should not

[1] H. of C., March 16, 1837 (*Parliamentary Debates*, 3rd Series, vol. xxxvii, pp. 562 sqq.). A. Prentice, *History of the Anti-Corn-Law League*, vol. i, p. 54.
[2] *England, Ireland and America* (*Works*, vol. i, pp. 31-2).

free-traders form as many counter-associations to combat their monopoly? It was possibly in consequence of this suggestion from Lancashire, that the London Radicals founded at the end of 1836 their Anti-Corn-Law Association. At the general election of 1837 the free-traders not only kept the two Manchester seats, they gained two others, Wigan and Oldham, and a few more votes would have returned Cobden for Stockport.[1] But these free-traders were not returned on a specifically free trade programme, and half the Lancashire members were still in favour of protection.[2] It was not until 1838 that the demand for free trade became insistent. In that year the price of corn rose from 55s. in January to 72s. in September, and after a temporary fall to 64s. reached 74s. in December, and in January almost 80s. This explains the rapid growth of the Chartist agitation. It also explains the birth of a parallel agitation for free trade.

In February 1838 the *Manchester Times* published an important article which seems to have been the manifesto of a group of propagandists. The writer, Prentice, lamented that the workmen wasted so much time and money in useless agitations for a reduction of the working day, an increase of wages, and the repeal of the Poor Law, and urged them instead to make 'one combined and energetic effort against the landowner's monopoly'.[3] He could, however, excuse the ignorance of the cotton spinners when he called to mind the disgusting apathy displayed by the Manchester Chamber of Commerce. Not once during the last two years had they raised their voice against a monopoly which was destroying British Trade.[4] On February 13, this lethargic body awoke from its long slumber and issued a declaration stating that the injustice of the present system must be brought persistently to the notice of Parliament and demanding the repeal of the Corn Laws.[5]

Its effect was felt in Parliament. Charles Villiers, a younger son of a noble family, and a friend of the Bullers and the Mills, who sat for the manufacturing town of Wolverhampton, asked for the appointment of a parliamentary committee to inquire into the Corn Laws. He renewed his motion annually and became

[1] A. Prentice, *History of the Anti-Corn-Law League*, vol. i, pp. 55–6. John Morley, *Life of Richard Cobden*, Popular Ed., p. 13.
[2] *Manchester Times*, July 7, 1838.
[3] A. Prentice, *History of the Anti-Corn Law League*, pp. 57–8.
[4] *Minutes of Evidence before Select Committee on Import Duties*, 1840, pp. 157 sqq.
[5] A. Prentice, *History of the Anti-Corn-Law League*, p. 59.

the accredited advocate of Corn Law repeal, as Grote of the ballot. No doubt when he made his motion, the agitation for free trade was as yet in its infancy, for he was obliged to lament the lack of public interest in the question.[1] But important papers in Manchester, Scotland and London were already conducting an unremitting campaign against the Corn Laws.[2] Ebenezer Elliott, the workman poet, was an avowed free-trader as well as a Chartist. In Lancashire 22,000 handloom weavers, probably under the direct instigation of the group of agitators who had inspired the article in the *Manchester Times*, signed a petition for the repeal of the Corn Laws.[3] And finally, when in August it became certain that there would be a bad harvest and that winter was likely to bring a famine in its train, the moment seemed opportune to execute the programme sketched in February by the *Manchester Times*.[4]

2

On September 10, sixty supporters of free trade gave a reception in honour of John Bowring, who had just returned from his travels, undertaken to study foreign conditions and which had taken him as far afield as Egypt. In the after dinner speeches, surprise was expressed that Manchester did not yet possess like London and several other English cities[5] its Anti–Corn–Law Association. But if such an association were not founded, it would be impossible to arouse the Chamber of Commerce from the slumber into which after its February manifesto, it had once more fallen. A small committee held a series of meetings. To

[1] H. of C., March 13, 1838 (*Parliamentary Debates*, 3rd Series, vol. xli, pp. 909 sqq.). See p. 911: 'It might be said that this was not a fit time to bring forward the question, because there was no excitement on the subject. But he thought that it was not wise to postpone the consideration of so important a subject until there would be neither calmness nor leisure to discuss it.' For the relations between Villiers and the Utilitarians, see J. S. Mill, *Autobiography*, pp. 77, 126, 128. *Greville Memoirs*, April 22, 1839: 'Charles Villiers who is a very leading man, and much looked to among them, probably, besides that he really is very clever, on account of that aristocratic origin and connection which he himself affects to despise, and to consider prejudicial to him.'

[2] *The Scotsman* and *Tait's Edinburgh Magazine* in Edinburgh, the *Glasgow Argus*, the *Manchester and Salford Advertiser* and the *Manchester Times*; also Perronet Thompson's *Sun* in London.

[3] Prentice, *History of the Anti-Corn-Law League*, vol. i, p. 80. Cf. *The Times*, May 4, 1838, in the report of the Handloom Weavers Commission.

[4] *Manchester Guardian*, August 11, 1838: article entitled 'The Weather and the Corn Laws'; August 25, 1838: article entitled 'Prospects of the Harvest. The Corn Laws'.

[5] I have been unable to discover the places which had followed the example set at the end of 1836 by the London Association. *Tait's Edinburgh Magazine* for January 1838 (N.S., vol. v, p. 66) mentions the foundation of associations in the West of Scotland which were federated in a Central Anti-Corn Law Association for the West of Scotland.

obtain as wide a membership as possible it was decided that the subscription should be only 5s. By October 4, a hundred members had been enrolled. On October 11 a temporary committee was formed.[1]

It was not until the following week that Cobden's name was added to the list of members. He had spent the whole of September travelling in Germany. Before his departure he had been extremely depressed by what he called the 'dense ignorance' of English working men, and was sure their enthusiasm could be aroused only for some quack panacea.[2] The decision taken in his absence by his Manchester friends appears to have changed his attitude completely. We find him no longer willing to take the Chartist agitation too seriously. If it roused the country from its apathy so much the better. No doubt the Radicals were ignorant and self-opinionated, but were they any worse in these respects than the ruling classes? 'I think the scattered elements may yet be rallied round the question of the corn laws.'[3]

On the face of it free trade was a more attractive programme than the Chartist manifesto. The Chartists offered the people the franchise which no doubt the new electors might use later to win all sorts of benefits, but which in itself did nothing to improve the material conditions of the poor. The free-traders without troubling themselves with political claims promised the poor an immediate and tangible boon, cheap bread. The Chartists might, it is true, reply that they agreed with the Manchester manufacturers in their demand for the repeal of the Corn Law, but regarded it as absurd to expect it from a Parliament elected on the existing franchise. But if that was in fact the position of the more moderate Chartists, who with Lovett were shortly to profess a social philosophy not easy to distinguish from that of Charles Villiers and Cobden, O'Connor on the other hand, who as an Irish landowner, had always been a declared protectionist, suddenly gave an altogether different direction to the Chartist movement. He was supported by the revolutionaries under the leadership of Bronterre O'Brien, who maintained that the repeal of the Corn Laws could do nothing to improve the labourer's lot, unless the wage system were first abolished.

[1] A. Prentice, *History of the Anti-Corn-Law League*, vol. i, pp. 64 sqq. *Report from the Select Committee on Import Duties, together with the Minutes of Evidence*, August 6, 1840, pp 157 sqq. (evidence of J. B. Smith).
[2] R. Cobden to W. Tait, August 17, 1838 (John Morley, *Life of Richard Cobden*, ed. 1876 vol. i, p. 127).　　[3] R. Cobden to his brother, October 3, 1838 (ibid., p. 126).

According to Ricardo's law of wages the workman received as the reward of his labour a wage just sufficient to keep himself and his family alive. If the cost of living fell as a result of the reduction of the import duties on food stuffs, the real wage received by the workman would not be altered. He would merely receive a money wage equal in purchasing power to his former wage, so that his real wage would remain the same. Fifteen years earlier, William Thompson, the co-operator, and the individualist Thomas Hodgskin, had made use of Ricardo's law to prove that the real cause of the poverty of the working class was the profit received by the capitalist. It was in vain that the free-traders adduced statistics to show that wages did not necessarily rise and fall with the rise and fall in the cost of food, that between 1833 and 1835, for example, though bread was cheap, wages had not therefore fallen, and that when the price of corn was subsequently doubled, they did not rise.[1] The advocates of free trade had too often used arguments which laid them open to the Chartists' attack. They were never weary of insisting that the golden rule of commercial success was what Cobden termed 'the talismanic law of cheapness'.[2] How, they asked, could the British manufacturer compete successfully with his foreign rival, if his workmen cost twice as much to feed? Evidently, replied the Chartists, the real object of the free-traders is not the improvement of the workers' lot but cheap labour.

Warned by the Chartist reply of the damage they might do their cause by such imprudent arguments, Cobden and his friends saw the necessity of giving another turn to their propaganda. Cobden, Bowring, and indeed all the members of the group who had visited America, had seen a vigorous attempt being made to compete with British manufacturers and they ascribed it to the system of protection which the British landlords had set up for their private gain. For it was only with their agricultural produce that the continental nations could purchase the products of English manufacture, and the Corn Laws excluded foreign corn from the British market. Since they were thus prevented from exporting their corn to England, they were unable to pay for the manufactured goods which England offered

[1] T. Tooke, *History of Prices*, vol. iii, pp. 51-3. *Report from the Select Committee on Import Duties*, 1840 (Joseph Whetstone's evidence).
[2] R. Cobden, *Russia*, chap. iv (*Works*, vol. i, p. 295).

for their purchase, and were compelled to manufacture for themselves. Thus the Corn Laws protected directly the British landowner, indirectly the foreign manufacturer.

The Continental nations were indeed not satisfied with the indirect protection they received from the Corn Laws. They maintained or even stiffened their own tariffs. It was in vain that the winegrowing regions of the South of France organized demonstrations in favour of a qualified system of free trade, the industrial North, more powerful than ever since the July revolution, would grant the British Government no more than the derisory concessions contained in the tariff of 1836, and as early as 1837 the French Government declared its intention to raise the duty on imported linen fabrics. The utmost concession the British merchants could secure was a delay of two years before the new tariff came into operation. In spite of all inducements to the contrary Russia was determined to protect her new born industries. Naples placed a duty of 100 per cent on all manufactured articles imported into the country. And even the Spanish Government, which we might have expected to be helpless in the face of British demands, clung to her old system of prohibitive tariffs. The Board of Trade could indeed boast of one success, the commercial treaty concluded with Austria in 1838. But it was balanced by the failure in 1836 of the negotiations for a commercial treaty with Prussia. And of all the Continental nations it was Prussia which at this very date dealt the severest blow to the British export trade. To protect German industries against the foreign importer the Zollverein had just united twenty-five million Germans in a single tariff system.[1]

Could British trade hope to find in America compensation for the loss of the European market which now appeared inevitable? There also the outlook was dark. In the United States the agriculturalists of the South had revolted a few years before against the system of protection forced upon them by the manufacturers of New England, and had secured a gradual reduction of the duties

[1] Only one European country remained completely open to British exports, namely Turkey. But Cobden, who evinced a sudden and most surprising admiration for Russian protection, had nothing but contempt for Turkish free trade. 'The very stringent laws, which Russia has passed against the importation of our fabrics, are indications of the same variety of character, evincing a desire to rival us in mechanical industry: whilst the apathy with which the Turk sees every article of our manufactures enter his ports without being stimulated to study the construction of a loom or spinning frame is but another manifestation of his inferior structure of intellect' (*Russia*, chap. i, *Works*, vol. i, pp. 187-8).

which in ten years time would bring them to the permanent figure of 20 per cent. But the tariff was due for revision in 1842; the Protectionists were preparing to avenge their defeat, and would certainly succeed, unless England responded to these concessions by equal concessions on her side. The situation in South America was the same. Brazil had declared against the extremely favourable commercial treaty of 1829, due to expire in 1844.[1]

No doubt there was truth in Owen's contention that the world was suffering from a surfeit of production. But according to the free-traders it was not the effect of causes inherent in the very nature of capitalism, but was due to a vicious distribution of the products. In England there was an excess of manufactured goods, a deficiency of agricultural produce, with the consequence that the former were cheap, the latter was dear. Elsewhere there was a deficiency of manufactured goods, an excess of agricultural produce, and the cost of the former was therefore prohibitive, the latter were dirt cheap. The responsibility for this state of affairs lay with the great English landlords, who had obtained the Corn Laws from Parliament. Only repeal these statutes, and allow the laws of supply and demand to operate freely between the British manufacturer and the foreign farmer. The British factories would soon recover their former prosperity. And the workman would secure, if not exactly cheap bread, his first necessity, employment.

3

Such were the arguments which, towards the end of this year 1838, the Chartist and Free Trade agitators were bandying to and fro, not in books or in the columns of the Press, but at public meetings before crowds of working men. Free-traders interrupted Chartist meetings, and invited the audience to carry an amendment to the resolution before the meeting and demand in addition to universal suffrage, the repeal of the Corn Law. The Chartists replied by interfering with free-trade meetings, which they persisted in representing as demonstrations organized by the middle classes against the popular cause.

The Chartists had in truth good reason to be alarmed by the rapid growth of the free trade movement. A certain Paulton who

[1] For a complete account of the situation, see *Commercial Treaties and Regulations of the several States of Europe and America, together with the Commercial Treaties between England and Foreign Countries*, 1841-2; also G. Poulett Scrope, *Memoirs o the Life of the Right Honourable Charles Lord Sydenham*, pp. 76 sqq.

during the summer of 1838 seems to have inaugurated the method
of free trade lectures, went on tour at the end of October, and
after speaking at Manchester visited Birmingham, where two
months later the corporation declared in favour of repealing the
Corn Law.[1] He then lectured up and down the country and carried
the campaign into the enemy's stronghold by visiting purely
agricultural counties such as Norfolk. In January he boasted that
he had spoken in seven counties and addressed a total audience of
45,000.[2] During the first fortnight of January, mass meetings were
held in Manchester, Leeds, and Liverpool.[3] Would the members
of Parliament and the Ministers yield? On January 28, 1839, an
event occurred which the opponents of the Corn Law hailed as a
presage of imminent victory. *The Times*, always alert to detect the
current of public opinion, and seemingly afraid lest it should be
anticipated by a Government it hated, declared in favour of free
trade. Hitherto it had barely mentioned the campaign of the
Manchester free-traders, and on the two or three occasions on
which it had referred to it, it had been to attack it most vehe-
mently.[4] Then all of a sudden, in a sensational leader, *The Times*
urged against the sliding scale, the very objection which after
1815 it had urged against the fixed tariff, and attempted to prove
that the present system, since it produced incessant fluctuations
in the price of corn, did not benefit even the landowners, and a
fixed tariff was therefore preferable to the sliding scale. Moreover, this fixed duty must be extremely moderate, no higher than
was sufficient to compensate for the special taxation to which
agriculture was subject. If the great landlords and the farmers
abandoned corn-growing as no longer sufficiently profitable, so
much the worse for them. For it was not the interest of the agricultural class alone, but of the entire nation that was at stake. Let
the Whigs beware of degrading the question to the level of party
politics; it was not from any considerations of party that *The
Times* denounced 'the oppressive system of the Corn Laws'.[5]

[1] A. Prentice, *History of the Anti-Corn-Law League*, vol. i, p. 77. A Chartist amendment
to the motion in favour of free trade proposed by T. C. Salt, was rejected by 34 votes
to 12 (J. Th. Bruce, *History of Birmingham*, vol. i, pp. 165–8).
[2] A. Prentice, *History of the Anti-Corn-Law League*, vol. i, p. 103.
[3] *Northern Star*, January 19, 1839 (Leeds meeting). A. Prentice, *History of the Anti-Corn-
Law League*, vol. i, pp. 95–6.   [4] March 22, 23, September 15, 1838.
[5] For the effect produced by this article, see *Greville Memoirs*, January 24, 1839: 'The
question of absorbing interest is now the repeal of the Corn Laws and the declaration of
war against them on the part of *The Times* has produced a great effect, and is taken as

During the following fortnight *The Times* abandoned its campaign against the Poor Law to attack the Corn Law, and became the official organ of the free trade movement. As the opening of Parliament drew near the campaign became more intense. Petitions were signed in every important town in the Kingdom. On January 22, the Anti-Corn-Law Association of Manchester was definitely founded and appointed its executive which was shortly to become the executive, not of a local association, but of a National League. It decided to adopt the procedure by which in 1812 the repeal of the Orders in Council had been obtained, and which the Chartists were employing at that very moment in their campaign for universal suffrage, and send delegates to London to take petitions to Parliament, watch the debates in the House of Commons, and when necessary help the speakers with their advice. Parliament met on February 6. During the long adjournment, both agitations had 'matured', and the moment had now arrived when the rival demands put forward by the people, were to be laid before their legal representatives. When the session opened the rival delegations sent respectively by the Chartist meetings and the Manchester Anti-Corn-Law Association met in London.

IV THE CHARTIST RISING OF 1839

I

The Chartist delegates were fifty in number. Of these fifty a bare majority were working men. They included three Justices of the Peace, representatives of the democratic magistrates Lord John had appointed during the last three years, six journalists, two doctors, a Nonconformist minister, a clergyman of the Established Church—the eccentric Dr. Wade—a large Birmingham manufacturer, and a considerable number of shopkeepers.[1] We must not, however, conclude that in this little Radical assembly the working men were necessarily the left wing, the traders and professional men the right. The most violent of the Chartist orators were of middle class origin, and when Lovett and his

conclusive evidence that they cannot be maintained, for the rare sagacity with which this journal watches the turn of public affairs.'

[1] *Life and Struggles of William Lovett*, p. 201. F. Dolléans, *Le Chartisme*, vol. i, p. 289. M. Hovell, *The Chartist Movement*, pp. 121-2.

friends decided to confine the membership of their London association to working men, their object was to keep out the demagogues. Nevertheless, even after the revolutionary campaign of the previous winter, the moderates were still predominant in the delegation. For reasons of economy it had been decided that a single delegate might represent several districts and these delegates had been chosen from Chartists domiciled in London. And the majority of the London Chartists were moderate.

The first question to be settled was the status the delegates should assume. Were they, as it might be argued from the terms of the resolutions passed at the meetings which had elected them, simply the bearers of a petition to Parliament who must wait until it had been examined and then dissolve? This was the view of James Cobbett, a son of the famous Cobbett, who was one of the two delegates from Manchester. But his contention was rejected in February, and he resigned.[1] Even had it been accepted the Convention could not have dissolved immediately: for the House of Commons could choose its own date to take the National Petition into consideration, and there might be a lengthy delay. Moreover, when the delegates examined the petitions entrusted to their charge, they found that they were far from having obtained the success on which they had reckoned. They had expected 1,000,000 signatures, had received only 600,000. In these circumstances they decided to send 'missionaries' up and down the country to collect further signatures. What were the remainder of the delegates to do in London meanwhile?

The revolutionaries maintained that the Convention, since it had been elected at public meetings by a body of electors more numerous than the Parliamentary electorate, constituted the only Parliament in England with valid credentials, the true 'People's Parliament'. They therefore contended that the Convention should refuse to admit the authority of a 'rotten' Parliament. Though they were not a majority of the delegates, their contention flattered the self-conceit of many among their fellows, and they held meetings apart from the regular sittings of the Convention by which they influenced its decisions. At the same time their uncompromising language gave rise to several resignations; Dr. Wade and the Birmingham delegates resigned. The latter belonged to the body of moderate leaders who had inaugurated

[1] *Life and Struggles of William Lovett*, p. 203.

the Chartist movement a year before.[1] Their departure therefore strengthened the power of the revolutionaries in the Convention. It was further increased by the news which the 'missionaries' reported from the provinces. At Norwich pikes were being distributed. At Middleton in Lancashire, shots were fired every night by way of demonstration. At Rochdale the Radical Association had decided to furnish its members with pikes, guns, powder and bullets. There were, it was reported, 4,000 armed men at Rochdale, 6,000 at Oldham, 30,000 in the four towns of Hyde, Ashton, Newton Moor, and Stalybridge. Henry Vincent toured the south-west, urging the revolutionary labourers to march on London *en masse*. In the mining districts of Wales his visit produced a disquieting state of unrest. On May 3 the news reached London that the small Welsh town of Llanidloes had been occupied by armed revolutionaries.[2]

By degrees the extremists captured the Convention. As late as March 7 it formally repudiated Harvey and condemned all attempts to imitate the French Jacobins. But a month later, on April 9, it affirmed by a declaration of principle the right of every Englishman to carry arms. It was, however, with visible reluctance that it allowed itself to be carried away by the stream. It was careful not to give the signal for immediate revolution and was content to deliberate upon the further measures to be taken when Parliament rejected the National Petition. The manifesto issued in the early days of May, as the result of these deliberations, bore the stamp of its authors' indecision. It began by a frank invitation to the wage-earning 'slaves' to rise in revolt. An appeal followed to 'all friends of peace and order . . . and especially to the "middle class" '. The grant of universal suffrage was presented as the only means of avoiding a bloody revolution. 'We are contending for no visionary or impracticable scheme.

[1] M. Hovell, *The Chartist Movement*, pp. 131, 133.

[2] *The Times*, May 3, 6. 9, 10, and 11, 1839. R. G. Gammage, *History of the Chartist Movement*, p. 151. Nothing is said of this episode by Hovell or Rosenblatt. The history of the Chartist movement in North Wales has yet to be studied. It was probably a revolt of the small tenants against the introduction of the workhouse, and was unconcerned with the problems which had arisen in the manufacturing districts, resembling rather the Irish disturbances. See *Annual Register*, 1837, pp. 137, 145. The *Report of the Commissioners of Inquiry for South Wales*, 1844, though dealing with troubles slightly posterior to our period and concerned exclusively with the southern half of the Principality, throws some light on the causes of the discontent in the Welsh country districts, the heavy charges levied upon the peasantry by the Highway Trusts, the enforcement of the statute of 1836 dealing with the tithe, and the administration of the New Poor Law.

The principles of our Charter were the laws and customs of our ancestors, under which property was secure and the working people happy and contented.' And after all the Convention shrank from the responsibility of revolutionary measures. It was content to order 'simultaneous' meetings to be held on a fixed day throughout the entire country (this also in imitation of the procedure followed in 1819) and to announce that at these meetings the Convention would submit certain questions to the assembly. Would they be prepared to withdraw all their savings from the banks on a fixed date? To strike for a month, 'the sacred month', to compel the acceptance of the Charter? To take up arms to 'defend the laws and constitutional privileges their ancestors bequeathed to them'? To ignore at the next general election the legal poll, and elect by show of hands democratic candidates, who would proceed to London to function as the genuine representatives of the people?[1] That is to say, the Convention contrived at once to adopt and not to adopt the proposals of the extremists, and gained time by referring the matter back to the people, and asking them to decide at a later date whether or no they approved of the violent procedure suggested.

2

With the publication of the manifesto, battle was joined between the Government and the Chartists. When the conflict broke out, the Tories blamed the Liberals for having failed to show the necessary firmness and having made resistance a moral impossibility by the repeated proofs of weakness they had given since 1832. They could not form an alliance with the Irish agitators without paying the penalty in the indirect encouragement given to revolutionary agitation in England. Though the Cabinet was in a very difficult position, without an assured majority in Parliament or the country, it contrived nevertheless to retain office, avoid panic and get the better of the insurgents without having recourse to extraordinary legislation as the Tories had done twenty years earlier, or as they had done themselves in Ireland six years before. The Speech from the Throne had declared that the Government would be content with the strict execution of the existing laws, and counted for the maintenance of order upon the good sense and law-abiding spirit which distinguished

[1] See the full text of the manifesto, *Life and Struggles of William Lovett*, pp. 209 sqq.

the British people. Their optimism was justified by the event. The ministers did what was necessary, but nothing more than was necessary, to repress and prevent disorder.

Their first step was to mollify the Radical opposition in the House. Once more people were asking whether Brougham[1] or Lord Durham[2] would lead an organized Radical party. The *Morning Chronicle* declared a further measure of Parliamentary Reform necessary—the ballot, household suffrage, and triennial Parliaments—and threatened to withdraw its support from the Government unless concessions were made to the Radicals.[3] And we have already seen that in May an outbreak of ill humour on their part, had sufficed to produce a Cabinet crisis, and that it was only as the result of a court intrigue that Melbourne and Lord John had remained in office. What could be done to appease them? Melbourne agreed that in future the ballot should be regarded as an 'open' question, that is to say, a matter on which each member of the Cabinet was free to vote as he pleased.[4] And on June 18 a Cabinet minister voted for the ballot with his colleagues' approval.[5] Macaulay, who had just been returned for Edinburgh on a Radical programme, entered the Cabinet a few weeks later as Secretary for War. But the attitude the Cabinet adopted towards the ballot was a mere gesture and led to nothing. The motion was lost by a majority of over 100 votes.

Outside Parliament the Cabinet did its utmost to conciliate public opinion.

The previous year the ministers had declared war upon the trade unions. To institute an inquiry, as Parliament had done, into their alleged crimes, was to impeach them before the tribunal of the gentry and the middle class. Did the Government intend to go back on the statute of 1825? The Cabinet let the matter drop. The committee of inquiry published the evidence of the witnesses, but did not even draw up a report.[6] The Glasgow labourers,

---

[1] Croker to Sir Robert Peel, May 12, 1839 (C. S. Parker, *Sir Robert Peel*, vol. ii, p. 399): '. . . He means to be President not of the Council, but of the Republic.'

[2] *Quarterly Review*, January 1839, 'Political Affairs' (vol. lxiii, p. 275).

[3] *Morning Chronicle*, March 25, 28, 1839.

[4] Lord Melbourne to Lord John Russell, June 1839 (*Lord Melbourne's Papers*, p. 399). Cf. *Greville Memoirs*, April 6, 22, June 24, 1839.

[5] It was calculated that 17 members of the administration and of the Queen's household voted for the ballot, and only 12 against it (*Annual Register*, 1839, p. 279).

[6] *First and Second Reports from the Select Committee on Combinations of Workmen; together with the Minutes of Evidence*, June 4, July 30, 1838. Cf. Lord Melbourne to Lord John Russell, December 1, 1838 (*Lord Melbourne's Papers*, p. 385). See, on the other hand,

who had been found guilty in 1837, did not complete their sentence. The Government sought to detach the trade unions from the Chartist organizations and, as we shall see, achieved its object.

Socialism, that is to say, the doctrine of Owen, had been about 1833 the orthodoxy of the working class. Since that date Owen had lost the allegiance of the main body of trade unionists. Nevertheless, he continued his propaganda, in many respects revolutionary and frankly irreligious. But for Owen the forces which were to achieve what he termed the 'new moral world' were argument and example. If his aim was revolutionary, his methods were not. He was not even a democrat. Melbourne, who cared little for religious orthodoxy, presented him to the Queen, in memory of her father, the Duke of Kent, who had once patronized the reformer. One hundred and ninety-four persons were presented that day, but only three of the Queen's subjects had the honour to be personally presented, and of these Owen was one. The choice gave considerable scandal, and it was in consequence of the outcry raised on this occasion that the term 'socialism', hitherto confined to the working class, appeared in the leading Reviews, and was mentioned in Parliament.[1] Melbourne was wiser than his critics. Owen's 'socialism', in other words, co-operation, was welcome to the Government, because it presented the working classes with a counter-attraction to the revolutionary Jacobinism of the Chartists.

The agitation for universal suffrage, originally devised as a

Wellington's letter to Peel of December 18, 1839, which is intensely hostile to the trade unions and affirms the necessity of amending the legislation of 1825 (C. S. Parker, *Sir Robert Peel*, vol. ii, pp. 418–9).

[1] *Socialism exposed, or the Book of the New Moral World examined by Joseph Mather*, 1839. *The Progress and Tendencies of Socialism. A Sermon preached before the University of Cambridge*, November 17, 1839, by George Pearson, 1839. *Socialism as a Religious Theory irrational and absurd. Three Lectures on Socialism as propounded by R. Owen and others*, delivered at the Baptist Chapel, South Parade, Leeds, by John Eustace Giles, 1839. *Socialism in its moral tendencies compared with Christianity*, by John Eustace Giles, 1839. These pamphlets prove that at this date Socialism was treated rather as a system of irreligion than as a social Utopia. Cf. *Quarterly Review*, December 1839, 'Conduct of Ministers and Seditious Meetings. The Press, Socialism . . . Socialism and Chartism . . . are the natural and necessary developments—Chartism of Whig principles, Socialism of Dissent' (vol. lxv, p. 304); June 1840: '. . . Among the dregs of our population, though under no classical name, the same spirit is working. Socialism is a vulgar pantheism' (vol. lxvi, p. 115). The word appeared for the first time in *The Times*, October 21 (Socialism or the new Morality) and December 14 (the alarming advances of democracy, socialism and Popery, formidable alike to property, morality, trade, civil order and religious freedom). Cf. H. of L., January 16, 24, 27 and February 3, 1840 (*Parliamentary Debates*, 3rd Series, vol. li, pp. 510, 567, 928, 1176); also Archbishop Whately to Nassau Senior, January 28, 1840 (E. J. Whately, *Life of R. Whately*, vol. i, p. 451).

diversion from the anti-Poor-Law agitation, was once more at the close of 1838 combined with it. Would it be advisable to make some concessions to the enemies of the Poor Law? Many Radicals urged that course upon the Cabinet. The powers conferred upon the three commissioners by the statute of 1833 were due to expire. Was it not an excellent opportunity to go back upon an unpopular measure and place the normal operation of the Poor Law on another basis? The ministers rejected the advice and were encouraged in their refusal by the approval of Wellington and Peel, the leaders of the Conservative party so many of whose members had supported the attack upon the Poor Law. They agreed to continue the Commissioners' powers for one year only, not for three, as they had originally proposed.[1] But it was the sole concession made. Their powers were not diminished and the principle of the workhouse was maintained.[2] Some temporary and restricted relaxations, however, in applying it were granted, which were received with noisy delight by the opponents of the Poor Law, and in Lancashire and the West Riding of Yorkshire, where the attitude of the mob was particularly threatening, the Government delayed a long time before introducing the workhouse system.[3] In several large towns the new workhouses did not provide sufficient accommodation for the paupers during a period of unemployment. The guardians were therefore compelled to return to the system of outdoor relief. But it took the form of providing work on the roads or some other employment of public utility and the cost of these undertakings was borne by voluntary subscriptions, not by the rates.[4]

3

The disorders however, had reached a point at which conciliatory measures were insufficient. Order could be maintained only by the use of force in one form or another. It was at this time that Parliament at the request of the Government established

---

[1] An amendment which would have indirectly restored in certain cases the system of outdoor relief was almost carried, being passed once by the Commons (H. of C., July 29, 1839 (*Parliamentary Debates*, 3rd Series, vol. xlix, pp. 965 sqq.). Lord John Russell's attitude betrayed considerable embarrassment. See Wellington's indignant protests (*Greville Memoirs*, July 22, 1839).

[2] H. of C., July 15, 1839 (*Parl. Deb.*, 3rd Series, vol. xlix, pp. 353 sqq.).

[3] M. Hovell, *The Chartist Movement*, p. 87.

[4] For these relaxations introduced in consequence of the depression in trade, see *Annual Register*, 1837, Chron., pp. 143–5; 1838, Chron., pp. 200–1). *The Times*, December 22, 1838: '. . . the workhouse humbug is everywhere tumbling to pieces'.

in the English counties by a statute whose provisions have been already explained[1] a 'rural police', a *gendarmerie*. The nature of the opposition offered to the new bill by Thomas Attwood the Chartist, and the young Disraeli, an eccentric Ultra-Tory with Chartist sympathies, is now clear. The enemies of the Poor Law were in high feather. The new Poor Law, they had been promised, would empty the gaols, and rid the country of tramps and criminals,[2] and now, only five years after it had been passed, it was found necessary to set up a new system of police to deal with the increase of crime. It would in fact be some time before the new police Act could come into regular operation, and it could therefore afford no protection against the formidable preparations being made by the Chartists in the north. Nevertheless, the Government refrained from asking Parliament, as the Tories had done in 1817 and 1819, for special legislation to restrain the freedom of public meeting. Indeed, one of the restrictions imposed on the Press by the Six Acts of 1819 which was still in force was relaxed.[3] The Cabinet was content to take the necessary steps to enforce the existing laws. In April, Lord John gave the command of the Northern District to Sir Charles Napier, an officer equally known for his valour as a soldier and his Liberal views, and placed under his command about 6,000 men and 18 guns. As soon as the military arrangements had been carried out the Government issued on May 3 a proclamation against all who took part in drills with or without arms and the magistrates received orders to take the necessary steps to put down these illegal meetings. The proclamation was followed by a letter from Lord John which the Chartists regarded as a declaration of civil war. He authorized the formation of a civil force for the protection of life and property, and undertook to provide arms to those who made application according to the prescribed form. On March 10, Henry Vincent was arrested in London for the speeches by which he had provoked the riots in Wales. Though the Chartist delegates went forward with their plans, they were alarmed by the growing hostility of the middle class. The grand jury to whom the case of Stephens had been submitted found a true bill against him and pronounced on oath the 'Convention' an

[1] See above, p. 220.
[2] *The Times*, July 22, 26, December 6, 18, 1839. Police bills were passed for Birmingham, Manchester and Bolton (after the riots in July), 2 and 3 Vict., cap. 87, 88, 95.
[3] 2 and 3 Vict., cap. 12.

illegal body.[1] When on May 6 the delegates marched in pairs with the red rosette in their buttonholes to Thomas Attwood's lodging and brought him, wrapped around an enormous roller, the National Petition bearing 1,200,000 signatures, he made reservations as to certain points of the programme, refused to introduce a bill in regular form, and called upon the Chartists to issue an explicit declaration repudiating the use of physical force. The Cabinet crisis followed and the Tories were within an ace of taking office. O'Connor took advantage of it to revive a proposal he had first put forward on April 30 and asked the Convention to transfer its sessions on Monday, May 13, to Birmingham. The removal was equally acceptable to the timid and the hot heads in the Convention. The timid were afraid that, if they remained in London, they might be arrested *en masse* by a Tory Government. The advocates of violence—that is to say, following O'Connor—hoped to withdraw the movement from the influence of the moderates and their leader Lovett. It was therefore from Birmingham that the Convention issued the manifesto of May 13. It was decided that if favourable answers were returned by the 'simultaneous meetings' to the questions submitted, the delegates should meet at Birmingham to give effect to their decision. When Parliament refused, as it no doubt would, to take the National Petition into consideration, the Birmingham Convention would formally repudiate its authority and if necessary would summon 500,000 armed men to march upon London.

The simultaneous meetings were held, and the Chartists who attended returned affirmative answers to the questions asked by the Convention. Was this the prelude to a revolution on the French pattern? Far from it. Indeed a glance is enough to reveal the difference between the conditions which obtained in the two countries. In Paris on the very eve of the day when the Chartists migrated to Birmingham, Barbès and Blanqui had attempted an armed rising and had actually held the Hotel de Ville for several hours. It was no doubt a ludicrous affair and was quickly snuffed out. Nevertheless, it was the caricature of a revolutionary upheaval which had succeeded in July 1830 and would succeed again in February 1848. In a country where the administration was highly centralized a revolutionary minority which got possession of the executive machinery was able to

[1] *Life and Struggles of William Lovett*, p. 205.

change the Government within twenty-four hours. The situation in England was totally different. London did not occupy the same position relatively to the country at large as Paris did in relation to France. Moreover, the seat of the revolutionary propaganda was not London, but the manufacturing districts. And in those industrial centres remote from the capital, the Chartists were advocating a new method of action altogether unlike that employed by the French revolutionaries, namely, the simultaneous economic revolt of the entire working class, a general strike, which by the concerted action of the proletariat would bring the entire work of the nation to a standstill.

4

Unfortunately for the Chartists the new strategy was not easy to carry out. It could succeed only if it obtained the unanimous support of the working class. But whenever did an entire nation agree to make a revolution? A revolution is always the work of an active minority taking advantage of favourable conditions. The Parisians have understood this, the conditions have been favourable, and for almost a century Paris has been the Mecca of revolution. The Chartist leaders on the contrary sought to initiate a revolution by pushing the great mass of the proletariat into a general strike for political ends. But even before they reached Birmingham, they must have noticed that as soon as the revolutionaries began to capture the movement, the masses began to forsake it, and in the provinces as well as in London.[1] The South remained as it had always been, apathetic.[2] In April the Chartist emissaries had been mobbed, and Vincent was nearly lynched. Scotland had always turned a deaf ear to the advocates of 'physical force', and the Scotch workmen now repudiated their violence more decidedly than ever. What was the situation in those English districts which the Chartists regarded as their most favourable battle field, Birmingham, the Midlands, the West Riding, Lancashire and the Northern Counties? From Worcestershire, Warwickshire, Staffordshire, Durham, and even from the West Riding where O'Connor had made his headquarters, for the past month the Convention had received discouraging reports. In

[1] *Greville Memoirs*, April 30, 1839.
[2] *The Times*, April 11, 13, 1839. M. Hovell, *The Chartist Movement*, pp. 129–30.

Wales, no doubt, the attitude of the people was more revolutionary, but Wales was not England.[1]

But the geographical distribution of Chartism tells us very
little. It is more important to understand its moral and intellectual
significance in 1839. For the popularity of the Marxist philosophy
of history has given birth to mistakes which it is difficult and therefore important to dissipate.

The first of these is the following. According to Marx the
impoverishment and despair of the working class was bound to
increase with the progress of machinery, and as its inevitable
result. Chartism was therefore the revolt, largely subconscious, of
the operative against the machine by which he was being enslaved.
In fact the main body of the revolutionary host did not work in
the factories. A considerable section consisted of the miners of
the North and West. Even larger numbers were drawn from
the hosiers of Nottingham and Leicester, the silk weavers of
Spitalfields, the weavers of woollen stuffs in Yorkshire, and the
cotton weavers of Lancashire, all of whom worked with hand-
looms at home. Their numbers far from decreasing were actually
on the increase, a fact which aggravated the lamentable deteriora-
tion of their economic position. Treated as outcasts by the
operatives of the factory, and receiving wages whose amount was
only an eighth of theirs, they called upon the State to interfere and
fix a minimum wage. They were asking for a remedy even worse
than the disease. For it was only by accepting a starvation wage
that they could withstand the competition of machinery. The
fixing of a minimum wage would have completed their ruin and
sealed the victory of the machine.[2] In a sense they were in truth
victims of machinery, but only indirectly and because they were
obliged to compete with the workers in the factories, who were
better paid and more contented.[3]

[1] See above note to p. 313.
[2] See a letter from Ebenezer Elliott to Mr. Tait which reproduces a letter from Edward
Sunderland, stuff weaver of Leeds, to Fielden and Oastler (*Tait's Edinburgh Magazine*,
November 1839, p. 253).
[3] For the decline of the hand-loom weavers, see a very interesting document, an auto-
biographical piece, hidden in a theological brochure. 'A short account of the life and
hardships of a Glasgow weaver; with his opinion upon the question at present in hot
dispute between Churchmen and Voluntaries, written by himself.' Containing also
Remarks by David Maclure, printer, author of a letter to Dr. Wardlow, 1834. For the
economic position of the hand-loom weavers, see H. of C., March 7, 1833: speeches by
John Fielden, Wynn Ellis and Gillon (*Parliamentary Debates*, 3rd Series, vol. xvi, pp. 365,
367); March 9 and July 28, 1835 (ibid., 3rd Series, vol. xxxviii, pp. 715 sqq., and vol.
xxix, pp. 1152 sqq.); July 4, 1837 (ibid., 3rd Series, vol. xxxviii, pp. 1790 sqq.); March

It was indeed because they received good wages that the factory operatives had been able to form the powerful Trade Unions, against which the employers, towards the close of 1837, had contemplated war. In self defence the Unions, when Chartism began its career, had been drawn into the movement. After a Radical meeting at Bury the *Northern Star* greeted the first example of a Trade Union with sufficient intelligence and courage to declare political action one of its legitimate objects,[1] and throughout the summer the Chartist mass meetings had been nothing less than Trade Union festivals, at which squadrons of Trade Unionists marched with drums beating, and headed by their banners. But when the Chartist agitation became once more an agitation against the workhouse, when the Unions were assured that the danger of official persecution had passed and when O'Connor and O'Brien had assumed the leadership of the movement, they withdrew, and Chartism degenerated into an insurrection of the rabble. As a delegate regretfully admitted, it was only among the worst-paid workers that Chartism found unanimous support. Those who earned thirty shillings a week, cared nothing for those who earned fifteen and the latter cared as little for those who earned five or six shillings. Like the middle class, the working class had its aristocracy.[2]

19, 1838 (ibid., 3rd Series, vol. xlvi, pp. 871 sqq.). For the different methods suggested by which a minimum wage could be fixed by law and especially for Fielden's plan, see *Report from Select Committee on Hand-Loom Weavers' Petitions, with Minutes of Evidence and Index*, 1834, pp. iii-iv; also *Report* . . ., 1835, pp. xiv-xv. Both reports are favourable to the proposal. Four years later the opposition to every form of state interference between masters and men had become stronger, and the *Report of the Commissioners on the Condition of the Hand-loom Weavers*, 1841, unreservedly condemns it (p. 49). The Commission recommends the repeal of the Corn Laws and the laws passed to prevent attempts by the trade unions to set up a tyranny over the workmen. Valuable information as to the condition of the hand-loom weavers will be found in a summary form in Michel Chevalier's *Cours d'Economie Politique*, 1842, pp. 167 sqq.

[1] *Northern Star*, March 31, 1838. Cf. July 7, 1838: '. . . Antecedently . . . the different bodies of Trade Unions considered their order sufficiently protected by the rules of their respective associations, and they rested satisfied with the protection which these rules yielded to their society, and therefore became negligent of their political duties from a fanciful reliance upon their associated strength . . . The trades did not formerly join in public meetings, but, for the reasons stated, they now do . . . To the trades and New-castle societies both English and Irish, we are indebted for the splendid and astonishing meeting which took place on Thursday last . . .'

[2] Meeting of the Birmingham Convention, July 16, 1839 (Dolléans, *Le Chartisme*, p. 1379). Cf. *Annual Register*, 1838, Chron., p. 206: '. . . trade unions . . . are scarcely ever resorted to, except by those who habitually receive high wages; and they almost invariably make their appearance when trade is prosperous.' The wages which the *Annual Register* in this passage calls high, ranged from 28s. to 31s. and from 30s. to 35s. a week. See also the *Morning Chronicle*, September 10, 1840 (the subject of the article is the general strike in Paris): 'Neither in England nor in France does the discontent manifest itself

We must now expose the second mistake, also due to the study of Marxism. Since Chartism was a revolt of the working class against industrial capitalism, and since Marxism is regarded as the most adequate ideology of this revolt, a doctrine akin to the teaching of Marx is instinctively sought as the basis of Chartism. Now it is certainly true that in so far as the Poor Law of 1834 was inspired by individualist principles, every revolt against it can be regarded as more or less vaguely tinged by what we should now call socialism. But, unfortunately for the thesis in question there were already in 1839 professed Socialists fully conscious of their position, who advocated the abolition of private property and the substitution for capitalism of a thorough-going co-operative system, and it never occurred to anyone to confuse this Socialism with Chartism. Lovett and a few of his friends had been, and possibly still were 'socialists', but they gradually lost faith in Socialism, until they finally reached an individualism closely akin to that of the Utilitarians. O'Connor, the hero of Chartism, was a convinced individualist, Owen, the founder of Socialism, an enemy of Chartism. Of the Chartist leaders, only one, O'Brien, seems to have wished to introduce into the movement doctrines borrowed from Babeuf and Owen. And even he explicitly repudiated Communism. He recognized every man's right to possess as his private property the produce of his labour. The only social reform he appears to have desired, was the abolition of private ownership of land.[1] And the agents of the Anti-Corn-Law Association could remark as a favourable sign the fact that the Chartist revolutionaries, after denouncing all capitalists indiscriminately, were led unconsciously to unite with themselves in attacking the landlords alone.

In reality Chartism was not a creed. It was the blind revolt of hunger.[2] The despair of the populace was inflamed and allayed in turn, as the harvest was good or bad. The English are not a

strongly in the more intelligent and skilled operatives. In both countries, there is a sort of working class aristocracy, which the rest aims at being equalized with. . . . In the Chartist Congress the difference of feeling became distinctly marked in the discussions. The Trade Unions of London, embodying the élite of the operatives, always stood aloof from the agitation. . . . They were appealed to again and again, to no purpose.'

[1] See an excellent account of Bronterre O'Brien's social theories in Rosenblatt, *Social and Economic Aspects of the Chartist Movement*, pp. 115 sqq.

[2] Raikes to Wellington, May 29, 1841: '. . . The English require to be better *fed* than the French. Those who aim at popularity with the latter only appeal to their vanity: the former are to be won by their bellies' (L. Raikes, *Private Correspondence with the Duke of Wellington and other Distinguished contemporaries*, p. 277).

people of revolutionary temper, quick to take up with any theory which provides a justification for their destructive passions. The mass meetings which were attended by vast crowds were amazingly peaceful.[1] When torchlight meetings were prohibited, the workers evaded the prohibition by meeting without lights and in silence.[2] When all open air meetings were prohibited, and the local authorities refused the Chartists the use of the Town Hall, they invaded the churches on the Sunday morning. But they were guilty of no disorderly conduct or looting. They were content to force their poverty upon the notice of the rich. They did not intimidate, they merely asked for pity.[3] When we told the story of the popular risings of 1816 and 1819, we called the reader's attention to the discrepancy between the revolutionary theories of the leaders and the purely economic demands of the masses. The situation had not changed in the interval, except that in London the revolutionary leaders had lost ground. The only creed which could win a hearing from the crowds of working men was the Christian creed as preached by the Nonconformist sects. When the Chartist agitation began, the Nonconformist ministers found themselves able to extend their sympathy to the movement, for the Chartists were then seeking to unite all sections of the poorer classes on a programme of political Radicalism. The situation entirely changed in the course of 1839. Many lovers of order refused to listen any longer to Tory calumnies, and acknowledged the services rendered by these churches of the lower middle class. For it could not be denied that their ministers, in spite of the social ostracism which was their lot at the hands of polite society, were active supporters of the ruling classes in their struggle with the spirit of revolution.[4]

[1] Louis Blanc, *Revue du Progrès*, vol. ii, p. 249 (1839): 'The Chartists constitute the vanguard of English democracy. In their meetings they copy even the external forms of French democracy. But for the vast majority of the nation the meetings were rather a show than a serious demonstration, the audience gathered to hear the speakers as an agreeable pastime, and traffic could move freely across the public places where they were held.' Cf. *Life and Opinions of General Sir Charles James Napier*, by Lieut.-General Sir William Napier, vol. ii, pp. 39, 43, 49.
[2] R. G. Gammage, *The History of the Chartist Movement*, p. 153.
[3] R. G. Gammage, ibid., p. 153; *Annual Register*, 1839, p. 304. See also *The Times*, August 21, 1839, which quotes from the *Leeds Intelligencer*. At Bradford the working men attended St. James's Church, having previously sent a deputation to the Rev. Mr. Bull, as had been done in other instances, requesting accommodation, and that a certain text (Amos viii, 4–8) might be the subject of the discourse.
[4] A few typical extracts from the *Christian Advocate*, the organ of the 'political dissenters', written when the Chartist agitation was at its height, will give an idea of the attitude of Nonconformity. June 3, 1839 (account of the annual meeting of the Congregational

5

On July 1, the Convention reassembled at Birmingham. It had received from its electors the mandate to make preparations for the 'sacred month', that is to say, for a general strike. It postponed the matter until the House of Commons had discussed the Petition, that is to say until July 13, and decided to return to London where the delegates met on the tenth. On July 12, the Commons, after a half-hearted speech by Attwood in support of the Petition, a spirited rejoinder by Lord John, and an eccentric speech by the young Disraeli,[1] refused by a majority of 237 to 48 Radical votes, to take the Petition into consideration. The following day, the Convention took action, and proclaimed a 'sacred month' to begin on August 12. At Birmingham, where for the last fortnight the excitement had been at fever heat, and where on the 8th, the arrival of additional police, draughted from London, had caused a preliminary skirmish, serious riots broke out on the 15th. Every shop in the most important street was looted. Then the ministers decided to adopt severe measures. Since the National Petition had been duly taken to Parliament and received by the House, the agitation had no longer any legal justification. Numerous arrests were made.[2] The prosecutions did not stimulate the Chartists to more vigorous action. On the contrary, the movement collapsed.

On July 16, the Convention adopted a temporizing resolution,

Union): 'The Rev. J. A. James referred to the numerous revival meetings lately held in this country. Will it be believed by a large portion of the members of the Establishment in this country—that portion that considers the Dissenters as little else than a political faction—that forty Dissenting ministers could meet in three days' solemn public service and private conference, without a passing allusion to the questions which have been agitated with so much bitterness of spirit.' May 27, 1839: 'Ten thousand troops would not be removed from Ireland, nor a rocket-brigade sent to Birmingham for nothing! Yet it seems difficult to reconcile all this with the comparative insignificance of the Chartist meetings, and the somewhat contemptible tranquillity that has followed their note of preparation for open hostility.' July 15, 1839: 'Far be it from us to apologize for the violence of Chartism: but that is the puling of children compared with the dangers which must ensure, if, under the guise of free and popular institutions, we must longer continue to exclude the people from the fair enjoyment of those physical and moral blessings, which, under the providence of God, we are able, and bound, to confer upon them.' On July 22, after denouncing in scathing terms 'the atrocious conduct of the Birmingham rabble', the *Christian Advocate* declares that the rising 'sprang, no doubt, from the loins of that anti-poor-law agitation which the Tory Press has so much encouraged'.

[1] H. of C., July 12, 1839 (*Parliamentary Debates*, 3rd Series, vol. xlix, pp. 220 sqq., 236 sqq., 246 sqq.).

[2] 443 *condemnations* in 1839-40, according to Lovett (*Life and Struggles of William Lovett*, p. 238); 543 according to Rosenblatt (*Social and Economic Aspects of the Chartist Movement*, pp. 205-6).

declared itself unable 'to take the responsibility of dictating the time or circumstances of a strike' and appointed a committee of five of its members to draw up a manifesto, defending its retreat. It appeared on August 6, and explained almost in so many words that a general strike was impossible without the co-operation of the trade unions, and that the unions had turned a deaf ear to the appeal of 'their more distressed brethren'.[1] August 12 passed without any disorder worth mention. On September 6, the Convention pronounced itself dissolved. In October, at a banquet given in their honour at Edinburgh, Liberal statesmen took credit for having suppressed Chartism with no other weapon than 'the good *sense* of the country' and boasted that 'Chartism *had vanished into smoke*'.[2]

Suddenly on November 6, when Chartism seemed almost a thing of the past, Londoners read in their morning paper that on the day before, a serious rising had occurred at Newport, a town on the border of South Wales. Several thousand Chartists had besieged the Town Hall. Nothing short of a battle had been fought. Later the news arrived that a general insurrection had been arranged to begin simultaneously in Yorkshire and Wales. The projected rising had not taken place in Yorkshire, because O'Connor had taken fright at the last moment and recalled his orders. But his order countermanding the revolt had not reached Wales in time, and the Chartists had risen on the appointed day. It was a feeble affair. The Mayor, assisted by a few important persons of the neighbourhood, and twenty-eight soldiers under the command of a lieutenant, successfully held in check a mob of rioters armed with guns and pikes.[3] Ten Chartists were killed in

[1] 'It is the deliberate opinion of this Council, that unless the trades of Great Britain shall co-operate as united bodies with their more distressed brethren, in making a grand national moral demonstration on the 12th instant, it will be impossible to save the country from a revolution of blood. . . . Under these circumstances, we implore all our brother Chartists to abandon the project of a sacred month. . . . We also implore the united trades, if they would save the country from convulsion, and themselves and families from ruin, to render their distressed brethren all the aid in their power, on or before the 12th inst., towards realizing the great and beneficent object of the holiday' (R. G. Gammage, *History of the Chartist Movement*, p. 155).

[2] See the report of the speeches, *Quarterly Review*, December 1839, vol. lxv, p. 294.

[3] Stanhope (*Conversations with Wellington*, p. 195) records under November 13, 1839: 'The Duke gave us a full account of the Newport revolt. There is one thing, he said, always to be borne in mind in this country, and that cannot be impressed too much, though in France it does not prevail, at least not at all to the same degree, that, whenever people do what they know is wrong and against the law, they become most terribly frightened, and run away. How else can you account for thirty men putting to flight six thousand?' J. West, however, in his *History of the Chartist Movements*, pp. 143-4, casts doubt on the alleged number of the rioters, and concludes, 'For a precisely parallel case, see Falstaff's account of his adventure in Shakespeare's Henry IV, Part I, Act 2, Scene iv.'

the riot and fourteen tried for high treason. At the head of the latter group was the organizer of the revolt, John Frost, who until March, had been one of Lord John's Justices of the Peace. O'Connor disappeared for a time from public life and returned to Ireland.

When Parliament reassembled in February 1840, Conservatives were naturally not wanting in both Houses, who lamented the recent disturbances, and blamed the weakness of the Government. But if their fears had been genuine, distinguished members of the bar, and Conservatives to boot, Sir Frederick Pollock and Goulburn, would hardly have come forward to defend the Chartist prisoners at their trial. The nature of the defence is easily guessed. The speeches, and even the acts, of the Chartists were no worse than the speeches and acts of the Radicals in 1832, when, with the entire approval of the Whig Cabinet, they were seeking to compel the surrender of the House of Lords and the passage of the Reform Bill. Among the magistrates entrusted, in July, with the task of restoring order in Birmingham, were former delegates of Chartist meetings. And Frost himself had been a magistrate until the authorities took alarm at his conduct, and had been fined for taking part in meetings which Lord John had at first expressly recognized as legal. The argument was unanswerable. But the inference is plain. If the Tories were so successful in exploiting the fear of Chartism, it was because they were not very afraid of it themselves.

All over the country Chartist workmen were promising, in their hatred of the Whigs, to help the Tories at the next election. 'Conservative Working Men's Associations' continued to enroll new members in Yorkshire and Lancashire. In a brilliant essay, Carlyle drew the moral of the Chartist rising. Although the Chartist programme was itself Radical and political, he regarded the rising as a token that political Liberalism and even Radicalism were bankrupt. According to him it proved that the social question was thrusting the political into the background, and that the modern world was tending towards a system, at once monarchical and aristocratic, a paternal government invested with religious awe. And for the Tory public this work was the more valuable, because Carlyle owned allegiance to no political party.

If the ruling classes had been momentarily alarmed at the beginning of 1839, their fears were dissipated as soon as the

Chartists were obliged to proceed from words to deeds, and the full extent of their weakness was revealed. This was plainly no French revolution, but simply one of those widespread popular movements which had been common in the manufacturing districts of the north during the period immediately following Waterloo, and of which the nation was now growing weary.[1] Greville was right in June 1837, mistaken in December 1838. Nothing happened. In England, nothing ever did happen.

During the entire spring and summer of 1839, Parliament devoted ten hours to the government of Ireland and Jamaica for every hour it spent upon the danger of revolution at home. Now the Convention had broken up, the Chartist leaders were safe in prison, and the nation was thinking of nothing but the Queen's marriage. Nor had the Chartist agitation improved the position of the Radicals in Parliament. On the contrary, the Conservatives were now taking the offensive, and asking for a restriction of the franchise established in 1832. Lord Stanley introduced an Irish Registration Bill, which, on the plea of putting an end to the glaring scandals which attended the compilation of the registers in Ireland, sought to make it more difficult for the small-holders to obtain the franchise, and thus, indirectly, to reduce the number of Catholic electors.[2] It was only by employing for months every device of Parliamentary management, that the Government prevented his bill from becoming law.

[1] See the interesting article by a French disciple of Fourier who visited England at this period, and whose evidence (*La Phalange*, August 15, 1837) is above suspicion, since he regarded the Chartist movement 'or rather the ideas which it was inculcating upon the lower classes', as a force capable of pulling down the entire social fabric of Great Britain. He continues, however, 'That is the decided opinion which I have reached during my visit to this country, in spite of the imperturbable confidence displayed by the upper and middle classes', and a little later, 'The English are so far from sharing my view of the agitation that whenever I mention the Chartists to an Englishman—"the Chartists," they say, "who in England ever bothers his head about the Chartists? It is only in France that any notice is taken of them."' 'Before I conclude,' continues the writer of the article, 'I must tell you of an episode which has given me no little amusement and is very characteristic. Only imagine; Feargus O'Connor, a little while ago, speaking at a mass meeting, propounded *an infallible method of effecting a revolution*. I will wager my readers ten thousand to one they will never guess what that infallible method was . . . to empower the Association to bring fifty republicans from Paris and pay them 5s. to 10s. a week from the funds of the Association so long as they remained in England. "I should like to advise you," he added, "to settle in every large town where we wish to establish the movement, some ten to twenty of them according to the size of the place, and I promise you that once these good fellows are here, things will begin to look up".' A Pole named Beniowski was believed to have been the organiser of the abortive rising in November (M. Hovell, *The Chartist*, p. 177); cf. the documents quoted in my article 'Chartism' (*Quarterly Review*, July 1921, vol. ccxxxv, pp. 71 sqq.).

[2] H. of C., February 25, 1840 (*Parliamentary Debates*, 3rd Series, vol. lii, pp. 615 sqq.).

V PROGRESS OF THE AGITATION FOR FREE TRADE

I

Since popular agitation always turned, as though by some decree of fate, to the advantage of the Conservative Opposition, what resource was left to the Liberals and the moderate Radicals? They might attempt to recover their popularity by playing off the Anti-Corn-Law agitation against the Anti-Poor-Law agitation, and in the language of a Nonconformist journalist, try whether 'Manchester might not prove a match for Tamworth'.[1] What then, while the Chartist movement failed, had been the fortunes of the counter-movement organized by the partisans of free trade?

Undoubtedly the delegates who on February 4, 1839, met in Brown's Hotel, exactly opposite the Houses of Parliament, to bring up the petition for free trade and ensure that it should be seriously discussed, entertained at first considerable expectations of success. For, five days after the conversion of *The Times*, Lord John, the leader of the Commons, had addressed a letter to an Anti-Corn-Law meeting held in his constituency, in which he declared himself in favour of replacing the sliding scale by 'a fixed and moderate duty'.[2] This surely was a sign that the ministry was being converted to the views of Manchester.[3] But the delegates were quickly disillusioned. Their failure was as complete as the Chartists' and more rapid. The question of the Corn Laws was raised during the debate on the Address, by Brougham in the Lords, and in the Commons by G. W. Wood, President of the Manchester Chamber of Commerce. The Cabinet had invited Wood to move the adoption of the Address. It was intended as a compliment to the Manchester Chamber of Commerce, and the free-traders of the district. But Wood had always been extremely lukewarm in the cause of free trade, and it was in fact owing to his opposition that the Chamber of Commerce had delayed so long before committing itself. He therefore painted a very rosy picture of the state of British trade generally, which he depicted

---

[1] *Patriot*, March 18, 1839: 'Can it be doubted by whom the Chartists have been encouraged in their insane violence? But Manchester will be a match for Tamworth yet.'
[2] *The Times*, January 26, 1839.
[3] Sir James Graham to Sir Robert Peel, January 30, 1839: 'Every day throws fresh light on the intention of the Government to raise the question of Corn Laws' (C. S. Parker, *Sir James Graham*, vol. i, p. 277).

as extremely prosperous, and in particular of the cotton manufacture.[1] Peel was quick to take full advantage of his speech: if
British trade was really so flourishing, what justification was there
for the alarmist language of the Anti-Corn-Law Association?[2] A
few days later, Brougham on February 18 in the House of Lords,
and Villiers on the 19th in the House of Commons, moved that
in view of the numerous petitions which had been presented to
Parliament, both Houses should appoint committees to inquire
into the question. They delivered brilliant speeches. Nevertheless
the motion was rejected in the Lords by show of hands, and in the
Commons though it secured a far larger number of votes than in
the previous session, 174 instead of 97, it was rejected by a majority
of 189.[3] Peel again took the offensive, and his oratory won
another success. The debates had been expected to last two or
three days. The business was despatched in a single sitting. The
delegates reassembled, adjourned *sine die*, and decided to return to
their homes. A month later they were again in London to support
with their presence a new motion introduced by Villiers. Like the
former it was rejected.[4] The Cabinet showed signs of retreat. *The
Times*, reassured as to their intentions, displayed no further
interest in the question of the Corn Law. Like the Chartists the
free-traders had no other resource except to appeal to the country.

They decided to combine without further delay the local
associations in every town which had sent delegates to London, in
a single organization, which took the title, soon to become
famous, of the Anti-Corn-Law League. Manchester continued to
be their headquarters. Since the December election the opponents
of the duties on corn had controlled the Corporation.[5] Since the
annual election had been held the previous February, they had
also controlled the Chamber of Commerce; every member who
had failed to give active support to the cause of free trade—they
were sixteen out of twenty-four, Wood at their head—had been
unseated and replaced by an enthusiastic free-trader.[6] It was in

[1] H. of C., February 5, 1839 (*Parliamentary Debates*, 3rd Series, vol. xlv, pp. 55 sqq.).
[2] H. of C., February 5, 1839 (ibid., 3rd Series, vol. xlv, pp. 104–6).
[3] H. of C., March 15, 1838 (ibid., 3rd Series, vol. xli, p. 946). February 19, 1839 (ibid. 3rd Series, vol. xlv, p. 691).
[4] H. of C., March 12, 13, 14, 15, 18, 1839 (ibid., 3rd Series, vol. xlvi, pp. 333 sqq., 441 sqq., 628 sqq., 715 sqq., 805 sqq.).
[5] *Manchester Guardian*, December 15, 1838: 'Of 8,000 entitled to vote, 3,500 voted. Except in a single district which elected six extreme Radicals (Chartists), the free-traders were everywhere returned uncontested.'
[6] A. Prentice, *History of the Anti-Corn-Law League*, vol. i, pp. 110 sqq.

Manchester that the organ of the League, the *Anti-Corn-Law Circular*, was published. The first number appeared in April. And it was in Manchester that the Free Trade Hall was erected in Saint Peter's Fields, on the very site where in 1819, the battle of Peterloo had been fought. It was an enormous edifice, built to house the meetings of the League, 150 feet long, 105 broad, and occupying an area of 15,750 square feet. Banquets could be given in the Hall, with places laid for 3,800 guests. On the wall which rose behind the President's Chair, the word Justice was emblazoned in fiery letters, a yard high. And the walls were hung with 20,000 yards of pink and white calico.[1]

Mass meetings were held to gather signatures to monster petitions. Lecturers were sent into the country districts at the League's expense, to win the agricultural labourers and the farmers, by attempting to prove that under the tariff system set up in 1828, they also were sacrificed to the interest of the landlords. In the manufacturing centres, the propaganda had to contend with attempts at violent obstruction by the Chartists who were often in the pay of the Tories. In the country districts, the missionaries of free trade were subject to organized persecution at the hands of the squire, the parson and their dependants. But in spite of these obstacles, the free-traders saw their propaganda increasingly successful, and even began here and there to employ the language of revolution. According to the calculation of Prentice in his *History of the League*, during the single year 1840, 800 lectures were delivered, over 1,000,000 pamphlets and leaflets distributed, 200,000 copies of the *Anti-Corn-Law Almanack*, and 330,000 copies of the *Anti-Corn-Law Circular* sold.[2] The same year the League collected almost 1,500,000 signatures to its petition for the total repeal of the Corn Laws. It is of interest to remark by way of contrast, that two petitions for the grant, not of universal, but merely of household suffrage, together obtained only 22,000 signatures.[3]

2

As a result of the League's activities, a new Radical party came into existence. It drew its members from the manufacturers both large and small, the middle class and even the working class. The moral force section of the Chartists, disgusted by the violence of

[1] A. Prentice, *History of the Anti-Corn-Law League*, vol. i, p. 142.
[2] Ibid., vol. i, p. 173.   [3] *Morning Chronicle*, August 14, 1840.

Wesley who had organized a campaign of propaganda, had copied intentionally or unintentionally the Wesleyan model. No doubt free trade was not in itself a doctrine which made an appeal to the heart. Cobden was a Utilitarian, and when he tells us that his sympathies are with the Protestant religion, it is an entirely unemotional preference dictated by political reasons: he regarded the Protestant as more favourable than the Catholic system to the development of industrialism.[1] But Bowring whose visit to Manchester in September 1838 occasioned the foundation of the Anti-Corn-Law Association, was a Christian of the emotional type and an active member of the Unitarian body. John Bright, a member of the provisional committee of the Association, was a Quaker. And when the League was formed the pastors of the different Nonconformist bodies made haste to join it.

Anxious to keep their flocks from the snares of the revolutionary Chartist and the Tory demagogues who were proving dangerously attractive, they were tired of preaching a prudence which was purely negative. The programme of the League offered them a way out of the difficulty. They could now teach their people a doctrine which was not a doctrine of class strife, but on the contrary, of peace between classes and nations alike. God had willed that all mankind should be one. Why therefore should evil laws range men one against the other? He had caused the earth to bear sufficient corn to feed the entire human race. How then dare man forbid corn to be brought from regions where there was a superabundance, to feed the hungry in a land where the harvest was scanty? In 1841, to take the place of the *Patriot* and the *Christian Advocate*, which had ceased to exist, the Nonconformist sects founded a new organ, *Miall's Nonconformist*, which adopted as its motto 'The Dissidence of Dissent and the Protestantism of the Protestant Religion'. Its publication is of importance in the history of thought because it was in its columns that Herbert Spencer would shortly address the public for the first time. The editorial which introduced the first number argued that if, since 1832, the Nonconformists had exercised so little influence on the political life of the nation, it was because they had failed to look beyond the particular interests of their sects. It was the object of the new paper to represent, 'not a class but principles', the 'religious' principle of 'justice to all men,

[1] *England, Ireland and America*, chap. ii (*Works*, vol. i, pp. 55 sqq.)

freedom for all men, peace between all men'; in other words the full application of the principle of free trade.[1] On August 17, a 'Conference of Ministers of Religion' opened in Manchester, to discuss the question of the Corn Laws, in which 650 clergymen of various Christian denominations took part. Among them were Nonconformists, Socinians and Catholic priests. But only one Anglican parson accepted the invitation. The Wesleyans refused to attend in obedience to the rule of their Church, which forbade ministers to take part in any political agitation whatsoever. Bunting however, at that time the Sovereign Pontiff of the sect, in his reply to the invitation of the organizers, publicly declared himself in favour of repealing the Corn Laws. The deliberations lasted three days, and the Conference affirmed by a unanimous vote that the Corn Laws were 'a great national offence against that Being by whom kings reign and princes decree justice'.[2] Free trade was becoming a religion.

3

The agitation was successfully floated. How would it influence future legislation? The shocking condition of the national finances which grew worse every year, presented an obvious handle to the criticisms of the free-traders, criticisms which the Liberal cabinet could silence, if they would but perform the promises they had made when they took office at the end of 1830. Why had they delayed so long? Every year the cost of the army and navy was greater than the year before. It had never been so low as it had been in the budget introduced by Peel during his brief tenure of office. Since then it had continuously increased. The expenditure upon the army increased fairly slowly, rising from £6,400,000 in 1835 to £6,600,000 in 1840; for the ordnance the rate of increase was higher, £1,100,000 to £2,000,000, and the naval expenditure rose more rapidly still, from £4,000,000 to £5,500,000. It was the cost of Palmerston's policy. But even in

[1] *The Nonconformist*, April 14, 1841: 'At present we have government in excess. Every limb of the nation is pinioned by acts of parliament. . . . Nothing is left to spontaneous growth. Restriction meets us everywhere—regulates our markets, impedes our commerce, cripples our industry, paralyses our religion. These, in our opinion, are the natural fruits produced by mistaking the proper objects of government. The utmost liberty, compatible with social order, we take to be the inalienable right of all men.'

[2] A. Prentice, *History of the Anti-Corn-Law League*, vol. i, pp. 233 sqq. See a sympathetic report of the Conference in the *Morning Chronicle*, August 18, 19, 20, 21, 23; also a sarcastic report in *The Times*, August 19, 20, 21, 1841.

1835, before these increases had been made, the free-traders were complaining that the Whigs had spent too much money on the navy.[1]

Not only had the national expenditure become heavier, the depression of trade had reduced the revenue. The Chancellor of the Exchequer was no longer in the fortunate position of Lord Althorp, who disposed of a surplus every year, and could therefore grant the reductions of taxes the public demanded. On the contrary, as the need to remedy the growing deficit became more urgent, the more unlikely it became that a prudent government would dare to adopt the method Sir Henry Parnell had formerly advocated, and sacrifice immediate receipts in order to revive trade, and thus restore in the end a satisfactory balance.

The budget of 1836 was the last in which the Chancellor of the Exchequer was able to make any sensational reduction of taxes. He consolidated and reduced the tax on paper, reduced the stamp tax on newspapers and abolished Lord Althorp's additional tax of 50 per cent on the sale of intoxicants. In 1837 no reductions were made. In 1838 there was an admitted deficit which had to be made up by the issue of Exchequer Bills. In 1839 Parliament compelled the Chancellor of the Exchequer to introduce penny postage. But it was evident the following year that he had been mistaken in his forecast that since trade had improved, the financial position must improve in consequence. When the budget of 1840 was drawn up, the receipts were estimated at £46,700,000, the expenditure at £49,432,000, that is to say, a deficit was expected of £2,732,000. To make it up, Baring, who had just succeeded Spring Rice at the Exchequer, increased the assessed taxes by 10 per cent, the customs and excise duties by 5 per cent, and placed a new tax of 4d. a gallon on spirits. Even if all these taxes could be levied immediately, the budget could be balanced only by further borrowing to an amount Baring estimated at £395,000. Since, however, several months must pass before the new taxes came into full operation, he proposed to borrow an additional £850,000. This spelt the complete and frank sacrifice of every financial principle the Liberal party had professed on its advent to power.

After this financial defeat the free-traders transferred the contest to another field. Ever since the campaign against the Corn Laws

[1] R. Cobden, *Russia* (*Works*, vol. i, p. 320).

began, their defenders had never tired of pointing out that corn was not the only article of commerce protected by a tariff against foreign competition. Woollen stuffs, to take an example which particularly affected the textile industry, were subject to a far heavier duty than that imposed on raw wool. The Manchester manufacturers however had been careful to declare in favour of universal free trade. They knew that these duties which proved so awkward when they were arguing against the Corn Laws were not needed to protect the manufactures of England, already secure against foreign competition. Nor did the objection in any way apply to the cotton manufacture, since the duty which protected it was so slight that it was impossible to compare it with the heavy duty, a duty which did in fact hamper trade, levied on raw cotton from America, for the benefit of the West Indian planters. The delegates of the Anti-Corn Law Meetings had hardly arrived in London, when on February 5, 1839, they made for the first time a definite pronouncement on the question.[1] On March 18, after their petitions had been rejected, they appointed on Cobden's motion a sub-committee of five members to carry out with the least possible delay a statistical investigation into the operation of the existing tariffs, discover what were the duties, whether on manufactured articles or on articles of food, which could be considered protective, and advise upon the best methods of bringing the results of their inquiry before the public.[2] And at the suggestion of the Anti-Corn-Law League, Hume asked the House of Commons to appoint a Committee to investigate the operation of the tariff system.[3]

It was appointed. Among its members were Hume himself, Villiers and Sir Henry Parnell. In spite of the opposition of a protectionist minority, the committee soon declared itself satisfied by the evidence which had been given, and issued a report drawn up by Hume, a Radical theorist and an uncompromising free-trader. He reviewed the tariffs set up in 1833. Articles of commerce were arranged in 1,150 distinct classes, for each a special duty was provided, and of these, seventeen accounted for 94½ per cent of the receipts. What was the use of charging a duty on the remaining 1,133? Further, was the interest either of the

[1] A. Prentice, *History of the Anti-Corn-Law League*, vol. i, p. 108.
[2] *The Times*, March 19, 1839.
[3] H. of C., May 5, 1840 (*Parliamentary Debates*, 3rd Series, vol. liii, pp. 1308–9).

British producer or the British consumer best promoted by the choice of these seventeen articles? The attempt to make the customs a source of revenue, that is to say, to encourage the import of the articles on which duty was paid, and at the same time to use them as a means of protection, that is to say, to discourage imports, was self-contradictory. The principle on which a sound tariff should be based was to impose duties on a small number of articles selected so as to restrict consumption as little as possible, and therefore to provide the largest possible revenue. Even more interesting perhaps than Hume's report, was the evidence given by certain witnesses, by John Macgregor, one of the Joint Secretaries of the Board of Trade, James Deacon Hume, who had just retired after thirty-eight years' service in the Customs, and eleven years at the Board of Trade, and George Richardson Porter, the head of the Statistical Department of the Board of Trade, established in 1832. It was principally on the evidence of these three government officials, that Hume based his recommendations. Evidently the Board of Trade had been converted to the economics of the Manchester school.

4

It was therefore widely believed that the entire inquiry had been decided, arranged and controlled by the Cabinet.[1] The belief went far beyond the truth. There were, no doubt, in the Cabinet, convinced free-traders. We have already seen that at the beginning of 1839, Lord John had caused a sensation by his public declaration against the Corn Law. On the whole he was adopting the very policy against which he had fought when still a young man, on its first adoption by Lord Liverpool about 1820. He was attempting to divert the people from claims whose revolutionary character alarmed him, by adopting the programme of reform put forward by the Liberal economists. But he could satisfy their wishes only by making a frontal attack on the landlords, and it was not surprising that he failed to gain the support of the majority of his colleagues, who were themselves country gentlemen, some of them even great landowners. Moreover Melbourne was in every respect a more timid statesman than the head of the Tory Cabinet twenty years earlier. He refused to yield an inch to Lord John's

[1] H. of C., April 5, 1841, Herries' speech (*Parliamentary Debates*, 3rd Series, vol. lvii, p. 914).

views.[1] This was the explanation of the Cabinet's attitude in 1839, when it disappointed the free-traders' hopes. In 1840 he was equally obdurate, and if, when speaking in the House of Lords, he used the hesitating language to be expected from the head of a ministry divided against itself, he expressed the opinion that to raise the question or even institute an inquiry would involve the country in the danger of revolution.[2] In the Commons, when Villiers brought forward his annual motion for an inquiry into the operation of the statute of 1829, his opponents first contrived to stop the discussion by raising a question of procedure, and on a second occasion drowned the defenders of free trade by a storm of noisy protest. The motion was rejected by 300 to 167 votes.[3]

No doubt the very violence of Melbourne's language and the tactics of obstruction to which the defenders of the Corn Law had recourse in the Commons, could plausibly be interpreted by the free-traders as favourable signs which proved that their opponents were afraid. When the session opened, Graham had expected that the ministers would make the establishment of a fixed duty their official programme, invite defeat and appeal to the country on the question.[4] During the debate on Villiers' motion, a Radical member, named Warburton, predicted that it would be carried in 1841 by an overwhelming majority.[5] But all this did not alter the stubborn facts that Melbourne's opposition was as inflexible as ever, and Villiers' motion had secured fewer votes than it had obtained in 1839; and when the session closed the free-traders were extremely disheartened to find that their campaign of petitions though so brilliantly organized had borne little fruit. 'I fear,' wrote Baines, 'that *nothing but famine* will extort from them their monopoly'.[6] In August, the *Morning Chronicle* reluctantly admitted that the public were calm, even apathetic, and that the Anti-Corn-Law agitation had reached a 'temporary lull'.[7] The publications issued by the committee of inquiry into import duties do not appear to have been noticed

[1] Lord Melbourne to Lord John Russell, December 29, 1838; January 18, 20, 21, 23, 29, 1839 (*Lord Melbourne's Papers*, pp. 387 sqq.).
[2] H. of L., June 11, 1840 (*Parliamentary Debates*, 3rd Series, vol. liv, pp. 1040 sqq.).
[3] H. of C., April 1, 2, 3, 1840 (ibid., 3rd Series, vol. liv, pp. 315 sqq., 432 sqq., 481 sqq.). May 26, 1840 (ibid., 3rd Series, vol. liv, pp. 563 sqq.).
[4] Sir James Graham to Arbuthnot, February 28, 1840 (C. S. Parker, *Sir James Graham*, vol. i, p. 293).
[5] H. of C., May 26, 1840 (*Parl. Deb.*, 3rd Series, vol. liv, p. 627).
[6] E. Baines, Jun., *The Life of Edward Baines*, p. 260.
[7] *Morning Chronicle*, August 29, 1840.

in any of the important London papers, and Prentice, who published long extracts in the *Manchester Times*, admitted that 'even in Manchester' few people displayed any interest in the work of the committee.[1]

The apathy of the public is explained by the fact that towards the close of the year 1840 their attention was preoccupied by the eastern question, and in December the brilliant diplomatic victory won by Palmerston seemed likely to remove all the difficulties which beset the Cabinet's domestic policy. When Parliament reassembled on January 24, 1841, foreign politics were almost the sole theme of the speeches delivered during the debate on the Address. In the Lords, Wellington agreed with Brougham, and in the Commons, Peel agreed with Hume, in regretting that Palmerston had jeopardized so lightheartedly the good understanding which had existed between France and England. 'A cordial and good understanding between England and France was,' he declared, 'essential to the peace and the welfare of Europe.' He hoped that twenty-five years of peace had taught the lesson that the maintenance of peace was for all alike not only 'an inestimable advantage' but 'a great moral obligation', and that the 'new material interests' which had arisen during that period were sufficiently strong to prevent any future explosion of warlike passions.[2] To censure the foreign policy of the Whig administration, Peel had borrowed the pacifist language of Cobden. But for the moment Palmerston's position seemed impregnable, and his fellow ministers, though their personal dislike of their colleague was as bitter as ever, hoped for several days that his popularity would strengthen the position of the Government. They were speedily disillusioned. Four by-elections were held during the early part of February.[3] They were all unfavourable to the Whigs, although three of the four constituencies had been represented by a Whig since 1837. These defeats following, as they did, many others suffered during the past year, were a serious matter for a ministry whose majority in the House was infinitesimal. And their gravity was increased by the fact that the Anti-Corn-Law League had a share in bringing them about. After the defeat of Villiers' motion in April 1840, the members of the League had decided to

---

[1] A. Prentice, *History of the Anti-Corn-Law League*, vol. i, p. 165.

[2] H. of C., January 26, 1841 (*Parliamentary Debates*, 3rd Series, vol. lvi, pp. 95–6).

[3] Walsall, February 2; Canterbury, February 3; East Surrey, February 8; Monmouthshire, February 9.

take concerted action at elections. 'Dissociating' themselves 'from all political parties', they pledged themselves to do their utmost to secure the return of candidates in favour of repealing the Corn Laws.[1] At Sudbury in June they had won their first victory; the candidate supported by the League defeated the Tory candidate. But at Walsall on February 2, 1841, they took a bolder step. The Liberal candidate, who had several important connexions among the Whig aristocracy, refused to declare himself opposed to the Corn Laws. He was compelled to retire, and his place was taken by J. B. Smith, the President of the Manchester Chamber of Commerce.

The Tory candidate, however, defeated his Manchester opponent by a small majority. The ministers were now placed in an awkward dilemma. They could not hope to keep for long a majority in the Commons. When they lost it they would be obliged either to resign or dissolve Parliament; and in either case a general election was unavoidable. With what programme should they go to the country? If they yielded to the pressure of the League they would endanger the unity of the party without even the hope, as the Walsall result had proved, of securing a majority. If, on the other hand, they persisted in their refusal to make the repeal of the Corn Laws a Cabinet question and, true to the policy they had adopted in 1834, continued to treat it as an 'open' question, they would be faced in many constituencies with the organized opposition of the League. The free-traders would either abstain from voting or run independent candidates. And that would spell disaster.

For three months longer the debates dragged out. The Cabinet introduced a bill to continue for ten years the operation of the Poor Law of 1834.[2] There was an assured majority in favour of the bill, but it was opposed by a large number of speakers, Ultra-Radicals and Ultra-Tories, who urged with the utmost acrimony

[1] With the free trade programme, however, they combined a programme of parliamentary reform. See *Manchester Times*, September 19, 1840: Free trade; triennial parliaments; one-third of the members to be elected annually; the ballot; and redistribution of seats, and the right of voting to all who can read and write. The *Morning Chronicle*, December 23, 1840, mentions the foundation at Leeds of a Parliamentary Reform Association with a programme of five points which reproduced in a modified form the six points of the Charter. This further programme was, however, an after-thought, a bid for the support of the moderate Chartists. For the League's new strategy, see A. Prentice, *History of the Anti-Corn-Law League*, vol. i, pp. 158, 169, 174, 175, 184 sqq.).

[2] H. of C., January 29, 1841: Lord John Russell's speech (*Parliamentary Debates*, 3rd Series, vol. lvi, pp. 155 sqq.).

all the stock arguments against the tyranny of the three Commissioners and the barbarity of the workhouse. The Tories welcomed their speeches, and when a seat fell vacant for the borough of Nottingham, John Walter, the editor of *The Times*, came forward as a candidate. Nottingham was one of the citadels of the Liberal party. Nevertheless, Walter, who contested the seat exclusively on the Poor Law question, was returned. It was a warning to the Cabinet that opposition to the Poor Law was still a living issue. They must be prepared at the next election to face an alliance of Tories and Chartists on the Anti-Poor-Law programme.

Lord Stanley now reintroduced his Irish Registration Bill.[1] The Cabinet decided to oppose it by bringing forward a measure of its own. The Government bill, introduced by Lord Morpeth, admitted the necessity of controlling more strictly the compilation of the registers, but to prevent an excessive reduction of the electorate in the Irish counties proposed to reduce the property qualification from £10 to £5.[2] The bill was a gross blunder. It was barely three years since Lord John had declared in a speech which obtained considerable notoriety that the Reform Bill of 1832 was sacrosanct. Now to please O'Connell he was prepared to amend it on an important point in the case of Ireland. Lord Morpeth's bill was read before Lord Stanley's. But the Cabinet secured this advantage by a majority of five only.[3] When the clause extending the franchise in the Irish counties was read, it was amended in debate by the Government and amended by the Opposition; and, in spite of these amendments, rejected by a majority of 300 to 289 votes.[4]

5

A dramatic surprise followed. On April 30 Baring brought in his budget. He began by explaining that the financial situation was worse than he had expected when he had made his estimates the year before. He had estimated the expenditure at £49,432,000, the receipts at £48,641,000; that is to say, a deficit of £858,000. But if the expenditure had been slightly less than he had anticipated, the receipts had been very much less. The actual deficit was £1,840,000. Owing to the increased cost of the army and

[1] H. of C., February 2, 1841 (*Parliamentary Debates*, 3rd Series, vol. lvi, pp. 220 sqq.).
[2] H. of C., February 4, 1841 (ibid., 3rd Series, vol. lvi, pp. 274 sqq.).
[3] H. of C., February 25, 1841 (ibid., 3rd Series, vol. lvi, p. 1126).
[4] H. of C., April 29, 1841 (ibid., 3rd Series, vol. lvii, p. 1274).

navy and the special expenditure necessitated by the situation in Canada and China, he estimated the expenditure for the new year at £50,731,000. Taxation, however, would produce a revenue of no more than £48,310,000. There would therefore be a deficit of £2,421,000, of £1,700,000, if certain special expenses which were not recurrent were left out of consideration. Baring did not propose any new taxes, such as the succession duty on real estate, which Hume had proposed in 1840, or an income tax. He proposed to improve the national finances not by additional taxation, but by adopting the daring method advocated by the free-traders, and reducing the existing duties.

Under the present tariff an import duty of 10s. was levied on colonial timber, of 55s. on foreign. Baring revived Lord Althorp's plan, and proposed to raise the 10s. duty to 20s. and reduce to 50s. the 55s. duty. Colonial sugar paid a duty of 24s. per cwt., foreign sugar a duty of 63s. Baring adopted in a slightly modified form a proposal made in 1840 by a Radical member named Ewart,[1] and while keeping the duty on colonial sugar at the existing figure reduced the duty on foreign to 36s. From the increase which he expected in the imports of foreign timber and sugar, he anticipated an additional revenue of £1,300,000. He had still to find £400,000. Instead of looking for new sources of revenue to make good the deficit, Baring attacked the third great monopoly, not colonial this time but British—the corn monopoly. He proposed to reduce the duties on the import of corn. The reduction was not indeed formally included in the budget, but even before Baring introduced the budget, Lord John had given notice to the House of Commons that on May 31 he would invite the House 'to consider the acts relating to the trade in corn'.[2]

Is it possible to discover any of the reasons which finally induced the Cabinet to take this startling decision? Although its deliberations were never revealed, there is good reason to believe that the course of events was as follows. The Conservatives maintained that the ministers had drawn up their budget in a hurry, in March or even in April, to escape from their dangerous Parliamentary predicament. They even charged them with preparing

[1] H. of C., June 25, 1840 (*Parliamentary Debates*, 3rd Series, vol. cv, pp. 77 sqq.). Ewart had proposed that the duty on foreign sugar should be reduced to 34s. Cf. H. of C., June 28, 1839 (ibid., 3rd Series, vol. xlviii, pp. 1021 sqq.), for Ewart's first motion on the Sugar Duties.
[2] Ibid., 3rd Series, vol. lvii, p. 1294.

two budgets at the same time, 'one for fine, and the other for bad weather' and producing the second when they saw a storm brewing.[1] The ministers emphatically denied the charge and they are entitled to credit. It is probable that even before Parliament met several ministers had demanded a free trade budget. For the past two years Lord John had been urging a reduction of the duties on corn, and the section of the Cabinet in favour of free trade had been asking for a simultaneous attack on the three great interests.[2] It was not therefore surprising that at the beginning of 1841 Lord John, who for the past four months had been humiliated and flouted in the Cabinet by Palmerston, should attempt to take his revenge.

At the beginning of January a Radical journal, the *Spectator*, published as a supplement a very extensive summary of the report issued the year before by Hume's Committee. Thirty thousand copies were sold.[3] This piece of propaganda was presumably encouraged by the free-traders in the Cabinet. And the very day on which Parliament opened, the *Edinburgh Review* devoted a long article to the work of the Committee and demanded a radical reform of the tariff system.[4] Everybody believed the article was inspired by the Cabinet.[5] But it was significant that the *Edinburgh Review* did not suggest that the reform should be immediately incorporated into the budget. It proposed that the same procedure should be adopted as in the case of the new Poor Law, and a Royal Commission appointed to inquire into the question. If this procedure were followed, the Commission could not issue their report, at the earliest, before the summer, and however quickly the matter were despatched the reform could not be effected until 1842. This is a clear proof that the ministry had not yet reached a definite decision. It was still feeling the pulse of the public. In

[1] H. of C., June 4, 7, 1841 (*Parliamentary Debates*, 3rd Series, vol. lviii, pp. 1239, 1264, 1266-7. Sir Robert Peel's speech; Lord John Russell's reply).

[2] Lord Sydenham's Diary, September 21, 1839: '. . . in England there is little to be done by me. At the Exchequer all that can be hoped is to get through some BAD TAX. There is no chance of carrying the house with one, for any great commercial reform, *timber, corn, sugar*, etc.' (G. Poulett Scrope, *Life of Lord Sydenham*, p. 102).

[3] *Spectator*, January 2, 1841. H. of C., April 30, 1841: speeches by A. Chapman and Hume (*Parl. Deb.*, 3rd Series, vol. lvii, pp. 1365-6).

[4] *Edinburgh Review*., January 1841, 'Customs Duties—Effects of the Protective System' (vol. lxxii, pp. 418 sqq.).

[5] *Quarterly Review*, June 1841, 'The Budget and the Dissolution' (vol. lxviii, pp. 243-5). This report was made the subject of an article in the *Edinburgh Review* of last January, attributed to two official pens . . . This article was published just at the opening of the Session.

all probability the proposal to reduce the duty on corn still met with an obstinate resistance within the Cabinet, and as regards the duties on sugar and timber the Government were waiting for the replies of the colonial governors they had consulted. This would explain the silence of the Speech from the Throne on the question of finance.

On February 2 the Cabinet laid before the Commons a bill by which rum from the East Indies would pay the same duty as rum from the West Indies, which received a preference.[1] It was another attempt to test public opinion. How would the West Indian planters and their friends in Parliament receive this first attack on their interests? At the same moment Baring was submitting to his colleagues the first draft of his budget, in which he dealt with the duties on sugar and timber.[2] The rum bill was well received by the House of Commons, and Peel delivered a speech in favour of free trade, which received the praise of *The Times*[3] and must have been very encouraging to the Cabinet. But Baring's draft did not touch the duties on corn. On February 9, in a memorandum submitted to his colleagues, Lord John protested against the omission.[4] It was at this very moment that the Whigs were losing a series of by-elections. It is difficult not to connect Lord John's memorandum with these defeats.

Lord John's immediate proposal, however, went no further than a modification of the sliding scale. When was the budget of 1841 adopted by the Cabinet in its final form, in which it included a revision of the duties on corn and the substitution of 'a fixed and moderate' duty for the sliding scale? Statements made by ministers would lead us to believe that it was the second half of February. But these statements are extremely vague,[5] and only

---

[1] H. of C., February 2, 1841: Labouchere's speech (*Parliamentary Debates*, 3rd Series, vol. lvi, pp. 204 sqq.).

[2] Sp. Walpole, *Life of Lord John Russell*, vol. i, p. 368. In this draft Baring made the same mistake as Lord Althorp had made in 1831, and to lessen the inequality between the duties on timber of different origin, proposed to raise the duty on Canadian timber.

[3] H. of C., February 12, 1841 (*Parl. Deb.*, 3rd Series, vol. lvi, pp. 617 sqq.). *The Times*, February 15, 1841.

[4] Sp. Walpole, *Life of Lord John Russell*, vol. i, pp. 368–9.

[5] H. of C., May 7, 1841: Lord John Russell's speech (vol. lviii, p. 18). In this speech Lord John Russell informs us that on April 30 he received from Lord Sydenham (Poulett Thomson, now Governor-General of Canada under that title) a reply to a letter from London informing him of the Cabinet's decision. This letter can hardly be identified with the letter of March 21, published by Poulett Scrope (*Life of Lord Sydenham*, pp. 88–9). It must therefore have been written between March 22 and 25, for it can hardly have left Quebec at any later date. It was on April 7, 10, and 19 that bodies of Canadian merchants, to whom the decision of the Cabinet had been communicated by Lord Sydenham, began

two facts are certain. About the beginning of March a campaign of petitions was opened in favour of a general reform of the tariff.[1] It was probably instigated by the Cabinet. Simultaneously, Labouchere, who had replaced Poulett Thomson at the Board of Trade, laid before the House of Commons a comprehensive scheme to reform the system of tariffs to which colonial trade was subject.[2]

The object of the measure was to abolish the restrictions imposed in the interest of the British exporter which hampered trade between the colonies and foreign nations. In other words, the Government wished to compensate in advance the West Indian and Canadian merchants for the very considerable sacrifice it intended to ask from them. Liberal speakers insisted that the bill did no more than give effect to the recommendations of the committee of 1840. They also pointed out that they were only carrying to its conclusion the policy the Tories had initiated so successfully when Huskisson was President of the Board of Trade.[3] They obviously hoped by raising the question of free trade to divide and thus weaken the Conservative Opposition. Perhaps Lord John believed that the leader of the Opposition, Peel, would be obliged, on the issue of free trade, to support the Government's policy.

He was mistaken. In the Cabinet he had gained the victory, a double victory. A victory over Melbourne, who gave way after holding out for two years. A victory over Palmerston, who was forced into the background while Lord John became once more the leading Liberal statesman. To leave the Church alone, keep the question of parliamentary reform in the shade, concentrate

to show alarm at the threat to their interests (*Correspondence between the Secretary of State for the Colonial Department and the Governors of the British Possessions in North America, relative to proposed Alteration in the Duties on Timber*, 1841). When could the letter from London informing Lord Sydenham have been written? Between February 15 and 20; in other words, within a few days of Lord John's memorandum. This suggests that Lord John's statement was deliberately vague, and the budget which was communicated to Lord Sydenham was the first draft which revised the duties on sugar and timber, but not the duty on corn. In that case our questions remain to be answered: At what date (no doubt before March 11) was the reform of the duties on corn incorporated into the budget? At what date (possibly after March 11) was it decided to replace the sliding scale by a 'fixed and moderate' duty?

[1] *Morning Chronicle*, March 10, 13, 20, April 27, 1841. H. of L., April 29, 1841; H. of C., March 10, 28, April 30, 1841 (*Parliamentary Debates*, 3rd Series, vol. lvii, pp. 1166, 1242, 1294).

[2] H. of C., March 12, 1841 (ibid., vol. lvii, pp. 148 sqq.).

[3] See Herries' speech in praise of Huskisson (H. of C., April 5, 1841, ibid., 3rd Series, vol. lvii, p. 905); Lord John Russell immediately took hold of the handle presented by this speech (ibid., p. 909).

upon a programme strictly economic, and take up the task of financial reform which Sir Henry Parnell had preached in 1830 and Lord Althorp had failed to carry out in 1831, this was his new policy, which he had successfully imposed upon the Cabinet. But the victory was not won until it had obtained the assent of Parliament and the nation. Here he failed.

6

The debate upon the budget began on May 7, and from the 7th until the 18th the House of Commons debated the reform of the sugar duties. It was one of those imposing and solemn debates which were the pride of the British Parliament. Forty-eight speakers addressed the House, among them Lord John, Lord Stanley, and Peel, and it was unanimously agreed that Lord John's speech was a masterpiece. But several members of the Whig aristocracy who were landlords, and therefore in favour of protection, deserted the Government. The Conservative Opposition exploited against the Cabinet the anti-slavery feeling of the country. Did the Government propose to give a preference to Brazilian sugar grown by slave labour, over West Indian grown by free labour? When the division took place on the 18th the Government obtained 281 votes, the Opposition 317. The Government was therefore in a minority of 36.

Two courses were open to the Cabinet: to resign immediately, or to continue in office, bring the question of the corn duties to a division and then, but not before, appeal to the country. Melbourne was in favour of the former alternative. He was a believer in Protection and felt himself being pushed by his colleagues where he had no wish to go. But once more he gave way. The debate on the Poor Law Bill was adjourned; on May 20 Baring asked the House of Commons to pass the customary duties on sugar, and Lord John announced that on June 4 he would submit the question of the Corn Laws to the decision of the House. Peel, however, did not leave him time to fulfil his intention. Confident now of victory, he asked the House of Commons to declare that the Government no longer possessed its confidence, and that its continuance in office violated the spirit of the Constitution. The debate continued a week and was concluded on June 4, the very day on which Lord John had intended to raise the question of the Corn Laws; 312 members voted for Peel's resolution, 311 against it. The Cabinet was obliged to choose one of two courses: to resign or dissolve Parliament. It chose the latter.

Lord John's proposal which the Cabinet had adopted was to impose a fixed and moderate duty on imported corn, not to abolish the duty entirely. The members of the League blamed his timidity. But the free-traders in Parliament, headed by Villiers, declared themselves satisfied. Only Grote stood out and refused to compromise. In spite of inevitable concessions the cause of free trade had won an undeniable victory. For Lord John announced his intention to propose a fixed duty of 8s. a quarter, that is to say, a duty lower by 2s. than that which Ricardo had been willing to accept twenty years earlier.[1] The Manchester League had been in existence for little more than two years, and it had compelled the Whig Government to espouse its cause. But the attempt to breathe fresh vigour into a party so exhausted by endowing it with an entirely new programme on the eve of a general election came too late. The election which began on June 28 and ended on July 17 was a catastrophe for the Liberals. As was a foregone conclusion in every election, they kept a majority in Scotland and Ireland; but it was reduced. And had it remained as large as it had been in 1835 and in 1837, it could not have compensated for the overwhelming majority the Conservatives obtained in the English constituencies. The Liberals lost ground even in the boroughs which were divided almost equally between the two parties. But the Conservatives swept the counties, which returned only 23 Liberal members as against 136 Conservatives. The elections left the Conservatives with a clear majority of 76.[2]

The sudden conversion of the Cabinet to the repeal of the Corn Laws was regarded by the public as a mere electioneering manoeuvre, and the manoeuvre failed. Peel won at last the victory for which he had waited and worked so many years. But was his victory after all the victory he had sought? When the Reform Bill was passed in 1832 he had expected that the Radicals, the opponents of the monarchy, peerage and Church, would be re-

[1] H. of C., May 7, 1841 (*Parliamentary Debates*, 3rd Series, vol. lviii, p. 16). We must, however, bear in mind that the 10s. duty formerly proposed by Ricardo had been intended to compensate the landlords for the special burdens to which they were liable, and that it might reasonably be claimed that these burdens had been considerably lightened in the interval by the reform of the Poor Law and the abolition of several taxes.

[2] For the election of 1841, see an excellent article by Duvergier de Hauranne, 'De la dernière session du Parlement anglais et du prochain ministère' (*Revue des Deux-Mondes*, August 1, 1841, vol. xlix, pp. 341 sqq., especially pp. 372–3, 375).

turned in larger numbers at every successive election. But he refused to believe that the venerable institutions of the country had lost their power over the hearts of Englishmen, and had waited patiently for the day when he would gather into the ranks of a Conservative party led by himself, the survivors of the old Tory party and the old Whig party, when both alike had perished. The event had belied his forecast.

The Radicals had failed either to form a third party independent of the two historic parties, or to absorb the Liberal party. Their programme of administrative and ecclesiastical reform had not been realized, the Liberal Parliament had always voted for a compromise, and the compromise had very often been formulated by Peel. Moreover, the Radicals had been overwhelmed by the revolutionary violence of the Chartists, and discredited, like the Liberal administration itself, by the alliance which O'Connell had forced upon them. The history of the period since the Reform Bill proved that England, which the attraction of the French revolution of 1830 had temporarily deflected from the orbit she pursued in isolation from the movement of the continental nations, was already returning to her regular path. The Liberal party, yielding to the pressure of the Anti-Corn-Law League, was now appealing to the electorate on a programme, of reform no doubt, but of reform as understood by the middle class, Liberal, inasmuch as it was a declaration of war upon the monopoly of the landlords, but nevertheless 'Conservative' in the sense in which Peel understood the term. For it left intact the entire constitutional edifice of the country, indeed strengthened it by diverting public attention to reforms of a different nature,[1] a programme which was no more than a somewhat bolder application of the policy which Lord Liverpool's ministry had pursued so successfully for several years before the crisis of the Reform Bill. The Conservative party, on the other hand, had become once more a Tory party in the stricter and more uncompromising sense of the term. To defend the political and economic privileges of the landlords, it was prepared to welcome any allies against the middle-class industrialist, was even willing to conclude the pact

[1] Lord Sydenham to Lord John Russell, May 24, 1841: '. . . You have taken a bold step. . . . It has everything to recommend it, in what it touches, and in what it lets alone. It does *not* meddle with religious prejudices: it does *not* relate to Ireland: it does not touch on any of the theoretical questions of government on which parties have so long been divided' (Poulett Scrope, *Life of Lord Sydenham*, p. 89).

with the followers of O'Connor which ever since Walter's election was known as the 'treaty of Nottingham'.[1] Peel made no objection when the candidates of his party adopted in the constituencies this policy of alliance with the Ultra-Radicals which he refused to adopt himself in the House and in many English boroughs, it was by declaring themselves opposed to the factory system and the workhouse that the Conservative candidates secured sufficient support to win the election.

All his antecedents had unfitted Peel to be the leader of such a party, and during the important debates which had preceded the election many speakers had noticed the incongruity and called attention to it. His speeches were carefully scrutinised in the hope of finding some augury of his conversion. It was sometimes remarked that he adopted an intentional obscurity and refused to commit himself as to his future policy. Or if he expressed himself clearly, loopholes were detected in his statement. No doubt he rejected the idea of a fixed duty, but he was prepared to accept a modification of the sliding scale and that modification might be such as to give the agriculturalists, at the present price of corn, an even smaller measure of protection than they would have received from Lord John's 'fixed and moderate duty'. Moreover, he had once already changed front on the question of Catholic Emancipation after agreeing with the Ultra-Tories to denounce it as a revolutionary measure. Members who put forward these considerations in the House were often inspired by feelings of hostility, or at least were speaking in sarcasm.[2] But this was not always the case, and there were many who evidently felt that when the great decision must finally be made, they would not look to Peel in vain.[3] And it would be to Peel they would look

[1] H. of C., June 2, 1841: Handley's speech (*Parliamentary Debates*, 3rd Series, vol. lviii, p. 1042).

[2] See the frankly hostile speech by Handley, a Protectionist Whig (H. of C., June 2, 1841, ibid., 3rd Series, vol. lviii, pp. 1036 sqq.). Lord John's speech necessarily hostile (H. of C., June 4, 1841, ibid., 3rd Series, vol. lviii, pp. 1197–8), and the speech delivered by Sir John Hobhouse, which was conceived in the same vein as Lord John's, but was more friendly to Peel (H. of C., May 21, 1841, ibid., 3rd Series, vol. lviii, pp. 854–5).

[3] See especially the speech of the Radical, Wakley: 'The right hon. Gentleman, it must be admitted, possessed great capacity and was at the head of a great party in that House, the right hon. Gentleman commanded powers which caused him to be in the highest degree capable of rendering services to this kingdom; and he would therefore entreat the right hon. Gentleman to . . . let them know boldly and distinctly what it was they were to expect from him and his supporters, if they should come over to that side of the House. He could tell the right hon. Gentleman, that if he would promise more than the present Ministry, he, for one, would vote for him, and no one would give him

rather than to Lord John. If England, after the crisis from which she had just emerged, were to regain her balance, and find it in a liberty expressed by economic rather than by political formulas, formulas wholly British and utterly un-French, the creation of Adam Smith and Ricardo, they preferred to believe that it would be Peel, not Lord John, who would have the honour of leading his country into the new era of plenty and social peace.

a more cordial and hearty support' (H. of C., May 24, 1841, ibid., 3rd Series, vol. lviii, pp. 717–18). Cf. another speech by Wakley (H. of C., June 7, 1841, ibid., 3rd Series, vol. lviii, pp. 1278), also a speech by Ewart, delivered after the election (H. of C., August 25, 1841, ibid., 3rd Series, vol. lix, p. 116). Many Radicals exasperated with the Whigs agreed with the forecast of the policy of a Tory Cabinet which Sir William Molesworth had expressed three years earlier: 'I do not believe, Sir, that we shall ever again have a Government acting upon Tory principles. If the Tories were under the responsibility of office, they would be as Liberal as the country: they would be controlled by the Opposition just as the Government is controlled, the only difference being that whereas the guiding opposition is at present Tory, it would then be Liberal' (H. of C., March 6, 1838, *Parliamentary Debates*, 3rd Series, vol. xli, pp. 489–90). Lord Sydenham wrote on September 21, 1839: '. . . If Peel were in, he might do this, as he could muzzle or keep away his Tory allies and we should support him. If he got in, and he had courage, what a field for him!' (Poulett Scrope, *Life of Lord Sydenham*, p. 102).

Index

M

353

M*

INDEX

Corn Laws, 92; *Agitation for Repeal*, 301–11, 329–35; origin of, 1836, 302; anti-Corn Law associations, 302–5; Manchester anti-Corn Law Association, 305–6, 311, 348; National Anti-Corn Law League, 311, 330–4, 377, 340–1, 349; Lancashire headquarters of anti-Corn Law campaign, 303; meetings, 309–10. 331; lecture campaign, 310, 331; Press campaign, 305; arguments of, 306–9; petitions, 311, 331, 346; national petition, 331; motion for fixed corn duty defeated, 1837, 302–3; Villiers' annual motion for committee of enquiry, 304–5, 339; delegation in London, 311, 329–30, 337; committee of enquiry refused, 1839, 330; appointed, 1840, 337; committee's report, 337–8; anti-Corn Law campaign broadens into general free-trade movement, 336–7; Cabinet divided and hesitating, 338–9; defeat in the Commons, 1840, 330; public indifference, 339–40; electioneering campaign, 1840–1, 340–1; Cabinet introduces free-trade budget, 1841, 342–5; defeated on free trade, 347–8; free-trade election lost, 1841, 348; relations of anti-Corn Law agitation with Chartism, 301, 304, 306–7, 309; a Radical diversion to anti-Poor Law agitation, 329; relations with Utilitarianism, 332; supported, 310; then abandoned by *The Times*, 330; supported by Nonconformists, 335; by Conference of Ministers of Religion, 335; Peel's attitude towards, 345, 347, 350–1

Corn Prices, 181, 301–2

Corporations, Municipal Reform of, 212–7

Cotton industry, 271–2; crisis, 278–9; supports free trade, 303, 329, 337

Coulson, W., 123

Country gentlemen and farmers, *see* Agriculturalists

Cousin, Victor, 106

Crisis, Economic, *see* Trade and Bank Crisis

Crisis, Political, 40–7, 55–9; *see also* Agitation

Croker, John Wilson, 38

Cumberland, Ernest Augustus, Duke of, from 1837 King George V of Hanover, 162, 191, 241

D

Dickens, Charles, 288

Disestablishment, *see* Anti-Clericalism, Agitation, Church of England, of Scotland, of Ireland

Dissenters (*see also* particular denominations), numbers of, 62n.; political power of, 62; unrepresented in reformed Parliament, 62–3; attack privilege of Church of England, 42, 133–5; disunited, 154–5; attack fails, 165, 209–10; attack slavery, 239–41;

attitude to factory reform, 114–15; marriage of, 167–8; university question, 169–70, 199–200; educational discrimination against, 221; conciliated by Peel, 178–9; representation in new municipalities, 215; appointed as magistrates, 216; popularity among working class, 324; attitude to Chartism, 324; support free-trade campaign, 334–5

Disturbances, *see* Agitation

Disraeli, Benjamin, 99, 155n., 190, 220

'Droits de l'Homme' Society, 43

Duncannon, Lord, 13, 25

Duncombe, T. S., 49n.

Durham, John George Lambton, Earl of, 13, 56, 142, 172, 196, 236–41

E

East India Company, loses monopoly of Chinese trade, 86

Ebrington, Lord, 198

Education, National, 104–7, 113–14, 126–7, 221–4

Egypt, 74–5, 256–60, 264–7

Eldon, John Scott, Earl of, 8

Elections, General:
1830, 4–5
1831, 32–3
1832, 60–1
1835, 179
1837, 241
1841, 348

Elements of Political Economy, 143

Emancipation of slaves, *see* Slavery

English National Society, 107

Evangelicals: religious revival, 51–2; anti-slavery efforts, 81, 84–5, 232; work for factory reform, 112–22; advocate Church Reform, 136–8, 140, 207; moral reform, 162; religious education, 221, 224; power of, 1833, 162–4; in Church of Scotland, 164–5

Evans, Colonel, 49n., 95

Ewing, Marshall, 135

Exports: to Spain, decrease of, 78; statistics, 1836–40, 278n.

F

Factory Reform (for Factory Acts, *see also* Acts of Parliament), 16–17, 107–19,284, 332–3

Factory System, agitation against, 283–6, 299–30, 349–50

Falmouth, Lord, 364

Faraday, Michael, 104

Ferdinand VII, of Spain, 76

Fielden, John, 65, 110–12, 117, 118, 220, 287, 301n., 321n.

357

Finance, *see* Budget, Bank of England, Army, Navy

Foreign Policy: Wellington, 5–6, 251; Palmerston, 19–20, 71–8, 251–68, 340

France, 3, 4–7, 19–20, 39, 43, 59, 73–9, 106, 108, 119, 189, 251–69, 340

Free Trade, 79, 88–91, 338–51; *see also* Corn Laws

Froude, Richard Herell, 145, 147

G

Gascoyne, General, 31, 48

Germany, Zollverein, 310

Gladstone, William Ewart, 190, 209

Glenelg, Charles Grant, Baron, 189, 235

Graham, Sir James, 13, 25

Grand National Trades Union, 44–6

Greece, 75, 251

Grenville, Lord, 21

Grey, Charles, Baron and Earl; political character of, 12; refuses to assist Tory Government, 11n.; takes office, 12; prepares to introduce reform bill, 12; settles Belgian question, 1831, 20; decides to introduce reform bill, 22; opposes ballot, 25; pledges himself to reform bill, 40; opposes large creation of peers, 26, 46–7; asks for a creation of peers, 55; resigns with his Cabinet, May 1832, 55; resumes office, 57; accepts Irish Coercion Act, 129–30; refuses Irish disendowment, 160; opposes distestablishment, 164; supports Nonconformist access to universities, 166; decides to renew Coercion Act, 171; resigns, 171; favours Stanley's centre, 186; retires from active politics, 187

Grote, George, 65, 70, 237, 291, 304, 305, 333, 351

Guizot, François Pierre Guillaume, 75, 251, 260–1, 265–7

H

Habeas Corpus Act, suspended in Ireland, 131

Harewood, Lord, 81

Harrowby, Lord, 47 *and n.*, 49n., 53

Harvey, Daniel Whittle, 294, 296, 300, 324

Henley, Lord, 138

Hetherington, 18, 44, 116, 294

Hill, Rowland, 274–5

Hobhouse, Henry, later Baron Broughton, 22, 26–7, 56, 94–5, 107, 125, 189

Holland, 4, 1920, 50, 73, 77–8, 256–8

Howick, Lord, 13, 187, 189

Hume, Joseph, 84, 113, 139, 150, 197, 219, 224, 227n., 238, 250, 262, 293–4, 304, 339–40, 341, 343

Hunt, Henry, 16–17, 27

Huskisson, William, 9, 97, 274

I

Ibrahim Pasha, *see* Pasha, Ibrahim

India, British, 227–30, 269

Industry, *see* Trade

Ingilby, Sir W., 94

Inglis, Sir Robert, 106

Ireland, Secretaries for: Lord Stanley, 13, 143; Littleton, 143; Lords Lieutenant: Lord Normanby, 198; Lord Ebrington, 198; Tory majority returned, 1830, 3; agrarian riots, 1831, 18; disturbances in 1832, 3, 128–30; 1834, 167; O'Connell's agitation, 1831, 17–18; agrarian outrages after 1835, 198; agitation for Home Rule, 129–30; Home Rule demanded by O'Connell, 168; Habeas Corpus Act suspended, 131; Irish Coercion Act, 131; renewed and modified, 172–3; parliamentary victory of O'Connell, 173; Irish votes turn scale against Tories, 1835, 180–1; O'Connell's agitation dropped, 1835, 198; government of Ireland left to O'Connell, 1835–41, 197–9; agitation against Church of Ireland, especially tithe, 18, 130, 134, 151; state reform of Irish Church, 139–40; Irish tithe bill, 170–4, 186; Irish Tithes Act, 204; Orange Lodges, 160–1; unpopularity of Irish in England, 151–2, 196; popular education in, 106–7; Poor Law in, 211–12; municipal corporations, reform of, 214–16; Irish Registration bill, 329, 342; Ireland purchases British yarn, 271

Iron manufacture, 274

Irreligion: opposition to fast day, 52; anticlerical attitude, *Morning Chronicle*, 52; irreligious attitude of Liberal intelligentsia, 156; decline of, 218; Owen's propaganda, 316

Irving, Rev. Edward, 51–2

Italy, 19, 74–5

J

Jamaica, 80

Joint Stock Companies, 279, 284; *see also* Banks, Joint Stock

Judicial System, reform of, 100–1

K

Keble, Rev. John, 145–9

Kent, Duchess of, 242–4

L

Landsdowne, Lord, 12, 13, 176, 189

League, Anti-Corn Law, 310, 320–2, 338, 340–1, 349–51

Leopold I, King of the Belgians, 244, 247–8, 250, 255, 263–4

Libel, in parliamentary reports, 269

Liberals, *see* Whigs

Lichfield, Lord, 187
Ligue de la Résistance Bretonne, 43
Liverpool, Lord, 137
Llanidloes, riot at, 313
Londonderry, Lord, 79
Louis Philippe, King of the French, 3, 5, 6, 74, 78–9, 253–6
Lovett, William, 294, 297–8, 298n., 301, 306, 312, 320, 324, 331–2
Lyndhurst, Lord, 54, 57, 177, 192
Lytton, Edward Bulwer, 65, 101, 105, 115n.

M

Macaulay, Thomas Babington, Lord, 38, 50, 110, 152n., 229–30, 262n., 289n., 315
Machinery, manufacture of, 274–5
Magistrates, appointment of, 216–8; jurisdiction diminished, 123; increased, 221
Mahmoud, Sultan, 75
Mahon, Lord, 61n.
Malthusianism, 120–2
Maria, Donna, Queen of Portugal, 74–7
Marriage, of non-Anglicans, 167–8, 202–4, 214
Marx, Karl, 270n., 323
Meetings, Public, of sympathy with Paris revolutionaries, 1830, 4; of political union, 1832, 45; against First Reformed Parliament, 1833, 68; illegal mass meetings in London, 1833, 97; to protest against house and window taxes, 93n.; London demonstration of protest against Dorchester sentences, 118; against New Poor Law, 1834, 128; of Dissenters against Anglican privileges, 150–1; at London Tavern in favour of Disestablishment, 130; against New Poor Law, 290; Chartist, 311, 314, 320, anti-Corn Law, 213, 332
Mehemet Ali, see Ali, Mehemet
Melbourne, William Lamb, Viscount: political views, 194–5; as Home Secretary, 1830, 46; suppresses riots, 1831–2, suppresses agrarian disorders, 1834, 118; as Prime Minister, July 1834, 173; opposes Lord John Russell on Irish Disendowment, 174, 204; engineers his own dismissal from office, November 1834, 175; attacks Dissenters, 178; forced to accept Radical support, 179; favour's Stanley's centre, 187; returns to office, April 1835, 188; forms Cabinet, 189; accepts Radical-Irish alliance, 194; opposes new peerages, 194; appoints Liberal Churchmen, 208–9; views on appointments of magistrates, 217; subservience to Peel, 226; introduces Jamaica bill, 241; resigns, 242; resumes office, 246; relations with Queen Victoria, 240–9, 251; with Prince Albert, 250–1; attitude in bedchamber crisis, 244–6; fails

to make army promotions subject to War Office, 190; averts Cabinet crisis, 1840, 266; opposes ballot, 293; makes it an open question, 317; patronizes Robert Owen, 318; maintains New Poor Law, 318; refuses to adopt free trade, 330; yields, 342–6; see also 48n., 255n.
Methodists (see also Dissenters), numbers of, 154; political attitude of, 152–4; support denominational education, 225, 355; support free trade, 336; also 117n.
Metropolitan Trades Union, 44
Metternich, Count (see also Austria), 253n., 254, 262
Mexico, 251
Miguel, Dom, 75–6, 78
Mill, James, 55, 139, 141, 227, 229, 232, 293
Mill, John Stuart, 5, 45, 101n., 105n., 156, 158, 228–9, 232, 238, 299
Molesworth, Sir William, 65, 226n., 229–33, 238, 297, 302, 332, 351n.
Monopolies, Liberal attack upon, 85–6
Moore, Thomas, 161
Morpeth, Lord, 111
Mulgrave, Lord, see Normanby, Constantine Henry Phipps, Marquis of
Münchengrätz, Congress of, 74, 76

N

Naples, 308
National Political Union, 45, 49n., 56
National Union of the Working Classes, 44–6
Navy Estimates, 1830 and 1834, 96; 1835 and 1840, 335
Negroes, see Slavery
New South Wales, 230–1
New Zealand, 232, 286
Newcastle, Duke of, 41, 110
Newman, Rev. John Henry, 146–9, 160–2, 209
Newport, Chartist insurrection at, 326
Nicholls, George, 210
Norbury, Lord, 197
Normanby, Constantine Henry Phipps, Marquis of, 197; Lady, 244

O

Oastler, Robert, 107, 109, 116–17, 289–91, 293n., 298, 300, 333
O'Brien, Bronterre, 299, 306, 322–4
O'Connell, Daniel, 19, 27, 33, 65, 106, 131–2, 136, 139, 143–4, 153, 159–60, 169–73, 187, 190, 196–9, 203 and n., 210, 215, 242, 243–5, 261n., 292, 294–5, 297, 301
O'Connor, Feargus, 295, 297–8, 301, 306, 319, 322–3, 327, 328n., 350
Opium War, 227–8
Opposition, Tory, see Tories; Liberal, see Liberals; Radical, see Radicals

INDEX

R

Radical, 18

Radicals, encouraged by French Revolution, 1830, 5; agitate for revolutionary reform, 17; attitude towards first reform bill, 27; to second reform bill, 36–7; to third reform-bill, 49*n.*; increased representation in Parliament, 1833, 63–6; agitate against reform bill settlement, 68; adopt in various degrees utilitarian programme, 68–9, 99–100; press for universal education, 105–7, 221–2; unite with Tories against Whigs, 109; attitude towards disestablishment, 134–5, 139–40, 141–2, 152–3, 159; alliance with O'Connell, 153, 188; gain seats at Whig expense, 1835, 180; gains, 1833, 195–6; losses, 1837, 195; disunited, 195–6; defeated by O'Connell, 198; partial victory on municipal reform, 214; Colonial policy of, 225–32, 236–8; condemn transportation, 231; attack Jamaica bill, 240–1; loyalty to Victoria, 242; oppose Palmerston's Russian policy, 261–2, 340; campaign against House of Lords, 290; for the ballot, 290–1; attitude towards Chartists, 297, 300–1; opposes Chartism by anti-Corn Law agitation, 301; Whig Cabinet's overtures to, 315; New Economic Radical party, 331–40; failure to form third party or absorb Whigs, 349; Ultra-Radicals agitate for revolutionary reform, 44–6; split with moderate Radicals, 45; criticize Factory Act, 116; oppose New Poor Law, 128–9; oppose police, 220; campaign for universal suffrage, 291–5; *see also* Utilitarians, Chartism

Railways, 219, 275–8

Rebellion: Belgium against Holland, 1830, 7; Poland against Russia, 1831, 20; Modena Parma and Romagna, 1831, 20; Jamaica slaves, 1832, 80; Lower Canada, 1838, 235–8; Upper Canada, 1838, 235; Jamaican Legislature against Parliament, 1839, 240; Chartist, 313, 326–7

Reform bills and Act, first reform bill, 22–32; second, 32–40; third, 47–50, 53–9, 98

Registration, Civil, 201, 211–12

Religious Revival, Evangelical, 51–3, 161–4; Anglo-Catholic, 145–9, 159–62, 209–10; general, 207–10

Revenue, *see* Budgets

Revolution: *for* England, *see* Agitation, Popular; Crisis, Political; Rebellion; Reform bills and Act; French, July 1830, 3; in Switzerland and various German States, 1830, 6

Richmond, Duke of, 13, 172

Riots, *see* Agitation, Popular; Crisis, Political; Rebellion; Reform bills and Act; in France, 8, 43, 58–9, 119, 319

Ripon, Lord, 171

Roads, administration of, 127*n.*, 219

Roebuck, John Arthur, 64, 105–6, 126, 157, 163*n.*, 196, 221, 223, 261*n.*, 289*n.*, 292, 295, 297, 300, 302, 332

Romilly, John, 64

Rose, Rev. Hugh James, 145–7

Rotunda (Blackfriars Bridge), 11

Russell, Lord John, character of and political position, 13, 23–30, 33, 38–9, 47–9, 58*n.*, 140*n.*, 142, 143, 168, 171, 175, 177, 186–9, 194, 194*n.*, 198, 200–3, 216–17, 220, 223–4, 236, 237*n.*, 240, 247*n.*, 264–6, 291, 300, 311, 317*n.*, 318, 325, 327, 333*n.*, 338

Russia, 20, 72, 75, 188, 227, 250, 257–60, 267, 308

S

Sadler, Michael Thomas, 109–10, 116, 210, 290

Saint Germain l'Auxerrois, 43

Saint-Simonians, 158

Saxony, 6

Scotland, Church of, *see* Church of Scotland; municipal reform in, 212–14

Senior, William Nassau, 100*n.*, 120, 124

Sibthorp, Colonel, 37*n.*

Slavery, emancipation of slaves, 80–4, 233, 239–40, 247

Smith, Sydney, 209

Smith, Thomas Southwood, 100, 141, 115, 212

Socialism, 44–5, 289, 292, 316, 323

Société aide-toi le ciel t'aidera, 43

Society for National Regeneration, 117

South Africa, *see* Cape Colony

South Australia, 232

Spain, 75–8, 250–2, 263, 308

Spencer, Earl, *see* Althorp, Lord

Spencer, Herbert, 115

Stanley, Lord, 13, 47, 82–4, 130, 132, 142, 144, 172, 177, 179, 187–8, 235, 255*n.*, 328, 342, 347

Stephens, Rev. James Rayner, 154, 287–8, 298–300, 318, 333

Sterling, John, 45*n.*, 51*n.*

Stockmar, Baron, 246, 248–50

Strikes: Manchester cotton spinners, 16; Glasgow, 1838, 294; projected strike against payment of taxes to support reform bill, 56–7; General Strike proposed by Owen, 1834, 117; by Chartists, 297, 311–13, 318–20, 326

Sutton, Sir Charles Manners, 55–6, 57, 64, 181

'Swing, Captain', 7

T

Tallyrand, Perigord Charles Maurice de, 76–7, 188, 253, 257

Tamworth Manifesto, 178

362

W